W9-AZY-502

ECONOMICS: AN INTRODUCTION TO THE WORLD AROUND YOU A BOOK OF READINGS

Dennis J. Weidenaar
Emanuel T. Weiler

Purdue University

Addison-Wesley Publishing Company
Reading, Massachusetts • Menlo Park, California
London • Amsterdam • Don Mills, Ontario • Sydney

Preface

The readings in this collection are intended to assist you and encourage you to

- Think about the goals you want your economic system to achieve;
- Understand the particular set of economic institutions currently being used to achieve these goals (institutional economics);
- Measure the success or failure of a particular set of economic institutions in achieving these goals (applied economics);
- Invent new economic institutions which will best achieve the goals you think are important.

To achieve these goals we have compiled a set of readings which

- Describe economic institutions which have been created to achieve specified goals;
- Present varied viewpoints on current economic issues;
- Illustrate how economic analysis can be used to clarify issues.

You may think that it is overly ambitious to expect you, a student taking a first economics course, to appraise the economic institutions you see around you. But consider that many people who have never had *any* course work in economics are actively involved through the political process in changing the mix of institutions which govern economic activity.

In using these readings, you will profit by first reading the summary. This will give you an idea of what the reading is about. Then we suggest you read the questions to alert you to important issues in the reading. Finally, read the article carefully and answer the questions.

Keep in mind that all economic institutions are made by human beings and therefore can be changed by human beings. If you are going to be a full participant in a society, you should know how it works and what might be done to make it work better.

West Lafayette, Indiana   D.J.W.
January 1976   E.T.W.

Contents

The International Economy

Reading 1

Some Conjectures on Policy Problems of the 1970s*

By Kermit Gordon

Summary

Ten years ago some social thinkers—but, to be fair, I must say not many economists—had discerned a new menace to social peace called automation. Somehow this newly discovered force was destroying jobs so fast that work itself was in danger of becoming obsolete, and we faced the challenge of designing a new society in which work would figure only incidentally. It is embarrassing today to recall that automation would have drawn many votes in 1963 as one of the major economic problems of the 1960s.

With this cautionary example in mind, I approach with humility and diffidence the task of identifying some of the major economic policy problems that are likely to absorb our attention through the remainder of this decade.

Key Questions to Consider

- What are the five major economic problems the author sees confronting society in the 1970s?

- Why is the present international economic system an unstable one?

- How successful has the tax system been in redistributing wealth?

* Reprinted with permission from *The American Economic Review* (Papers and Proceedings) **LXIV,** No. 2 (May 1974), 125–128.

Some Conjectures on Policy Problems of the 1970s

A quick way to acquire a suitable modesty about our capacity to see clearly ten years ahead is to review the state of the predictive art a decade ago. The effects are sobering.

Ten years ago some social thinkers—but I must say to be fair, not many economists—had discerned a new menace to social peace called automation. Somehow this newly discovered force was destroying jobs so fast that work itself was in danger of becoming obsolete, and we faced the challenge of designing a new society in which work would figure only incidentally. It is embarrassing today to recall that automation would have drawn many votes in 1963 as one of the major economic problems of the 1960s.

With this cautionary example in mind, I approach with humility and diffidence the task of identifying some of the major economic policy problems that are likely to absorb our attention through the remainder of this decade.

International Economic Problems. We live in an increasingly interdependent world in which the institutions and arrangements that nurtured and sheltered this interdependence have broken down. World trade has been growing much faster than world income; international investment, whether via the multinational corporation or otherwise, has expanded stead-

ily; money and capital markets of the industrialized countries have become integrated to an unprecedented degree. But at the end of the era during which these links were being forged, we saw the collapse of an international monetary system based on gold, dollars, and fixed exchange rates, and we saw large fissures appear in a trading system that was characterized by increasing liberalization and nondiscrimination and that was shaped under American leadership and lubricated by U.S. balance-of-payments deficits.

The present situation is clearly unstable. The United States has lost the dominance that enabled it to exercise effective leadership in the creation of new institutions and arrangements, and other sources of leadership have not yet appeared. The increasing fragility of the global economy comes at a time when both North-South economic relations and East-West economic relations are in flux. Though the developing countries as a group have enjoyed a high rate of economic growth, they are troubled by problems of rapidly rising population, unemployment and maldistribution of income. The grievances they feel against the industrialized countries are intensified by a rising spirit of nationalism. Clearly the donor-client attitudes which characterized the foreign aid relationship in years past have come to an end. The developing countries are convinced that the terms of trade have been rigged against them, and they can be expected to use whatever means are available to improve their relative price position.

At the same time, the Communist countries are seeking more intimate trade and credit relationships with the rest of the world. This development will raise again the complex of questions concerning the mechanisms of economic intercourse between state trading countries and capitalist countries that have been discussed since the end of the Second World War but never resolved.

Inflation.   Some economists squirm a bit when they hear themselves characterizing inflation as one of our gravest economic ills. They probably have in mind a hypothetical society in which all money claims are indexed to the cost of living, and they suspect that life in such an economy might be quite tolerable. But whatever life might be like in such an imaginary society, inflation is clearly perceived by the American people as a major social disorder. When a sharp rise in the price level coincides with rising real per capita consumption, it must follow that many people are better off than they were before; yet the evidence seems to indicate that most people *feel* worse off, including many of those who are demonstrably better off. It is dangerous to dismiss as irrationally grounded the socially corrosive effects of inflation.

We should take small comfort from the fact that in recent years we have one of the better price records among the industrialized countries. In recent years we have had, on American standards, an unacceptable rate of inflation in recession, in recovery, and in expansion—a process complicated by two dollar devaluations, a world food shortage, and an energy crisis. I know of no neat theory of inflation that fits the facts of the last five years—neither aggregate demand, nor money supply, nor labor power, nor oligopoly power, nor bottlenecks, nor expectations—though I could easily be convinced that all played a part.

Until someone discovers the Rosetta stone that unlocks the mysteries of the inflationary process and prescribes the appropriate aggregate or structural

measures to combat it, I suspect we will continue to see the intermittent use of the blunt device of direct governmental intervention in private wage and price decision making. I for one am not prepared to write off such interventions as inherently mischievous. A great deal depends on the temperature of the economy at the time the intervention occurs, the scope of the program, the skill and integrity with which the intervention is managed, and most of all, on the moral authority of the governmental intervenor. But however we cope or fail to cope, it seems likely that the inflation problem will remain high on the American agenda in the years ahead.

Performance of the Public Sector.   Economists at all points in the opinion spectrum can rally round the proposition that government at all levels ought to be performing much better than it is. The main but not the only impetus to this convergence of opinion was, as we all know, the pervasive disappointment with the results of the new social programs of the 1960s.

In retrospect, we see now that the federal government of the 1960s attacked the complex social problems of the era with the implicit conviction that common sense or simple deductive reasoning was sufficient to design public programs that would cure social ills. Only when it was recognized that the disbursement of large sums of money does not necessarily solve problems did attention begin to turn toward the search for strategies and techniques that work.

This search for ways to translate public dollars into visible social gains will, I think, be a principal concern of public policy thinking throughout the 1970s and beyond. Let me give just one example, albeit a very important one. To move people to act in a desired fashion, one can either order them to do so or make it worth their while to do so. That is, one can choose between administrative regulation on the one hand and a system of incentives or disincentives operating through the market on the other. There is a place in the governmental system for each strategy, but in most cases we seem to go the regulation route without weighing carefully the pros and cons of each approach.

The search for effective strategies to treat social ills will rarely lend itself to armchair analysis. Often the only way to find out what works is to try out alternative strategies on an experimental basis. The social experimentation approach, though difficult, expensive, and time-consuming, deserves to be a major element in the effort to improve the performance of the public sector.

The problems are not going to evaporate, nor is government going to get smaller. It simply has to do better.

Distributive Equity. The quest for greater equality of opportunity and the quest for reduction in the inequality of results are closely related but are not, of course, synonymous.

The problem of improving equality of opportunity relates mainly, but not wholly, to minority groups and women. It is a safe bet that minority rights and women's rights will continue to occupy a central position on the national agenda of economic problems throughout the 1970s. The two movements went through an unsteady initial period, but both have clearly settled down to an effective strategy of skillful and persistent application of pressure combined with appeals to conscience.

The broader problem, the distribution of income and wealth throughout the economy, is more diffuse and ambiguous. For my part, I doubt that the present degree of inequality of income and wealth is necessary to safeguard the motivations and incentives which drive the system. Some forces are at work to moderate the degree of income inequality, such as the minority and women's movements and the great expansion of government transfer payments and subsidized services to low-income groups. But earlier visions that saw the spread of unionization and collective bargaining and of higher education as equalizing forces are held today with considerably less fervor.

The tax system is potentially a powerful device for reducing nonfunctional inequalities in income and wealth. Yet the total American tax system today does not appear significantly to alter the pretax distribution of income, nor does our present system of death duties seem to have much effect on the distribution of wealth. Given the inertia of our tax system, it would require a major crystallization of public opinion to achieve changes in the tax system that would serve even moderate redistributive ends. My tea leaves do not tell me whether such a crystallization is in prospect in this decade.

Environment, Energy, Resource Depletion, and Economic Growth. Though these are by no means a single problem, they are linked together in a network of interconnections. We are now well beyond that rapturous early period during which some apparently felt that purity of heart and worthiness of motives were capable of cleaning up the environment. As the problems have shaken down, it has become clear that environmental progress involves painful choices, complex trade-off problems, and a critical evaluation of fundamental strategies and techniques. Despite occasional and even major setbacks to the cause, the environmental issue probably possesses staying power: any movement grounded in an alliance of youthful activists and middle-class conservationists is likely to continue to make itself heard.

The long-term dimensions of the problems of energy and resource depletion are not nearly so clear. If only free markets ruled the world, it would be possible without great difficulty to visualize the kind of economic and technological measures—working through economizing, substitution, and innovation—that would be required for a smooth adaptation to the gradual depletion of particular wasting resources. But the world is also influenced by monopolies, international politics and ideologies, and military force. The crisis we are now passing through, however it may be resolved, is bound to alter fundamentally the way the United States and the rest of the world think about long-term energy and wasting-resource problems. True, there is probably no internationally traded commodity other than oil in which the potential for coercion and gouging is as great, but there are probably a few other commodities the monopolistic control of which is capable of causing significant disruption. Many of us would have said even as recently as a year ago that measures to achieve the goal of national self-sufficiency in energy sources would cost us dearly and would do great harm to the world trading system. Today it is much more difficult to build a case for a free trade policy in oil.

Any forecast made in the midst of an imposed world oil crisis is almost certain to be distorted by short-term perceptions. But it takes no great acumen to say that the policy problems associated with energy sources and wasting resources will be with us in one form or another in the years ahead and will occupy a position high on the economic policy agenda.

For the sake of completeness, it is necessary to take note of the view of those who would halt economic growth as a means of saving the natural environment and slowing the depletion of resources. This could be a prescription, not for throwing out the baby with the bath water, but for throwing out the baby instead of the bath water. But whatever the merits, the no-growth debate is likely to continue to stimulate analysis and arouse passions throughout the decade.

Reading 2

Internal and External Functions of the Council of Economic Advisers*

By Herbert Stein

Summary

Economists who participate in the policymaking process have, in my opinion, two responsibilities. First, they should try to identify themselves so that people will understand from what political standpoint they speak. Second, they should try to tell the truth. Our profession has only a few truths. They are mainly of the order of "There is no free lunch," "Things are seldom what they seem," "We live in a world of scarcity," and "To live is to choose." We should try to tell these truths to the people. The president appreciates having his economic advisers tell him the truth, even when it is unpleasant. The people will also, I believe, respect economists for telling them the truth.

Key Questions to Consider

■ What are the inside and outside functions of the Council of Economic Advisers (CEA)?

■ What does Dr. Stein have in mind when he states, "Members of the Council of Economic Advisers do not have to leave the room when the political consequences or political feasibility of proposed economic policies are being considered"?

■ What responsibilities do policymaking economists have?

* Reprinted with permission from the author. The article appeared in *Monthly Labor Review* **97,** No. 3 (March 1974), 42–43.

Internal and External Functions of the Council of Economic Advisers

The Council of Economic Advisers has both an inside function and an outside function—communicating inside to the President and other Administration officials and communicating outside to others. The inside function is by far the more important. I will start with some precepts for behavior in the inside role.

1. The Council should present to the President and other officials the best economic information and analysis it can. That is obvious. One implication is that the Council should select its staff solely on the basis of professional competence.

2. The honest, objective "options paper" is the noblest work of the Council of Economic Advisers. The President must be given a fair account of the pros and cons of all the eligible choices. The Council must be sufficiently aware and respectful of the differences of opinion among reasonable men to do this. It must be able to distinguish between the strength of its own convictions and the probability of truth.

3. In a process where there is opportunity for different positions to be advocated, the Council should be prepared to choose a position and argue it vigorously. In choosing its position the Council should give particular weight to those long-run, indirect, and general consequences of policy which are likely to be underestimated by others who have special interests or who are not economists. The Council should try to distinguish between those aspects of its conclusion that stem from economic analysis and those it justifies on other grounds.

4. Members of the Council of Economic Advisers do not have to leave the room when the political consequences or political feasibility of proposed economic policies are being considered. Most political discussions are based on what economists call casual empiricism. Any middle-aged economist who has spent his life in an economics department or other political organization, who knows something about history, and who reads the newspapers can contribute to that.

The trouble with politics is that so much of it is bad—not in the sense of being immoral, which it isn't, but in the sense of not working, and of being a poor predictor. For good economics to be overridden by good politics may sometimes have to be accepted. But for good economics to be overridden by bad politics is a tragedy which should be resisted as far as possible.

5. A Council member, as long as he remains a Council member, should be prepared to give advice about the operation of the policy that exists, even if it is not his preferred policy and even if he is at the same time urging its revision. To think that this can-

7

not be constructively done, and that a person can only work well in a world made in his own image, is childish. It is especially childish for economists, whose whole stock in trade is how to make the best of a given situation.

Now let me turn to some guidelines for the behavior of the Council of Economic Advisers in their external function, that is, in communicating to the public outside the Administration:

1. The President and the country are entitled to explanation and defense of the President's economic policies. Without public understanding, even the best policies will not work or will not survive. The Council of Economic Advisers is qualified to perform this function because it understands at least as well as anyone else the reasons for the President's policies. Of course, the Council does not perform this function alone; others in and out of the Government participate in it.

2. The key requirement in the Council's explanation and defense of the President's economic policies is honesty. There are people who think that explaining and defending the President's economic policies is inconsistent with honesty, especially when the President is not their hero. But surely a reasonable, unbigoted person, not overwhelmed by his own conceit, will not take this position. There are honest arguments to be made on many sides of most issues. Democratic process requires that these honest arguments be heard, including the President's. There are also plenty of dishonest arguments around, and the Council should not use them.

3. The Council is not required to go into hiding during political campaigns. It is during such campaigns that public education on economic issues is most needed. But a campaign is not an excuse for abandoning the basic rule of honesty. During campaigns a certain depreciation of the verbal currency goes on, which everyone seems to understand and to discount, and which apparently does no great harm. However, I don't believe that members of the Council should participate in it. It risks too much confusion about the Council's role.

4. On the whole, Council members should not tell jokes in public. The press won't understand them.

I have suggested nine commandments for the conduct of the Council of Economic Advisers. To go to 10 would be presumptuous. Everything I have said can be summed up in the word I have used several times—"honesty." That word seems to be going out of style, and is being replaced by another one, "credibility." These are quite different ideas. "Honesty" is telling the truth. "Credibility" is saying what the listener expects you to say. The Council should seek to be credible, but not at the expense of being honest.

The subject under discussion here—the behavior of the Council of Economic Advisers in the world of policymaking—is part of a larger subject—the behavior of all economists in that world. Surely singling out the CEA for discussion here does not mean that a lower standard of honesty, objectivity, and integrity is required of other economists—of Presidents of the American Economic Association, of professors, or of economic journalists. In fact, the danger that the Council of Economic Advisers will mislead the public for political reasons is smaller than that other economists will do so. The members of the Council are instantly recognized as appointees of the President, who have participated in making his policy, who believe in him and in the policy. What they say is understood in that light, and people can discount it as they think fit. In fact, since whatever the Council says is filtered to the public through adversary media, the discount is likely to be too great rather than too little. But people don't know what discount to apply to the utterances of economists identified only as "professor," which is not to say that no discount is needed.

Economists who participate in the policymaking process have, in my opinion, two responsibilities. First, they should try to identify themselves, so that people will understand from what political standpoint they speak. Second, they should try to tell the truth. Our profession has only a few truths. They are mainly of the order of "There is no free lunch," "Things are seldom what they seem," "We live in a world of scarcity," and "To live is to choose." We should try to tell these truths to the people. The President appreciates having his economic advisers tell him the truth, even when it is unpleasant. The people will also, I believe, respect economists for telling them the truth.

Reading 3

Shortages: A Necessary Evil Of the Future?*

By Donald L. Raiff

Summary

Their grocery carts colliding, two shoppers at the local supermarket scramble for the last roll of paper towels. Across the street, a long line of automobiles waits for gasoline. These and similar scenes have been publicized by the popular press as examples of recent material shortages in the U.S. economy.

To some people, today's "shortages" portend more empty shelves in the local markets as well as depletion of "necessary" raw materials. Yet, government price controls appear to have been a fundamental cause of the product shortages.

The future of shortages depends largely on the application of price controls. Calls for such controls depend on the citizenry and their understanding of the costs and benefits of such actions. Fortunately, continued regulation of prices by government fiat is not a certainty. When forced to choose between shortages and price rises, it is not clear that the consumer will choose the former. Some shoppers would prefer to pay 60 cents for a gallon of gasoline rather than not be able to buy gas if the price were set at 35 cents per gallon.

Relative prices—the price of one good as compared to all other goods—are a powerful tool in the market's attempts to balance future demand and future supplies as well as current quantities. As such, they generate incentives that affect production of desirable goods and the conservation of scarce resources. It would be better to harness these motives to help accomplish social objectives than ignore their existence and appear indignant when they throttle well-intentioned efforts by government.

Key Questions to Consider

- What is the relationship between shortages and prices?

- How do price controls create shortages?

- What is the relationship between exhaustible raw materials and shortages?

---

* Reprinted with permission from *Business Review*, Federal Reserve Bank of Philadelphia, October 1974, pp. 13–23.

Shortages: A Necessary Evil Of the Future?

Their grocery carts colliding, two shoppers at the local supermarket scramble for the last roll of paper towels. Across the street, a long line of automobiles waits for gasoline. These and similar scenes have been publicized by the popular press as examples of recent material shortages in the U.S. economy.

To some people, today's "shortages" portend more empty shelves in the local markets as well as depletion of "necessary" raw materials. Yet, Government price controls appear to have been a fundamental cause of the product shortages. Holding prices down encourages heavy demand for goods and discourages suppliers from increasing their output. Thus, current shortages need not suggest continuing problems provided the future is free of price controls.

But what about the chance that market forces may fail us and that we will eventually run out of a "necessary" raw material? Although this scenario is a possibility, economic analysis suggests a *more likely path*—increases in the prices of materials in short supply relative to those that are not so scarce. The higher price of the scarce commodities will then make it more practical to conserve remaining supplies and search out substitutes.

Some citizens may actually prefer shortages to the price rises necessary to clear the market. They want to allocate goods by nonprice methods during normal times as well as for periods of a national emergency to protect certain groups such as the poor. However, in these instances, a better solution would be to have the Federal Government provide the poor with income through direct transfers, while allowing price movements ot provide incentives for conserving resources and allocating available commodities.

SHORTAGES: THE NATURE OF THE BEAST

Perplexed Charlie Consumer asks: "How can anyone blame the Government for the product shortages? Our gasoline shortage resulted when OAPEC (Organization of Arab Petroleum Exporting Countries) tried to slap an embargo on oil shipments to America. So, the Arab exporters were the culprits, weren't they?"

OAPEC members played a key role in originally decreasing the quantity of oil brought to the U.S. market and causing the initial scarcity. *Yet, neither smaller supplies nor larger demands by themselves imply shortages. Only if prices are unable to move upward will decreased supply or increased demand promise a shortage.* Thus, the Federal Government turned the initial scarcity into a shortage by preventing price rises to the consumer.

When studying shortages an economist zeroes

11

in on prices. In his view, there's a situation of excess demand—a shortage—when at the current market price consumers demand more of a product than the market can immediately supply. If there is a shortage at this price, economic theory holds that the market price will eventually move upward to a level that eliminates the shortage (see Box 1). The shortage will vanish as higher prices cause buyers to reveiw their spending plans and cut back on those items becoming relatively more expensive. Also, profit-motivated suppliers will find the higher prices an incentive to increase the amount they bring to market.

Would there necessarily be a shortage if a large number of suppliers suddenly withheld their product from the market? No. If prices were allowed to move upward, this would allocate the available items as well as provide suppliers incentive to stop their withholding action. Thus, newsmen observing the situation would report rising prices, but no lengthening of the waiting lines or shrinking inventories of goods.

"Everyone seems to be able to obtain the amount they desire to purchase" would be the report because the "symptoms" of shortages would not be evident to the newsmen.[1]

Arguments that rising prices will not eliminate the shortages imply that consumers and producers make decisions independent of the price level. However, as long as either the supply or demand is even slightly responsive to price changes, a price increase will eventually eliminate the shortage.[2] The price will rise to a market-clearing level—the level which will

---

[1] Rising prices should not be called a symptom of shortages but rather the normal market adjustment to a decrease in supply or increase in demand. The main shortage symptom is when consumers are unable to obtain the amount they are actively trying to purchase.

[2] The precise process which generates the rise in the market price is probably a combination of unsatisfied demanders offering higher prices and suppliers raising their selling prices as they notice the unsatisfied demand.

Box 1   # What about Localized One-time Shortages?

The product shortages referred to in the text of this article are those experienced across regions in the U.S. by large numbers of firms or large numbers of consumers over a long period. Other localized shortages occur occasionally because of one-shot breakdowns in the distribution process, an inability to anticipate consumer demand over short periods, and/or an unwillingness to vary certain prices daily.

If a bread truck breaks down so that its normal Monday store deliveries can't be made until Wednesday, shoppers will most likely find a shortage of bread. Prices will probably not be raised on Monday to allocate the available bread because the grocer would be accused of taking advantage of a bad situation—windfall profits. Unless the supply, for at least this Monday and Tuesday, responded to higher prices, the grocer would probably plead for continued goodwill for himself and bad feelings for his supplier, while leaving prices unchanged.

Attending a theater for the opening of a highly publicized movie may provide another example of a local shortage—theater seats. Why shouldn't the theater manager raise the admission to discourage some of the demanders, save the long lines, and eliminate the uncertainty of such an admission policy based on queues? A number of reasons enter the manager's judgment to change his pricing policy. How would he get this information out to his potential market? Since the demand may differ between the 7 and 10 o'clock shows, he would have to vary his price to attract just enough people to "fill the house." For the sake of simplicity and goodwill, he may decide to keep the price unchanged and allocate by way of long lines. In this way any disappointment of a potential movie-goer is usually voiced against the people ahead of him in line rather than the price setter—the theater manager.

spur producers to supply exactly the quantity demanded by customers. It is true that the size of the hike necessary to clear the market hinges on the market participants' sensitivity to price changes.

PRICE CONTROLS IN A CHANGING ECONOMY INSURE SHORTAGES

The demands of both domestic and foreign consumers, as well as the supply intentions of firms and labor, can change—sometimes rapidly. Increases in demand and/or decreases in supply will raise the level of the market-clearing price. If Government controls hamper the free movement of market prices, these prices are prevented from doing their double duty—*rationing the available commodity among competing shoppers and providing the necessary incentive for businessmen to expand their output.* Without the assistance of upward price movements, demanders will not be able to find adequate supplies of the products they desire. Nonprice rationing schemes such as queues and, in some instances, black markets will spring up to allocate the available commodities. Suppliers may even attempt to cut costs by changing the product (see Box 2).

Changing Demands Alter Market-Clearing Prices. The idea that the amount demanded of most goods will rise as the price of that product falls and vice

Box 2 Controls Germinate A New Allocation Device and Product Alternatives

On August 15, 1971, the U.S. Government dramatically enlarged its efforts to control reported market prices (wages are the price for labor services).* This price control effort clamped ceilings on many of the prices of items sold in the United States. Some of the ceiling prices changed as the Federal effort moved through its various phases. But the relevant question is whether the official ceiling was below the price which would have equated the quantity supplied with the quantity demanded—the market-clearing price. If so, the quantity must be allocated through a nonprice method (such as—first come, first serve), and/or suppliers may cut costs by altering the product.

For illustrative purposes, consider the most recent example of price ceilings in the face of a large decrease in supply—the automobile fuel market, during the first quarter 1974. Evidently the quantity brought to the coastal markets by the suppliers was neither as great as that sold in similar periods a year before nor as great as the contemporary quantity demanded, given the posted prices. During this period posted prices were allowed to rise a few cents—as the Cost of Living Council and then the Federal Energy Office allowed increases in crude oil costs to be passed along. But this allowable price increase did not consider the effect of a decreased quantity brought to market and the price rises *necessary* to induce users to buy a reduced amount. Consequently, customers experienced rationing by other methods such as queuing, maximum purchase sizes, and sales only on alternative days depending on the odd or even number on the license plate.

Besides the nonprice allocation schemes, the purchased product changed. Before the oil embargo last year, gasoline was sold as a "joint product" with the services of windshield cleaning and a check under the hood "with a smile." In addition, sellers vied to make sure the consumer had a 24-hour daily option on such purchases. With Federal orders controlling the pump price, sellers profited only by curtailing costs and thus the services supplied. The result was shorter hours (7 A.M. to 10 A.M. was frequent in the Philadelphia area) and less frequent delivery of the ancillary services accompanied by attendants' smiles.

---

* Before 1971, the U.S. Government has regulated prices for such products as electricity, telephone services, and even a bank's depository services.

versa is a familiar one. However, there can also be an "increase in demand" for the product. This increase in demand means that consumers want even more of the commodity at the current price than they wanted previously. They are also willing to pay more for the same amount of the product than they would have earlier. For example, what would happen within a community if each person receives an unexpected $5,000 tax rebate? Suppose also there exists in this community a small combination manufacturing and retail business for mahogany furniture called Ethan's Place. This firm's handcrafted Early American line is the "luxury" many residents want to buy with their new-found dollars. Before receiving the rebate, they just couldn't afford the purchase, but now many more can. This increase in demand for furniture will be recognized first in the retail outlet, as floor samples are sold in an attempt to satisfy the growing number of back orders. The owner's natural response would be to increase production, but the manufacturing plant is already operating with a full shift of workers. To expand output, Mr. Ethan must pay his laborers time and a half for overtime, and this will increase costs per unit of furniture. If the firm is to expand output to meet the increased demand, it must charge a higher price to cover these rising per-unit costs and maintain profits. A general premise for any firm is that unless output can be expanded without increasing per-unit costs, increased demand will force prices upward until the market is cleared with increased output.[3]

But Movements Are Stymied by Price Controls. If prices are fixed by Government fiat, the market response would be stymied. The owner of the furniture-manufacturing outlet will spot the increased demand

in the same way—increased orders and lower inventories. But, *if his per-unit costs rise* with any increase in the quantity brought to market, he will not increase the amount supplied because doing so is unprofitable. He cannot recover higher unit costs by raising prices because of Government price controls. The result is a shortage of this Early American furniture, and an upsurge in cocktail party inquiries as to why Mr. Ethan doesn't increase production and eliminate the shortage.

The U.S. natural gas industry is a good example of the actual problems caused by price controls during a period of rising demand. The agreement to fix prices at the wellhead goes back to 1954—a time when natural gas was plentiful at the market price.[4] As possible uses of the product were expanded, demand increased yet prices were held down by the Federal Power Commission, at least relative to other fuels. The accelerating popularity of natural gas and its accompanying scarcity seems to stem from the U.S. Government's effort to hold down the price of natural gas. The low price spurred demand but failed to provide sufficient incentive to increase production.

While the price of natural gas rose 20 percent between 1950 and 1970, that of coal soared 80 percent, and that of heating fuel jumped 33 percent. In 1972 the cost of heating a home with gas in U.S. averaged 29 percent less than heating by fuel oil and 52 percent less than the cost of heating by electricity. As a result, consumers are now using natural gas faster than reserves are being discovered, natural gas inventories are declining, and in some areas new hookups are not being accepted. Prior to 1969, the annual addition of new reserves of gas exceeded production in the United States. But from 1968 to 1972,

[3] Over long periods, firms can adjust their production technology and possibly lower the per-unit costs of production and even new firms may enter the industry. But not all industries have technological breakthroughs or gain large economies by increasing the number and size of firms. Those *without* such breaks rely on increased prices to justify increased production.

[4] In 1938 Congress passed the Natural Gas Act for the purposes of placing pipelines selling natural gas in interstate commerce under the regulatory authority of the Federal Power Commission. The act was specifically made inapplicable "to the production or gathering of natural gas." Sales of gas at the wellhead by independent producers thus continued unregulated by the FPC until the 1954 Supreme Court decision in *Phillips Petroleum Co. v. Wisconsin.*

the annual addition of new gas reserves averaged only 47 percent of the production from existing reserves. In 1973, reserves totaled only 270 trillion cubic feet— a 12-year supply at current use levels.

Although there has been a steady decline in the production of existing gas reserves, an estimate for "potential" natural gas supplies (that is, gas not yet in proved reserves, but either identified or predictable according to acceptable geological knowledge) in the United States as of December 1972 is 1,146 trillion cubic feet. The significance of these "potential" natural gas supplies becomes apparent when it is understood that 1,146 trillion cubic feet is more than 49 times America's consumption in 1973. Thus, the natural gas shortage resulted *not* from an inadequate domestic resource base, but from the lack of an economic incentive to remove gas from the ground because of controlled wellhead prices.[5]

Supply Changes Can Alter the Market-Clearing Prices.

Other forces that can alter the market-clearing price are changes in supply. If demanders' plans are unchanged, a "decrease in supply" will force a rise in the clearing price. This decrease in supply means that suppliers reduce their output at current prices. Similarly, they must get a higher price for their goods to maintain their original level of output. For example, what happens in the furniture town referred to earlier if there's no tax rebate, but rather the suppliers of mahogany are able to conspire and double their price for the wood needed in Mr. Ethan's manufacturing prices? Now, his per-unit costs increase across the board regardless of his level of output. Recognizing the need to pass along this input-cost rise to maintain his profits, he quickly decides that only a price increase can keep him in business. The level of demand

for the furniture has not changed; therefore, some people considering future purchases will be discouraged by the higher price and buy something else instead, thus decreasing final output.

But Movements Are Stymied by Price Controls.

If posted prices are fixed by Government fiat, the market response is blocked. The supplier recognizes the need to increase prices in the same way—his cost of raw mahogany has increased. With the option of raising prices sealed off, he exercises other options which may involve cutting unit costs even to the extent of lowering product quality or changing its design. If he cannot discover a way to attain an acceptable rate of return over the longer haul, he will go out of business.

Beef is a good example of an industry that experienced supply shifts while under Federal price controls in 1973. As cattle feed prices rose throughout 1973, suppliers attempted to pass on their cost increases through slaughtering, packaging, and retail sales to the consumer. Some shoppers switched to less-expensive foods and bought less beef. However, cattlemen were generally able to pass along their cost increases until meat prices were frozen in late March (continuing through September 10). The meat industry, faced with a lid on retail prices and few quick cost-cutting measures, essentially shut down the slaughtering and packaging of production.

Some retailers, to stay in business, sold beef at a loss while attempting to make their profit on other products carried in their markets. However, in general, sparsely filled meat counters were the order of the day, despite the continued relative abundance of cattle.

Problems in Domestic Markets for Products Traded Internationally.

A ceiling price will also produce shortages when there are two markets for a single product—one controlled, the other uncontrolled.

Consider the United States's domestic and export markets. Firms export if the price they can obtain in foreign markets exceeds that obtainable at home. The

---

[5] See "Toward an Adequate Natural Gas Supply" published by the Gas Supply Committee, 1725 DeSales Street, N.W., Washington, D.C., September 1973, Sections II-III; and "Federal Oil and Corporation Gas Proposals," Legislative Analysis No. 18 (Washington: American Enterprise Institute for Public Policy Research, 1974).

difference must be wide enough to cover differential shipping and marketing costs between the two markets. Suppose that for some reason—increases in demand or decreases in supply—the world price of a product increased. In the domestic market, effective Government intervention may keep the U.S. price from rising. However, it cannot keep the world price from rising relative to the prevailing U.S. price. If the spread between the domestic price and the value of the item in the foreign markets becomes wide enough to cover exportation costs, the American firm may find it more profitable to sell to foreigners abroad rather than to purchasers at home, as the latter are limited in the price they can offer. This situation will swell exports and probably shrink domestic supplies for all products affected.

The aluminum industry illustrates this point. Aluminum will be facing a severe "capacity crunch" during the next several years. The beginnings of a tight supply situation can be followed through two periods. First, the industry's profitability declined during the sluggish period of demand at the beginning of the 1970s. Second, during the subsequent period of booming sales, the industry failed to attain a return on investment large enough to justify the new facilities required to meet the projected demand of the mid-decade. It is the latter period where price controls played a role.

Domestic and foreign demand for aluminum recovered sharply in 1972, and the supply situation became very tight in 1973. With supplies tightening, the selling price for ingot aluminum in the spring of '73 finally reached the published price of 25 cents per pound, ending more than three years of selling at a price discounted below the list price. Continued price recovery was thwarted by the establishment of a 25-cent ceiling price under Phase IV. Under the program, further increases were to be limited only to those necessary to cover cost increases incurred during 1973.

During the last half of 1973, as the foreign price climbed to 42 cents per pound, the United States became a net exporter of aluminum for the first time since 1970. In December the Cost of Living Council permitted a 16-percent increase—from 25 to 29 cents per pound—in the base price of primary ingot. The Council acknowledged that the action was necessary to encourage the expansion of domestic capacity and reduce the differential between foreign and domestic prices. In short, the Council moved to let the aluminum price rise to alleviate domestic shortages.

THE FUTURE IN TERMS OF EXHAUSTIBLE RAW MATERIALS

It might appear that some necessary resources are going to be exhausted, given our current rate of consumption. But in a competitive market the incentives would more likely insure the development of substitutes or conservation of presently available resources. If the demand for nonreproducible resources increases—as is being generally forecast—the market-clearing price for the resources will very likely increase.

Price appreciation of scarce resources will feed back on the production costs of final products using such material. A rising price of one final product relative to another gives consumers an incentive to cut back on their use of the good becoming more expensive. Producers of the good becoming relatively dear may then find it more profitable to develop new production technology using substitute raw materials.

Suppliers of raw materials that are becoming more expensive have the incentive to search for and develop additional sources of these materials. It is possible that some locations—identified by geologists but previously too costly to work—will now be tapped because the higher price makes them profitable (see Box 3). The development effort may also generate technological breakthroughs in the process of mining the raw material and even in geological efforts to discover the location of resource deposits.

Private ownership is important to the conservation of resources. Suppose a firm has private rights to land containing some raw material; expectations that

Box 3   # Projecting Resource Demand and Reserves

Since World War II, a number of technical studies have made projections about future resource usage and attempted to quantify the amount of raw materials available in the United States and the world.* In doing this, the analysts have had to forecast and incorporate the effects of growth, technological innovations, and changes in consumer preferences. These forces of change will alter the market-clearing price of a resource relative to its substitutes. It is this relative price which is crucial to the production and consumption decisions made everyday.

Taking present studies as the starting point, it might be useful to examine how they project future demand and arrive at a concept of reserves. As an example, consider the 1973 report compiled by the National Commission on Materials Policy. The demand until the year 2000 is estimated to repeat the growth experienced from 1950 through 1970. The cumulative demand 1971–2000 is calculated by adding up the consumption in each year. This technique ignores the effects of new movements in relative prices simply because these shifts were judged too difficult to estimate; as such, this is reason to doubt the accuracy of the estimated demand.

To set a framework for discussion of nonreproducible raw material supplies, the study defines the amount listed as *reserves* as that quantity known to be available using processes less costly than the current open market price. These reserves are available without any new price changes or technological breakthroughs. However, there are some quantities, call them *identified resources*, which are essentially well known as to location, extent, and grade, but too costly to mine presently. Presumably these resources will be exploitable in the future under changed economic conditions or with improvements in technology. For each commodity, there may be a third classification of quantities undiscovered but predictable according to accepted geological knowledge. Call this third group *hypothetical resources*.

To understand some of the implications of these data, assume there exists some hypothetical commodity, RAMAT. This hypothetical material is typical of those commodities whose cumulative demand projection substantially exceeds their current reserves, say the average of those in the Table. This average ratio of probable cumulative demand to reserves of these resources is 5.2. At first glance, we would expect to run out of RAMAT before the end of the current decade. However, as the reserves are used up, suppliers will find themselves able to raise prices to allocate dwindling supplies over future years. As the open market price of RAMAT rises, demanders will cut back on their quantity demanded and suppliers will find it in their interests to bring forth some of the identified resources and even to explore more of the hypothesized resources. Depending on the size of the identified reserves, their costs of recovery and the findings from further exploration, a shortage at 1971 prices could turn into abundance at 1980 prices.

---

* See the following resource comparisons with expected consumption in J. Frederic Dewhurst and Associates, *America's Needs and Resources*. Twentieth Century Fund Report 1947; *Resources for Freedom*, Report of the President's Materials Policy Commission (Washington: Government Printing Office, 1952); Hans H. Landsberg *et al.*, *Resources in America's Future* (Baltimore: Johns Hopkins Press, 1963); *Material Needs and the Environment Today and Tomorrow*, Final Report of the National Commission on Materials Policy (Washington: Government Printing Office, 1973).

Reserves at Current Prices Do Not Tell the Whole Story

(A) Commodity	(B) Units[1]	(C) Probable cumulative demand 1971–2000[2]	(D) U.S. reserves at 1971 prices[2]	(C/D) Demand relative to reserves	(E) Identified resources	(F) Hypothetical resources
Aluminum	Million S. T.	370	13	28.5	Very Large	KDI [3]
Antimony	Thousand S. T.	822	110	7.5	Small	Small
Asbestos	Million S. T.	43	9	4.8	Small	Insignificant
Barium	Million S. T.	31	45	.7	Very Large	Very Large
Beryllium	Thousand S. T.	28	28	1.0	Very Large	Huge
Boron	Million S. T.	5	40	.1	Very Large	Huge
Bromine	Billion lb.	12	17	.7	Huge	Huge
Copper	Million S. T.	93	81	1.1	Large	Large
Feldspar	Million L. T.	38	500	.08	Huge	Huge
Fluorine	Million S. T.	39	6	6.5	Small	Small
Gold	Million tr. oz.	293	82	3.6	Large	KDI [3]
Gypsum	Million S. T.	726	350	2.1	Huge	Huge
Iodine	Million lb.	269	225	1.2	Very Large	Huge
Iron	Billion S. T.	3	2	1.5	Very Large	Huge
Lead	Million S. T.	34	17	2.0	Large	Moderate
Lithium	Thousand S. T.	183	2,767	.07	Huge	Huge
Mercury	Thousand flasks	1,730	75	23.1	Small	KDI [3]
Molybdenum	Billion lb.	3	6	.5	Huge	Huge
Natural Gas	Trillion cu. ft.	1,098	279	3.9	Moderate	Large
Petroleum	Billion bbls.	276	38	7.3	Large	Large
Phosphorus	Million S. T.	208	39	5.3	Very Large	Huge
Planinum	Million tr. oz.	16	1	16.0	Moderate	Large
Potassium	Million S. T.	216	50	4.3	Very Large	Huge
Silver	Million tr. oz.	4,400	1,300	3.4	Moderate	Large
Sulfur	Million L. T.	514	75	6.9	Huge	Huge
Talc	Million S. T.	52	150	.3	Very Large	Huge
Tungsten	Million lb.	1,000	175	5.7	Moderate	Moderate
Uranium	Thousand S. T.	1,240	130	9.5	Large	Large
Zinc	Million S. T.	62	30	2.0	Very Large	Very Large

[1] S. T. = Short Tons, L. T. = Long Tons, lb. = pounds, tr. oz. = troy ounces, kg. = kilograms, bbls. = 42 gals.

[2] As estimated by U.S. Bureau of Mines, 1973.

[3] Known data insufficient.

Source: *Material Needs and the Environment: Today and Tomorrow.* Final Report of the National Commission on Materials Policy (Washington: Government Printing Office, 1973), pp. 4B-8 to 4B-9.

the price of that resource will rise rapidly in the future provide an incentive to conserve it.[6] In a sense, the company can *save* by holding stores of this commodity rather than dollars. As long as the expected rate of growth in the value of this commodity exceeds *the interest rate* plus any costs of holding this resource, the commodity is worth more undeveloped than developed. Under these conditions, if the owner develops the resource, sells it, and buys investment securities at the existing rate of interest, he will have less money than if he waits a year before developing and selling it. As such then, the market-clearing price and expectations about its movement can stimulate conservation as well as more rapid development of resources, depending on the direction of expected movements. This scenario also highlights the importance of the level of the interest rate in determining the conservation of raw materials—and it suggests a potential danger in regulating interest rates over any long period.[7]

THE CLAMOR FOR GOVERNMENT ACTION

What about the poor? Some people favor price controls—regardless of the shortages caused—because they claim that the poor are "unfairly" squeezed out in the distribution of commodities by "high prices." Others might argue that controls would be necessary in times of natural disasters to insure distribution of goods to the affected parties. Still others would point to their need during wartime to insure the allocation of resources to the national effort and not some profitable venture which appears not to assist in winning the war.

It is true that prices discriminate according to the ability to pay. Not that the rich will consume all commodities, but with their superior ability to pay they will probably end up with more of the available goods and services. If society wants to change this distribution, there are more efficient methods than Federal price controls. First, it is not clear that the poor will be better off in the longer run when a nonprice allocation scheme is substituted for price rises.[8] Second, price controls shrink the size of the total "pie" of goods and services available by hamstringing the incentive necessary to increase output by suppliers.[9] An "unsatisfactory" distribution of income could be better solved by using government as a vehicle to tax the nonpoor and give income to the poor through transfer payments. This would save the efficient product-allocation scheme and allow society to see more explicitly the costs of accomplishing this social goal.

During times of natural disasters, people may be more willing to sacrifice personal wealth to the common good of helping those caught in the disaster. Thus, a democratic government might be used as a vehicle to marshal the personal resources of the "unaffected" and distribute them to the "affected." However, attempts to hold down prices for the benefit of those less able to pay will encourage everyone to consume more of available goods. Also the incentive to produce more—usually desirable at such times—will

---

[6] Establishing ownership is an important ingredient in finding the best *method and level* of conservation for our raw materials. It is not the fact that a resource has economic value that leads to its depletion, but more important how it is owned. For example, fish and beefsteak both have economic value, but the stock of New England coastal fish is being depleted while cattle survive. The fish are owned by "everyone," while cattle are owned by individuals (or agents of the individuals) who have the right to keep others from slaughtering them. Hence, they can capture the value at some time in the future, which cannot be assured under common ownership.

[7] To some this may seem a far-out connection between the financial markets and conservation of resources, but as long as financial securities are alternative investments to holding real assets the connection exists.

[8] For a discussion of this in terms of rental housing, see Howard Keen, Jr. and Donald L. Raiff, "Rent Controls: Panacea, Placebo, or Problem Child?" *Business Review* of the Federal Reserve Bank of Philadelphia, January 1974, pp. 3–11.

[9] The goal could be just the opposite—enlarging the output available for distribution. Investment in productive education and machinery enlarges the economy's ability to produce and for this reason some people are urging government to provide investment tax credits.

be stifled as low prices hold down the profit incentive.[10]

During wartime every citizen is supposed to pay the price of victory through the personal sacrifices asked by government. However, it would be wise for government to avoid institutions which are inefficient and hinder the incentives to increase productivity and conserve in consumption. Price controls are such an institution. It would be better for government to bid away from other uses the resources needed to win the war. The resulting increases in income to suppliers of equipment (and manpower) would provide incentives for them to heighten their efforts. Rising prices for material and labor would also encourage conservation of resources in nonwar endeavors. If any changes in the resulting distribution of income were desirable, this could be handled through income taxes.

---

[10] For a reconstruction of the housing market after the San Francisco earthquake of 1906 and discussion of the necessary role of prices in such markets, see Milton Friedman and George J. Stigler, *Roofs or Ceilings? The Current Housing Problem* (Irvington-on-Hudson, N.Y.: Foundation for Economic Education, 1946).

NECESSARY EVIL? NOT UNLESS PRICES ARE STRIPPED OF THEIR POWER

The future of shortages depends largely on the application of price controls. Calls for such controls depend on the citizenry and their understanding of the costs and benefits of such actions. Fortunately, continued regulation of prices by government fiat is not a certainty. When forced to choose between shortages and price rises, it is not clear that the consumer will choose the former. Some shoppers would prefer to pay 60 cents for a gallon of gasoline rather than not being able to buy gas if the price were set at 35 cents per gallon.

Relative prices—the price of one good as compared to all other goods—are a powerful tool in the markets' attempts to balance future demand and future supplies as well as current quantities. As such, they generate incentives that affect production of desirable goods and the conservation of scarce resources. It would be better to harness these motives to help accomplish social objectives than ignore their existence and appear indignant when they throttle well-intentioned efforts by government.

Reading 4

Meat Prices*

Summary

The sharp increases in retail meat prices in recent months have been the subject of much discussion. The increases have had a major impact on total consumer outlays since meat expenditures account for about one-third of the average family food budget. Reflecting their disappointment at these higher costs, some people have accused farmers, meat packers, and grocery stores of "gouging consumers" by forcing meat prices up. These views are generally stated without a full understanding of the underlying economic processes involved in price determination.

This article presents an economic analysis of the forces which have led to meat price increases. The analysis emphasizes the function of the market system in pricing meat, in allocating meat products to consumers, and in allocating resources to meat production.

Key Questions to Consider

■ Who is to blame for the price increases in meat? Explain.

■ What factors have caused the demand and supply curves to shift?

■ How does time enter into the economic analysis of meat price determination?

* Reprinted with permission from *Review,* Federal Reserve Bank of St. Louis, **55,** No. 5 (May 1973), 17–20.

Meat Prices

The price of food remains a topic of much concern to consumers, government officials, and the food industry. In the past six months food prices have increased at an exceptional 20 percent annual rate. Since meat purchases represent a substantial portion of consumer expenditures on food, it seems reasonable that meat prices would receive more attention than price increases for other items. The persistence of this situation has prompted publication of the following abridged and updated version of an article which appeared in the October 1972 issue of this Review.

One can only distribute and consume what has been produced, this is an elementary truth.[1]

The sharp increases in retail meat prices in recent months have been the subject of much discussion. The increases have had a major impact on total consumer outlays since meat expenditures account for about one-third of the average family food budget. Reflecting their disappointment at these higher costs, some people have accused farmers, meat packers, and grocery stores of "gouging consumers" by forcing meat prices up. These views are generally stated without a full understanding of the underlying economic processes involved in price determination.

This note presents an economic analysis of the forces which have led to meat increases. The analysis emphasizes the function of the market system in pricing meat, in allocating meat products to consumers, and in allocating resources to meat production.

ECONOMIC ANALYSIS OF PRICE DETERMINATION

An economic approach to determining prices of meat or any other commodity holds that changes in meat prices at grocery stores result from a series of market factors rather than arbitrary decisions by farmers, meat packers, wholesalers, and retailers. Behind retail price increases is often found greater consumer demand as indicated by a rising volume of sales. When the demand for a commodity increases, the first change one typically observes is a higher sales volume which results initially in a reduction of inventories. In order to restore depleted inventories retail grocers increase their meat orders from packers hoping to continue selling a larger volume at the prevailing price. Upon receiving increased orders for meat the packers in turn increase their rate of meat slaughter and seek to restore meat animal inventories by additional purchases from farmers. Since the prevailing price only provides sufficient incentive for producing the current number of animals, additional animals are not available for immediate delivery at current prices. As packers compete among themselves in an attempt to obtain more animals, they raise their offering prices to farmers.[2]

In the short run the number of animals available for marketing is relatively fixed. The number of ani-

[1] Leonid I. Brezhnev, First Secretary of the Soviet Communist Party (*New York Times*, May 29, 1971).

[2] See Armen A. Alchian and William R. Allen, *University Economics*, 3rd ed. (Belmont, California: Wadsworth Publishing Company, Inc., 1972), pp. 95–97.

Table 1

Estimated Meat Expenditures as Percent
of Total Consumer Outlays
(Dollar Amounts in Billions)

	Total personal consumption expenditures	Total meat expenditures	Meat as percent of total
1950	$191.0	$14.2	7.4%
1955	254.4	16.4	6.4
1960	325.2	20.0	6.2
1965	432.8	24.1	5.6
1970	616.8	35.0	5.7
1971	664.9	36.5	5.5
1972	721.0	43.3	6.0

Source: Calculated from U.S. Department of Agriculture and
U.S. Department of Labor data

mals on farms cannot be increased rapidly and the increase in meat production per animal is relatively limited. In other words, the supply of meat is "inelastic" with respect to price in the short run; only a small percent increase in quantity will be forthcoming with a relatively large percent increase in price.

Table 2

Importance of Meat in the Food-at-Home Budget
(Percent of Food-at-Home Outlays)

	Red meat	Poultry	Fish	Total
1960	28.3%	4.1%	2.9%	35.2%
1965	27.8	4.1	2.9	34.7
1970	31.1	4.3	3.3	38.7
1971	31.3	4.2	3.4	38.9
1972	27.9	3.4	3.1	34.4

Source: Calculated from U.S. Department of Agriculture and
U.S. Department of Labor data

Over the longer run, however, the supply of meat is more "elastic," meaning that with each incre-

mental increase in price, a larger quantity will be offered than in the short run. Given sufficient time, farmers and ranchers find it profitable to expand their meat animal breeding herds and produce additional animals for slaughter. The fact that the long-run meat supply is more elastic than the short-run supply means that a given increase in demand for meat has a smaller impact on prices after passage of some time. Nevertheless, any increase in the demand for meat involves a rise in the price paid by consumers. The higher price equates the larger amount demanded with the amount supplied.

Conversely, declines in meat demand, or advancements in production technology which tend to increase supply, result in lower prices. More meat animals are offered to packers and more meat to consumers than can be sold at previous prices. Prices are thus marked down by retail grocers until the quantity of meat demanded by consumers equals the amount supplied.

DEMAND FOR MEAT HAS INCREASED

Demand for meat has increased substantially in recent years, as evidenced by the fact that consumers have purchased larger quantities of meat at higher prices. Factors contributing to the greater demand include rising per capita incomes, increased food subsidy programs, and a larger population.

Both Consumption and Prices Have Risen

During the period of rapid increase in average meat prices from 1964 to 1972, total meat consumed rose from 42 to 52 billion pounds. Per capita consumption rose from 224 to 253 pounds. The rise in per capita consumption was at a faster rate during this period of rapid price increase than during the previous 14 years (1950–64) when prices were relatively stable.

The fact that meat consumption has increased reveals little about meat demand without information on prices.[3] Meat consumption, like consumption of any other commodity or service, depends in part upon its price. Given no change in the demand, a decline in meat prices will induce consumers to purchase a larger quantity. For example, a larger volume of meat production caused by livestock cycles or by unusually favorable weather conditions will increase the supply and result in lower prices. The lower prices will induce some consumers to purchase larger quantities of meat. Conversely, a cyclical or seasonal decline in meat output will cause an increase in meat prices, which will in turn cause some consumers to substitute other types of food for meat and reduce their meat purchases. These short-run changes in supply can cause price changes without a change in demand. Such short-run changes in supply have no doubt been a factor in the irregular upward course of meat prices since 1964. However, consumers have purchased larger quantities of meat at higher prices per pound indicating that demand has increased.

Food Subsidies Have Increased

Larger Government issues of food stamps to the lower income groups and increased donations of meat products to schools, institutions, and low-income families occurred during the recent upswing in meat prices. Total issues of food stamps rose from $0.7 billion in 1969 to $3.6 billion in 1972. Federal outlays on the school lunch program have more than tripled during the last three years, rising from $227 million in 1969 to $788 million in 1972. Food distributions to low-income families, institutions, and others also have increased, but at a lower rate than the school lunch programs. Total Government outlays for the Federal

food programs, including food stamps, food distribution, and money donated for food purchases, rose from $1.2 billion in 1969 to $3.5 billion in 1972. In 1969 Government outlays for these programs amounted to only 1.4 percent of the total costs of food used at home by all consumers. By 1972 these outlays amounted to more than 3.6 percent of total food-at-home costs.

MEAT SUPPLY

Over the longer run, production technology and imports have tended to increase the nation's meat supply and offset part of the impact on prices of the rising demand for meat. As shown in Charts I and II, meat production plus net imports have risen at a sufficient rate to provide consumers with increasing quantities

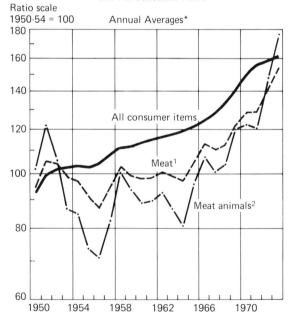

Chart I

Price Trends — Meat, Meat Animals, and All Consumer Items

Ratio scale
1950-54 = 100   Annual Averages*

Sources: U.S. Department of Agriculture and U.S. Department of Labor
[1] Includes beef and veal, pork, lamb and mutton, poultry, and fish.
[2] Includes beef cattle, hogs, and sheep.
*1973 based on average of first two months.

---

[3] Economists explain a larger quantity of a good being purchased in two different ways. One way is for the *demand schedule to shift* to the right, indicating a *greater quantity* will be taken *at each price*. The other way is a *movement along a given demand schedule*, indicating that price changes are the result of a shift in the supply schedule. The latter means that *larger quantities* are purchased *only at lower prices*. Both schedules may also shift simultaneously.

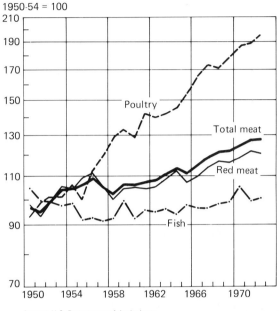

Chart II

Trends in Per Capita Meat Consumption

1950-54 = 100

Source: U.S. Department of Agriculture

at less than average price increases for other consumer items. From 1950 to 1972, red meat and poultry production combined rose from 25.9 to 48.1 billion pounds, a 3 percent annual rate of gain. Production of red meat rose from 22.1 to 37 billion pounds, an annual rate of 2.4 percent, while output of chickens almost tripled. Meat imports in 1972 were equivalent to 6 percent of domestic red meat production, whereas imports were insignificant in 1950. Meat import controls were relaxed last year, and if they are not reimposed, rising meat production in other nations, along with rising domestic meat production efficiency, should have an even more favorable impact on the nation's meat supply in future years.

Between 1950 and 1972, when meat consumption was increasing rapidly, prices of meat animals rose 1.7 percent per year, and red meat prices rose 2.1 percent per year. Broiler prices declined 1.6 percent per year. In comparison, the consumer and general

price indexes rose at average annual rates of 2.7 and 2.9 percent, respectively.

CONCLUDING COMMENTS AND SUMMARY

The data indicate that meat prices in recent years have been determined largely by basic supply and demand conditions. With the exception of the Government crop control and price support programs and import restrictions, the meat industry has generally operated in a competitive, free enterprise atmosphere.

The meat industry meets a major competitive test of easy entry and exit. The industry is not hampered by rules and regulations such as chartering, licensing, or long periods of apprenticeship. Virtually all are free to enter all phases of meat production and distribution. It has numerous participants in all stages of production and distribution. The efficient prosper and the inefficient fail. This incentive has permitted the price mechanism to bring into equality the quantity of meat supplied and demanded at a relatively high level of consumption per capita and at prices which have risen only moderately compared with other consumer items.

If people want more meat they will bid up the price and the higher prices of meat will provide the incentive for increased production. Productive resources will flow freely to this sector when anticipated returns are attractive. The higher meat prices in recent years have been necessary to attract the additional resources used in producing the larger volume of meat demanded by consumers. If prices had been set arbitrarily at a lower level, a smaller volume would have been produced and some consumers would have had less meat. Therefore, in the absence of a responsive price system in which the quantity supplied and the quantity demanded are equated, the available quantity must be rationed among consumers by some other means.

In summation, the fact that meat prices have increased sharply in the past year, and have generally risen since 1964, is not a sufficient reason for the belief that the consumer is being taken advantage of or that the meat industry is callous or inefficient. The meat industry is reasonably competitive and takes advantage of developing technology. Meat production has increased at a high rate since the upward trend in meat prices began in 1964. Consumers have demanded a higher level of meat production per capita, and have paid a higher price for the increased output.

The higher prices were necessary to provide incentive for producers to supply the amount of meat demanded. Without the higher prices output would have been less. Unforeseen events such as livestock cycles and unusual weather conditions may cause livestock and meat prices to fluctuate around their long-run equilibrium levels. However, given the generally competitive conditions in the industry, the market price of meat is always near that level required to match production with consumer demand. The recent price increases were probably no exception to this general rule.

Reading 5

Congested Parks—
A Pricing Dilemma*

By Dan M. Bechter

Summary

In the last few years, newspapers and magazines have called attention to the problems caused by record numbers of people crowding into some of our national parks. Although the gasoline shortage may ease this crowding somewhat, the state and local parks may experience even heavier use as a result. It is easy to conclude that these congestion difficulties justify creating new parks. This conclusion, however, may not be justified. Economic analysis can help us see the nature and probable consequences of the park crowding problem. This article demonstrates the use of such analysis.

Key Questions to Consider

■ In what ways can a market shortage be alleviated?

■ If private camps are substitutes for public parks, what is the nature of the relationship between an increase in price for the services of one and demand and supply of the other?

■ One of the difficulties in this analysis is the definition of park services. How will the definition you use affect your analysis?

* Reprinted with permission from *Monthly Review*, Federal Reserve Bank of Kansas City, June 1971, pp. 3–5.

Congested Parks—
A Pricing Dilemma

In the last year or two, newspapers and magazines have been calling attention to the problems caused by record numbers of people crowding into some of our national parks.[1] Yellowstone and Yosemite are receiving most of the publicity, but other national recreation areas are suffering similar popularity troubles. Many state and local parks, too, are being strained to accommodate rapidly increasing attendance. It is easy to conclude that these congestion difficulties justify creating new public parks and expanding outdoor recreation facilities in existing ones. Additions to supply would seem appropriate, considering the rising demand. Yet, the apparently inadequate recreational capacities of various public parks may reflect something other than a lag in adjustment of supply to demand. Governments may be distorting the recreation market by charging too little for the recreational use of public parks. Such an improper pricing practice would be misallocating resources. Some groups would be benefiting—perhaps those that are not intended to—at the expense of others. Economic analysis helps show the nature and probable consequences of the park crowding problem. It also helps reveal the complex and indirect influences on public park fees, the choices of consumers, and the markets for all recreational goods and services.

WHEN DEMAND CROWDS SUPPLY

Overflowing visitation at a public park provides a textbook display of a shortage. Park crowding means insufficient park space—or types of park space, such as camping space, driving space, fishing space, etc.—to satisfy outdoor recreationists. They want more. Their wants, however, depend directly on what they must pay. The existence of a shortage says only that the quantity demanded exceeds the quantity supplied at the going price. Excessive park crowding, therefore, reflects a park entry or a park privilege fee that is below the one that equates the amount of park space consumers want to the amount available. Chart 1 clarifies the explanation.

Chart 1 shows a set of demand and supply relationships for camping spaces in a hypothetical public park. Demand curve D_1D_1 shows that the lower the price, the larger the number of park camping spaces desired on an average summer day.[2]

---

[1] See, for example, Paul Friggens, "Last Chance for Yellowstone?" *Reader's Digest*, March 1971, pp. 190–96.

[2] Assume away (as unnecessarily complicating here) the likelihood that campers prefer some of the park's campsites to others.

Chart 1

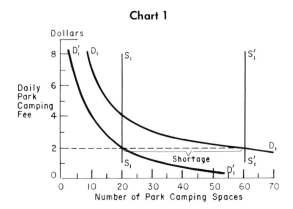

Vertical line S_1S_1 indicates the number of camping spaces in the park—assumed to be an invariable quantity in the very short run. Now, suppose park officials set the camping fee at $2. Clearly, quantity demanded (60 spaces) exceeds quantity supplied (20 spaces), or a shortage of 40 spaces prevails at that price.

What happens to the 40 camping families whom the park cannot accommodate? Those who can return home may disappointedly do so. Others may not show up, having heard about or previously experienced the shortage. Still others may try to squeeze and shoehorn into the camping area, or pitch their tents in unauthorized areas of the park. Some may find other public or private places to camp nearby. The remainder may stay in motels, sleep along the road, or drive all night.

As can be seen, selling a good or service below the market-clearing price—where demand equals supply, or $4, in the example—simply requires other forms of rationing or adjustment, such as first come, first served, which places a premium on arrival time. Some of these adaptations, in effect, increase the cost of the outdoor recreation experience. They make the consumer spend extra time and money guaranteeing himself participation in the leisure activity. Other adjustments, such as crowding into available space, make outdoor recreation less fun.

The shortage shown in Chart 1—or any market shortage, for that matter—can be reduced by (a)

increasing price, (b) increasing supply, (c) decreasing demand, or (d) a combination of the preceding. Before considering these solutions, consider a part of what is going on outside the park.

Chart 2 shows another set of supply and demand curves—those for camping spaces on private land near the hypothetical public park. Currently, entrepreneurs are making 18 such spaces available, charging the going-market price of $2.50. Note that quantity demanded equals quantity supplied at this price—no shortage here. On a day of normal demand, everyone who wants to camp in a private area can do so. Some of this demand for private camping space depends, of course, on overflow from the public park. Assuming that campers prefer locations within the park to those outside, it might seem strange that some are willing to pay the extra half dollar charged by private campgrounds. It must be remembered, however, that the park cannot satisfy demand at $2. Also, note that a sizable portion of the left tail of demand curve D_1D_1 (Chart 1) lies above $4, indicating that several campers are willing to pay more than this amount for places inside the park. Some of these people certainly would be willing to locate outside for less when the park is full.

Now, consider each of the solutions to the shortage of public park camping spaces. Suppose first that the park authorities raise their camping fee to $4 (Chart 1). The shortage immediately disappears.

Chart 2

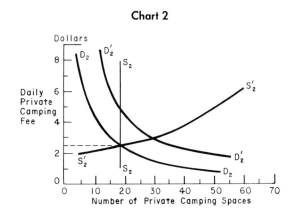

Everyone wanting a space at this price within the park finds one, because quantity demanded declines from 60 to 20 spaces. In addition, because of the increase in the park's camping fee, more people will decide in favor of the less expensive private facilities. Demand curve D_2D_2 for private camping spaces (Chart 2) will shift over to $D_2'D_2'$. For awhile, there will be a shortage of private camping spaces, and campground owners may raise their prices. Eventually they will expand, or new private campgrounds will open. This is what colored curve $S_2'S_2'$ shows—the number of camping spaces private landowners will supply, given the opportunity to adjust to various prices. As can be seen, the market price settles at $3 a space, where quantity demanded = quantity supplied = 29 spaces.[3] ($S_2'S_2'$ slopes upward to the right, showing that costs per space increase as space is increased.) Furthermore, the market for motel rooms, and other markets, will be affected. This example only looks at the market for the most obvious substitute for public camping spaces.

Suppose that instead of increasing price, the park officials increase the number of camping spaces from 20 to 60 in Chart 1, shifting supply out to $S_1'S_1'$. Again, the shortage disappears. As a result, how-

ever, the private campgrounds may be driven out of business. (In Chart 2, D_2D_2 shifts left—not shown.) Other markets, too, are affected.

Instead of increasing the number or the price of park camping spaces, the park authorities (Federal, state, or municipal) may try to alleviate the crowding —the shortage situation—by reducing demand for these spaces. (D_1D_1 would shift left to $D_1'D_1'$ in Chart 1.) This could be done by allowing the quality of the park facilities to run down. Or, another public park could be established nearby, thereby relieving the pressure on the existing one. Subsidization of private campgrounds, to lower their costs and to encourage their expansion and improvement, offers still another means of reducing the demand for space in the hypothetical public park.

Each of these alternatives affects the outdoor recreation market differently. If camping conditions in the public park are allowed to deteriorate, for example, the demand for private campground space in the vicinity might rise as the desirability of these private areas increases relative to those in the park. On the other hand, the region may become less attractive as an outdoor recreation area, especially if the whole park deteriorates, and private enterprise also may suffer declines in demand. Creating more public parks or subsidizing private outdoor recreation areas in the region should, at least in the short run, decrease demand for space in individual parks. In the region as a whole, however, such measures will likely encourage more outdoor recreation by reducing its time-and-money cost to consumers.

---

[3] A more complete treatment of these adjustments would include probable increases in the demand for park camping spaces brought about by increases in the price of private camping spaces, and so on, back and forth, until an equilibrium is reached.

Reading 6

Airport Congestion: Can Some New Cures Get Off The Ground?*

By Howard Keen, Jr.

Summary

For many Americans, traveling by airplane isn't as much fun as it used to be. As if the energy crisis weren't enough of a nuisance, there's the seemingly insoluble problem of traffic congestion, not just on highways but runways too. Taking off in flight from a large airport is becoming almost as big as hassle as battling freeway traffic to reach it. More and more air travelers are victims of airports that can't handle air traffic at peak hours. As a result, congestion and delay mount as planes are backed up waiting to land or take off.

The most obvious solution to this problem—building more runways—is running into some turbulence. Land in the right location is scarce and airports experiencing the most congestion are those in areas already crammed with homes and factories. The costs of land, construction, and financing are soaring. Concern for preserving the environment imposes additional limitations. Even without these problems, the time needed to construct new airports can be as much as ten years.

One way to bail out of this problem is to extract more use from airports already in existence. If existing facilities can be used more efficiently, the obstacles to airport expansion don't have to spell "stacked up." And the key to this efficiency is putting a price on runway space.

Key Questions to Consider

■ What would be the effect on the amount and timing of airport facility usage if airport authorities auctioned off the rights to using runways and landing facilities?

■ What is the effect of government regulation in this industry?

■ How are the inefficiencies of the current pricing system reflected?

■ How do the two solutions offered, variable congestion charges and exchangeable landing rights, differ? Which do you prefer? Why?

* Reprinted with permission from *Business Review*, Federal Reserve Bank of Philadelphia, February 1974, pp. 3–8.

Airport Congestion: Can Some New Cures Get Off The Ground?

For many Americans, traveling by airplane isn't as much fun as it used to be. As if the energy crisis weren't enough of a nuisance, there's the seemingly insoluble problem of traffic congestion, not just on highways but runways too. Taking off in flight from a large airport is becoming almost as big a hassle as battling freeway traffic to reach it. More and more air travelers are victims of airports that can't handle air traffic at peak hours. As a result, congestion and delay mount as planes are backed up waiting to land or take off.

The most obvious solution to this problem—building more runways—is running into some turbulence. Land in the right location is scarce and airports experiencing the most congestion are those in areas already crammed with homes and factories. The costs of land, construction, and financing are soaring. Concern for preserving the environment imposes additional limitations. Even without these problems, the time needed to construct new airports can be as much as ten years.

One way to bail out of this problem is to extract more use from airports *already in existence*. If existing facilities can be used more efficiently, the obstacles to airport expansion don't have to spell "stacked up." And the key to this efficiency is putting a price on runway space.

CONGESTION IS COSTLY

Congestion is a big waste. It wastes time and lost time is costly. Delays during take-offs and landings impose costs on airport users and, to some degree, on non-users. Most obvious are the costs of aircraft operation, especially apparent when planes are "stacked" waiting to land. This results in extra costs of fuel and extra wear and tear on the mechanical parts of the aircraft. In the case of planes with a crew, extra salary expenses are another cost of congestion. These extra operating costs resulting from congestion come out of the pockets of the aircraft owners initially but are bound to find their way into prices charged air travelers.

Time Is Money. Passengers also experience costs from delays. If delays prevent them from earning money, the cost of the delay to them is represented by these foregone earnings. Conversely, if the delay time would have been used for leisure activities, then the cost of the delay is given by the value passengers place on their leisure. These are the *opportunity costs* of delay. Congestion resulting in delays rules out the opportunity to use time in alternative ways. (See Box for the differences in opportunity and operating costs

Box   **Runway Customers Differ**

Users of airport runways, control tower facilities and ground service and storage areas fall into two major categories. *Air carriers* are aircraft which provide scheduled air transportation over specified routes. They are certified by the Civil Aeronautics Board (CAB) and consist largely of passenger-carrying airlines. *General Aviation* is the label given all civil aircraft not classified as air carriers. General aviation includes smaller corporate jets, recreational and instructional aircraft.

In general, the *opportunity costs per plane* of air carriers is greater than those of general aviation since air carriers have many more passengers. Furthermore, the operating costs are higher for air carriers as they are more costly to fly and require greater crew expenses than general aviation.

As a rule, general aviation has lower opportunity and operating costs per plane than air carriers and, as a consequence, imposes higher delay costs on air carriers than in the opposite situation. While general aviation contributes to peak-hour congestion at large airports, so do air carriers. In 1968 almost half of U.S. airports enplaning a million or more passengers per year experienced congestion because of peaking of flights, and air carriers made up more than 60 percent of peak-hour traffic at half of these congested airports.*

---

* U.S., Congress, Senate, Committee on Commerce, *National Airport and Airway System: Report to Accompany S. 3641*, 90th Cong., 2d sess., 1 July 1968, p. 89.

---

of the two major users of airports—air carriers and general aviation.)

More Pollution. Planes in the air and on the ground add to air and noise pollution. Those waiting to land and take off merely compound pollution. While this may be a problem only near airports, extra pollution costs can be substantial.

Higher Accident Risk. Finally, a flock of planes in the air waiting to land has a higher accident risk than only a few planes. Increased danger of accidents raises the cost of control tower operations because crowded skies require more careful monitoring of air traffic. Moreover, passengers, crews, and nonusers of airports are endangered by this increased accident risk.

An idea of the magnitude of these delay costs can be drawn from a few attempts to estimate them. In 1968 U.S. airlines put their costs resulting directly from delays at roughly $52 million annually.[1] This didn't include attempts to value the opportunity costs of passengers. A study which did attempt to estimate these costs found that delays at New York City's three major airports alone during April 1967 to March 1968 amounted to almost five million minutes or $50 million.[2] Delay costs for the U.S. as a whole would be much higher. The old adage that "time is money" is certainly applicable to time lost from airport congestion.

WHAT'S HOLDING UP THE LINE?

Federal Subsidies and Pricing. Public airports are not operated for the purpose of making a profit. The revenue goal is typically to cover costs. Consequently, the price charged for using runways and landing facilities is designed to raise revenue rather than force airport users to pay the full economic costs of using the facilities. Congestion is the result.

---

[1] U.S., Congress, Senate, Committee on Commerce, *National Airport and Airway System: Report to Accompany S. 3641*, 90th Cong., 2d sess., 1 July 1968, p. 51.

[2] Ross D. Eckert, *Airports and Congestion: A Problem of Misplaced Subsidies* (Washington: American Enterprise Institute for Public Policy Research, 1972), p. 18.

The bulk of airport revenue is from fees other than runway charges. Nonrunway revenues are from rentals, concessions, parking, and fuel sales. This part of airport operations uses facilities (terminals and access roads) which are not Federally subsidized.[3] The predominant method of granting concessions is to award them to the highest bidders. Here price allocates a limited number of concessions among competing demanders.

Runways (which receive Federal subsidies) are *not* allocated by price. Rather, they are open to all users on a first-come, first-serve basis. Fees charged airplanes to use runways are essentially a residual—to cover the difference between airport expenses and nonrunway revenues.[4] The typical charge is a landing fee based on aircraft weight.

So, in effect, users of airport runways and landing facilities are subsidized in two ways. One is through Federal grants and the other through revenue from other phases of airport operations such as terminal concessions. This means that there is no pressure on airport operators to charge runway users prices that reflect in any way the cost of resources used in landing and taking off or external costs (costs imposed on others who are delayed). With runway charges no higher at popular hours than at less popular times, it's not surprising that there's a waiting line.[5]

Moreover, the treatment of air carriers and general aviation with respect to landing fees is uneven. All large "hub" airports charge air carriers landing fees based on gross landing weight. General aviation, by comparison, is charged no landing fee whatsoever at 21 percent of large hub airports. Landing fees, when charged, don't vary according to the time of landing, the cost of airport resources used up, or the delay costs imposed on other users.

Government Regulations. Domestic interstate airfares are under the control of the Civil Aeronautics Board (CAB). One result of CAB policies is that air carriers have little chance to compete for passengers by offering lower prices. Except for some lower promotional fares and night fares on certain routes, interstate airfares are uniform across arrival and departure times. Consequently, there's a strong incentive to resort to competitive scheduling to attract passengers. Most airlines rank passenger preferences (along with good equipment utilization) high on their list of scheduling considerations. Passengers, given little incentive in the form of lower airfares, prefer to land or take off at a few concentrated hours. This results in an uneconomically large number of arrivals and departures at peak hours.

INEFFICIENCIES RESULT

The upshot of current subsidy and regulation policies is a pricing structure that encourages inefficiency and congestion. Prices that aren't designed to ration the available runways and that don't provide information about users' preferences result in inefficient use of

---

[3] Public airports have received Federal subsidies for runway construction and development since 1946. Through 1969 over $1 billion in matching grants went to over 2,000 airports. Current programs call for annual disbursements of $310 million in Federal monies for fiscal years 1974–75.

[4] Runway fees could make up the bulk of airport revenue if terminal and other ancillary concessions were of low market value. However, this is not the general rule at the larger airports which experience most of the congestion. See Michael E. Levine, "Landing Fees and the Airport Congestion Problem," *Journal of Law and Economics* 12 (1969): 79–108.

[5] This is not to say that, *on average*, landing fees are necessarily too low. While fees may not cover the full cost of providing runways and control tower facilities, the total

revenues generated for a community by air travel may be highest when runways are priced below cost. This can occur if low landing fees make flying less expensive, thus increasing the number of travelers. More travelers would mean additional revenues to other terminal facilities as well as many other local businesses.

existing airport facilities.[6] This inefficiency is manifested in several ways.

There are too many peak-hour flights in relation to the number the facilities can handle. This "excess demand" originates with both air carriers and general aviation. Airport facilities are strained and the costs from congestion—lost opportunities, aircraft operation, pollution and accident risk—mount.

Inflexible runway charges can also lead pilots to use the longest runways available, regardless of their real landing requirements. When airports have runways of different lengths, pilots usually prefer the longer ones because of the extra measures of safety they afford. However, the use of longer runways by small planes can delay air carriers waiting to land since the shorter runways are often inadequate to handle the commercial passenger craft.

Passengers and general aviation pilots have little opportunity to indicate how much they value delay-free use of airports at any particular time. It's likely that some would be willing to pay much more for less congestion—an indication that the opportunities lost from delays are worth a lot to them. Others may feel that their money cost and the cost of delays usually encountered are in about the right balance to suit their tastes. But as long as landing fees and airfares remain fixed, these preferences can't be fully expressed.

Airport investment suffers from this lack of information. The "need" for investment in additional facilities depends upon how much the additional facilities are worth to the ultimate users. Without this information, the chances of misguided investment are high.

In addition to inefficient use of individual airports, the overall airport system is used less efficiently. When airports are available to all users at below-cost prices occasionally, there's a preference for more modern, conveniently located airports. Even if landing fees were somewhat higher at large public airports than at smaller public or private airfields, quality of services, ease of access, and location still may outweigh any small price differences. What results is relative disuse of airports that could handle much more air traffic—especially general aviation. This avoidance of smaller private or public airports discourages investment in them to accommodate future air traffic growth.

SOME PROPOSED CURES

Several solutions to the problem of crowded airports have been offered. After taking a look at what causes airport congestion, it's no surprise that the indicated solutions focus on the pricing structure faced by airport users. Various twists could be added to proposed solutions, but mainly they fall under two major categories: variable congestion charges and exchangeable landing rights.

Variable Congestion Charges. Variable congestion fee proposals are in the form of either variable landing fees or variable passenger fees. Landing fees that vary with the time of day (or even with the day of the week)—with higher fees for peak-congestion hours—would tend to discourage congestion. Those not valuing peak-time use will be encouraged to land and take off at nonpeak hours. Air traffic would flow more evenly over a 24-hour period instead of being concentrated at a few popular hours. Since airport "capacity" is usually viewed as the facilities needed to handle *peak-hour use*, pressure for expansion to higher levels of capacity would be lessened.

---

[6] Price isn't the only rationing device—available supplies can be rationed by quotas too. In fact, both the Civil Aeronautics Board and the Federal Aviation Administration have quotas and quota-like policies in effect to alleviate congestion. However, quotas are far less efficient in providing information about air travelers' preferences than are prices. See James C. Miller, III, "Short-Run Solutions to Airport Congestion," *Atlanta Economic Review*, October 1969, pp. 28–29; and Eckert, op. cit., pp. 34–38.

Pressures on air carriers to overschedule at peak hours would be reduced by varying landing fees. Reluctance by the CAB to permit differential airfares (to jibe with differential landing fees) might impede passing the incentives from airlines to their passengers. But there needn't be a complete blockage. Airlines could cut costs by reducing in-flight services or the number of peak-hour flights. With more fully loaded planes, the same number of passengers could be handled with fewer flights. In this way, airline passengers would have some (although limited) way of expressing how much they value airport use at peak hours compared to less-congested times.

Variable landing fees can also be expected to alter the time and location of airport use by general aviation. In 1968 peak-hour landing fees at New York City's three major airports were raised from $5 to $25 for aircraft seating fewer than 25 people (mostly general aviation).[7] The results were striking: general aviation use at peak hours dropped by almost a third. Apparently, the peak-load value to a third of general aviation of these airports compared to nonpeak hours or less desirable airports was minimal.

Besides reducing congestion at heavily used airports, variable landing fees should result in more use of airports that currently are shunned. There would be incentives for increased use of smaller airports at peak hours (and even during nonpeak times if landing fee differentials were higher than they are now). With higher fees for general aviation at large hub airports, public and private airports in relative disuse now might become more attractive.

Variable passenger fees are another form of variable congestion charges. With these, differences in price would affect air passengers directly. Passengers would have to pay more to arrive or depart at peak hours than at nonpeak times. These charges could be in the form of variable airfares, but congestion could be effectively reduced even if airfares remained as they are now.

Either the airlines or airport operators could levy a surcharge on passengers arriving or departing at peak times. Since not all airports experience the same degree of congestion, this type of surcharge could be applied selectively only where it's desirable to reduce peaking of flights. In this way the structure of airfares would not have to be changed at all. Congestion surcharges would merely be tacked onto regular ticket prices.[8]

Exchangeable Landing Rights. A second type of proposed solution involves turning the right to use runway and landing facilities into a commodity. This "good" would then be sold to the highest bidders. The idea is to take a time slot—say half an hour—and offer a given number of landings to be handled—say 50. These 50 landings could then be awarded to the 50 highest bidders. As with variable landing fees, the willingness and ability to pay the price would determine use of airport facilities.

Users would have a way of indicating how much they value airport use at different times. The more they value use at a particular time, the more they would bid for that time slot. As circumstances change, landing rights could be traded just as other goods and services are exchanged in everyday market transactions. Airport authorities, after selecting the number of slots for a given time period, would auction them

---

[7] Airports receiving Federal aid must be available to the public without undue discrimination. Since the increase in landing fees favored larger planes at peak hours, a legal question was raised. In *Aircraft Owners and Pilots Association* v. *Port Authority of New York*, 305 F Supp. 93 (1969), it was ruled that this structure of landing fees was a reasonably valid method for using available facilities efficiently. Eckert, op. cit., p. 56.

[8] To have a maximum impact on congestion, variable passenger fees would have to be combined with some method of limiting general aviation traffic at peak hours. Either variable landing fees or surcharges at peak hours could accomplish this. If low-cost or no-cost access were still available to general aviation while air carrier traffic were reduced, peak-hour use by general aviation might even increase.

off. Both air carriers and general aviation would then bid for them.[9]

Like variable landing fees, exchangeable landing rights would result in less-wasteful use of airport resources. By offering only a limited number of operations at any one time, airport operators will force air traffic to be spread more evenly over a 24-hour period. Just as important, with landing and take-off slots granted to the highest bidder, users could indicate how they value the use of airports. Not only will this assure that scarce facilities go to those valuing them the most, but it will also give airport operators indications of the "need" for airport investment. Finally, congestion costs would be lowered, the necessity for continued expansion would diminish, and resources could be diverted to other uses.

TIME FOR AN EXPERIMENT?

It would take some time to iron out the administrative wrinkles in the new system under either of these proposals. For example, air carrier landing fees are

---

[9] For a fuller discussion of exchangeable landing rights, see Eckert, op. cit., pp. 50–53.

set out in contracts with airport operators. These take time to negotiate, especially if a change in fees is proposed.

Even if these administrative details were taken care of, airport operators would still have basic decisions to make. With variable landing fees, there's no advance information to indicate how traffic will vary with flexible fees. And with exchangeable landing rights, it's not known how the bids would vary with the number of slots offered. Trial and error would supply answers.

There are guidelines, however. Fees should approximate the full costs of use as closely as possible. They should account for direct costs (wear and tear on runways as well as control tower operations) and indirect costs (delay costs imposed on others). In short, users should be charged higher fees during peak-load periods.

New airports can't be built forever, and airplanes can't stack up forever. For airplanes to have a better chance of finding a place to land, present airports have to be used more efficiently. The present pricing structure of airports *encourages* inefficiency and congestion. Variable congestion charges and exchangeable landing rights would *discourage* this waste while at the same time taking some of the headache out of air travel.

Rent Controls: Panacea, Placebo, or Problem Child?*

By Howard Keen, Jr. and Donald L. Raiff

Summary

The topic of rent controls evokes varied responses. Many people view rent controls as a solution—a panacea of sorts—for the nation's immediate and long-range housing problems. Others hold that such controls make little difference one way or the other. Still others (landlords, homeowners, and even some renters) see the controls as creating more problems than they solve, in other words, begetting a perpetual problem child. Clarification of the arguments concerning rent controls can be accomplished by examining some basic principles of economics.

Rent controls are not a panacea for the rental housing market. They neither improve its operation nor provide the incentives to insure that renters' demands will be met over the long haul. In the meantime, controls can be a placebo, that is, they delude society into thinking government intervention is beneficial.

In the longer run, rent controls beget a problem child. They deter suppliers from providing the quality and quantity of rental housing services tenants want and are willing to pay for. Rent controls do this by lowering the income stream of owners relative to what they would have received in an unfettered market. Thus, they provide an incentive for present owners to "disinvest" in housing by allowing their properties to deteriorate, as well as encourage new investors to steer clear of the rental housing market.

Key Questions to Consider

■ The various markets have characteristics which differentiate them from each other. What are the characteristics of the rental market which make it unique?

■ Shifts in supply and demand occur in the housing market as they do in most markets. What factors cause these shifts and how would the responses of owners and renters differ in the case of rent controls as opposed to the free market situation?

■ What are the spill-over effects of rent controls on the owner-occupied housing market?

* Reprinted with permission from *Business Review*, Federal Reserve Bank of Philadelphia, January 1974, pp. 3–11.

Rent Controls: Panacea, Placebo, or Problem Child?

The falling gavel signals the opening of a meeting of the Verdant Valley Tenants Association. The evening's program features the financier and builder of the community's largest apartment complex who will explain why he hiked the rents on his housing units. The guest of honor proceeds to explain about his increasing costs, the effects of not being able to pass on cost increases, and the increased demand for his units from employees of the new plant down the road.

Timothy N. Tenant opens the question-and-answer session, complaining about "exorbitant" rent increases and asking about the "shortage" of alternative rental housing units. The verbal jousting continues until boredom descends, and the meeting is adjourned. The issues remain unresolved, but the Association is more resolved than ever to seek relief through rent controls.

Meetings such as these could be occurring in communities throughout the land. Some levels of government are now feeling the political clout of tenant associations. Tenant groups regularly air their grievances before voter-sensitive city councilmen. Rent control measures have been debated in the halls of Congress. And, only recently in New Jersey the state Supreme Court upheld the legality of local rent controls ordinances.[1]

The push for rent control legislation appears at first glance to interest only tenants and landlords. However, if allocation problems arise in any sector of the housing market, all other sectors stand to be affected. Rent controls have costs which must be compared with their benefits both for renters and the rest of society. Understanding these costs and benefits requires knowledge of the probable effects of this form of government intervention on the price and availability of rental housing relative to that found in an uncontrolled housing market.

The topic of rent controls evokes varied responses. Many people view rent controls as a solution —a panacea of sorts—for the nation's immediate and long-range housing problems. Others hold that such controls make little difference one way or the other. Still others (landlords, homeowners, and even some renters) see the controls as creating more problems than they solve—in other words, begetting a perpetual problem child. Clarification of the arguments concerning rent controls can be accomplished by examining some basic principles of economics.

---

[1] *Inganamort et al.* v. *Borough of Fort Lee et al.*, 62 N. J. 521 (1973).

NOT NEW BUT LARGELY FORGOTTEN

Rent controls are nothing new to Americans. Uncle Sam used them from 1942 to 1952. In the late '50s and '60s only New York City had them. Then in '71 under Phase I, rents along with other prices were controlled. Phase II decontrolled about 45 percent of all rental units affected, and Phase III lifted controls on the remainder. Today under Phase IV rents remain uncontrolled, despite strong political pressures on Congress to revive them.

Demands for government intervention in the rental housing market appear to be one of the many reactions to escalating rental prices. If rents climb faster than before, then controls are presumably a way of harnessing these increases. Rents, as measured by the rental component of the Consumer Price Index, increased at an average rate of 1.6 percent per year from 1960 to 1969. The average annual increase from 1970 to 1972 was 4.1 percent.

RENT CONTROLS: A RESPONSE TO AN SOS FROM THE RENTAL HOUSING MARKET

In general, rent controls are a response to large or rapid hikes in rent; however, their specific purposes often are unclear and not uniformly accepted by their backers. Proponents claim that these controls prevent owners from "gouging" tenants with large rent increases. This dovetails with the idea that controls would prevent only "unreasonable" rent increases. (Of course, agreement might be difficult to reach among renters, owners, and the general public as to what is gouging or unreasonable.) But why do rent hikes in particular bring forth these claims of "gouging" and "unreasonable" increases? Part of the answer is that not everyone understands how the rental housing market operates. Another part is that the rental market has a couple of characteristics that leave renters feeling helpless when faced with stiff rent hikes, such as high relocation costs, information costs, and time-lags in changing the stock of rental housing.[2]

Consider, for example, the effect of relocation costs. Besides the problem of moving his belongings, a renter's living habits often undergo major disruptions whenever he has to move. Suppose Mr. Tenant estimates the cost of disrupting his daily habits and moving to a new apartment to be roughly $1,000. If at lease-renewal time Mr. Owner raises the rent above the value that Mr. Tenant places on his living quarters, then the renter might be expected to move. This would force Mr. Owner to compete with other landlords for new tenants. However, if the rent increase, computed over the full duration of Mr. Tenant's expected stay in this rental market, falls short of the relocation cost estimate of $1,000, he'll not move. In this instance, relocating would cost more than the rent saved by moving to the less expensive apartment.

Moreover, the cost of obtaining information on both sides of the rental housing market can be quite high if the information is needed quickly. Renters want to know about the location and quality of services they can expect for what they pay. Owners desire to know about potential renters to insure that rent payments will be made and the rented units won't be damaged. Gathering information is time-consuming. If needed quickly, obtaining it is probably expensive. Giving tenants plenty of advance notice for rent hikes allows more time to collect the necessary facts. This lowers the cost of securing the additional information. So over longer periods, owners and renters can make less costly adjustments to the pressures and incentives of market forces.

Meeting the housing demands of the market is not easy. Forecasting what renters will want in the

---

[2] These characteristics (see p. 44) cause the rental housing market to fall short of the economists' idealized notion of "perfect competition." The basics of "perfect competition" are many small buyers and sellers, a homogeneous product, free mobility of resources, and low market-information costs. The rental housing market meets only the first condition to a high degree. Apartment locations and surroundings differ widely, relocating can be expensive, obtaining information on other units takes time and effort, and building new units quickly is costly.

future, and making rapid adjustments to changes in demand are difficult. Building new units or converting existing ones to new uses takes time and money. If demand increases, this slow adjustment of supply over short periods will cause rents to rise more than they would if units could be created instantaneously.

If to the extent the immediate effects of market changes are not understood, rent increases from this source are likely to seem "exorbitant" and "unreasonable." Rent controls offer no real solution to these short-run problems (see Box 1). Rather, they just keep the market from allocating the existing rental housing units to demanders on the basis of the price they are willing to pay. This effect, along with others, can be seen by applying some basic economic principles.

WHAT'S LIKELY UNDER RENT CONTROLS

Shifts in the supply and demand for housing occur with and without rent controls. Landlords will see their property taxes, construction costs, and operating costs change. Demands for particular apartments and

units in specific locations shift whenever industry relocates or renters' preferences change. When this happens, prices change until a new market-clearing price is reached. At any price other than the market-clearing one, owners and renters would not agree to an exchange of rent money for housing. At a higher price owners would be willing to build more units or activate vacant ones, but renters would not desire more.[3] At a lower price renters would want more apartments, but owners would be unwilling to provide them.

In the rental housing market, the price is the monthly rent. Under recent and proposed rent control measures, however, rents would not be completely free to move, and they could rise only if approved under the selected cost pass-through arrangements (see Box 2). But what if these pass-through measures result in rental housing prices that do not satisfy both renters and owners?

---

[3] Businessmen hold inventories as a buffer against unexpected changes in demand. In many cases, apartment owners hold vacant rental units. This lowers their costs of adjusting to changes in present and future demand.

Box 1   ## Proposals to Increase Competition

Rent controls govern the stated rental price. But is that the problem on which their proponents wish to zero in? The effective price—stated price plus other costs necessary to secure the rental unit—would be the better target. No matter the level of the effective price, it will decline as the rental housing market becomes more competitive. Proposals which attack the problems of relocation and information costs will, if enacted and effective, provoke more competition among the owners and tend to lower the resulting rental price. For example, specific subsidies to renters to cover part of their normal relocation costs would allow renters to be more responsive to market changes. Programs to collect and disseminate information on the rental housing services available in a locality would lower renters' information costs, whether the programs are

backed by tenant associations or government resources. The same applies to surveys of employers and renters to assist owners in projecting the demand for current and potential units.

Some proponents of rent controls have taken a longer-range view, hoping that these controls could assist in providing decent rental housing for everyone who wants it at a reasonable price. On the surface this rental housing goal can be realized either by raising personal income or by lowering the rental price. However, lowering the rental price through rent controls will have feedback effects thereby reducing the supply of housing. A less disruptive approach suggests raising personal income rather than circumventing the market allocation scheme by controlling rents.

Box 2   **Sample Proposals for Rent Controls**

If the demands for rent controls are successful, the program set in motion will have certain major characteristics. Two model rent control bills and two rent control amendments to the 1973 extension of the Economic Stabilization Act can be considered representative of recent rent control proposals. One model rent control bill was prepared by the South Jersey Tenants Association and the other was prepared by the Apartment House Council—an affiliate of the New Jersey Builders Association. The proposed Congressional amendments (introduced March 20, 1973) are one by Senator Clifford Case of New Jersey and one by Senator Lawton Chiles of Florida. Four major provisions are found in each of these proposals. One is a set of rules established to pass through cost increases incurred by the owner. A second is that rents are controlled on all multi-family units except those being rented for the first time. A third characteristic is the establishment of a rent control authority to adjudicate disputes arising under the controls. A fourth is the mechanism which activates the powers of the rent control legislation.

A central issue in every legislative consideration of rent control is the pass-through of cost increases. If the landlord's costs increase and he's prohibited from raising his rents, eventually he'll go out of business. So generally all rent-control legislation enables the landlord to pass some of his increased costs on to the tenant. Each of the proposals allows complete pass-through of tax changes. Two of the bills afford similar treatment to capital improvements. Other cost increases are considered under the umbrella of specific formulas which range from allowing rent increases of 2.5 percent a year to one allowing a rate of change commensurate with movements in the Consumer Price Index.

Exempting new units from initial controls shows a concern for the effects of such controls on the construction of new rental units. If rents are set below the level which generates a satisfactory rate of return on the owner's investment, new sources of supply would be cut off. Yet proponents of rent controls fail to realize that controlling the rents after the first renewal causes uncertainty and lowers the likely stream of rental income. The increased uncertainty and lower expected revenue will deter the construction of new rental housing despite the original exclusion of units rented for the first time.

Another common characteristic is the appointment of a person or board, whose job it is to evaluate rent increases and enforce the controls against illegal hikes. Such a board might function by examining costs and rent changes or, depending on how it's structured, render judgments on rental complaints before it. The administrative expense of this board is a tangible cost of rent control, but this cost is probably small compared to the misallocation costs that can occur when the market is not allowed to operate.

The suggested mechanism that activates rent controls ranges from some measure of the relative housing supply to formal Congressional action. Local controls are activated when a survey estimate of the vacancy rate for rental housing goes below a specified level. Thus, they could come and go depending on the variance of local vacancy rates. The Federal controls would end with expiration of the Economic Stabilization Act.

How Will Owners Respond?   In the face of cost increases, profit-maximizing owners will attempt to increase rents if they are to supply the same amount of rental housing. Although this is at best a trial-and-error process, rent controls make matters more uncertain for the owner. Rent controls generally have some pass-through provision for rising costs. However, the owner cannot up the rent in excess of the pass-through allowances without convincing the rent control authority he needs the extra amount because of financial hardship.

The pass-through formula could allow all increases in supplier's costs to be passed on to the renters. But then what has the legislation contributed, other than creating work for those involved? Even if the pass-through allows rents to reach their market-clearing levels, such controls still have costs. Owners, renters, and the rent control board will respond to the new laws by using resources to understand and cope with the regulations. Without controls, this extra time, effort, and money could be put to other uses.

The costs of controls are compounded if the pass-through allowance prevents rents from rising to their market-clearing levels. When this occurs, rent can no longer perform two important functions. It cannot allocate the present supply of rental units among renters so that everyone who is willing to pay the new rent can get rental housing. Nor can it provide incentive for owners to increase the supply of housing to satisfy demand at the new price. Without the freedom to up the rent, the owner can maximize his profit (or at least minimize his losses) only by cutting costs, which usually means lowering the quality or quantity of his rental units. This is the expected response as the owner tries to protect his investment over the short run in the face of a binding rent ceiling. The resulting supply of rental housing services would be less than if rents were free to rise to market-clearing levels. Although current rent control proposals prohibit lowering quality for a given level of rent, the difficulty of policing such actions would increase the administrative and enforcement costs of rent control with questionable results on quality.

Controls inject an additional degree of uncertainty into investment in rental housing. This occurs even if an owner could charge as high a rent as the market would bear for a unit when leasing it for the first time. An important factor when considering a particular investment is the ability to alter it when market conditions change. Rent controls hinder the owner's ability to respond to changing market conditions. And, consequently, such controls—or even the possibility of their being enacted—could make construction of rental housing less attractive as an investment than it would be without them.

Over the long haul rent controls will tend to make would-be owners reluctant to invest in rental housing. Current owners would adjust prices until the controls ceiling impinges on their planned rent hikes. Then they'll adjust by trying to cut operating costs. On the heels of decreased operating costs comes less and lower-quality housing services.

How Will Renters Respond? Suppose a new plant opens in a community. As the plant hires more non-residents, demand for housing in the community increases. Presumably, part of this increased demand will be for rental housing. In an unfettered market, rent increases would induce tenants who do not value this location so highly to surrender their apartments and move to rental housing elsewhere. To some, this may be viewed as driving current residents out of their living quarters. But the market is simply allocating a scarce resource among competing demanders, so that those who most desire a particular type of housing can bid for it. The resulting rent increases also spur owners to provide more and better housing. But under a binding rent ceiling these adjustments cannot occur. Price can no longer provide the needed supply incentive nor be used as a rationing device.

Under rent controls, apartments might be handed out on a first-come, first-serve basis. However, opportunities for discrimination based on looks, race, religion, and a host of other nonmonetary characteristics would result. If renters can compete for housing services, using both monetary and nonmonetary methods, an owner who discriminates on non-price grounds risks losing rental revenue. When monetary methods of competing are severely limited, as they are under rent controls, the potential loss of revenues from nonprice discrimination is less. This would lower the cost of these forms of discrimination, thereby encouraging their use.

Tenants unable to obtain controlled units could

be forced to pay relatively high rents for uncontrolled units or share living quarters with other families. When tenants desire more rental housing than landlords are willing or able to provide, controls may allow some segments of the population to avoid economizing on rental housing while others might be forced to live penuriously. As a result, black markets and "under-the-table" deals become commonplace. The "have-nots," who value a particular unit more than the "haves" occupying it, might offer some payment in exchange for that unit. In this way the market would still operate, but the costs of arranging mutually agreeable exchanges would be raised.

Market-search costs form a lion's share of the total transaction costs. And it's difficult to see how rent controls would lower such costs for renters. Under conditions in which rent has been controlled at a level below the market-clearing price, potential renters would need to ascertain the types of allocating schemes employed. Then they must develop a *modus operandi* for enhancing their chances of getting the desired housing services. All of this is more likely to raise rather than lower renters' market-search costs.

Tenants who somehow obtain controlled units will spend less on rent than they would if rents could rise to market-clearing levels. This may sound like a good deal for those fortunate renters, but actually such fortune has indirect costs. In addition to the possibility of deteriorating quality of housing services, there's the problem of mobility. In terms of the freedom to change residence, rent controls can be expected to make renters less mobile. Rents that are held at artificially low levels would not force particular renters to economize on housing as they would if rents were free to rise. Renters now living in controlled units would have little chance of duplicating their current housing and its cost at a new location. This would create a premium on obtaining and *retaining* controlled units.

Wealth Transfers Can Result.   To the extent that renters spend less on housing at the expense of rental

housing owners, there is a net transfer of wealth from owners to renters. Adequate housing is a desirable goal, but there's no economic or sociological rationale for imposing the costs of such subsidies on owners of rental housing alone. Furthermore, there's no assurance that all renters are economically disadvantaged or that all owners are economically advantaged. The only empirical study found in the literature on this issue concluded that no evidence existed to indicate that tenants were poorer than landlords.[4] So if rent controls are intended to redistribute income from the rich to the poor, they're probably an ineffective vehicle for doing it.

Spillover to Owner-Occupied Housing.   The prices of owner-occupied housing are not regulated under rent control proposals. But this doesn't mean that this portion of the housing market will be unaffected by rent control. Since owner-occupied housing is a close substitute for rental housing, any imbalances in the latter market may alter the demand or supply for owner-occupied housing. As potential renters find they are unable to obtain rental units, they will turn to the ownership market to obtain housing. Some developers will cater to this demand and shift from supplying units for rent to units for sale. The ultimate effect on the price of these housing units depends upon the strengths of these shifts.

The spillover effects of rent controls do not have to be confined to the price and quantity of owner-occupied housing. Another spillover channel is possible through the property tax system. If the quality of controlled rental housing deteriorates so that its assessed value drops, then a heavier tax burden could fall on residential homeowners or other tax revenue sources. (See Box 3 on pages 45 and 46 for details of the major U.S. experience with rent controls.)

---

[4] D. G. Johnson, "Rent Control and the Distribution of Income," *American Economic Review* 41 (1951): 569–82.

Box 3   # The New York City Experience

New York City has had rent controls since 1943 and they remained basically unchanged until 1969. The characteristics of these pre-1969 controls are not identical with the proposals described in Box 2. Housing built after 1946 was not subject to rent controls.[1] The Office of Rent Control under the Housing and Development Administration administered the controls, and owners were permitted to hike rents when there was a change of renters. The rent hike was limited to 15 percent, but it could be less if the building in question was not violation-free. In some cases, rent reductions could be ordered. In addition, various cost pass-through allowances were permitted—major capital improvements, economic hardship of the owner, increased service, and rising labor costs. The triggering mechanism was a vacancy rate below 5 percent in the controlled sector. Surveys were conducted every two years to determine this rate, but it never climbed higher than 3.2 percent in the post–World War II period.

There is little evidence of any major problems in the rental housing market before 1960. In the early 1960s storm warnings appeared, and around 1965 Gotham's rental housing market plunged into a crisis. The pervasiveness of the crisis is evident in a 1970 study by the Rand Institute in New York City.

Vacancies are acutely scarce, construction is at its lowest level in many years; rents in the previously uncontrolled sector rose so rapidly in 1969 that a new form of control was imposed, and large numbers of recently habitable buildings have been reduced to shambles or withdrawn entirely from the market. Tenants are deeply dissatisfied either with the quantity of service provided by their landlords or with the rents demanded, or both. Landlords are equally dissatisfied with the yields of their property, the behavior of their tenants, the burdens of public regulation, and the illiquidity of their investments.[2]

Rent controls alone did not cause the crisis, but they contributed heavily because they prevented rents from rising in tandem with costs. This protected many tenants from major rent increases. Rand found that since 1945 the costs of supplying well-maintained rental housing rose about 6 percent per year, while rents moved upward only 2 percent per year.

When the costs of operating and maintaining rental housing began accelerating in 1965, the gap between costs of supplying rental housing and controlled rental revenues widened appreciably. The same Rand study discovered that in the first half of the '60s the stock of rental housing grew at an average annual rate of 22,000 units. But in the second half the available supply declined by an average of 7,000 units per year. Quality suffered too, according to the Rand Institute. From 1960 to 1967 the inventory of rental housing classified as "sound" increased 2.4 percent, while that rated "deteriorating" rose by 37 percent, and "dilapidated" by 44 percent. Moreover, about 80 percent of the housing inventory losses (for reasons other than merger or demolition) during 1966 to 1968 involved units in buildings classified as either "sound" or "deteriorating" but *not* "dilapidated" in 1965. It's not surprising that proposals to alleviate the city's rental housing shortages included drastic changes in rent controls ostensibly to reflect supply and demand forces better and revive incentives to supply rental housing.

Some persons did benefit from rent controls, however. Renters who obtained and retained controlled units spent less on housing than they would

---

[1] In 1969 the New York City Council passed a law which widened the coverage of rent controls to include housing built after 1946.

[2] Ira S. Lowry, ed., *Rental Housing in New York City. Volume 1, Confronting the Crisis* (New York: The New York City Rand Institute, 1970), p. 1.

have in the absence of such controls. Some of the monetary costs and benefits were examined in a study using 1968 data. It's estimated that the net benefit to families living in controlled housing was $270 million (an average of $213 per family). However, the cost to landlords totaled $514 million, and the cost of administering rent controls hit $7 million. So the estimated excess of costs over benefits to the market participants was $251 million.[3] Both "poor and nonpoor" alike received these benefits. It was estimated that in 1967 a family of four could manage a "low-to-moderate" standard of living in New York City on a gross income of $6,800 to $7,400. In that year about 45 percent of all renters living in controlled units had incomes above $7,000.[4]

---

[3] Edgar O. Olsen, "An Econometric Analysis of Rent Control," *Journal of Political Economy* 80 (1972): 1094.

[4] Ira S. Lowry, *et al.*, *Rental Housing in New York City. Volume 2, The Demand for Shelter* (New York: The New York City Rand Institute, 1971), p. 81.

It is easy to see how a premium can be attached to controlled units. Families who lived in rent-controlled housing in Manhattan in 1968 paid an estimated average of $1,200 less per year than they would have paid for the same housing in an uncontrolled market.[5]

While rent control in New York City was not the only cause of the housing crisis, several independent studies, including some commissioned by the City, concluded that the rent increase limitations were a major contributor. In response to this, the City adopted a major reform of its rent control law in mid-1970, and a New York State law, passed in the spring of 1971, decontrolled all controlled units vacated after June 30, 1971.[6]

---

[5] Ibid., p. xv.

[6] For details of the reformed rent controls, see Alan S. Oser, "City Details Rent Formulas for '72 and '73," *New York Times*, October 3, 1971, sec. 8, p. 1.

PANACEA, PLACEBO, OR PROBLEM CHILD?

Rent controls are not a panacea for the rental housing market. They neither improve its operation nor provide the incentives to insure that renters' demands will be met over the long haul. In the meantime, controls can be a placebo—that is, they delude society into thinking government intervention is beneficial. In fact, they start down the path of problem creation. With the usual demand increases, controls will initially aid renters living in controlled units—holding down their monthly payments—at the expense of the owners of controlled rental housing. This short-circuits the role of rent to provide incentive for tenants to economize on housing usage and for owners to meet the demand for housing services. All of this is done without coming to grips with the roadblocks to competition, such as relocation costs, inadequate in-

formation about alternatives, and time-lags in building new units.

In the longer run, rent controls beget a problem child. They deter suppliers from providing the quality and quantity of rental housing services tenants want and are willing to pay for. Rent controls do this by lowering the income stream of owners relative to what they would have received in an unfettered market. Thus, they provide an incentive for present owners to "disinvest" in housing by allowing their properties to deteriorate as well as encourage new investors to steer clear of the rental housing market.

Summing up, it seems the rent-control bandwagon "on its way to the happy housing grounds" could get stuck at a rundown tenement shack. And, that's reason enough for considering its destination before hopping aboard.

The Urgency of Minimum Wage*

By George Meany

Summary

In 1966 when the minimum wage of $1.60 an hour was enacted, it was the first time in history a worker who worked full-time, year round, at the minimum wage could provide something better than a life of poverty for his family. This is what the Fair Labor Standards Act was meant to do when it was enacted 35 years ago.

The confidence instilled in the minimum-wage worker by the 1966 amendments, a confidence which reflected his ability to provide an above-poverty level of living for his family, did not last long.

In the last few years the cost of living has continued to move upward at a rapidly increasing rate and the purchasing power of the $1.60 minimum wage has plummeted. By April 1973 the $1.60 an hour minimum wage, which looked so promising in 1966, was worth $1.19.

That is why organized labor regards an increase in the federal minimum wage to at least $2 an hour now as one of Congress' most urgent legislative matters.

Key Questions to Consider

■ According to the author, what do studies show about effects of minimum wage legislation on wages, prices, and employment?

■ Why is the AFL-CIO opposed to a subminimum wage for youth?

■ The author claims that in the long run, low wages actually reduce rather than create jobs. What is his reasoning?

* Reprinted with permission from *American Federationist*, AFL-CIO **80**, No. 7 (July 1973).

The Urgency of Minimum Wage*

In 1966 when the minimum wage of $1.60 an hour was enacted, it was the first time in history a worker who worked full-time, year round, at the minimum wage could provide something better than a life of poverty for his family. This is what the Fair Labor Standards Act was meant to do when it was enacted 35 years ago.

The confidence instilled in the minimum-wage worker by the 1966 amendments, a confidence which reflected his ability to provide an above-poverty level of living for his family, did not last long. In the last few years the cost of living has continued to move upward at a rapidly increasing rate and the purchasing power of the $1.60 minimum wage has plummeted. By April 1973 the $1.60 an hour minimum wage, which looked so promising in 1966, was worth $1.19.

That is why organized labor regards an increase in the federal minimum wage to at least $2 an hour now as one of Congress' most urgent legislative matters.

During the two-year delay while Congress has talked about, but not enacted, a new minimum, the price of onions has increased by 83 percent, potatoes 39 percent, chuck roast 34 percent and hamburgers, fish and eggs by 25 percent or more. These are all staples in the poor man's diet and there are no "cheap" substitutes for him to resort to.

The present $1.60 minimum wage means that the employed head of a family of four, working 40 hours a week, year round, would earn nearly $1,000 less than the government-defined poverty level for his family of $4,275 a year. Since the goal of the Fair Labor Standards Act when it was adopted almost 35 years ago was to insure that the lowest-paid workers and their families would not have to live in poverty, the $1.60 minimum wage means this country is far short of its commitment.

Two years ago the AFL-CIO stated that the minimum wage should be increased to at least $2 an hour immediately and coverage under the Fair Labor Standards Act extended to all workers, a recommendation supported by government statistics which showed that the number of poor persons in this country had increased in 1970, after declining throughout

* This article is based on the testimony by AFL-CIO President George Meany before a Senate Labor subcommittee. At the time of the testimony, the House had passed a minimum wage bill supported by the AFL-CIO, with Senate action yet to come.

the 1960s. The $1.60 minimum wage was worth less in 1971 than the previous $1.25 minimum rate was worth in 1966 when the law was last changed. Unless Congress helped minimum-wage workers, they had no recourse except welfare in a period of spiraling prices.

Two years later, all of these situations not only continue to exist, but have worsened.

Not all the provisions of the pending Senate bill are adequate to meet the needs which now exist. For example, $2 an hour today will not buy what $1.60 bought in 1966 or even in 1968. Nor will $2.20, a year from now, fully compensate for escalating living costs. The AFL-CIO supports a further increase a year after that to $2.50 an hour.

The Census Bureau in a report released in December 1972 showed that 25.6 million persons were "low-income" or "living in poverty" in 1971. This is 1.4 million more than in 1969. (Subsequent government figures on the 1972 poverty level show that the number of Americans below the $4,275 poverty level decreased in 1972, to 24.5 million. This entire decline was among whites—while the number of whites defined as poor dropped by 9 percent, the number of blacks living in poverty rose some 4 percent to 7.7 million, an increase of almost half a million. Overall, the 24.5 million figure means that about 1 of every 9 Americans is still living in poverty.)

These are not just numbers; they are people. Many of them are members of families where the father or mother works full-time, year round, but is unable to provide the family with even a minimum standard of living. Inflation has hit low-wage workers the hardest and many workers are questioning why they should continue to work when they can do little more for their families than those on welfare.

The Fair Labor Standards Act should also be broadened to cover all workers. The patchwork of exemptions included in the law means that almost 17 million workers are currently denied even its modest wage and hour benefits. An additional 6.5 million workers are in activities which have minimum wage protection but are exempt from overtime provisions.

"Low wages do not create additional jobs. In the long run they actually reduce the number of jobs by cutting into the purchasing power of the people who must spend all the money they can make."

—AFL-CIO TESTIMONY, *1973*

Many of the unprotected workers are among the hardest-working, poorest-paid employes in the country today. They work on small farms, in restaurants, in stores, in state and local governments. They work as domestics and for this work they are not even paid subsistence wages. Half of the household workers were paid less than $1 an hour in May 1971, according to a recent study of the Department of Labor—hardly the kind of wages which will increase the supply of domestics and meet the demand for such workers. All of these workers should be guaranteed "the minimum standard of living necessary for health, efficiency and general well-being," as stated in the law.

Whenever the question of updating the minimum wage law is under consideration, the same dismal predictions of resulting business shutdowns, massive unemployment and inflation are heard. As a result of these repeated complaints, Congress has ordered studies designed to measure any negative effects of minimum wage legislation after each change in the statute. Each study has proven how false these complaints were. Each study has consistently demonstrated widespread benefits for the economy as a whole, accompanied by substantial gains for those at the lowest end of the wage scale and only isolated instances of adverse effects.

These studies have been conducted under both Republican and Democratic Administrations and the findings have been consistent—the good effects have far outweighed any isolated adverse effects and the economy has benefited. We make no reference to the 1973 report of the Department of Labor because, in our view, this report does not contain "an evaluation and appraisal" of the minimum wages established by the act nor does it include recommendations for improving the statute.

However, Secretary of Labor James D. Hodgson said in his January 1972 report to Congress evaluating minimum wages: "On balance, the wage increases granted to 1.6 million workers to meet the $1.60 minimum wage standard had no discernible adverse effect on overall wage or price trends."

In his January 1971 report, Hodgson had stated: "Although the economic indicators just noted increased at a fairly rapid rate in the year in which the federal minimum wage for the newly covered group was raised 15 cents, it is significant that employment in retail trade and services—the industries where the newly covered group is largely concentrated and hence most likely to manifest some impact from the wage increase—fared better than industries unaffected by the statutory escalation in the minimum wage."

He concluded his summary with this statement: "In view of overall economic trends, it is doubtful whether changes in the minimum had any substantial impact on wage, price or employment trends. Of much greater significance, however, is the fact that the 15-cent boost did help 2 million workers recover some of the purchasing power eroded by the steady upward movement of prices which had started even before the enactment of the 1966 amendments."

In a previous report to Congress in 1970 by the then Secretary of Labor George P. Shultz, a similar conclusion was drawn. It stated that "Total employment on nonagricultural payrolls rose in 28 out of the 32 consecutive months between January 1967 and September 1969. In the most recent 12-month period, employment climbed 3.2 percent, from 68.2 million in September 1968 to 70.4 million in September 1969. Employment rose in all major non-agricultural industry divisions in the 12-month period between September 1968 and September 1969. In the retail, services

and state and local government sectors—where the minimum wage had its greatest impact in 1969, since only newly covered workers were slated for federal minimum wage increases—employment rose substantially."

With respect to price controls Secretary Shultz stated: "The steady upward movement of prices during the period studied reflects a continuation of the rising trend in prices which was in motion prior to the enactment of the 1966 amendments. There are strong indications that other factors, although possibly not entirely exclusive of minimum wage escalations, were major causes of price increases occurring during the period studied."

In the previous Democratic Administration, then Secretary of Labor W. Willard Wirtz drew substantially the same conclusions, stating in 1969 that "the increased minimum wage levels set in 1966 have not contributed to the current inflationary spiral to an extent which permits reasonable questioning of their net value in strengthening both the position of low-paid workers in particular and the economy in general."

In the face of these consistent reports by Secretaries of Labor—including Hodgson and Shultz—we believe Congress should reject the views of those who foresee economic collapse every time the FLSA is amended. Similarly, Congress should reject the voices of those who, while acknowledging the need for change, recommend only minimal increases in the minimum wage while and at the same time attempting to use the amendments as a vehicle for retrogressive exemptions.

For example, opponents of increases in the minimum wage have reacted to the positive findings in studies of minimum wage effects by shifting the point of their attacks. Most recently, the target has been a lower minimum wage for young workers.

The AFL-CIO is unalterably opposed to a subminimum wage for youth or for any other category of worker. The minimum wage represents a floor under wages, and no one—young or old, black or white, male or female—should be asked to work for less than the wage floor.

Because minimum wage opponents were placing the onus of high unemployment rates for youths on the Fair Labor Standards Act, a massive study on this subject was undertaken by the Department of Labor. The study failed to link youth unemployment to minimum wages. Hodgson stated the conclusions of his 1971 report: "A comprehensive study of the relationship between youth unemployment and minimum wages ... provides information useful in evaluating the teenage unemployment problem. A significant finding was that it was difficult to prove any direct relationship between minimum wages and employment effects on young workers."

The study itself, which was completed by the Department of Labor in March 1970, includes significant statements:

"The magnitude of the employment effects of minimum wage legislation probably has been small, as the studies included in this report underline, and consequently difficult to measure precisely ...

"Unlike Britain, France or Japan, American wage-setting institutions have generally developed the practice of setting a wage rate for a job regardless of who holds the job ...

"If a youth differential were instituted in the 1970s, it would be difficult to evaluate its effects without better data ... During the coming decade, the teenage population will increase 12 percent, compared with 40 percent in the 1960s. Assuming no major decline in economic activity, this slower rate of growth, alone, should help ease problems of absorbing teenagers into the employed labor force."

How this Administration—in the face of its own reports—can urge a subminimum wage for youth is beyond comprehension.

The AFL-CIO is concerned about the high level of teenage unemployment. We are concerned about all unemployment. The real problem—and Congress and this Administration must face up to it—is that the economy is generating too few jobs for all workers,

old as well as young. The answer is the creation of more jobs—not a "super low-wage" pool of exploitable young workers.

Low wages do not create additional jobs. In the long run they actually reduce the number of jobs by cutting into the purchasing power of the people who must spend all of the money they make.

Those people who seek a lower minimum wage for teenagers refuse to recognize that this action would actually mean the displacement of working heads of families, discrimination based solely on age, and higher profits for employers at the expense of young workers.

When Secretary of Labor Peter J. Brennan was seeking confirmation of his nomination by the Senate, he testified on Jan. 18, 1973: "I believe in a realistic and adequate (minimum) wage. I am aware of the problem of youngsters, many of whom have to pay their way through school, but I am fearful if we have a difference of wages with the youngsters and their fathers in the area where minimum wage is so important, this could create problems."

Senator Robert A. Taft (R-Ohio) then asked, "How do you feel about the youth differential?" In answer, Brennan said: "... If they are going to perform the same duties, the same responsibilities, I do not see why there should be any difference in the rate."

However, when Brennan testified before a House Labor subcommittee on April 10 he managed to present a proposal worse than that presented last year on behalf of the Administration. His proposal would result in employers firing fathers to hire sons, by extending the exemption from 18 to 20 years.

This proposal is put forth as a solution to the critical unemployment situation facing youths. As we read Brennan's testimony, the situation for the 16-17 year old group was deemed most "critical" because their unemployment rate was highest. The situation for the 18-19 year old group was deemed to be only "slightly less critical" because their unemployment rate was somewhat lower. Setting aside for the moment the fallacy of low-wage setting as a mechanism for creating jobs, it is important to know how many people in the 16–20 age category are looking for jobs and what kind of jobs they are seeking.

In April 1973, there were 4,174,000 unemployed. Of these, 3,189,000 were looking for full-time work. In the 16 and 17 year old group there were 606,000 unemployed but only 166,000 of them were seeking full-time jobs. In the 18 and 19 year old group, there were 501,000 unemployed, of whom 360,000 were looking for full-time jobs. While only about one-quarter of the unemployed 16–17 year olds were seeking full-time jobs and 72 percent of the 18 and 19 year olds were seeking such jobs, in the 20–24 year old group almost 90 percent of the unemployed were looking for full-time jobs. In the 20–24 year group, therefore, some 822,000 persons out of 938,000 unemployed were seeking full-time work.

It boggles the mind that government policy should be designed so as to move 16–17 year olds to the front of the hiring line, and 18 and 19 year olds just behind them, by allowing employers to pay them substandard wages, while placing a competitive disadvantage on the 20–24 year old group as well as on older unemployed workers who are not only more numerous but who are typically seeking full-time work.

In April 1973, the black unemployment rate was 9.1 percent while the white rate was 4.5 percent. The rate for veterans 20 to 24 was 9.3 percent, compared to the overall rate of 5 percent.

If the Administration were logical, it would be proposing a sub-minimum for black workers and another sub-minimum for veterans. The black teenage unemployment rate is higher than the overall rate for teenagers. So why not a separate minimum for black teenagers, lower, of course, than for white teenagers?

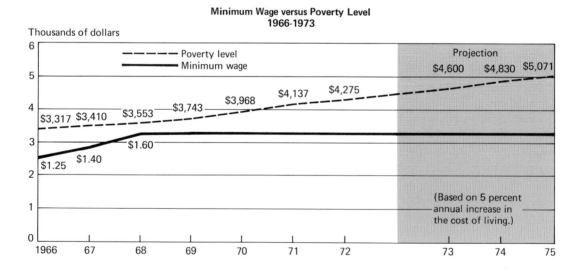

Minimum Wage versus Poverty Level
1966-1973

There is no logic to the Administration proposal. The only beneficiary would be the employer who would fire fathers in order to employ youngsters at a cheaper rate. And that type of employer deserves no break at all.

A growing economy and full employment are the only correct answers to unemployment. Discrimination in any form is wrong and cannot be tolerated. Increasing the minimum wage has proven an effective method of generating additional jobs through increased purchasing power. And that is what America needs now.

The goal and the hope of the Fair Labor Standards Act must be met and the federal minimum wage should be increased immediately to a point no less than is needed to support a family of four above the poverty level. Regularly scheduled increases to $2.50 an hour should be enacted to guard against further erosion of the living standard of workers receiving the federal minimum wage.

The same minimum wage rates should apply to all presently covered workers as well as to those newly covered by these amendments. The AFL-CIO rejects the idea of a differential in the minimum wage rates for agricultural workers or for any other groups of workers, such as household workers or government employes. Social legislation should not be used to create second-class citizenship. Arguments that expansion of coverage must be postponed if the minimum wage is increased should be rejected.

In both the 1961 and 1966 amendments, the minimum wage was raised and coverage was expanded to include substantial groups of low-wage workers. Following each of these changes, business prospered, the economy expanded and many workers had a floor placed under their wages for the first time.

The Administration is out of line in its view that to extend coverage to additional state and local government workers would be "at cross purposes" with efforts to restore the vitality of local government. The price of "vitality" of local governments is not—and must not be—depressed wages for government workers. Furthermore, Hodgson's 1971 statement evaluates the feasibility of applying a minimum wage to non-covered state and local government workers and concludes that this would require less of an adjustment than did coverage of schools and hospitals.

Previously the Department of Labor had reported to Congress that adjustment to wage and hour standards had been accomplished without difficulty by hospitals and schools.

The AFL-CIO also supports the repeal of many of the exemptions—both from the minimum wage and overtime provisions—which no longer can be justified, if they ever could.

Finally, Congress should join with us in refusing to place the burden of this Administration's economic failures on the workers. The enactment of the proposed Senate bill will demonstrate that Congress recognizes that workers are poor because they are paid inadequate wages, not because they are old, or young or black or women. They can move out of poverty only if they are paid enough.

Reading 9

When Minimum Wage Means No Wage At All*

Summary

There is a growing and politically diverse number of economists who are convinced that, by eliminating marginal job opportunities, the minimum wage is hurting people it is supposed to help, striking hardest at blacks and teenagers.

Key Questions to Consider

■ What evidence is there that minimum wage legislation fosters unemployment—especially among blacks and teenagers?

■ Is there any evidence contradicting this alleged relationship between unemployment and minimum wage legislation?

■ How does the employer react to minimum wage legislation?

_____

* Reprinted with permission from *Business Week,* May 15, 1971, pp. 82–84.

When Minimum Wage Means No Wage At All

Teen-agers, especially blacks, are hit the hardest by reluctance to hire.

Shortly before Christmas, 1929, Harvard University fired, without notice, Mrs. Katherine Donahue, Mrs. Hannah Hogan, and 18 other scrubwomen in the Widener Library rather than raise their pay from 35¢ to 37¢ an hour as demanded by the Massachusetts Minimum Wage Commission. To avoid paying the extra 2¢, Harvard replaced the women with men, who were not covered by the state's pioneering but weak minimum wage law.

As recounted by labor historian Irving Bernstein in *The Lean Years*, the case of the Harvard charwomen ended on a brighter note. Denouncing the university as "harsh, stingy, socially insensitive, and considerably short of the highest ethical standards of the time," a group of 268 students and alumni, headed by Corliss Lamont, raised $3,880 to compensate the discharged scrubwomen.

Minimum wage laws have come a long way since the early decades of this century, when they were first devised to halt exploitation of "the poor working girl." Now a federal minimum wage of $1.60 an hour covers some 46-million workers, and pressures are building to raise it to $2 and extend coverage to the rest of the labor force.

Inflation at Work. On the basis on which the minimum wage has generally been debated, there are good grounds for an upward shift. Inflation has wiped out nearly 17% of purchasing power since the floor was last raised in February, 1968. Today's minimum wage is less than half of average hourly earnings and provides the full-time worker with an income substantially below the federal poverty line.

But the debate has shifted in recent years, particularly among economists. A growing and politically diverse number of them are convinced that, by eliminating marginal job opportunities, the minimum wage is hurting people it is supposed to help, striking hardest at blacks and teen-agers.

"What good does it do a black youth to know that an employer must pay him $1.60 per hour if the fact that he must be paid that amount is what keeps him from getting a job?" asks Paul A. Samuelson. And Milton Friedman refers to the Fair Labor Standards Act of 1938, the base of the minimum wage, as "the most anti-Negro law on our statute books—in its effect, not its intent."

Where It Hurts. Samuelson's rhetorical question and Friedman's questionable rhetoric point up the kind of emotion generated by the minimum wage issue. But economists using the rigorously clinical, computerized techniques of econometrics come up with the same general idea. As Gene L. Chapin and Douglas K. Adie of Ohio University put it: "Increases in the federal minimum wage cause unemployment among teen-agers. The effects tend to persist for considerable periods of time. And the effects seem to be strengthening as coverage is increased and enforcement of the laws becomes more rigorous."

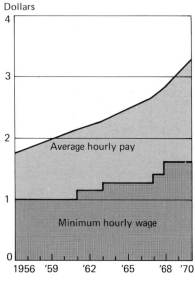

The minimum wage pushes upward

Dollars

Average hourly pay

Minimum hourly wage

Data: Bureau of Labor Statistics

The techniques, language, and variables used in their mathematical models may vary, but most other econometricians get the same result: a strong correlation, confirmed by repeated observations in the 1950s and 1960s, between youth unemployment and the minimum wage.

Finis Welch of the National Bureau of Economic Research and Marvin Kosters, now a senior staff economist with the Council of Economic Advisers, concluded in a Rand Corp. study last year that "minimum wage legislation has apparently played an important role in increasing the cyclical sensitivity of teen-age employment." They found that as minimums

rise, "teen-agers are able to obtain fewer jobs, and their jobs are less secure over the business cycle. A disproportionate share of these unfavorable employment effects accrues to nonwhite teen-agers."

The econometricians concede that the raw figures from the Bureau of Labor Statistics do not show these correlations. They note that the minimum wage usually has been raised when the economy has been swinging upward, which "washes out" much of the disemployment effect. Chapin adds that this phenomenon gives "politicians a chance to appear to be doing something the public wants with little cost." But a study by economists Jacob Mincer and Masanori Hashimoto at the NBER warns that many teen-agers are scared out of the labor force by lack of job opportunities and vanish into the gray area of hidden unemployment.

Labor Dept. study doubts that a rise in minimum wage is the whole explanation.

The BLS has shown deep concern about these findings and run its own econometric check of the results. In a Labor Dept. study titled "Youth Unemployment and Minimum Wages," Assistant BLS Commissioner Thomas W. Gavett notes that "while there is a significant relationship . . . where other variables are excluded, a look at the whole set of variables casts doubt upon the importance of minimum wages as an explanatory variable." But Gavett finds the lack of clear evidence "discouraging." He fears there is some basis for inferring that extensions of minimum wage coverage, not the rate itself, tended in the 1960s to offset benefits of federal manpower programs.

Opposing Views. Not all econometricians, to be sure, subscribe flat-out to the minimum wage-disemployment hypothesis. Ruth Fabricant of New York's City Planning Dept. found in a study at the Federal Reserve Board that the effect of minimum wage boosts on hours of work from 1954 to 1968 was "strongly negative," but the impact on the number of persons employed was "significantly positive" before the large increases in coverage and rates that took effect in 1967. Miss Fabricant explained that since minimum wage hikes are permanent and anticipated, "employers view them differently from other wage increases."

There is still another way to view minimum wage increases, and this is the approach taken by advocates. They find the econometric case unproven or too limited in scope. Gavett cites demographic changes that may far outweigh the wage factor:

■ The post–World War II baby boom, which swelled the teen-age civilian labor force by 49% between 1948 and 1968, compared with 30% growth in the entire work force.

■ A sharp decline in teen-age employment in agriculture from 734,000 to 394,000, with farm mechanization pushing large numbers of youths, especially blacks, into urban labor markets.

Of crucial significance are employers' own attitudes toward youth. A BLS survey in 10 metropolitan areas showed that employers shied away from hiring teen-agers because of limits on hazardous work, the military draft, and "undependability and lack of training." Others felt that youths have "unrealistic wage expectations." But the most striking finding was that a majority of the employers in nine areas "did not consider the minimum wage important in affecting their decisions" on hiring teen-agers.

Daniel H. Kruger, professor of industrial relations at Michigan State University, finds in his own experience as head of Michigan's Manpower Commission that "if an employer needs additional workers, he hires them even at the going minimum wage." Kruger adds that the FLSA already allows a lower minimum for full-time students. But BLS figures show that in 1969 employers availed themselves of only 42% of the 36-million man-hours authorized at the 85% student rate.

Solving the Dilemma. Kruger proposes a wide array of manpower and educational programs for dealing with youth unemployment, but he insists that the problem cannot be solved without coping with overall joblessness. And this, he says, requires changes in the nation's monetary and fiscal policies.

The same theme is resoundingly voiced by an old war-horse of the Roosevelt and Truman Administrations, Leon H. Keyserling, second chairman of the CEA. Keyserling, who wrote a study that provided the basis for the Employment Act of 1946, believes that higher minimums are essential to provide the consumer purchasing power needed to put steam in the present recovery.

Noting that House Ways & Means Chairman Wilbur Mills is said to be promoting the $2 minimum as an adjunct to President Nixon's proposed family assistance plan, Keyserling says: "It is an anomaly and economically ridiculous to set a minimum wage for full-time employed people lower than what you are coming to accept as a national consensus of what people should get if they can't be employed. The $2 minimum is much better than paying people to do nothing."

Reading 10

The Incomes of Men and Women: Why Do They Differ?*

By Mary Hamblin and Michael J. Prell

Summary

The economic inequality of the sexes has been a major focus of attention in the current resurgence of the Women's Movement in the United States. Among the demands women have voiced is "equal pay for equal work," and they have pursued this objective through legislative and judicial channels.

Economists have exhibited increased interest in the relative economic status of the sexes. A number of facets of this problem have been examined, but one of the thorniest questions has been the role of sexual discrimination in the determination of observed pay differentials. Although the literature on this subject can be traced back more than half a century, it has been only in the last few years that there have been the interest, theory, statistical technique, and data necessary to begin answering this question in a meaningful quantitative fashion.

This article summarizes some of the recent findings on the causes of the male-female income differential. The debate about these causes involves essentially three broad questions to which conclusive answers have not yet been found: (1) What part does occupational distribution play in explaining the observed sex differential in income? (2) How much of the sex differential is attributable to differences in male and female productivity? (3) How much of the observed sex differential is attributable to discrimination? Each of these questions is treated in turn.

Key Questions to Consider

▪ What is the magnitude of the differential in the incomes of males and females?

▪ What portion of this differential can be explained by occupational distribution and difference in hours worked?

▪ What does the evidence show about differences in absentee rates, turnover rates, and such factors between males and females?

▪ What types of discrimination exist and which of these appears to be most important in explaining the wage differential between the sexes?

▪ What portion of the wage differential can be attributed to sex discrimination?

---

* Reprinted with permission from *Monthly Review*, Federal Reserve Bank of Kansas City, April 1973, pp. 3–11.

The Incomes of Men and Women: Why Do They Differ?

The economic inequality of the sexes has been a major focus of attention in the current resurgence of the Women's Movement in the United States. Among the demands women have voiced is "equal pay for equal work," and they have pursued this objective through legislative and judicial channels. In the early 1960's, Congress responded with the Equal Pay Act of 1963 and Title VII of the Civil Rights Act of 1964, both milestones on the road to equal treatment for male and female workers. In 1972, Congress passed the Equal Rights Amendment to the Constitution, and that amendment is now traveling a stormy course through the state legislatures. The Nation's courts also have responded to women's pleas, issuing numerous orders to employers to rectify discriminatory policies in the hiring, advancement, and pay of women.

Against this background, economists have exhibited increased interest in the relative economic statuses of the sexes. A number of facets of this problem have been examined, but one of the thorniest questions has been the role of sexual discrimination in the determination of observed pay differentials. Although the literature on this subject can be traced back more than half a century,[1] it has been only in

the last few years that there have been the interest, theory, statistical technique, and data necessary to begin answering this question in a meaningful quantitative fashion. To date, however, little progress has been made in sorting out the complex set of sociological and economic factors behind male-female income differences. The conclusions reached by various researchers sometimes have differed strikingly—a rather distressing situation given that this has become an important issue of social policy.

This article summarizes some of the recent findings on the causes of the male-female income differential. The debate about these causes involves essentially three broad questions to which conclusive answers have not yet been found: (1) What part does occupational distribution play in explaining the observed sex differential in income? (2) How much of the sex differential is attributable to differences in male and female productivity? (3) How much of the observed sex differential is attributable to discrimination? Each of these questions is treated in turn, but it

---

[1] See, for example, Eleanor Rathbone, "The Remuneration of Women's Services," *Economic Journal*, Vol. 27 (March 1917), pp. 55–68; F. Y. Edgeworth, "Equal Pay to Men and Women for Equal Work," *Economic Journal*, Vol. 32 (December 1922), pp. 431–57.

will be useful to begin by documenting the magnitude of the sex differential in income.

THE MAGNITUDE OF THE SEX DIFFERENTIAL IN INCOME

In 1971, according to U.S. Census data, the median income of year-round, full-time female workers was $5,701, only 59.2 percent of the $9,631 median for male workers.[2] The ratio of mean incomes was even lower—56.4 percent—suggesting that female workers are particularly poorly represented in the higher income classes. In contrast, comparable data indicate that the ratio of nonwhite to white mean income was 66 percent in 1971, an interesting statistic in view of the greater attention that has been paid to the race differential than to the sex differential in income. Table 1 illustrates clearly the differences in income

Table 1

Total Income By Sex, 1971
Year-round, full-time workers

Total money income	Percent of males	Percent of females
$1 to $999	1.3	1.9
$1,000 to $2,999	3.0	8.2
$3,000 to $4,999	7.8	28.1
$5,000 to $6,999	13.7	30.3
$7,000 to $9,999	27.5	21.8
$10,000 to $14,999	29.6	8.1
$15,000 to $24,999	13.1	1.4
$25,000 and over	4.0	0.3
Median income	$9,631	$5,701

Source: U.S. Department of Commerce, Bureau of the Census: *Money Income in 1971 of Families and Persons in the United States*, Series P-60, No. 85.

---

[2] U.S. Department of Commerce, Bureau of the Census: *Money Income in 1971 of Families and Persons in the United States*, Series P-60, No. 85.

distribution by sex. Over two-thirds of year-round, full-time women workers had incomes of less than $7,000, compared with about one-fourth of male workers. More than 40 percent of male workers had incomes in excess of $10,000, but only 10 percent of female workers attained that income level.

Despite the legislation and litigation of the 1960's, there is no indication that the sex differential in workers' incomes was reduced during the decade. Indeed, the ratio of female to male median income was slightly higher, at 60.6 percent, in 1960 than it was in 1971. It perhaps should be noted that the ratio of about 60 percent has not only been fairly stable across time, but across various related data series as well. For example, the female-male nonfarm average hourly earnings ratio was 60 percent in 1959 and the "usual weekly earnings" ratio was 62 percent in May 1971.

While the median income figures are a useful indication of the relative economic statuses of male and female workers, they leave many questions unanswered. They provide no clues as to the causes of the sex differential in income and, in particular, they do not indicate whether or not male and female workers receive equal pay *for equal work*. An obvious first approach to both of these questions is to examine the occupational distributions of the male and female working forces.

OCCUPATIONAL DISTRIBUTION

The data in Table 2 make it quite apparent that differences in occupational distribution are an important factor underlying the observed sex differential in median incomes. A much larger percentage of female workers is concentrated in the lower paid occupational groups than is the case with male workers. For example, 53 percent of female workers are found in two relatively low-wage occupations: clerical workers and service workers. In contrast, only 14 percent of male workers fall in these categories. Table 2 also highlights another important phenomenon: there is a tendency for women to account for a large proportion of

Table 2

Median Income By Occupation and Sex, 1971
Civilian, year-round, full-time workers

Occupation	Median income in occupation	Male median income	Female median income	Percent of full-time male labor force	Percent of full-time female labor force	Female workers as percent of occupation group
Managers, Officials, and Proprietors	$12,192	$13,087	$6,970	15.8	6.4	14.6
Professional and Technical	11,395	12,842	8,515	15.7	18.6	33.4
Sales Workers	9,683	11,122	4,681	6.2	4.2	22.3
Craftsmen and Foremen	9,664	9,779	5,493	21.6	1.4	2.7
Operatives	7,274	8,069	4,884	17.7	13.9	25.0
Laborers (except farm)	6,932	7,063	4,486	4.8	.6	5.1
Clerical Workers	6,904	9,512	5,820	6.9	39.3	70.6
Service Workers	6,090	7,484	4,375	6.9	13.3	44.8
Farmers and Farm Managers	n.a.	4,915	n.a.	3.4	.2	2.2
Farm Workers	n.a.	3,806	n.a.	1.0	.3	10.8
Private Household Workers	n.a.	n.a.	2,328	n.a.	1.7	n.a.
	n.a.	9,631	5,701	100.0	100.0	29.8

Source: See Table 1.

the workers in the lower paid occupations, clerical and service workers again being a good example. Thus not only do women seem to find their way in disproportionate numbers into the lower paid occupations, the lower paid occupations tend to be those traditionally regarded as "women's work." The figures in Table 2 actually understate the prevalence of these two related phenomena in the United States. If more detailed occupations were shown, the image would be even sharper. For instance, closer examination of the professional and technical occupational group reveals that women are heavily concentrated in such lower paid subcategories as nursing and elementary school teaching.[3]

Researchers have attempted to assess the impact of occupational distribution on the sex differential in income, although the limited degree of disaggregation in available data is a barrier to precise quantification. Henry Sanborn, using 1949 Census data covering 262 occupational classes, concluded that differences in occupational distribution accounted for about 6 to 8 points of the 42 percentage point gap that existed in that year between median male and female wage and salary incomes.[4] Use of the 1949 Bureau of Labor Statistics data for more detailed occupational groups

---

[3] In 1970, nearly one-half of female professional and technical workers were registered nurses or elementary school teachers, and women comprised 97.3 percent of all registered nurses and 83.7 percent of all elementary school teachers. At the same time, less than 1 percent of women professional

and technical workers were lawyers, judges, or physicians, and they comprised roughly 7 percent of the populations of those occupations. These and many other data on occupational distribution may be found in the Council of Economic Advisers' recent report on "The Economic Role of Women," *Economic Report of the President*, 1973.

[4] "Pay Differences between Men and Women," *Industrial and Labor Relations Review*, Vol. 17 (July 1964), p. 534.

permitted him to attribute an additional 6 points to occupational distribution. Although Sanborn achieved a considerable degree of disaggregation, it seems likely that data based on even more detailed occupational breakdowns would yield a larger figure for the proportion of the sex differential explained by occupational distribution. Victor Fuchs has suggested that "if one pushes occupational classification far enough one could 'explain' nearly all of the differential." [5] His point apparently is that, when disaggregation of occupational groups is carried far enough, such a great degree of occupational segregation will be observed that the question of sex differentials in pay will have been reduced effectively to one of explaining the phenomenon of occupational segregation.[6] While studies of quite narrowly defined occupations suggest that disaggregation would have to be extreme in order to eliminate sex differentials, it is certainly true that explanation of the observed occupational distribution is essential to an understanding of the causes of the sex differential in median income.[7]

Length of Work Week

An important source of income differences that is closely related to occupational distribution is length of work week. In 1971, women employed full time on nonfarm wage and salary jobs worked an average of 39.9 hours per week—considerably less than the 43.6 hours averaged by similarly employed males.[8] Only

15 percent of women with full-time jobs worked overtime in May 1971, compared with 30 percent of men. These disparities are in large part attributable to the relatively greater concentrations of men in the blue collar occupations. Sanborn estimated the effect of differences in hours worked on the 42 percentage point pay differential he observed, and he found them to account for 10 points of the gap in 1949—the most important single identifiable factor other than occupational distribution *per se*. The Council of Economic Advisers recently estimated that the length of work week differential accounted for about 6 percentage points of the 1971 sex differential in median income— a smaller share than in 1949, but still very significant.[9]

CHARACTERISTICS OF FEMALE WORKERS

Even after adjustments have been made for the differences in hours worked and the direct effects of occupational distribution, there remains a sizable unexplained sex differential in pay. Innumerable reasons for this differential have been suggested by casual observers and careful students of the labor market. For convenience, the suggested reasons can be divided into two classes. First, there are those reasons that relate to the possibility that women are paid less than men for similar work simply because they are women—i.e., because of sexual discrimination. Second, there are those that relate to the possibility that women are paid less because of differences in various nonsexual characteristics between male workers and female workers. A few of these nonsexual characteristics are examined in this section, with discrimination being treated in a subsequent section.

---

[5] "Differences in Hourly Earnings between Men and Women," *Monthly Labor Review*, Vol. 94 (May 1971), p. 14.

[6] It might be noted that the claim has been made that men and women frequently do the same work in a firm, but with women holding less august and lower paid job classifications or titles.

[7] See John E. Buckley, "Pay Differences between Men and Women in the Same Job," *Monthly Labor Review*, Vol. 94 (November 1971), pp. 36–39; and Mary Hamilton, "Wage Discrimination on the Basis of Sex" (Mimeographed).

[8] Paul O. Flaim and Nicholas I. Peters, "Usual Weekly Earnings of American Workers," *Monthly Labor Review*, Vol. 95 (March 1972), pp. 30–31.

---

[9] See *Economic Report of the President*, 1973, p. 103. Adjusting simply for differences in hours worked may understate the impact of this factor on the sex differential in income. In 1971, among those who did work overtime, a greater proportion of men, 38 percent, received premium pay for doing so than was the case for women, 33 percent. Consequently, the impact on income of differences in overtime hours worked is greater than is implied by the length of work week ratio.

Absenteeism and Turnover

If, for any reason, female workers were less productive than male workers in the same job, profit maximizing employers would certainly wish to pay them less. If equal pay laws prohibited such a practice, employers would either resist hiring women or create artificial job title distinctions that might enable them to circumvent the legal constraints. A frequently encountered claim is that female workers tend to be less productive and more costly because they have higher rates of absenteeism and turnover. Although available data lend some credence to this view of female behavior, they also indicate that the view is somewhat exaggerated.

In the case of absenteeism, for example, there is evidence of only minor differences between male and female employee behavior. Government research indicates that age, occupation, and salary may be more important determinants of absenteeism than is sex.[10] In 1967, men between the ages of 25 and 45 lost 4.4 days per year due to illness, while women in the same age bracket lost 5.6 days—a difference of but 1.2 days per year. In the 45 and over age bracket, female employees lost fewer working days due to illness than men, making the overall averages 5.3 days per year for men and 5.4 days per year for women.[11] To be sure, illness does not account for all employee absenteeism. In particular, because of the different family roles typically assigned to men and women, women probably are more likely to take days off to care for sick children or to meet other household responsibilities. However, Labor Department data show that, during an average week in 1971, 1.4 percent of women and 1.2 percent of men did not report to work for reasons other than illness or vacation—certainly a small difference.[12]

The problem—or presumed problem—of employee turnover may have its greatest impact on female occupational distribution, but it might also affect relative pay. Employers, believing that there is a greater risk in investing in on-the-job training for female workers, might attempt to recoup their expected loss by paying women less. If the sex differential in turnover rates is an important factor in explaining the sex differential in pay, it is a testimonial to the power of myth over economic fact, for the existing data show the differences in turnover to be small. Labor Department figures reveal that voluntary "quit" rates for the sexes are not very different—2.2 per hundred male employees per month and 2.6 per hundred female employees in 1968.[13] Furthermore, it has been asserted that about one-half of this quit rate differential is attributable to the greater concentration of women in occupations where quit rates for both men and women are above average.[14]

Employers may magnify the quit rate differential in their minds, perhaps showing greater sensitivity to a woman's quitting to have a baby than to a man's quitting to take a better job, but whatever the psychological cause, there seems little basis in fact for the popular view of the size of the quit rate differential. Essentially, the same statement also can be made with respect to the absenteeism rates. Unfortunately, employers may act on their mistaken impressions, and there is a strong tendency for them to practice "statistical discrimination"—i.e., assuming that any given employee's behavior will conform to the employer's notion of average behavior for members of that employee's sex, rather than making careful assessment of the employee's motivation and past record. The likely gap between fact and employer belief makes it im-

---

[10] U.S. Department of Labor, Women's Bureau, *Women's Absenteeism and Labor Turnover*, 1969, p. 6.

[11] *Current Estimates from the Health Interview Survey, July 1966–June 1967.* U.S. Public Health Service Publication No. 1000—Series 10, No. 43.

[12] U.S. Department of Labor, Bureau of Labor Statistics.

Employment and Earnings (January 1972), Annual Average Tables A-20 and A-21.

[13] U.S. Department of Labor, Bureau of Labor Statistics, *Employment and Earnings*, various issues, 1968–69, Table D-3.

[14] Barbara R. Bergmann, "The Economics of Women's Liberation," in *Economics: Mainstream Readings and Radical Critiques*, ed. by David Mermelstein (New York: Random House, 1973), p. 331.

possible to quantify the impact of turnover and absenteeism factors on the sex differential in pay, and the authors are not aware of any attempts to do so.

Education

Among the factors for which quantitative estimates of impact have been made is education. Education might influence the sex differential in income either directly through an impact on productivity in a given job or indirectly through an effect on occupational distribution. In fact, as measured by years of schooling, education seems to be at most a minor force through either of these channels. Neither Sanborn nor Fuchs was able to discover a significant impact of years of schooling on the overall sex differential in median income or average hourly earnings. If anything, the average working woman appears to be slightly better educated than the average working man, but "greater education of working women than men tended to occur more in low paying than in higher paying occupations," according to Sanborn.[15] Furthermore, he found that "in the professional occupations, women were relatively concentrated in occupations where they had more education than men—nurses, social workers, technicians, and musicians and music teachers, while men had more education where they were relatively more concentrated—accountants and auditors, clergymen, civil engineers, and dentists." These observations are particularly interesting in light of the frequent suggestion that women's pay is lower than men's because women do not invest sufficiently in themselves—i.e., forego current consumption and use income to purchase education. What Sanborn found was a pattern of relatively heavy investment by women in the low-paid "women's work" occupations and a relatively low investment by women in the high-paid "men's work" occupations. If women face barriers to entry into certain occupations—real or

imagined—then this pattern of education investment might be rational or at least understandable.[16]

Age and Experience

One view of the labor market is that a certain diploma or other educational credential is merely a ticket of admission to an occupation. On-the-job experience is the critical vehicle for training and advancement. Unfortunately, data on years of experience in a job or occupation are usually hard to obtain, so other variables frequently have been used as proxies for experience in studies of the sex differential in pay. Age is one example of such a surrogate, though not a completely adequate one because, on average, women have fewer years of experience than men of the same age. As a consequence, it is not surprising that both Fuchs and Sanborn found age itself to be of minimal importance in explaining the observed sex differentials in pay.

However, both Sanborn and Fuchs deduced on other grounds that differences in work experience contributed significantly to the sex differential in pay. Women, at least in past years, have tended to enter and leave the labor force at early ages and then reenter at later ages. With this in mind, Sanborn estimated that differences in experience may have accounted for between 3 and 7 points of the 42 percentage point pay gap in 1949. Fuchs did not give a summary figure of the effect of experience on the sex differential in pay, but he did present evidence of its importance. He noted that women who have never married tend to have an age-earnings profile much like that of men, but that for married women with spouse present, the difference between male and female average hourly earnings increases with age. Re-

---

[15] "Pay differences between Men and Women," p. 536.

[16] Years of schooling may be an unduly heterogeneous variable for the purpose of explaining pay differentials. Some distinctions might be made between general education and vocational training, or between different college "majors," for example, but prior investigations have not done so.

searchers no doubt will want to examine more recent data comparable to Fuchs' 1959–60 figures to ascertain whether changes in female working patterns have altered the relationships between marital status and the age-earning profile. It seems likely, however, that as long as it is women who interrupt their careers to raise children, differences in work experience will give rise to a significant sex differential in earnings.

Length of Trip to Work

Another way in which the maternal role of women appears to affect the pay differential is via the length of trip to work. Women, presumably because of their duties at home, constrain themselves to jobs relatively close to their residences, and jobs in residential areas pay less on average than do the same jobs in nonresidential areas. Fuchs cites figures indicating that twice as large a percentage of female workers (18.1 percent) walk to work or work at home than male workers (9.3 percent). Since, regardless of sex, persons with such a short trip to work earn about 26 percent less than other workers, this implies at least a small difference between male and female average pay.

Race

One factor that might be expected to contribute to the sex differential in pay is race. Nonwhites constitute a larger proportion of the female labor force than of the male labor force, and as is well known, nonwhite workers tend to earn less than white workers. Interestingly, neither Sanborn nor Fuchs found race to be of any quantitative significance in explaining the sex differential in pay. This is primarily a reflection of the relatively small percentages of the male and female labor forces comprised by nonwhites (9 percent and 13 percent, respectively)—not a contradiction of the *a priori* logic involved.[17]

DISCRIMINATION

To this point, little more than casual reference has been made to the possibility that discrimination may be an ingredient in the creation of the observed sex differential in pay. Among those who have studied the sex differential there is fairly broad agreement that discrimination does play a direct role, but there is considerable disagreement on the magnitude of its contribution. It would seem fair to conclude, however, that discrimination is not a negligible factor.

In his seminal work, *The Economics of Discrimination*,[18] Gary Becker distinguishes between three types of discrimination: by employers, by customers, and by co-workers. The two studies most frequently cited in this article—those by Sanborn and Fuchs—minimize the significance of the first sort, employer discrimination. Presumably, the desire for profit outweighs most employers' willingness to pay male workers a premium wage in order to satisfy any tastes for discrimination they might have. Sanborn notes that there is no apparent correlation across occupations between the sex differentials in pay and the closeness of employer-employee relationships.

Fuchs cites a piece of evidence that points to customers rather than employers as the primary group of discriminators, namely, that the sex differentials in pay among self-employed workers are greater than those among private wage and salary workers. The opposite result presumably would be favored if employer discrimination were the stronger force. Fuchs is not convinced that discrimination is very important, but thinks that the strongest empirical case can be made with respect to customers. He, along with Sanborn, seems to be impressed by the large differentials that are present in many sales and service

---

[17] It might be noted that nonwhite women fare better relative to white female workers than do nonwhite males relative

to white male workers. In 1971 the median income of full-time, full-year nonwhite female workers was 88 percent of the white female median; for males the ratio was only 68 percent.

[18] Chicago: University of Chicago Press, 1971.

occupations. Customers apparently prefer waiters to waitresses in expensive restaurants and male to female auto mechanics, to mention two common examples.

Sanborn expresses the belief that discrimination by fellow employees is a significant force, but the hard evidence he is able to muster is limited. The fact that women are paid less than men in the managerial and foreman occupations might reflect the reluctance of fellow employees to accept female supervision. The apparent exclusion of females from many labor unions is also *prima facie* evidence of discrimination by potential co-workers, though in this case the sex differential in pay arises as a secondary effect of occupational or industrial segregation.

Studies to date do not seem to have proven that wage discrimination accounts for the portion of the sex differential in pay left unexplained by factors previously examined. However, it may be that the studies have inadequately explored the role of discrimination in occupational segregation. A major problem, here, is the difficulty encountered in distinguishing between discrimination and role differentiation. Women may be shut out of a given occupation by employer, customer, or co-worker discrimination, or they may not consider entering that occupation because society has designated such work as unsuitable for women. Certainly, there is only a thin line between discrimination and such sex-typing of jobs by society.

The courts and legislatures have, in recent years, acted to eliminate the sex-typing of jobs by employers. In addition, one of the major objectives of the Women's Movement has been to eliminate the socially induced psychological barriers that prevent women from pursuing many occupational goals. The potential impact on the relative economic statuses of the sexes of a change in attitudes about sexual roles is undoubtedly great. As Fuchs says, role differentiation, "which begins in the cradle, affects the choice of occupation, labor force attachment, location of work, post-school investment, hours of work, and other variables that influence earnings." [19]

The earlier-cited figures regarding the impact of occupational distribution on the sex differential in median income undoubtedly do not capture the full effect of occupational segregation. As previously noted, insufficient disaggregation of occupational categories masks some of the effect. However, occupational segregation affects not only the relative numbers of women in various occupations, but also the relative wage rates in those occupations. Segregation results in an "oversupply" of labor in female occupations and thereby drives down women's wages relative to those of men in male occupations where there is a resultant greater scarcity of qualified workers. In a perfectly competitive market, workers would flow from low-wage jobs to high-wage jobs, but if women are not allowed or do not allow themselves to do so, then the differential can persist.

SUMMARY

Women's earnings, whether measured as annual income or average hourly earnings, have averaged only about 60 percent of men's earnings during the past quarter century. This differential has been maintained despite momentous shifts in the composition of economic activity and increases in female labor force participation. Even though the sex differential in pay is greater than the race differential, it has received considerably less attention.

Research to date has made modest strides toward explaining the observed sex differential. The most important factor identified by analysts is the differing distributions of male and female workers across fairly broad occupational groups. Women are concentrated in relatively low-wage occupational groups. Furthermore, they tend to be found in occupations where opportunities for overtime and premium pay are relatively limited. Occupational distri-

[19] "Differences in Hourly Earnings between Men and Women," p. 14.

bution and hours worked may account for over half of the observed differential. If disaggregation of occupational categories is carried further, however, differences in distribution may account for an even greater portion of the income differential because considerable occupational segregation by sex is then discernible.

Productivity factors such as absenteeism and turnover should not be important in explaining the sex differential in pay because data indicate little difference in male and female behavior, although erroneous employer beliefs could introduce some discriminatory effect. Female attachment to the labor force, though perhaps strengthening, is sufficiently weak relative to that of males that it may account for part of the sex differential. Women, particularly those who are married, tend to have fewer years of work experience at any given age and, therefore, receive less pay. All told, however, experience and other productivity factors seem to account for only a small part of the sex differential in pay.

After considering occupational distribution and various productivity factors as well, there still remains a sizable unexplained sex differential in pay. What proportion of this residual might be attributed to discrimination is extremely difficult to assess. Based on research to date, perhaps a high estimate of the impact of wage discrimination by employers, customers, and co-workers would be that it accounts for a quarter of the 40 percent sex differential in pay. However, when the pervasive influence of role differentiation is considered, it seems clear that society's attitudes sharply limit women's economic opportunities. Significant progress toward closing the male-female income gap will be made if and only if there is a weakening of the individual and social biases that discourage women from entering high-pay occupations.

Reading 11

Profit Size and Measurement*

By Thomas M. Humphrey

Summary

The subject of profit is the focus of a bewildering array of opinions and a wide variety of interpretations. Popular views range all the way from a "fat cat" theory, which holds that profit arises from the rapacious exploitation of consumers and wage-earners, to a "seed corn" theory, which holds that profit is an indispensable source of capital expansion and economic growth. Economic theory, too, offers a diversity of explanations of profit. Does profit arise from monopolistic restrictions on output and access to the market? from unforeseen changes in demand and costs? from innovation? from the need to reward entrepreneurs for risk-bearing and decision-making? or from frictions that delay the adjustment of firms, industries, and markets to equilibrium positions following the disruptions of dynamic change? Economists cannot agree. Each of these explanations has its adherents. Most likely, none of the explanations will ever be unanimously accepted as the most correct.

With the purpose of dispelling some of the misconceptions about profit, this article discusses the size and behavior of corporate profits over the past 20 years and describes the chief empirical measures of profit.

Key Questions to Consider

- What are the four most widely used ways of measuring profit rates?

- Over time, how have profit rates behaved?

- What accounts for the drop in profit rates during the late 1960s?

- Why do some economists believe that profit figures have been overstated? How can these figures be corrected?

* Reprinted with permission from *Monthly Review,* Federal Reserve Bank of Richmond, **58,** No. 3 (March 1972), 9–13.

Profit Size and Measurement

The subject of profit is the focus of a bewildering array of opinions and a wide variety of interpretations. Popular views range all the way from a "fat cat" theory, which holds that profit arises from the rapacious exploitation of consumers and wage earners, to a "seed corn" theory, which holds that profit is an indispensable source of capital expansion and economic growth. Economic theory, too, offers a diversity of explanations of profit. Does profit arise from monopolistic restrictions on output and access to the market? From unforeseen changes in demand and costs? From innovation? From the need to reward entrepreneurs for risk-bearing and decision-making? From frictions that delay the adjustment of firms, industries, and markets to equilibrium positions following the disruptions of dynamic change? Economists cannot agree. Each of these explanations has its adherents. Most likely, none of the explanations will ever be unanimously accepted as the most correct.

The abundance of profit theories is matched by the profusion of misconceptions about the magnitude of profit. The average American apparently thinks that accounting profit per dollar of sales of manufacturing corporations is about seven times its actual level. This was revealed recently when the Opinion Research Corporation asked a sample of 1,000 adults what they thought the average manufacturer makes in after-tax profit as a percent of each sales dollar. The median response was 28.0%, far larger than the 4.0% margins actually earned by manufacturers in 1970.[1] Moreover, two-thirds of those questioned displayed further ignorance of the size of profit margins when they agreed that firms could pay a ten cent per hour wage increase without raising prices.

With the purpose of dispelling some of the misconceptions about profit, this article discusses the size and behavior of corporate profits over the past 20 years and describes the chief empirical measures of profit.

Measures of Profit. In economic analysis, relative magnitudes are usually more revealing than absolute magnitudes. Thus, although profit may be expressed as an aggregate dollar total, it is often more meaningful analytically when expressed as a ratio to, or percentage rate of return on, related economic variables. The most widely used profit rates are the ratio of corporate profit to: (1) net national product (NNP), (2) income originating in the corporate sector, (3) sales, and (4) stockholders' equity. The first two of these ratios are measures of profit's share in the aggregate income distribution. Note that the denomina-

[1] *Business Week*, December 18, 1971, p. 26.

tor of the profit/NNP ratio is more comprehensive than the denominator of the second ratio, which includes only that portion (roughly 60.0%) of the NNP produced by private corporations. The third, or profit/sales, ratio is the margin of profit on each dollar of sales. It also indicates the ratio of average price to cost per unit of output. For example, a profit/sales margin of 5.0% implies that unit cost is 95.0% of unit price. Finally, the ratio of profits to equity measures the rate of return on the book or historical value of owners' investment in the corporations.

Chart 1 shows quarterly figures since 1951 for each of these profit ratios. The profit rates on sales and on equity refer to manufacturing only, whereas the other two profit rates are for the entire corporate sector. In all cases profits are measured after taxes.

Notice that the profit rate on equity is about double or triple the profit rate on sales. The source of this disparity is the sales/equity or capital turnover ratio, which has a numerical value varying between two and three. Similarly, profit's share of NNP is approximately three-fifths the size of profit's share of income originating in corporations, reflecting the fact that only about 60.0% of the national product is produced in the corporate sector.

Behavior of Profit.   The information shown in Chart 1 reveals several noteworthy characteristics of the behavior of profit. First, profit rates are relatively low, contrary to the conviction held by many antibusiness critics and to the opinion of the man in the street. Over the entire 20-year period the share of profit in

Chart 1

Various Profit Ratios, 1951-1971

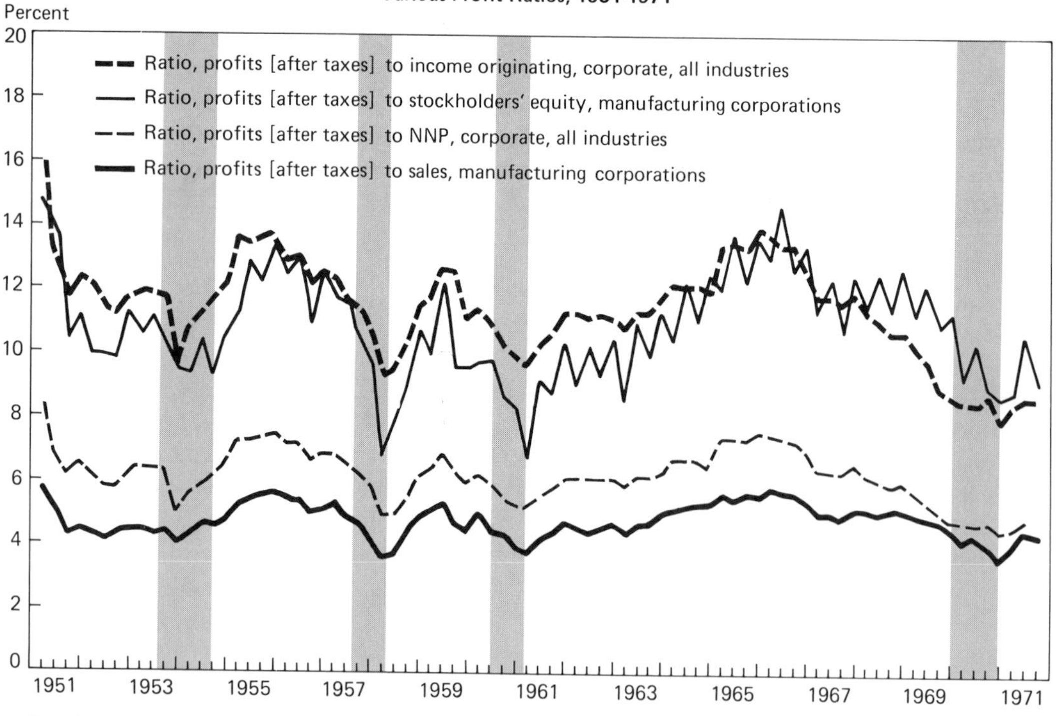

Note: Shaded areas represent periods of business recessions as defined by the National Bureau of Economic Research.

Sources: U. S. Department of Commerce, *Business Conditions Digest*; Federal Trade Commission, *Quarterly Financial Report for Manufacturing Corporations*.

NNP and in income originating in corporations averaged only about 6.0% and 11.0% respectively. Even in the relatively high-profit years of 1951, 1965, and 1966 these two ratios did not exceed 8.5% and 16.0%. Similarly, manufacturing profit per dollar of sales averaged only about 4.8% over the whole period and rarely exceeded 5.5%.

Second, the four profit rate measures have shown no appreciable upward or downward long-run trend. Apparently, price increases over the long run have been sufficient to prevent rising unit labor costs from encroaching on profit's share and profit margins. More precisely, the trend percentage change in the price level has been approximately equal to the difference between the percentage rise in hourly wage rates (including fringe benefits) and man-hour productivity.

Third, in contrast to their long-run stability, the aggregate profit measures exhibit noticeable short-run movements, generally rising in the recovery stage of the business cycle and falling in the boom and recession stages. Of the four series, profit's share of income originating in the corporate sector exhibits the most pronounced cyclical variation. As GNP rebounds sharply in the recovery stage, business firms normally experience declines in both unit fixed and unit labor costs, the former because of the spreading of overhead expenses over rapidly expanding output and the latter because of the registering of above-average gains in labor productivity. This decline in unit production costs leaves a growing share of sales revenue for profit. Profit's share may be further augmented if firms enjoying some degree of monopoly power respond to the increase in aggregate demand by raising prices as well as output.

In the boom and recession stages, however, profit's share falls as increasing costs absorb a growing proportion of revenues. Labor productivity growth slackens and wage increases accelerate causing unit labor costs to rise. Moreover, unit fixed costs stop falling in the boom, as firms approach their capacity output levels, and may rise in the recession, as businessmen cut back production. In short, during the boom and recession stages, rises in unit production costs tend to exceed price increases, thereby reducing profit's residual share of revenues per unit of output.

Fourth, profit rates suffered a drastic decline in the late 1960's. By 1970 profit rates had fallen to their lowest postwar levels. Accounting for the abnormally severe squeeze on profits were: (1) stagnant productivity growth; (2) wage increases substantially in excess of the limited productivity gains, with the consequent rise in unit labor costs surpassing the rise in selling prices; and (3) high unit fixed costs associated with depressed rates of capacity utilization (Chart 2).

In 1971, as the economy emerged from its fifth postwar recession, profit rates began to recover from their lows of the preceding year. Economists are predicting a substantial rise in the *dollar volume* of profits in 1972 as a result of the expected 9.0% expansion of GNP. Only modest gains, however, are anticipated for profit margins and profit's share of GNP. In fact, these gains are not large enough to bring the profit's share of GNP up to its 20-year trend value.

Overstated Profit Figures. Some economists believe that reported statistics on corporate profit, such as those appearing in Chart 1, represent a considerable overstatement of true profit. In other words, as low as measured profit has been in recent years, actual economic profit was even lower. These analysts argue that certain corrections should be made to the official profit figures to eliminate the upward bias. Any downward adjustment would, of course, establish the profit ratios at levels below those shown in Chart 1. Profit overstatement springs from two sources: (1) understated depreciation charges and (2) implicit interest costs contained in the profit figures.

Inflation and Historical Cost Depreciation. Historical cost amortization is one source of bias in the profit figures. Standard accounting practice spreads the original cost of capital equipment over its useful life by allocating to annual depreciation expense a portion of that original cost. In other words, the annual de-

Chart 2

Sources of the Profit Squeeze, 1966-1970

Rapidly rising wage rates combined with sluggish productivity growth to produce . . .

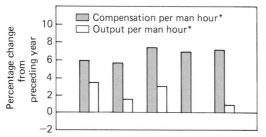

percentage rises in unit labor costs in excess of percentage rises in selling prices. These forces, together with...

falling rates of capacity utilization,

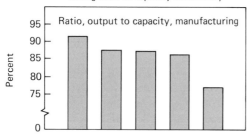

acted to squeeze profits' share.

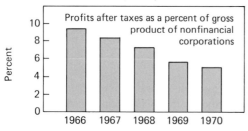

*Private nonfarm economy.

Sources: Council of Economic Advisors, *Economic Report of the President,* January 1972; *Survey of Current Business,* January 1972; *Federal Reserve Bulletin.*

preciation charge is expressed in terms of dollars of past, rather than current, purchasing power. When inflation occurs, past dollars differ from current dollars. Each past dollar is now equivalent to more than one current dollar in purchasing power. Prevention of inadequate amortization charges during inflation requires that the historical cost of depreciation be translated into current dollars of equivalent purchasing power. But this usually is not done. Consequently, depreciation expense is understated, and profit is overstated.

Similarly, profit distortion may result during inflation if accountants charge to current expense the prior-period acquisition cost of inventory used up in current production. This source of upward bias in profit could be largely eliminated if accountants expressed inventory consumption cost in terms of the inflated price level of the current period, instead of the lower price levels of the past. But this remedy is not always applied either.

The magnitude of profit overstatement resulting from the failure to fully adjust depreciation and inventory consumption expenses for inflation has been estimated by several analysts, including George Terborgh,[2] former research director of the Machinery and Allied Products Institute, and Solomon Fabricant of the National Bureau of Economic Research.[3] Terborgh's estimates indicate that the cumulative overstatement of profit since 1951 has been slightly in excess of $90.0 billion, with about $32.0 billion of the overstatement occurring in the three-year period 1968–1970 and $25.0 billion in the two-year interval of 1969–1970 alone. These sums represent errors of 18.0%, 31.0%, and 39.0% respectively of the corrected profit figures for the indicated years. Apparently the degree of profit distortion tends to vary

---

[2] George Terborgh, *Essays on Inflation* (Washington, D.C.: Machinery and Allied Products Institute, 1971), pp. 52–56.

[3] Solomon Fabricant, "Inflation and the Lag in Accounting Practice" in *Accounting in Perspective: Contributions to Accounting Thought by Other Disciplines* (Cincinnati: South-Western Publishing Company, 1971), pp. 139–141.

directly with the rate of inflation, which was 2.1%, 5.6%, and 5.9% respectively over the three periods.

Conclusion. Over the past 20 years reported profit rates generally have been lower than many people realize. Toward the close of the 1960's, moreover, some of these rates plunged precipitously and by 1970 had reached their lowest levels since World War II.

Removal of historic cost error further shrinks the profit rates, and when the element of implicit interest cost is extracted, they become even more slender. The cushion of pure surplus or residual profit, upon which business enterprise is often said to rest, has never been very thick, and in recent years it may have vanished altogether.

Reading 12

Free Enterprise Revisited—
A Look at Economic Concentration*

By Sheldon W. Stahl and C. Edward Harshbarger

Summary

In this article attention is directed at some broad aspects of economic concentration. This subject is one which many believe to be increasingly responsible for those monopolistic and restrictive practices which impair the ability of markets to perform effectively.

The growth of economic power is not a new phenomenon, but the increasing importance of economic concentration may be grasped by noting what has happened in the manufacturing sector during the post–World War II period. In 1947, the share of manufacturing assets held by the nation's 200 largest manufacturing corporations amounted to slightly more than 47 percent. By 1968, their share had risen to more than 60 percent. In roughly the same time span, between 1947 and 1967, their share of value added by manufacturing rose from less than one-third to more than two-fifths. Although such data, in and of themselves, cannot attest to noncompetitive behavior or practices by those corporations, such aggregate size would seem to many to be inimical to the competitive process.

Key Questions to Consider

■ What problems emerge as an economy evolves from an agrarian to an industrial state?

■ Under what circumstances will the free market *not* bring about correspondence between self-interest and the general welfare of society?

■ What market conditions are necessary for responsible competitive behavior?

■ Why do some people believe that "reasonably workable competition" might be difficult to maintain?

* Reprinted with permission from *Monthly Review*, Federal Reserve Bank of Kansas City, March 1973, pp. 10–16.

Free Enterprise Revisited—
A Look at Economic Concentration

In a recent book, *The Closed Enterprise System*, the authors observe that:

Americans have often set up models which do not exist, which have never existed, and which they may never permit to exist, yet which assuage our frontieristic, democratic spirit . . . our list of unachieved hyperboles is long. Among them must be included our faith in "the free enterprise system" and in the antitrust laws which supposedly maintain it. This phrase and the laws are of such vintage, and have been so repeated into catechism, that they are accepted on faith as part of the great American tradition. Yet, as with many of our democratic models, the reality is more apparent than actual. This book looks hard at the ideal of competition and antitrust, and concludes that it is time to state that the emperor has no clothes.[1]

Though this latter observation is perhaps somewhat dramatically overstated, there does appear to be mounting concern over the behavior of our economic institutions and of their consequences for the economy at large. In an address before a large audience of professional economists and finance specialists, Dr. Arthur F. Burns, Chairman of the Federal Reserve Board, took the view that market forces were no longer able to check rising prices and wages even when aggregate demand falls, as during a business recession. Alluding to certain institutional features of both labor and product markets which serve to reinforce these upward wage and price tendencies, Dr. Burns noted:

It will take courage for the Congress and the Executive to deal with the issues of structural reform in forthright fashion. The ground to be covered is difficult and enormous. We need to reassess the adequacy of our laws directed against monopolistic practices of business, the enforcement of these laws, the power of trade unions at the bargaining table, restrictions on entry into business or the professions, the restrictive practices of trade unions, the subsidies to farmers, the Federal minimum wage—particularly for teenagers, restrictions on the activities of financial institutions, the welfare system, import quotas, tariffs, and other legislation that impedes the competitive process. . . .

There is no quick or easy path to meaningful structural reform. But I see no real alternative if our national aspiration for prosperity without inflation is to be realized, while free enterprise and individual choice are being preserved.[2]

---

[1] Mark J. Green with Beverly C. Moore, Jr., and Bruce Wasserstein, *The Closed Enterprise System* (New York: Grossman Publishers, 1972), pp. xxi–xxii.

[2] Arthur F. Burns, "The Problem of Inflation," an address before the Joint Luncheon Meeting of the American Economic Association and the American Finance Association, Toronto, Ontario, Canada, December 29, 1972, pp. 21–22.

Admittedly, Dr. Burns' list of impediments is lengthy. It deserves attention not only by the professional academic economist, but also by those involved in formulating and executing public economic policies, as well as by the public at large which is so clearly affected by these constraints on the efficient operation of the free enterprise system. However, such a task is far beyond the scope of any single article. In this article—the first of several to deal with the subject—without minimizing the importance of any of those factors noted by Dr. Burns, attention will be directed at some broad aspects of economic concentration. This subject, though not explicitly mentioned above, is one which many believe to be increasingly responsible for those monopolistic and restrictive practices which impair the ability of markets to perform effectively. John M. Blair, from 1957 to 1970 the chief economist of the Subcommittee on Antitrust and Monopoly of the U.S. Senate, and earlier chief economist for the Federal Trade Commission, is one who strongly subscribes to this view. In his voluminous work on economic concentration, he states:

The action by President Nixon in freezing prices and wages on August 15, 1971, and subsequently establishing an elaborate system of price and wage controls was merely the logical response by government to the problems created by the growth in size and relative importance of the country's largest corporations. . . . It was the power of the large corporations to raise prices in the face of low and falling demand that set the stage for direct governmental intervention in the price-making process . . .[3]

More than two decades ago, the House Judiciary Committee sounded a similar warning when it concluded that:

The concentration of great economic power in a few corporations necessarily leads to the formation of large na-tion-wide labor unions. The development of the two necessarily leads to big bureaus in the government to deal with them.[4]

The growth of economic power is not a new phenomenon, but the increasing importance of economic concentration may be grasped by noting what has happened in the manufacturing sector during the post–World War II period. In 1947, the share of manufacturing assets held by the Nation's 200 largest manufacturing corporations amounted to slightly more than 47 percent. By 1968, their share had risen to more than 60 percent. In roughly the same time span, between 1947 and 1967, their share of value added by manufacturing rose from less than one-third to more than two-fifths. Although such data, in and of themselves, cannot attest to noncompetitive behavior or practices by those corporations, such aggregate size would seem to many to be inimical to the competitive process. Before considering certain broad aspects of concentration, it will be useful to review the rationale of a competitive market system, to place this phenomenon within an idealized free enterprise perspective.

SOME BASICS OF FREE ENTERPRISE

One of the dominant characteristics of a free enterprise economy is the wide measure of individual freedom it affords. Under such a system, economic wants are fulfilled largely through the private actions of individuals or groups of individuals in voluntary association competing both in the production and the exchange of goods and services in the marketplace. Clearly, however, as an economy evolves to progressively higher forms of organization in moving from an agrarian to a much more complex industrial struc-

---

[3] John M. Blair, *Economic Concentration, Structure, Behavior and Public Policy* (New York: Harcourt Brace Jovanovich, 1972), p. xiii.

[4] 81st Congress, 1st Session, House Judiciary Committee, Report to accompany H.R. 2734 (House Report No. 1191), 1949, p. 13.

ture, limitations on individual action are increasingly encountered. The present concern over economic concentration is a reflection of what often appears as a difficulty in reconciling the individual's freedom of opportunity to pursue a given economic course with the freedom of groups of individuals to voluntarily associate for the purpose of joint economic endeavors.

In the early stages of economic development, the inherent advantages of voluntary association are probably, and correctly, viewed in the attainment of the efficiencies in production which might result from specialization and division of labor. As the economy evolves to higher stages of technological sophistication, progress in productive techniques proceeds apace with progress in the forms of business organization and management. Thus, today's very large corporation, characterized by many plants and subsidiaries, is regarded by many as the natural outgrowth of voluntary association for economic pursuits. And, as was noted earlier, the growth of large labor unions is seen as a natural concomitant of corporate growth. Yet before one may safely assume that the gain in total output over time attributable to larger economic units has been costless, one must gauge both the gains and the losses in terms of the opportunities which such large-scale enterprises afford for individual initiative. For, as A. D. H. Kaplan observed:

Free enterprise has not only its historical (laissez-faire) implication of freedom from excessive control by the state; it also implies freedom from restrictive controls imposed by private domination of markets. The two are interdependent. The exercise of restrictive power by one segment of private enterprise over another must almost inevitably lead to intervention by government. The American tradition of reliance on a system of checks and balances to preserve political freedom has, as its counterpart in the economic sphere, a reliance on market competition. The preservation of competition may be viewed as a device for limiting the economic power of privileged groups to exploit others.[5]

---

[5] A. D. H. Kaplan, *Big Enterprise in a Competitive System* (Washington: The Brookings Institution, 1964), p. 43.

Thus, competition is pivotal in assuring both the viability of free enterprise and the promotion of the general welfare as a consequence of its performance.

ON COMPETITION IN MARKETS

In an economic sense, the term competition connotes the idea of smallness or insignificance of any individual economic unit as compared with the larger economic group within which it may operate. More broadly defined, it represents a process which involves exchanges in a market characterized by a wide range of choices among rival bids and offers. In a competitive economy, production is organized and orchestrated through a price system dependent upon the marketplace to determine values. The market brings together the disparate activities and decisions of buyers and sellers, and of producers and consumers. Those firms producing goods or services in greatest demand by consumers will tend to receive the highest prices relative to their costs, and thus will be the most profitable. Firms confronting little demand for their output will likely suffer losses. The more profitable the firm, the higher the prices it would be willing and able to pay for resources in order to expand its output. Since owners of resources would naturally seek the highest prices for those resources, it would logically follow that there would be a constant shifting of resources away from firms with weak demand—hence, lower resource prices—toward those firms with strong and growing demands. Thus, guided by the profit motive and operating under competition in free markets, the pursuit of self-interest may be reconciled with the broader public interest.

The merits of competition are apparent to most of us; it has been described by some as "the whip of efficiency." But it should be understood that whatever the actual or potential good of competition, it will not, under all circumstances, automatically bring about a perfect correspondence between self-interest and maximizing the general welfare. For example, economists have long recognized that, in certain special cases, competition may be inconsistent with efficiency. When increases in the scale of operations result in a continual decline in a firm's costs—a phenomenon known as economies of scale—the fewer the number of firms in that industry, the lower will be their respective costs of production. In the extreme case, the optimum scale of plant relative to the size of the market to be served may be so large as to insure continually decreasing costs within the relevant range of output. Here, competition would be undesirable.[6] Such a situation, given free entry and aggressive competition, would likely degenerate into cutthroat competition with each of the participants cutting their prices below their costs, resulting in the largest firm becoming the ultimate survivor. Indeed, where such instances of "natural" monopoly occur—as is typical in the field of public utilities—the rationale is clear either for direct government regulation or direct public provision of that good or service.

Indeed, in addition to cases of natural monopoly, a wide range of public enterprises have been removed from the aegis of private competitive markets on the grounds that since certain "public goods," such as police and fire protection, education, transportation, postal services, etc., must be generally available to a community, such enterprises are vested with a uniquely public interest. Under private ownership, it is held, a divergence might arise between the public interest and the exclusively private interests of the individual buyers and/or sellers. Where private behavior might impose high social costs on the public, these affected activities are usually excluded from the private competitive struggle.

It can be seen then, that whatever the merits of competition, there may be clear instances in which it may be undesirable. Even where it is clearly desirable, society must always be aware of its responsibility to set forth rules under which competition may be permitted. For, as J. B. Clark and J. M. Clark observed:

In our worship of the survival of the fit under free natural selection, we are sometimes in danger of forgetting that the conditions of the struggle fix the kind of fitness that shall come out of it; that survival in the prize ring means fitness for pugilism; not for bricklaying nor philanthropy; that survival in predatory competition is likely to mean something else than fitness for good and efficient production; and that only from a strife with the right kind of rules can the right kind of fitness emerge. Competition . . . is a game played under the rules fixed by the state to the end that, so far as possible, the prize of victory shall be earned, not by trickery or self-seeking adroitness, but by value rendered. It is not the mere play of unrestrained self-interest; it is a method of harnessing the wild beast of self-interest to serve the common good—a thing of ideals and not of sordidness. It is not a natural state, but like any other form of liberty, it is a social achievement, and eternal vigilance is the price of it.[7]

One can see, perhaps, in today's aroused concern over the social responsibility of private enterprise, the logical consequence of the Clarks' warning sounded more than six decades ago.

Although the question of what is socially responsible economic conduct is as yet unresolved, there is a reasonable agreement among the economics profession as to those necessary market conditions conducive to responsible competitive behavior. This list would include a sufficient number of buyers and sellers of essentially homogeneous goods, services, or resources, so that a meaningful choice among alternatives would exist, and none would be able to influence the market price. A second condition is that of free entry to and exit from the market unimpeded by restrictions either deliberate or otherwise, as in the case of high capital costs of entry for business, or various

---

[6] The term "optimum scale" refers to that scale of plant, given the existing state of technology, which results in the greatest net economies of scale. In a technical sense it is defined as the low point on the firm's long-run average cost curve.

[7] John Bates Clark, John Maurice Clark, *The Control of Trusts* (New York: Macmillan, 1912), pp. 200–201.

union barriers to entry into certain trades. In addition, no seller should be able to attain so strong a position that he would lack the incentive either to lower his costs, change his prices, or improve the product in order to enhance his profits position. As a corollary, no single firm should be so secure that it could dictate the conduct of other firms in the market and thereby restrict or narrow competition.

If these conditions were met, economists would describe such markets as approximating "pure competition." At the other market extreme would be the structure of "pure monopoly," where market power would be complete and price behavior would be determined solely at the discretion of the monopolist. In fact, it is clear that neither pure market form exists to any appreciable extent in the U.S. economy. Nonetheless, the study of competitive markets does furnish us with a logical point of departure not only to study variations from some theoretical norm, but, because there is a good deal of competition in the United States, the study of competitive markets helps to provide valid answers to a variety of economic questions. If, in fact, as a general rule, pure competition did exist throughout the economy, the fullest measure of economic efficiency would be realized, with both output and resource utilization maximized and prices and costs to consumers minimized. Therefore, the study of imperfect competition should proceed with the view of identifying, and hopefully ameliorating, those circumstances which generate aberrations from the competitive norm so that the overall operating efficiency of the American economy might be improved. It is within this context that the subject of economic concentration has received increased attention.

IMPERFECT COMPETITION AND CONCENTRATION

There are a number of widely held propositions about bigness and the concentration of resources therein which suggest that reasonably workable competition

might be difficult to achieve. For example, it is held by many that in numerous markets, buyers and sellers are so few or so large that no effective choice among alternative sources can exist. In such cases, the large are said to be able to dictate the conduct of the small within that same market. Such conditions would warrant alarm since diffusion, rather than concentration, of economic power has been regarded as the economic counterpart of political freedom in a democratic society. Whether such excessively disproportionate concentration of economic power does exist can only be determined by patient investigation on an industry-by-industry basis. Such investigation will form the substance of subsequent articles. The purpose at hand is to outline some observations about a market structure which would be amenable to the growth of industrial dominance and concentration of economic power.

A market situation in which there are so few sellers that the activities of one are of importance to others in that market is referred to by economists as oligopoly. In such a market, sellers will react to the market activities of any one seller, and their actions will, in turn, have repercussions on him. Thus, the individual seller, in his actions over price, output, advertising, or product improvement, must consider the reactions of rival sellers. In the words of Fritz Machlup:

The oligopolist usually thinks of certain firms as his rivals; he knows they are watching him or at least will notice his "competitive" actions; he believes he can hurt them or make them angry or cause them to take an action they would not take but for what he has done.[8]

Profits within an industry provide incentive for new firms to enter that industry. Under conditions of competition, the entrance of new firms will result in lowering of the market price as the output or supply of that industry expands. At the point where the new

---

[8] Fritz Machlup, *The Economics of Seller's Competition* (Baltimore: Johns Hopkins Press, 1952), p. 352.

market price no longer exceeds long-run average costs for the individual firms, profits will disappear, and entry will cease.[9] The same freedom of entry which eliminates profits under competitive conditions plays an equally key role by its absence in sustaining oligopoly and any profits which are being earned within that market structure. For when entry into an oligopolistic industry is relatively easy, unless the market is so limited that the number of firms required to serve it are very few, with each firm forced to take account of the actions of the other firms, the entry of many new firms will transform an oligopoly into something more closely resembling competition. Thus, barriers to entry are probably the single most important determinant to perpetuating oligopoly.

It has already been established that under conditions of oligopoly, an individual firm experiences a great deal of uncertainty about how its rivals will react to the firm's individual price-output changes. The less the single firm knows about the likely reaction of rivals, the greater is its uncertainty over the appropriate price-output decision to make. In the extreme, its very existence in the industry might be compromised by unpredictable actions by its rivals which might lead to price wars. Under these conditions, the allure, indeed the necessity for some form of collusion —either tacit or explicit as with cartels—is very strong for the market participants. And, suffice to say, free entry and collusive oligopoly represent a contradiction in terms. Because barriers to entry are the

major means for maintaining or establishing a market structure amenable to economic concentration, the nature of such barriers is important in determining the extent to which viable competition may in the future be extended to markets where presently it may be largely absent.

Restrictions on entry of new firms may be of two general types. The first may be a natural barrier, or inherent in the nature of the industry. A second type of restriction may be artificial in that it is imposed either by the firms in the industry or from without, but with the same effect of limiting the number of firms in the industry. Conceivably, while natural barriers would seem to imply a certain inevitability regarding the absence of effective competition in an industry, artificial barriers suggest that the absence of effective competition in an industry might be ameliorated by removal of such barriers. One example of a natural barrier to entry was noted earlier and involves the smallness of the product market relative to the optimum scale of plant for a firm in that industry. A second type of natural barrier exists when a large and complex scale of plant is needed, necessitating very heavy capital outlays, as in the automobile industry. Under such constraints, competition within the industry clearly will be limited.

Artificial barriers to entry may take many forms. Patent rights to machines or technological processes, or cross licensing arrangements between certain firms in an industry which exclude others serve to inhibit firm numbers. Frequently, excessive governmental regulation, as in the case of transportation, has the effect of protecting and limiting the number of competitors in a given industry. Similarly, local governments may promulgate numerous building codes or licensing laws which, though designed to protect the public, effectively restrict competition in local markets. Where existing firms in an industry control access to strategic raw materials, a further artificial barrier to new entry is operative. Predatory pricing policies by established firms in an industry represent yet another means of discouraging potential or prospective new entrants. By means of any or several of

---

[9] The concept of profit in economics is quite different from that generally used by the public-at-large. Economic profit is a pure surplus in excess of all costs of production which the firm may incur, where such costs include the obligations incurred for all resources used equal to the amount those resources could earn in their next best alternative use. This element of total costs is referred to as the "opportunity costs" of those resources and is typically excluded from the traditional accounting concept of costs in determining a firm's profits. Thus, economic profits exist only when, after accounting for all opportunity costs of resources used, a surplus remains. It is this surplus which attracts entrance of new firms, and it is their entrance into the industry which extinguishes such "profits."

these artificial barriers, freedom of entry by new firms may be blocked and competition lessened. To avoid costly price wars, competition under oligopoly typically is nonprice competition involving extensive advertising and quality and design variation in order to differentiate the firm's product in the eyes of consumers. Over time, such tactics become largely defensive and have the effect of maintaining, rather than altering, respective market shares, at considerable cost to the consumer.

This review of oligopoly clearly indicates that, in contrast with more nearly pure forms of competition, the public loses through higher prices and restrictions on output and the utilization of resources. Furthermore, it is this type of market structure with which writers on the subject of economic concentration are concerned. As Mason has observed in discussing the decline of competition, writers on the subject of concentration of control:

... appear to mean ... that at some critical point in the development of many if not most industrial markets a decline in the number of sellers, the growth in the size of some of them, or collusion between them has led to the substitution of some one of a variety of monopolistic responses for a competitive response of firms to the market situation. Markets in which buyers and sellers customarily act without too much regard for the results of their action on the market situation or on the actions of their rivals have given way to markets in which at least some sellers, by reason of their size, are forced to take account of the probable effects of their action.[10]

The term "concentration of economic power" clearly implies some disproportionate distribution of influence over economic decisions. However, as noted earlier, concentration of economic power is not necessarily synonymous with overall concentration or concentration in the large. Rather, it takes on economic significance only insofar as it relates to concentration

in particular markets. For it is the relative size distribution of firms in a particular market that may give insight into the nature of the competitive process in that market. Nonetheless, while a high degree of concentration is a necessary condition for noncompetitive market behavior, it may not be a sufficient condition. Thus, a few large firms jointly sharing a given market may behave in a competitive fashion. However, both the weight of theory and a sizable body of empirical evidence do strongly point to the conclusion that higher concentration is associated with less competitive markets.

If concentration in the large does not necessarily imply concentration in particular markets, it may be equally true that concentration in particular markets is not synonymous with substantial overall concentration. For example, assume the economy were composed of a large number of markets, each of which was very small in relation to total output, but with substitution between markets possible. It would be possible, then, to have a relatively small number of firms account for a large share of the supply in each market, yet by conventional measures of overall concentration, none of the firms would bulk large since they would be small in relation to the whole economy. And, under these circumstances, a single firm's discretion over prices and output would be limited. Thus, the broad economic implications of such concentration would be measurably different than where large markets were marked by a high degree of concentration with fewer possibilities for market substitution and with greater discretion over prices and output.

A CONCLUDING NOTE

The American economy is characterized by a substantial number of large markets that are nationwide in scope. Hence, concentration in those markets would have a significant effect on the overall behavior of the economy. Thus, the measurement of concentration in particular markets is of more than merely intellectual

---

[10] Edward S. Mason, *Economic Concentration and the Monopoly Problem* (Cambridge: Harvard University Press, 1957), pp. 46–47.

interest. Such an examination not only may help to identify those areas in which effective competition is impeded, but may serve also as an input in channeling public policy efforts into avenues which will enhance market competition and economic efficiency. To this end, subsequent analyses will focus on the extent of concentration in particular markets—both agricultural and nonagricultural.

Reading 13

Economic Concentration— Some Further Observations*

By Sheldon W. Stahl and C. Edward Harshbarger

Summary

Economic concentration is not a new topic of public discussion. In the late 1930s and early 1940s, the hearings and findings of the Temporary National Economic Committee (TNEC) were highly informative and led to much public discussion on the structure of the American economy. In particular, the study appeared to confirm that there was an observable tendency in the industrial sector of the economy for prices to be inflexible, and, given changes in aggregate demand, adjustment in production rather than prices was the dominant response in many industries. It was observed that in periods of depressed economic activity, production dropped most while prices dropped least, a finding that clearly contradicts classical competitive behavior. Since that time, similar inquiries have been regularly undertaken, and the question of the extent to which the concentration of economic power has impaired the ability of markets to perform effectively is again under more active consideration. The analysis which follows will be concerned with the extent to which economic concentration does occur in particular industries or markets, as well as with some of the economic consequences of such concentration.

Key Questions to Consider

- What are concentration ratios? Why are they significant?

- What has happened to concentration ratios in manufacturing in the post–World War II period?

- What factors tend to cause overstatement and understatement of concentration ratios?

- What relationships appear to be evident between concentration and the effectiveness of monetary and fiscal policy?

* Reprinted with permission from *Monthly Review*, Federal Reserve Bank of Kansas City, January 1974, pp. 3–11.

Economic Concentration—Some Further Observations

Economic concentration is not a new topic of public discussion. In the late 1930s and early 1940s, the hearings and findings of the Temporary National Economic Committee (TNEC) were highly informative and led to much public discussion on the structure of the American economy. The two-year study by the TNEC, "Investigation of Concentration of Economic Power," was prompted by concern over the economy's protracted inability to satisfactorily recover its forward momentum. In particular, the study appeared to confirm that there was an observable tendency in the industrial sector of the economy for prices to be inflexible, and, given changes in aggregate demand, adjustment in production rather than prices was the dominant response in many industries. It was observed that in periods of depressed economic activity, production dropped most while prices dropped least, a finding that clearly contradicts classical competitive behavior.

Despite the importance of these findings, the onset of World War II relegated considerations of structural imperfections in the economy to a decidedly low priority. Similarly, postwar economic concerns, as well as the Korean war, further inhibited investigations of our economic structure. By the latter 1950s, however, with the performance of the American economy again causing public concern, congressional hearings into "administered pricing" focused renewed attention on the matter of market power.[1] Since that time, similar inquiries have been regularly undertaken, and the question of the extent to which the concentration of economic power has impaired the ability of markets to perform effectively is again under more active consideration.

In an earlier issue of this *Review*, the theoretical relationship between economic concentration and a highly competitive free enterprise system was dis-

---

[1] The term "administered price" is generally credited to Gardiner C. Means and was initially defined as a price set for a period of time and a series of transactions. Over time, however, the concept has been broadened to attempt to explain the different behavior of market prices and so-called administered prices during a predominantly demand inflation, as well as to explain the seemingly contradictory phenomenon of simultaneous inflation and excess unemployment. See, for example, G. C. Means, *Industrial Prices and Their Relative Inflexibility*, S. Doc. No. 13, 74th Cong., 1st Sess. (1935); National Resources Committee, *The Structure of the American Economy, Part 1, Basic Characteristics* (Washington, D.C.: Government Printing Office, 1939); *The Corporate Revolution in America* (New York: Macmillan Press, 1964), pp. 101–17; Senate Subcommittee on Antitrust and Monopoly, *Hearings on Administered Prices. Part 9* (Washington, D.C.: Government Printing Office, 1959), pp. 4745–60; and "The Administered Price Thesis Confirmed," *The American Economic Review*, June 1972, pp. 292–306.

cussed.[2] The analysis which follows will be concerned with the extent to which economic concentration does occur in particular industries or markets, as well as with some of the economic consequences of such concentration.

CONCENTRATION RATIOS

Between 1947 and 1967, the share of value added by manufacturing accounted for by the nation's 200 largest manufacturing corporations rose from less than one-third to more than two-fifths. As impressive as these aggregate data may be in pointing toward the growth of large enterprise in our economy, they do not shed much light on the extent of economic concentration within particular industries or product classes; here, one can make use of concentration ratios. These ratios typically refer to the share of output accounted for by the four largest firms in an industry and are customarily expressed in terms of the value of shipments.[3] The economic significance of these measures lies in the fact that established theory clearly suggests that where a relatively few firms may possess a sufficiently large share of the market, none can or will remain indifferent to the actions of the others and their response to changes in market demand conditions will be quite different than if there were more numerous competitors. This behavior was amply documented in the TNEC hearings.

Since the concentration ratios refer to shares of output within certain industries or product classes, and since these categories are derivatives of the Standard Industrial Classification (SIC) system of the Bureau of the Census, knowledge of the basic char-

acteristics of the SIC system is helpful for a better understanding of the interpretation of the data on economic concentration. The SIC system has been developed over a period of many years through government and private industry cooperation. Under this system, as the coding proceeds from a 2-digit basis to a 5-digit basis of classification, the scope of the category becomes progressively narrower. For example, the two digits 20 designate a "major industry group," such as Food and Kindred Products. By adding a third digit, 201, the "industry group," meat products, is identified. The term "industry" refers to the 4-digit (2011) category encompassing meat packing plants, while the addition of a fifth digit (20111) denotes a "product class," fresh beef.

The classification system seeks to establish clearly separable spheres of economic activity so that the common characteristics shared by those in that group would make it unique and readily distinct from other spheres. Thus, within a given industry, those included largely would share a similarity of processes, end products, and materials used, and the producers would be expected to compete with each other in the marketplace. For the economist, however, the idea of a market is somewhat broader than the narrowly defined industry concept of the SIC system; this difference should be explained to place the usefulness of the concentration ratios in better perspective.

The general view of a market is one of a number of buyers and sellers of the same product or substitutable products which possess certain uniquely similar physical characteristics. However, in defining a market, the economist is not particularly interested in whether commodities are physically similar in order to determine whether they are substitutes, but whether different products might feasibly serve the same purpose even if they are physically dissimilar. For example, metal cans and glass containers are classified under the SIC system as being in two different industries, but both products effectively are substitutes and would more often than not fall within a single market. In this instance, the relevant industry is defined too narrowly—the substitutes are found in

---

[2] Sheldon W. Stahl and C. Edward Harshbarger, "Free Enterprise Revisited—A Look at Economic Concentration," *Monthly Review*, Federal Reserve Bank of Kansas City, March 1973, pp. 10–16.

[3] At times, these ratios might reflect the share of output accounted for by the eight largest firms in an industry. However, they most commonly refer to the share of the four largest firms and will be so used in this article.

different industries—and, therefore, the concentration ratios for each will tend to overstate the actual degree of concentration in those markets where the two products are substitutes and effectively compete for the buyers' dollar.

The interpretation of concentration ratios should be circumscribed by another factor which might result in overstatement of market concentration. Census concentration ratios are based on data from the Census of Manufactures, and these relate only to U.S. production. Since sales in domestic markets include imported goods as well, concentration ratios may tend to overstate the case in those industries where imports are of considerable importance. In the case of automobiles, for example, imports increasingly are becoming a competitive factor. However, where they represent "captive imports," or imports which are produced in overseas factories owned by domestic companies, any overstatement of concentration through excluding imports would tend to be offset to some extent.

Several factors which might contribute to an understatement of concentration in the ratios should also be noted. Because large firms frequently specialize in the production of one or just a few products of an industry, the production of individual products within an industry is generally more highly concentrated than is the industry as a whole. For example, if a farmer wishes to buy a tractor, he confronts a market in which the share of output accounted for by the four largest producers of this 5-digit product class is substantially higher than is the concentration ratio for the 4-digit industry "farm machinery and equipment." An additional factor which contributes to understatement is that such ratios are drawn from national data when tabulated from the Census of Manufactures. Given the existence of many regional or local markets, a concentration ratio derived for the nation as a whole will tend to understate the degree of concentration which might prevail in a more limited market. Where the product is highly perishable, or where transportation costs are relatively high, the national concentration ratio may not be a good indicator of local market conditions. Thus, while the

concentration ratio for "bread and bakery products" for the nation as a whole may not suggest a high degree of concentration, the share of the four largest companies within a given metropolitan area may be so high as to noticeably impede competition among the sellers in the local market.

What is the net effect of the possible overstatement and understatement of market control as expressed in concentration ratios and how may the ratios be correctly interpreted in various instances? Bain took the view that on balance, there is

. . . some net average tendency for Census industry concentration measures to understate the degree of seller concentration within the numerous theoretical industries into which existing enterprises should be grouped. We are not in a position to estimate in precise quantitative fashion the average degree of understatement which is involved. It is probably significant but moderate.[4]

Given the substantial growth in imports which has occurred since the above observation was made, the average degree of understatement has probably been reduced.

TRENDS IN CONCENTRATION

The manufacturing sector of the economy accounts for about one-third of all output as measured by the Gross National Product (GNP). Conventional wisdom has long assumed that the effective interplay of competitive forces within this area largely determines the outcome with regard to the composition, production, and distribution of output. In recognizing that competitive market forces are most likely to generate a more satisfactory economic outcome for society as a whole, trends which may suggest a diminution of competitive market forces are of particular interest. For this reason, the recent work of John M. Blair

---

[4] Joe S. Bain, *Industrial Organization* (New York: John Wiley and Sons, 1959), p. 119.

deserves particular mention.[5] Blair's work on economic concentration reveals a wealth of data on the subject and provides incisive analysis as well. The discussion which follows draws from Blair's work and the authors wish to acknowledge their debt.

Data on concentration trends are shown in Table 1 for various industry groups during the post–World War II period through 1967, the last year for which published Census of Manufactures data are available. The table is based on an analysis of a number of industries with a value of shipments of more than $1 billion, and with concentration ratios that changed three or more percentage points during the period 1947–67. The Food and Kindred Products group clearly was an area of increasing concentration; seven of the 10 large industries showed increases. The decline in the small independent brewer is clearly evident in the sharp increase in concentration in the malt liquor industry. Also, given the growing importance of soybean products as a source of protein, the sharp reversal of a declining trend in concentration since 1958 in soybean oil mills is of particular interest. At the same time, the advent of the large commercial feed-lot and the changing technology of the meat-packing industry involving a proliferation of smaller, more specialized plants is attested to by the decreasing concentration ratios for that industry throughout the postwar period. The Textile and Apparel groups were marked by generally increasing concentration, with eight of nine industries showing gains, against a decline for only a single industry.

In the Primary Metals group, two industries showed an increase in concentration for the period, although the changes have been rather moderate since 1958. For the largest industry in this group, blast furnaces and steel mills, the ratio fell after a sharp rise in concentration between 1947 and 1954. Nonetheless, as of 1967, the four largest firms in that industry still accounted for nearly half the output, a degree of

concentration which remained unchanged between the 1963 and 1967 Census dates. The Transportation Equipment group is dominated by the motor vehicles and parts industry which accounts for more than one-half the group's output. Within this industry, the disappearance of a number of automobile manufacturers may be clearly seen in the very sharp rise in concentration between 1947 and 1954. As of 1967, the four largest firms continued to account for nearly four-fifths of the total output. Even in those two industries in the group where there was a decline in concentration relative to 1947, the trend was somewhat irregular and the concentration ratios as of 1967 still reflect substantial market power by the four largest firms.

The growing market dominance of the large firm is apparent in the photographic equipment and supplies industry. On the other hand, the Chemicals and Allied Products group was one in which decreases outnumbered increases in concentration among three of its four large industries. The general tendency for declining concentration is also apparent in the six large industries in the Fabricated Metals and Non-electrical Machinery groups, as well as in the Printing and Publishing group, a development which reveals nothing about the extent of regional concentration. The Tobacco and Petroleum Products groups are both dominated by single large industries, cigarettes and petroleum refining. In both these industries, the decline in concentration occurred between 1947 and 1954. Since that time, no change in the dominant industries has been evident.

The data in Table 1 reflect concentration trends among a relatively limited number of large industries. Table 2 provides data which illustrate the trend of concentration among smaller and medium-sized as well as large industries, and includes a much larger sample than Table 1. There are more than 400 industries for which 1963 and 1967 Census concentration ratios are available. However, because of SIC revisions dating from 1963, only 191 industries remained comparable throughout the entire 1947–67 period. In addition, 18 other industries that remained

---

[5] John M. Blair, *Economic Concentration, Structure, Behavior and Public Policy* (New York: Harcourt Brace Jovanovich, 1972).

Table 1

Concentration in Industry Groups for Selected Years
(percent)

	1947	1954	1958	1963	1967		1947	1954	1958	1963	1967
Food and kindred products						*Transportation equipment*					
Increasing						**Increasing**					
Prepared feeds for animals and fowls	19	21	22	22	23	Motor vehicles and parts*	56	75	75	79	78
Bread, cake, and related products	16	20	22	23	26	**Decreasing**					
Confectionary products	17	19	18	15	25	Aircraft engines and parts	72	62	56	57	64
Malt liquors	21	27	28	34	40	Railroad and street cars	56	64	58	53	53
Bottled and canned soft drinks	10	10	11	12	13	*Instruments; miscellaneous products*					
Flavorings, extracts, and syrups	50	53	55	62	67	**Increasing**					
Soybean oil mills	44	41	40	50	55	Photographic equipment and supplies	61	n.a.	65	63	69
Decreasing						Games and toys	20	18	13	15	25
Meat-packing plants	41	39	34	31	26	*Chemicals and Allied Products*					
Ice cream and frozen desserts	40	36	38	37	33	**Decreasing**					
Distilled liquor	75	64	60	58	54	Industrial organic chemicals	n.a.	59	55	51	45
Textiles; apparel						Plastics materials and resins	44	47	40	35	27
Increasing						Pharmaceutical preparations	28	25	27	22	24
Weaving mills, cotton	n.a.	18	25	30	30	**Increasing**					
Weaving mills, synthetic	31	30	34	39	46	Toilet preparations	24	25	29	38	38
Knit outerwear mills	8	6	7	11	15	*Tobacco; petroleum products*					
Men's and boys' suits and coats	9	11	11	14	17	**Decreasing**					
Men's dress shirts and nightwear	19	17	16	22	23	Cigarettes	90	82	79	80	81
Men's and boys' separate trousers	12	12	9	16	20	Tobacco stemming and redrying	88	79	73	70	63
Women's and misses' suits and coats	n.a.	3	3	8	12	Petroleum refining	37	33	32	34	33
Women's and children's underwear	6	8	8	11	15	*Printing and publishing*					
Decreasing						**Decreasing**					
Knit fabric mills	27	17	18	18	15	Newspapers	21	18	17	15	16
Lumber, stone, clay, and glass						Periodicals	34	29	31	28	24
Increasing						*Fabricated metals; nonelectrical machinery*					
Logging camps and logging contractors	n.a.	8	13	11	14	**Decreasing**					
Decreasing						Metal cans	78	80	80	74	73
Glass containers	63	63	58	55	60	Sheet metalwork	21	19	15	11	10
Primary metals						Screw machine products	17	11	9	5	6
Increasing						Miscellaneous fabricated wire products	20	18	13	13	11
Gray-iron foundries	16	26	24	28	27	Valves and fittings	24	17	17	13	14
Iron and steel forgings	24	27	31	30	30	Ball and roller bearings	62	60	57	57	54
Decreasing											
Blast furnaces and steel mills	50	55	53	48	48						

Table 2

Distribution of Changes in Concentration Ratios
Number of Industries

Size of industry (Value of shipments in millions of dollars)	1947 (or 1954) to 1963	1947 (or 1954) to 1967
Increases		
$2,500 or over	4	9
$1,000 to $2,500	13	14
$500 to $1,000	14	18
Under $500	54	54
Total	85	95
Less than 3 percentage points	43	39
Decreases		
Under $500	44	30
$500 to $1,000	17	21
$1,000 to $2,500	13	15
$2,500 or over	7	9
Total	81	75
Total	209	209

Source: Bureau of the Census, Department of Commerce, *Concentration Ratios in Manufacturing, 1967, Special Reports, 1970*, Pt. 1, Table 5, taken from Blair, p. 23.

comparable beginning in 1954 have been included, for a total of 209 industries constituting more than one-half of the value added by all manufacturing industries.

The 1971 *Economic Report of the President* expressed the view that there was little objective evidence that economic power had increased in recent times. Yet, Table 2 shows that, with the introduction of 1967 Census data, industry concentration has risen.

Those industries in which concentration ratios changed by less than three percentage points are shown separately so that attention might be focused on those industries with more significant changes. In the period 1947(or 1954)-63, there were 85 increases, 43 cases of relative stability, and 81 decreases in concentration ratios. Thus, increases had been roughly offset by decreases. The inclusion of 1967 data clearly changes that picture. Industries with an increase in concentration ratios number 95—a gain of 10 over 1963; there is relative stability in 39 cases; and, decreases number 75—a net loss of 6 from 1963. It is interesting to note that of the 10 increases in concentration between 1963 and 1967, one-half took place in the very large industries with shipments of $2.5 billion or more. At the same time, the number of small industries with declining concentration in the period of 1947(or 1954)-63 fell off sharply—from 44 to 30—in the 1963–67 period. Thus, the data do show that concentration among the large industries has risen.

ANOTHER ASPECT OF CONCENTRATION

It has been recognized for some time that substantial economic power can impede the market's effective operation. Competition among the few will produce quite different results than under the assumptions of classical competition among the many. The early TNEC hearings illustrated this, but the implications for public policy were not grasped for a variety of reasons set forth earlier. However, the behavior of prices among concentrated industries during the recession of 1969–70 provides anew evidence of the difficulties besetting the traditional stabilization tools

---

◄ * The 1967 concentration ratio for motor vehicles and parts, as published by the Census Bureau, is 76%. However, it excludes automotive stamping plants operated by automobile producing companies, which had formerly been included in the motor vehicle and parts industry. For the year 1963 the Bureau has compiled ratios both including and excluding these stamping plants; the figures were 79% and 77%, respectively. Therefore, to retain comparability, the published ratio for 1967 has been increased 2 percentage points to 78%.

n.a. Not available.

Source: Bureau of the Census, Department of Commerce, *Concentration Ratios in Manufacturing, 1967, Special Reports, 1970*, Pt. 1, Table 5, and Blair, p. 21.

of monetary and fiscal policy in slowing inflation in our current economic environment. The policy implications of these difficulties might again be ignored in the face of evidence showing that concentration is diminishing, but with clear evidence to the contrary the 1969–70 experience presents a strong reason to reassess economic policy assumptions and actions.

Beginning late in 1968 and continuing through most of 1969, a combination of monetary and fiscal restraint was applied to the American economy in an attempt to reduce the rate of inflation. In part as a consequence, a reduction in aggregate demand did occur—aggravated by a major strike in the auto industry late in 1970—culminating in the recession of 1969–70. At the same time, prices not only continued to rise, but their rate of increase accelerated. In this connection, the price behavior of certain concentrated industries is quite instructive. Table 3 compares price changes for 347 product classes with Census concentration ratios for the industry groups within which those products are found. These products comprise more than one-half the value of all manufacturing output. The price changes are shown for the period between December 1969 and December 1970, these dates having been officially designated by the National Bureau of Economic Research as the beginning and the trough of the 1969–70 recession.

During this recession, classical competitive behavior was evident in only 52 product classes where prices clearly fell. These declines ranged from 2 percent to more than 5 percent. Of these declines, almost half occurred in the Farm, Food, and Tobacco group and the bulk of them were in excess of 5 percent. Among the other product classes, 65 remained relatively stable—with price changes of from +2 percent to −2 percent. However, for the remaining 230 product classes—or nearly two-thirds of the total sample—prices rose. In fact, more than one-half of these price increases were at a rate of 5 percent or more. Thus, it appears clear that a good deal of perverse price behavior occurred during this recession, behavior which does not comport with the kind of competitive performance suggested by classical economic theory.

A closer look at the data confirms that the extent of such perverse behavior is clearly related to the degree of economic concentration which pertains. For example, the preponderant share of price decreases—about four-fifths—were associated with concentration ratios of under 25 percent, or from 25 to 49 percent. On the other hand, only one-sixth of the price declines occurred where concentration ratios were 50 percent or more. At the same time, price increases were dominant in the moderate to highly concentrated product classes, and conspicuously less so where concentration ratios were under 25 percent.

A CONCLUDING OBSERVATION

Even in an economy marred by structural defects, reconciling the goals of high production and employment with relative price stability still depends, to a considerable extent, upon appropriate monetary and fiscal policies. Yet, one need not wholly accept the structural hypothesis for persistent inflation to recognize that we can no longer formulate and implement public policy largely under the classical economic assumptions regarding the existence of competitive markets. The data on industrial concentration in the foregoing analysis suggest a trend toward increasing market power. To this factor there must be added the growing power and restrictive practices of certain trade unions, import quotas, tariffs, subsidies, and other legislative impediments to the competitive process. Their net effect is to impart a noticeable inflationary bias to the economy, particularly in the light of the ongoing commitment to the attainment of high levels of production and employment. To the extent that competitive markets have been impaired, the problem of inflation has become more pronounced. The present disappointing experience with economic controls should convince us that a fundamental reappraisal of the nation's economic structure, and a serious effort to remedy its structural defects to permit freer operation of the marketplace, is long overdue.

Table 3

Concentration Ratio and Percentage Price Change of 347 Product Classes
December 1969 to December 1970

Industry grouping	Total	Increases 5.0% and over	2.0% to 4.9%	Changes of less than +2.0% or −2.0%	Decreases −2.0% to −4.9%	−5.0% and over
Farm, food, and tobacco						
50% and over	21	12	5	3	1	—
25% to 49%	32	12	7	3	3	7
Under 25% *	29	12	2	1	1	13
Total	82	36	14	7	5	20
Textiles, apparel, and leather						
50% and over	9	1	2	3	—	3
25% to 49%	14	1	1	7	3	2
Under 25%	11	1	6	3	1	—
Total	34	3	9	13	4	5
Lumber, furniture, and paper						
50% and over	6	3	3	—	—	—
25% to 49%	15	3	3	6	1	2
Under 25%	13	—	5	3	4	1
Total	34	6	11	9	5	3
Chemicals and petroleum						
50% and over	12	—	2	8	2	—
25% to 49%	15	8	5	2	—	—
Under 25% †	1	—	1	—	—	—
Total	28	8	8	10	2	0
Stone, clay, and glass						
50% and over	10	4	3	3	—	—
25% to 49%	5	2	3	—	—	—
Under 25%	3	3	—	—	—	—
Total	18	9	6	3	0	0
Primary metals						
50% and over	26	12	5	6	2	1
25% to 49%	12	6	4	0	—	2
Under 25% ‡	2	1	—	—	1	—
Total	40	19	9	6	3	3

Industry grouping	Total	Increases 5.0% and over	2.0% to 4.9%	Changes of less than +2.0% or −2.0%	Decreases −2.0% to −4.9%	−5.0% and over
Machinery and fabricated metal products						
50% and over	21	10	9	2	—	—
25% to 49%	27	14	11	2	—	—
Under 25%	8	5	2	1	—	—
Total	56	29	22	5	0	0
Electrical machinery						
50% and over	19	6	8	5	—	—
25% to 49%	14	9	2	1	1	1
Under 25%	2	1	1	—	—	—
Total	35	16	11	6	1	1
Transportation equipment						
50% and over	3	3	—	—	—	—
25% to 49%	1	—	—	1	—	—
Under 25%	—	—	—	—	—	—
Total	4	3	0	1	0	0
Miscellaneous						
50% and over	7	2	1	4	—	—
25% to 49%	5	—	4	1	—	—
Under 25%	4	1	3	—	—	—
Total	16	3	8	5	0	0
All product classes						
50% and over	134	53	38	34	5	4
25% to 49%	140	55	40	23	8	14
Under 25%	73	24	20	8	7	14
Total	347	132	98	65	20	32

* Includes 19 farm product classes.

† Includes one product class, wastepaper.

‡ Includes two product classes of scrap metal.

Source: Prices: Bureau of Labor Statistics, Department of Labor, Wholesale Price Index; Concentration ratios: *Concentration Ratios in Manufacturing Industry, 1963*, 1966, Pt. 1, Table 4, reprinted from Blair, pp. 546–47.

Reading 14

Social Costs—
The Due Bill for Progress*

By Sheldon W. Stahl

Summary

Progress is defined as "a journeying forward, a gradual betterment; especially the progressive development of mankind." In this regard, many probably view progress and growth—particularly economic growth—as nearly synonymous. The high priority which public policy assigns to the goal of economic growth clearly suggests that it serves as a proxy indicator of progress or of our gradual betterment.

Perhaps GNP, more than any other single indicator, has come to be viewed as the measure of our national well-being. It has been endowed with a tangible form in the shape of a GNP clock in the lobby of the U.S. Department of Commerce in Washington—a symbol of the importance we attach to things economic. Little wonder, then, that so many tend to equate a rising GNP with a rise in both our national and individual well-being. Yet, there are those who would question this view. Even as national income has grown, disaffection and discontent have dogged the path of economic growth, and debate grows over the wisdom of our course. In part, this probably represents the fact that, as we progress, our expectations rise faster than the actual improvements in our standards of living. But perhaps an even more noteworthy reason for a growing discontent, amid so much material progress, is the increasing realization that such progress is not without its cost in the form of a deterioration in the quality of life.

Key Questions to Consider

- What are social costs?

- What are externalities?

- How has the absence of property rights for air and water resources affected their use and with what effects?

- Why has society only recently grown anxious over the disamenities of growth?

- What is meant by "internalizing" externalities?

---

* Reprinted with permission from *Monthly Review*, Federal Reserve Bank of Kansas City, April 1972, pp. 13–19.

Social Costs—
The Due Bill for Progress

Progress is defined as "a journeying forward, a gradual betterment; esp: the progressive development of mankind." In this regard, many probably view progress and growth—particularly economic growth—as nearly synonymous. The high priority which public policy assigns to the goal of economic growth clearly suggests that it serves as a proxy indicator of progress or of our gradual betterment. Thus, publication of the various economic indicators commands more than a cursory interest. In particular, the annual *Economic Report of the President* and report of the Council of Economic Advisers is seen as a most comprehensive reference source as to the Nation's economic well-being and, by inference, our own. Within its pages may be found a wealth of data on production, employment, prices, trade, incomes, and so forth. Our system of national income and product accounts reduces the complexities of the marketplace to intelligible proportions and measures the varying contributions of the market participants to the economic whole. The results of these market-oriented activities —our progress or lack of it—are summarized in the data on the gross national product (GNP).

Perhaps, more than any other single indicator, GNP has come to be viewed as the measure of our national well-being. It has been endowed with a tangible form in the shape of a GNP clock in the lobby of the U.S. Department of Commerce in Washington—a symbol of the importance we attach to things economic. Little wonder, then, that so many tend to equate a rising GNP with a rise in both our national and individual well-being. Yet, there are those who would question this view. Even as national income has grown, disaffection and discontent have dogged the path of economic growth, and debate grows over the wisdom of our course. In part, this probably represents the fact that, as we progress, our expectations rise faster than the actual improvements in our standards of living. But perhaps an even more noteworthy reason for a growing discontent, amid so much material progress, is the increasing realization that such progress is not without its costs in the form of a deterioration in the quality of life. It is here that the matter of social costs intrudes, as was explicitly recognized in the 1971 *Economic Report of the President*. In discussing how our economic system might make its maximum contribution to national well-being, the *Report* acknowledged that:

The success of our economic system in achieving this goal requires that the full social cost be paid for the use of resources.[1]

---

[1] *Economic Report of the President* (Washington: U.S. Government Printing Office, January 1971), p. 107.

The concept of social costs and its relationship to progress as we have defined it will be explored in this article.

THE NATURE OF SOCIAL COSTS

In general, "social costs" may be defined as:

. . . all those harmful consequences and damages which third persons or the community sustain as a result of the productive process, and for which private entrepreneurs are not easily held accountable.[2]

Additionally, social costs include disamenities traceable to various governmental or public activities for which those bodies are not effectively held accountable. As such, these costs are not necessarily uniform in their incidence. In certain instances, their impact may be immediate. At other times, the social losses of production may not be readily visible, so that only after a long period of time are injured parties made aware of their loss. Social costs may affect only a limited group, or they may fall on all members of society. In the latter instance, where the loss is distributed over a great many persons, the costs to any single member of that group may be relatively small. If they are small enough, the individual may not find it worthwhile to act against the offending party. These varying kinds of social costs would include those associated with occupational injuries or disease, environmental pollution of the air or water, noise pollution, depletion of natural resources, and the costs associated with rapid technological change. Such a list undoubtedly could be expanded. Although these examples may portray the kinds of social costs generated, it is even more important to understand how these costs arise.

An identification of money costs with total costs is implicit in the valuation system which characterizes our market economy. If a transaction has consequences—or spillovers—that are not reflected as a money cost, they fall outside the market's valuation process. They are regarded by economists as "externalities." For example, if the costs of industrial pollution or industrial disease or disability are not charged to the seller who generates these costs, the market will ignore such externalities in determining exchange value. Social cost and economic cost will diverge in this instance, and the output of the firm will be underpriced in comparison with its true social costs. Such underpricing encourages a greater level of consumption than would pertain at some higher price in which all costs would be included.

Until recently, the decision largely to omit externalities from the economic cost calculus rested mainly on two basic assumptions. The first was that the market-place was highly objective in assigning exchange values in determining costs of production. In the absence of such objective market criteria, it was held that any evaluation of the social damages or social losses caused by private production—the externalities—would necessarily involve highly subjective value judgments, thereby rendering any conclusions from such an exercise equally arbitrary or subjective. The second assumption for largely ignoring spillovers or externalities was that they were thought to be of no major import, or at least only occasionally so, in the overall determination of costs. Both assumptions appear to be wanting. In the first instance, the danger of introducing subjectivity into economic analysis is not eliminated by choosing simply to disregard social costs. Such a decision, premised on their presumed noneconomic nature, implies that all social damages have zero value. Such a judgment is at least as subjective as that assumed in evaluating social costs. The other assumption, that externalities were only of occasional importance, also suffers in the light of current experience. If and when certain spillover effects become overly burdensome, remedies will be sought from government in the form of legislation or through regulatory actions. In either case, costs which were formerly external or noneconomic become internalized, or economic, in the cost structure. The

---

[2] K. W. Kapp, *The Social Costs of Private Enterprise* (Harvard University Press, 1950), p. 14.

growing concern over the quality of our air and water is an illustration.

The absence of any clear-cut property rights for the air or for much of our water resources has led to their being regarded by industry and individuals as essentially free goods. The release of wastes into either or both the air and the water, therefore, was viewed as involving no cost to the user. Society accepted this arrangement as long as the wastes did not exceed the assimilative capacity of the environment. Up to that point, the environment handled waste disposal at no apparent cost either to the user or to society at large. When the ability of the environment to handle this task was exceeded, pollution imposed real costs and clean air and water were no longer viewed as free goods to society. Despite the fact that no two parties in society might subjectively assign the same values to clean air or water, the increasing burden of environmental pollution prompted society to exercise its collective value judgment in calling for government action to provide relief. In this fashion, certain externalities, once largely ignored, have found their way into our value system.

OUR GROWING CONCERN

In a section of the 1971 *Economic Report of the President* dealing with national priorities and national output, it is noted that:

While the Nation has been engaged in a new and earnest soul searching about the role of growing material affluence in the good life, it is probably true that in general the American people prefer a rapid growth of GNP and its consequences.[3]

However, an important qualification to this statement appears shortly thereafter:

This is not to say that growth of measured GNP is an absolute to be furthered at all costs. As individuals and as citizens we clearly do many things that reduce the growth of GNP, and we fail to do many things that would accelerate it. This is perfectly reasonable; growth of GNP has its costs, and beyond some point they are not worth paying. Man wants more than is counted in GNP. People's values change. Conditions of life change. These may lower the point beyond which more growth of GNP is not worth its costs. Even so, growth of GNP would still be an objective about which we are not indifferent.[4]

This concern over growth and its attendant costs was manifest in the example of air and water pollution cited earlier. It is equally clear that numerous other aspects of growth process are also undergoing considerable scrutiny. Whether or not the observation that the American people generally prefer a rapid growth of GNP and its consequences will be borne out will depend on the results of that investigation.

As our population grows, increasing apprehension is felt over the limited supply of certain exhaustible natural resources needed to satisfy the demands occasioned by more people. The costs for those natural resources have risen, and may be expected to rise even more, as poorer deposits of mineral resources have been extracted and as water and other resources are recycled. The costs, whether in terms of added environmental damage or in terms of preventing such damage, also may be expected to rise. Growing material affluence, a product of rapid economic growth, would further intensify the future demands to be made against our shrinking resource base.

As growth continues, the trend toward increasing urbanization also is likely to continue. Yet the concentration of people and economic activity in ever-larger urban centers has pronounced costs of its own. Traffic congestion, noise, as well as air and water pollution, all increase with city size. Limited recreation areas become overtaxed and less accessible, and privacy diminishes. More time is spent in commuting. Expenditures for police and fire protection, street maintenance, welfare, and for waste disposal increase.

---

[3] 1971 *Economic Report*, p. 88.

[4] *Ibid.*

In short, the amenities which life, and urban life in particular, may afford are harder to come by and grow more costly.

It may be observed that these disamenities of growth always have been present in varying degrees. Why has society grown so anxious over them now? The answer may be traceable to a more rapid rate of growth and change than in earlier years. Just as our natural environment has been strained by the heightened demands of growth and change, so too may the assimilative capacity of our society in general be strained in the context of rapid changes. Alvin Toffler, author of the book *Future Shock*,[5] coined the terms to describe the shattering stress induced in individuals when they are subjected to too much change in too short a period of time. In a sense, then, our society may be suffering from a form of collective future shock as it is confronted with the phenomenon of rapid change and the acceleration in the rate of growth of the disamenities which accompany such change. In questioning the desirability of growth, it may be that society is looking to the future and reexamining its value system and its standards for defining progress. If so, it is worthwhile to look at some of the implications which might follow from such a reexamination.

SOME IMPLICATIONS

There has clearly emerged in our society a recognition that the pursuit of growth and the attainment of a desirable quality of life present us with some mutual contradictions. The need for making choices and for changes in our attitudes and in our institutional structure is increasingly evident. If a consensus has not yet emerged on what the tradeoff between growth and qualitative considerations should be, there has come about an awareness that the way we grow and the uses we make of our growth require a searching reexamination.

Viewing growth from the perspective of global environmental problems, economist Kenneth Boulding posits the concept of the "Spaceship Earth." [6] This view holds that there are finite limits to the assimilative capacity of the environment and that growth will test those limits in some unspecified, but not greatly distant, future period. Given these circumstances, growth should be retarded. In stressing that the closed earth of the future will require different economic principles than those which governed the open earth of the past, Boulding distinguishes between what he refers to as a "cowboy economy" and the "spaceman economy." The former is associated with the open economy of the past and the latter with the closed economy of the future. He observes:

The difference between the two types of economy becomes most apparent in the attitude towards consumption. In the cowboy economy, consumption is regarded as a good thing and production likewise; and the success of the economy is measured by the amount of the throughput from the "factors of production," a part of which, at any rate, is extracted from the reservoirs of raw materials and noneconomic objects, and another part of which is output into the reservoirs of pollution.... The gross national product is a rough measure of this total throughput....

By contrast, in the spaceman economy, throughput is by no means a desideratum, and is indeed to be regarded as something to be minimized rather than maximized. The essential measure of the success of the economy is not production and consumption at all, but the nature, extent, quality, and complexity of the total capital stock, including in this the state of the human bodies and minds included in the system. In the spaceman economy, what we are primarily concerned with is stock maintenance, and any technological change which results in the maintenance of a given total stock with a lessened throughput (that is, less production and consumption) is clearly a gain. This idea that both production and consumption are bad things rather than good things is very strange to economists, who

[5] Alvin Toffler, *Future Shock* (New York: Random House, July 1970).

[6] Kenneth E. Boulding, "The Economics of the Coming Spaceship Earth," *Environmental Quality* (Baltimore, Md.: Resources for the Future, 1966).

have been obsessed with the income-flow concepts to the exclusion, almost, of capital-stock concepts.[7]

In this regard, it is rather interesting to note an observation made by social philosopher John Ruskin more than 100 years ago.

It is popularly supposed that it benefits a nation to invent a want. But the fact is, that the true benefit is in extinguishing a want—in living with as few wants as possible.

I cannot tell you the contempt I feel for the common writers on political economy, in their stupefied missing of this first principle of all human economy—individual or political—to live, namely, with as few wants as possible, and to waste nothing of what is given you to supply them.[8]

Whether or not one fully accepts the "Spaceship Earth" concept, the debate on the social costs of growth reflects our growing concern and our desire for a practical solution to the dilemma. It is here that economists suggest that perhaps the best solution to the problem lies in internalizing externalities. By so doing, the cost of the disamenities and the undesirable side effects of the production process would be made to fall on those responsible for them. By raising the marginal costs to those producers, and thereby the prices to consumers of those products, the resultant price rise would cause fewer units to be consumed, thereby retarding growth of those products which have the highest social costs of production. Along with greater use of the pricing mechanism, increased efforts will have to be made to deal with those cases which may not be readily amenable to pure price solutions. For example, added governmental prohibition or regulation of certain activities may be required in the larger public interest. In addition, more innovative use of the tax structure and of public expenditures may be called for to provide incentives for minimizing future social costs, and for undoing the environmental damages resulting from past production.

Once the principle and practice of internalizing the external costs of our environmental amenities is accepted, greatly enhanced growth in the field of environmental pollution abatement would almost certainly follow. Changing our cost calculus to reflect the social costs of production in the prices which we will have to pay for these products will clearly alter the composition of GNP in the direction of increased quality. Such a mix would contain more environmental amenities but less material output.

However, redirection of growth need not involve its cessation. High social costs are not a function of growth per se, but of the way we have grown. Internalizing social costs will aid in redirecting growth toward a more socially desirable mix. Even with this new mix of output, the rate of growth need not suffer if we vigorously apply ourselves to the task of productively reemploying those resources freed as the flow of production of those goods with high social costs—and higher prices—is retarded. As already noted, growth in pollution abatement will most certainly absorb some of these resources. And the opportunities for further employment gains will grow as we turn to the urgent problems of reclaiming our land and waterways; improving transportation, education, and health services; eliminating poverty; and rebuilding our cities. As we consider these problems, special emphasis should be given to insuring that the poor be afforded an opportunity to share the improvement in the quality of life. Given the higher price tags that an improved quality of life might well carry, it becomes of special importance to promote more effective measures to redistribute income and economic opportunities in order that all may share the benefits of a better life.

The decisions about the uses to which our national product will be put will not be arrived at easily. The continuous debate over the appropriateness of our national priorities should make that clear. But the current thrust to redirecting growth toward improving the quality of our lives seems more likely to grow

[7] Ibid., pp. 8–10.
[8] John Ruskin, "Time and Tide," English Prose of the Victorian Era (New York: Oxford University Press, Inc., 1938), p. 1016.

than to abate. If this is so, then one might reasonably expect that the future might well hold for us a much better and more humane state of being than the present. As a guidepost along the path to that society, one might take note of the views expressed in a report of the Economic Council of Canada several years ago.

The long-term record of the growth of material wealth in today's high income countries has been impressive. But this growth does not proceed without social costs, and it has been tending to throw into sharper focus a growing array of problems and needs relating to both the quality of life and to an appropriate sharing in the fruits of economic progress. Illustrative of the issues which have become the subject of increasing social concern are: the problem of poverty in the midst of affluence; the needs for better access to high standards of health care and to opportunities for maximum educational advancement for all individuals in the society; increased air and water pollution in an age of greatly advanced scientific capabilities for dealing with these problems; increased urban congestion and blight concentrated especially in centres of the highest average of income and wealth; and the greatly increased needs for recreational facilities and enlarged cultural opportunities in conditions of reduced working time and increased leisure. In these and other fields, there has emerged an increasing awareness that under conditions of high income and well sustained economic growth there are both needs and opportunities for devoting proportionately greater resources to the maintenance and improvement of the quality of life. More generally, there has also emerged a strong conviction that economic growth and development cannot be regarded as satisfactory if the rising output and income which it generates is not widely shared among all groups and all parts of the country. A more equitable distribution of rising opportunities, income and wealth has thus become a more prominent objective of modern industrial economies along with other basic economic and social goals.[9]

---

[9] Economic Council of Canada, *Third Annual Review: Prices, Productivity, and Employment* (Ottawa: Queen's Printer, November 1966), p. 21.

A CONCLUDING OBSERVATION

In a very real sense, we have seen that social costs are, in fact, the due bill which must be paid for progress. By omitting them from our conventional cost calculus, we underpriced what we defined as progress and wastefully consumed it to the detriment of our natural environment and of those other amenities which add to the quality of our lives. In our current concern over the social costs of growth, we are asking questions which go to the root of the relationship between man and his institutions. Our present concern was clearly foreseen more than two decades ago by K. W. Kapp, who wrote:

An economic system which shifts part of the costs of production to third persons, and a body of doctrine which disregards these social costs, are in opposition to one of the most fundamental tenets of our professed humanistic ideals: respect for the human personality. Instead of being treated in his own right the individual becomes a mere instrument in the interest of long-run progress or whatever other "cause" if we fail to consider the human costs of production. This neglect of the individual needs to be remedied not only at the level of social legislation but also at that of economic theory, and it is within this broader context that the analysis and elimination of social costs offers a challenge to the economist.[10]

One might demur that it is to society at large, not merely to the social scientist, that the challenge is directed.

---

[10] Kapp, p. 20.

Proper Policies Could Improve Functioning of Market Economy*

By Clifford L. Fry

Summary

A new dimension has been added to economic concerns in recent years. Historically, a major concern has been for policies that would stimulate a nation's economic growth. To this has now been added an increasing awareness of the consequences for the environment of maintaining many policies aimed primarily at economic growth.

The environmental consequences of growth—such as water and air pollution and the rising noise level—have become of widespread concern. Many consider the situation a fundamental economic problem.

To clarify the problem and begin reaching for a solution, it is necessary, first, to examine the economic system that has allowed pollution of the environment to develop as a seemingly inevitable and certainly unintended side effect of growth. In the United States, that means an examination of the market economy. After defining the market characteristics that encourage pollution, it becomes possible to clarify some of the economic consequences of often espoused antipollution policies and to formulate criteria for evaluating pollution control programs.

Key Questions to Consider

- What are private costs? What are social costs? What are marginal social costs and marginal private costs?

- In what sense is pollution a cost the public must incur over and above the factor-input costs?

- What are the three approaches suggested for attacking pollution problems?

- How do the concepts of marginal benefit and marginal cost provide a guide for policy decisions?

* Reprinted with permission from *Business Review*, Federal Reserve Bank of Dallas, October 1973, pp. 1–5.

Proper Policies Could Improve Functioning of Market Economy

A new dimension has been added to economic concerns in recent years. Historically, a major concern has been for policies that would stimulate a nation's economic growth. To this has now been added an increasing awareness of the consequences for the environment of maintaining many policies aimed primarily at economic growth.

The environmental consequences of growth—such as water and air pollution and the rising noise level—have become a widespread concern. Many consider the situation a fundamental economic problem.

To clarify the problem and begin reaching for a solution, it is necessary, first, to examine the economic system that has allowed pollution of the environment to develop as a seemingly inevitable and certainly unintended side effect of growth. In the United States, that means an examination of the market economy. After defining the market characteristics that encourage pollution, it becomes possible to clarify some of the economic consequences of often espoused antipollution policies and to formulate criteria for evaluating pollution control programs.

THE MARKET ECONOMY...

Consumers in a market economy base their decisions partly on their personal preferences and buying power. But market prices are also a major factor influencing their decisions. The higher the price of an item, the greater the sacrifice a consumer must make for it in terms of other consumption that he has to forgo.

Producers' decisions are also affected by market prices. And because prices affect a producer's revenues and costs—and, therefore, his profits—they are a primary determinant of the final allocation of resources.

A simple example will illustrate the point. Assume that consumer tastes change and demand for one

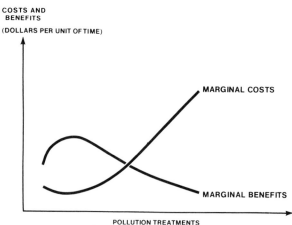

Marginal costs of cleaning up pollution eventually outweigh marginal benefits

COSTS AND BENEFITS

(DOLLARS PER UNIT OF TIME)

MARGINAL COSTS

MARGINAL BENEFITS

POLLUTION TREATMENTS

(UNITS OF POLLUTION REMOVED PER UNIT OF TIME)

item rises while demand for another falls. The results are twofold: a shortage of the first item that puts upward pressure on its price and a surplus of the second item that puts downward pressure on its price.

As the prices shift, production of the first item becomes relatively more profitable. Producers devote more resources to its production and fewer to the production of the second item. But in deciding to respond to the change in demand, a producer must compare the costs of increased output of the first item —or a shift to its production—with the expected revenue.

Theoretically, so long as the additional revenue from selling more of the item exceeds the additional costs of production, he will increase output. And if the market is perfectly competitive, he will continue to expand production until the additional costs of producing a unit of the item exactly equal its market price.

... AND THE ENVIRONMENT

The problem regarding the environment enters in connection with producers' costs. All the costs to this point have been *private costs*—the producer's out-of-pocket costs for such items as labor and materials and his implicit costs for use of such resources as the plant and equipment he owns and could, otherwise, rent to someone else.

Most of these costs are paid in money and are, therefore, thought of in terms of money. But there is another sense in which they are true costs. Because resources used by the producer for one purpose cannot be used for others, the cost of allocating scarce resources to the production of one item is the loss of production of another. This loss, however, does not always equal the total cost to society.

The *social cost* of an item is the private resource cost incurred by the producer plus any additional loss of resources that can be attributed to the production but is not paid for by the producer. Correspondingly, the resources sacrificed from other endeavors in the production of an additional unit of the item are the *marginal social costs* of producing that item.

Ideally, marginal private costs would equal marginal social costs. That, however, is not always the case. When marginal social costs exceed marginal private costs, there is a loss in resources that exceeds the loss indicated by private costs.

This loss in resources is a cost the public must incur over and above the factor-input costs directly incurred by the producer. One example of this extra cost, which arises when decisions made in the marketplace are based on private costs that do not fully reflect social costs, is pollution.

The implications of such a situation are many. The primary implication, however, is that more resources are devoted to pollution-causing activities than would be the case if all costs were incurred by producers and paid by consumers.

Take a situation, for example, where a manufacturing company operates a plant on the banks of a public stream and dumps its wastes into the stream. The company incurs many private costs by paying suppliers for the resources used in production. But because no one owns the waterway, no one can charge the company for dumping its wastes in the stream. And since this resource cost is not counted among the producer's costs, it is not reflected in the prices charged for the product.

Yet, when waste has built up in the water to a point where the stream is being destroyed—from the standpoint of either economic usefulness or environmental health—the public is losing an important scarce resource. And there is nothing inherent in the market system to reverse the destruction—at least, in time to prevent a significant loss of the resource.

Just as businesses make their decisions on the basis of private costs, so do consumers. In deciding between two goods that provide the same level of satisfaction, consumers can usually be expected to choose the lower-priced one. And in cases where the social costs of production exceed the market price, consumers may actually encourage pollution by picking the lower-priced good.

Only when pollution increases to the point of impinging on private costs and, thereby, exerts upward pressure on market prices do consumers consider substitutes. This, unfortunately, rarely happens before society incurs serious environmental problems. And these problems are usually irreversible in the short run and, sometimes, even in the long run.

In situations where social costs exceed private costs because of pollution, reliance on the free market can lead to an overproduction of goods with which pollution is associated. In its 1972 report to the President, the Council of Economic Advisers stated:

The basic environmental problem, for example, is that some resources, like air, are common property and consequently the private economic system does not put a price on their use. The result is overuse or misuse—such as the dumping of excess pollutants into the air.

The council went on to suggest, however, that solutions to the problem can be defined in the framework of a market economy:

The lesson of all this is not *laissez-faire*. There are conditions where a functioning price system does not naturally exist and has to be created or simulated.

ONE APPROACH TO THE PROBLEM

There are, doubtlessly, many ways of attacking pollution problems. Most, however, seem to center on three basic approaches. All can be explored in terms of a single example—water pollution.

Returning to the situation of a manufacturing company that dumps its wastes into a stream, one way to lessen the pollution would be for the public to undertake construction of a plant to treat the industrial waste. Such an approach might eliminate the pollution, but it has some inherent disadvantages.

With construction financed presumably out of general tax revenues, there would be no direct increase in the manufacturer's production costs and, therefore, no cost-induced price increase for his product. And without this price increase, no pressure for a reduction in the amount of the good demanded

would be initiated from the supply side of the market.

Some reduction in demand might result, of course, from the increase in taxes required to build the treatment plant, but the reduction would probably be slight. Just how effectively such an approach would influence the demand side would depend on the proportion of taxpayers that bought the product of the offending plant, the extent of the tax increase, and the sensitivity of demand for the product to changes in disposable income.

The greatest limitation of this approach, then, is that, with no direct implications for change in either production costs or consumer prices, the costs of pollution are still incurred by the public at large rather than being incorporated in the market price of the product. And, of course, to the extent that some taxpayers are not consumers of the good produced at the polluting plant, the program subsidizes those that are.

Consumers have no incentive to shift demand to less polluting products. The producer has no incentive to change either production methods or the volume of goods produced. And little change in the amounts of waste produced by the plant can be expected.

ANOTHER APPROACH

Another approach would be to require the company to adopt certain pollution standards. This approach would eliminate the need for public construction of a waste treatment plant. Instead, the company would be required to change its production technique to reduce the volume of pollutants.

Although some flexibility could be built into the pollution standards, there would probably be instances in which a company could not make the necessary changes in the time allowed and would, presumably, have to stop production. Considerations of the availability of substitute goods, any social benefits of having adequate supplies of the good produced by the polluting plant, and any problems connected with closing the plant—such as unemployment, loss of capital equipment, or costs of relocation—would, therefore, have to be taken into account in formulating standards.

Revamping a plant to meet disposal requirements will almost certainly result in corresponding increases in its production costs. If the goods could have been produced at a lower cost initially without polluting the stream, the producer would presumably have already done so. And if a technique with less pollution is not known, the producer will have to incur the cost of searching for it. For the company to stay in business, at least part of these costs of meeting pollution standards—which will vary with the particular industry and the severity of the restrictions—must be passed on to consumers as higher prices.

Transfer of resources represents another cost resulting from this approach. It takes time and money to retool a plant or move equipment from one company to another. And when new production techniques are forced on a producer, some specialized equipment is probably rendered obsolete. In the long run, these changes will bring higher prices, which, in turn, will lead some consumers to consider other goods with an eye to reducing their use of the goods in question.

AND A THIRD APPROACH

The third alternative is in most direct harmony with efforts to devise a better-functioning price system. It would involve two stages: the cost of waste treatment would be estimated, and, then, this estimated cost would be levied on the polluting company. Imposed as a tax on units of waste discharged—and possibly varied if marginal cleanup costs could be related directly to the volume of discharge—the levy could be used to build and maintain a waste treatment plant.

With production that resulted in pollution now costing more than production that did not, the company would be encouraged to update its plant as fast as new equipment and techniques became available. And with the tax cost reflected at least partially in

the price of the product, consumers could decide whether they wanted the product enough to pay the full cost of its production.

If there were not enough consumers willing to absorb the higher costs resulting from pollution control, the company might have to stop production altogether. In such a case—and assuming there were social benefits to be derived from the good—the public might want to consider alternatives to doing without the product. It would still have the option, for example, of financing waste treatment out of general tax revenue to keep a company in business.

This third approach to pollution problems represents an effort to create a functioning price system where one does not exist. By placing more reliance on the price system for the allocation of resources, this approach is more nearly consistent with the proper functioning of a market economy.

Where suitable technology is available for cleaning up pollution, revenue from the pollution tax can be used for that purpose. Meanwhile, the company is given an incentive to develop more pollution-free production techniques.

In the case of many water pollution problems, the technology for pollution treatment does exist. And policies consistent with the conceptual framework of the third alternative have been proposed.

Application of this approach, however, need not presuppose knowledge of how to reverse the adverse consequences of continuing pollution. By raising the cost of producing the polluting product and, thereby, reducing its production and consumption, a pollution tax can hold pollution to acceptable levels.

Proposals for such a pollution tax have already been made in connection with the use of electricity and automobiles. Progressive taxation on the use of electricity, it has been argued, should be substituted for declining unit-cost structures that encourage consumption. Similarly, taxes based on the pollution capacity of automobiles have been proposed.

While reduction in output would come at a cost to the public, so would continued deterioration of the environment. When the deterioration has become so great that the state of the environment is more important than the loss of some production, this application of the third approach becomes simply a matter of choosing the "lesser of two evils."

A GUIDE FOR POLICY

Problems of formulating adequate pollution control policies are complicated by the difficulties of assigning dollar values to the excess of social costs over private costs. A suitable conceptual framework is available, however, to provide a guide in choosing between proposed policies.

Both benefits and costs are involved in cleaning up pollution. The costs are fairly easy to identify. They are the dollar costs of resources used in the cleanup—presumably with no complicating side effects, such as pollution from the cleanup itself.

It is the benefits that pose identification problems. Since the benefits of a cleanup include not only the restoration of natural resources for purely productive use but also such noneconomic matters of general welfare as ecological balance, the abatement of noise and odors, and a reduction in threats to personal health, dollar values are hard to assign.

It seems clear, however, that where effluences have been treated very little and pollution has become a serious problem, the public can reap substantial benefits from efforts at cleaning up the environment. With each additional effort, more benefits may be achieved. But at some point, about as many benefits will have been obtained as can be without enormous additional effort.

Using the economic tool of marginal analysis, the benefits of pollution control can be viewed in terms of its *marginal benefit*—the benefit from removing an additional unit of pollution from the environment for a definite length of time. This might measure, for example, the gain to society from removing a ton of pollutants from the atmosphere for one day. Costs can be considered in terms of the *marginal cost* of such benefits—the dollar cost, again, of removing a unit of pollution for a specific period.

Since the marginal benefits of eliminating pollutants rise rapidly relative to the cost of such efforts until some point where the relationship begins to reverse itself and every additional benefit costs progressively more to achieve, the most efficient allocation of resources to pollution control can be plotted. The slope of the marginal cost curve depends on many factors, such as the type of production involved in the cleanup and the structure of the market for inputs to the cleanup. After a point, however, marginal costs will begin rising steadily, reaching their maximum only after the marginal benefits have been tapering off for some time. By contrast, marginal benefits rise initially and then normally level off and begin slowly tapering downward.

The optimal level of pollution control would be at the intersection of these curves—at the point where marginal benefits exactly equal marginal costs. Until then, although the difference is narrowing, the benefits of removing another unit of pollution always exceed the costs. After the point of intersection, the marginal costs exceed the marginal benefits.

This simple technique of analysis has ready application to policy decisions. In 1971, for example, the Senate passed an amendment to the Federal Water Pollution Control Act requiring absolutely no discharge of pollutants into streams by 1985. The cost of achieving this zero discharge goal has been estimated at $316.5 billion. But it has also been estimated that as much as 95 percent of the pollutants flowing into lakes and streams—and possibly as much as 99 percent—could be eliminated at a cost of $118.8 billion. This means the bill would require a marginal cost of nearly $200 billion to eliminate from 1 to 5 percent of the water pollution—and that after the achievement of what is considered high-quality water.

CONCLUDING COMMENTS

Any effective environmental policy will necessarily impose hardships on the economy, for such a policy would be designed to change behavior and resource-use patterns. There is now general agreement that some changes are necessary, but they will undoubtedly be costly and often difficult to make.

Discussions, usually in engineering or ecological terms, have already resulted in broadly accepted proposals for alleviating some of the problems of a deteriorating environment. Some of these proposals have been enacted into laws, and new laws are to be expected.

Hopefully, these laws can be designed to make prices reflect the true relative costs of products. Such an approach seems to be the only way to continue placing primary reliance on a market economy to allocate resources and yet escape from those environmental problems that have been the unintended consequences of choices made in a free market.

Reading 16

Income Distribution and Its Measurement*

By Thomas M. Humphrey

*Part I. Distribution among the Factors of Production**

Summary

Economic analysis in recent years has focused increasingly on the question of income distribution. Analysts tackling the subject generally distinguish between *size* distribution and *functional* distribution of income. *Size* distribution refers to the division of income among families and individuals classified by income brackets. *Functional* distribution denotes the division of the national income among the factors of production—land, labor, capital, and entrepreneurship—that combine to produce it.

The paragraphs that follow outline the evolution of distributive share analysis in economic thought, discuss the behavior of the functional distribution of income in the United States, and describe some of the methods and measures employed by researchers who study it. The second part of this reading discusses the size distribution of income.

Key Questions to Consider

■ What is the difference between *size* and *functional* distribution of income?

■ What purposes did the distribution of income serve according to the classical economists? What does contemporary income distribution analysis focus on?

■ How was national income distributed in 1970, by percentage? How does this compare to earlier periods?

■ How do the experts explain the long-term rise in labor's relative share of national income?

■ What is known about the short-run movements of distributive shares?

---

* Excerpt from *Monthly Review*, Federal Reserve Bank of Richmond **57,** No. 8 (August 1971), 7–16. The article appearing here is a considerably abridged version of the original. Reprinted with permission.

Income Distribution and Its Measurement

Part I. Distribution among the Factors of Production

Economic analysis in recent years has focused increasingly on the question of income distribution. There are a number of reasons for this resurgence of interest in a subject which occupied much of the attention of nineteenth century economists. In the first place, public concern over the problem of poverty has stimulated efforts to determine whether the gap between the poorest stratum and the rest of an increasingly affluent society is narrowing or widening. Second, recent experience with inflation and unemployment has generated a suspicion in some quarters that these two economic evils may have resulted in a significant redistribution of purchasing power among socioeconomic groupings. Then, too, the steadily increasing emphasis on human capital in economic analysis has pointed up the connection between education and productivity on the one hand and income on the other, suggesting that wide disparities in income levels might indicate large long term losses of output for society. Finally, the increasing quantity and quality of national income data has enabled researchers to undertake empirical evaluation of long accepted but largely untested theoretical models of distributive shares.

Analysts tackling the subject generally distinguish between *size* distribution and *functional* distribution of income. *Size* distribution refers to the division of income among families and individuals classified by income brackets. *Functional* distribution denotes the division of the national income among the factors of production—land, labor, capital, and entrepreneurship—that combine to produce it.

The paragraphs that follow outline the evolution of distributive share analysis in economic thought, discuss the behavior of the functional distribution of income in the United States, and describe some of the methods and measures employed by researchers who study it. A second article, to appear in a future issue of the *Monthly Review*, will discuss the size distribution of income.

EARLY DISTRIBUTIVE SHARE ANALYSIS

Traditionally, economists have devoted more attention to the functional than to the size distribution of income. Early nineteenth century economic analysis was dominated by the view, associated largely with David Ricardo, that the study of distributive shares held the key to the understanding of the entire economic mechanism, including the forces determining the rate and character of economic growth. To the Classical Economists of nineteenth century England, who took their cue largely from Ricardo, the distribution of income served three purposes. It divided the recipients into mutually exclusive economic groups, identified by their function in the production process; it served as an indicator of the relative welfare of the respective groups; and it defined the social classes that would play key roles in the economic evolution of the nation. Economic development was looked upon as a drama in which the actors were grouped by economic function, serving specified socioeconomic roles. For example, the working class not only supplied labor but, through procreation, insured the existence of labor supplies in perpetuity. The industrial class was associated with accumulation and the capital-supplying function, while the landed aristocracy exercised stewardship over land, a scarce and increasingly remunerative resource. On the basis of this model, British economists predicted that excessive procreation by the laboring class would combine with diminishing returns in land cultivation to bring bare minimum subsistence wages to labor, zero profits to capitalists, riches to landowners, and eventually cessation of growth for the economy as a whole.

Karl Marx, writing later in the century, also identified each factor of production with a distinct social class. Following the classical tradition, his analysis assumed that no income recipient could belong to more than one economic group, supply more than one type of productive resource, nor receive more than one type of factor income. A laborer could not simultaneously be a capitalist, nor a capitalist a laborer. In Marx's scenario, accelerating antagonism between an ever growing laboring class doomed to subsistence wages and an increasingly exclusive and wealthy capitalist class meant the eventual end of traditional capitalist socioeconomic organization, along with its political superstructure. By the time Marx systematized his model of class conflict, however, a new breed of classicists were weaving an intricate analysis demonstrating that the free market would achieve distributive justice and harmony by providing each factor of production with a reward just equal to its contribution to total output. Each of these nineteenth century

doctrines implied that the lines separating the factors of production also marked the division of social classes. Only later, with an increasingly widespread ownership of property and a growing degree of social mobility did this identification of social classes and economic function disappear from professional analysis. Today economists find it useful to retain the original division of the factors of production, but without the presumption of social class identification.

In recent decades the focus of distributive share analysis has shifted away from discussions of welfare. The blurring of factor ownership classes has forced the virtual abandonment of functional distribution as a welfare indicator. The factors of production, although analytically separate and distinct, are now seen as overlapping at the ownership level. Modern economists, unlike their classical predecessors, recognize that individuals often own and supply several types of productive resources. For example, it is not unusual to find the same individual receiving wage income from his employer, rent income from property leased to tenants, interest income from bonds and savings deposits, and dividend income from equity shares in the capital assets of corporations.

Contemporary income distribution analysis focuses on explanations of the alleged constancy of relative shares. This focus derives largely from economists' study of the Cobb-Douglas aggregate production function. A production function expresses the technological relationship between output and the associated inputs used in the production process. The Cobb-Douglas production function relates national output to only two factors of production, labor and capital, and implies that factor-income shares will be constant regardless of the amounts of the two inputs existing in the economy. In the Cobb-Douglas model, changes in the ratio of labor to capital resulting from dissimilar growth rates of the two inputs would have no effect on factor shares. The widespread acceptance of this model among economists has helped to foster the presumption of constant factor shares.

DISTRIBUTIVE SHARES IN 1970

The statistical series which most closely corresponds to the economist's concept of factor shares is published by the Department of Commerce in the *Survey of Current Business*. This series shows the distribution of the national income (prior to government taxes and transfers) by type of payment. The percentage breakdown for 1970 is as follows:

Employee Compensation	75.0%
Proprietors' Income	8.4%
Corporate Profit	9.6%
Interest	4.2%
Rental Income of Persons	2.8%
Total	100.0%

The lion's share of national income goes to employees, with corporate profits and proprietors' income running a distant second and third, respectively, and interest accounting for most of the remainder.

The relative size of the slice of the national income pie claimed by labor resources is especially noteworthy in view of the vital and conspicuous role played by capital resources in the production process. One might expect capital resources to claim a large part of the income generated by the world's most "capitalistic" economy. However, a quick calculation from the above figures indicates that approximately 82% of the national income pie was distributed to labor resources, leaving only 18% to be claimed by capital resources. This estimate was made by counting employee compensation as labor-resource income and all profits, interest, and rent as capital-resource income, and by dividing proprietors' income into labor and capital income in the proportion which the share of employee compensation bears to the combined shares of profits, interest, and rent (75.0 to 16.6). Too much faith should not be placed on the accuracy of these figures. For example, probably 3 or 4 percentage points of the 75 percentage point employee compensation share consists of salaries of corporation executives, not usually considered as labor

income in the ordinary sense. Furthermore, the allocation of proprietors' income is arbitrary. Nevertheless, the order of magnitude of the estimates is correct and it may safely be said that, in 1970, between three-fourths and four-fifths of the national income pie went to sellers of labor services.

MEASUREMENT AND INTERPRETATION

Although the Department of Commerce's classification of distributive shares is the best the economist has to work with, it is imperfectly suited to his needs. For example, two of the income claims, proprietors' income and corporate profits, are classified by type of business institution rather than by type of economic resource to which payment is made. This and other discrepancies between theoretical concepts and empirical measures create a host of problems for the researcher in his analysis of the behavior of relative shares.

LONG-TERM TRENDS

Formidable measurement problems notwithstanding, the bulk of the research on functional income distribution has been devoted to explaining the secular behavior of relative factor shares. Table 1 shows estimates of the percentage distribution of national income since 1900. The data for the period since 1929 were developed by economists in the Department of Commerce. Data for earlier years are the estimates of several scholars, including Simon Kuznets of Harvard, D. Gale Johnson of the University of Chicago, and Irving Kravis of the University of Pennsylvania.

The table indicates that over the century the measured wage share has risen substantially, largely at the expense of the proprietor share and only slightly at the expense of the combined shares of interest, rent, and corporate profits. Although the relative shares, as measured, display a moderate degree of stability over the 25-year post–World War II period, the figures in Table 1 do not reveal the "remarkable constancy" which economists often proclaim as the most conspicuous characteristic of distributive shares.

Table 1

Distributive Shares (Percent) of Total in
U.S. National Income, 1900–1970
(Decade Averages of Shares for Individual Years)

Decade	Employee compensation	Proprietors' income	Corporate profits	Interest	Rent	Total
1900–1909	55.0	23.7	6.8	5.5	9.0	100
1910–1919	53.6	23.8	9.1	5.4	8.1	100
1920–1929	60.0	17.5	7.8	6.2	7.7	100
1930–1939	67.5	14.8	4.0	8.7	5.0	100
1939–1948	64.6	17.2	11.9	3.1	3.3	100
1949–1958	67.3	13.9	12.5	2.9	3.4	100
1954–1963	69.9	11.9	11.2	4.0	3.0	100
1963–1970	71.7	9.6	12.1	3.5	3.2	100

Source: Irving Kravis, "Income Distribution: Functional Share," *International Encyclopedia of Social Sciences*, Volume 7 (New York: Macmillan and Free Press, 1968), p. 134. Reprinted with permission of the Publisher from THE INTERNATIONAL ENCYCLOPEDIA OF THE SOCIAL SCIENCES, David L. Sills, Editor. Copyright 1968 by Crowell Collier and Macmillan, Inc.; *Business Conditions Digest*.

Most of the research effort has been devoted to investigation of the trend in labor income. The disparate trends of corporate profits (up from 7% to 12%), interest (down from 5.5% to 3.5%), and rent (down from 9% to 3%) have received relatively little study. Researchers, in their eagerness to test the conclusions of two-factor economic models, have tended to consolidate all non-labor shares into a "property income" category whose overall stability conceals the divergent behavior of its constituent parts.

Explanations of the Trend of Labor's Share. How do the experts account for the secular rise in labor's relative share as measured in the national income accounts? Two alternative explanations have been offered. The first emphasizes structural alterations in the product-mix and industry-mix of the economy. This explanation, which appears in the work of E. F. Denison of the Brookings Institution and D. Gale Johnson, implies that the data can be reconciled with the theory of constant shares by showing that income distribution would remain unchanged in the absence of shifts in the composition of output. The second explanation, advanced by Irving Kravis, stresses the differing supply and demand conditions in the markets for labor and capital. Each of these explanations is discussed in greater detail below.

Structural Changes. The major structural shifts affecting labor's share include (1) the rise in the proportion of wage earners to proprietors as the corporate form of enterprise increasingly supplanted the individual proprietorship, (2) the growth in the importance of the government sector, and (3) the shift from land-intensive agriculture production to the production of labor-intensive services. Empirical techniques have been devised to measure the influence of each of these factors on the growth of labor's share.

Secular Changes in Input Supply and Demand. An alternative explanation of labor's rising share goes behind the facade of "structural changes" to focus on the changing conditions of demand and supply in labor and capital markets. This explanation, associated chiefly with Irving Kravis, lumps all non-labor income into one category (capital income) and emphasizes *total* demand for labor and capital rather than the *structural* changes discussed above.

In addition to explaining the rise in labor's share, Kravis' demand-supply approach reconciles the following developments that have occurred in the American economy since the early 1900s: (1) a six-fold rise in the capital stock, (2) a doubling of the man-hour inputs, (3) a more than threefold rise in the real wage rate, and (4) a virtually unchanged real rate of return on capital. Kravis concludes that these trends are due primarily to differences in the responsiveness of the supplies of labor and capital to increases in demand as well as to the tendency for businessmen to substitute relatively low-price capital for relatively high-price labor.

THE CYCLICAL BEHAVIOR OF DISTRIBUTIVE SHARES

Although relatively little research has been done on the short-run movements of distributive shares, many economists believe that the evidence is sufficient to establish a definite cyclical pattern for the employee compensation, fixed income (rent and interest), and corporate profit shares. The wage and fixed income shares appear to rise in periods of falling economic activity and to decline in periods of expansion. The share of profits, on the other hand, apparently rises in prosperity and falls in depression. These cyclical patterns were most conspicuous in the 1930's. During the contraction of 1929–1932, the shares of wages and interest spurted but the profits share fell sharply. With the progress of recovery after 1933, the wage

and interest shares sagged and the share of corporate profits rose.

These same cyclical patterns appear in the post–World War II period, although with diminished intensity. Table 2 shows the percentage income shares at the peak and through dates of all postwar cycles, as established by the National Bureau of Economic Research. The table clearly reveals the pro-cyclical behavior of corporate profits share and the counter-cyclical behavior of the employee compensation, rent, and interest shares. In each cycle, the corporate profits share was higher at the peak than at the trough. In all but one of the cycles the employee compensation, interest, and rent shares were higher at the trough than at the peak.

Overhead Costs, Unit Profits, and Distributive Shares. Economists have advanced several hypotheses to account for the observed cyclical behavior of the relative shares. The most plausible hypothesis holds that the pro-cyclical behavior of profits' share results from the relation between profits per unit of output and unit overhead costs. This relation varies with changes in aggregate output. During economic expansions, increased production induced by rising aggregate demand enables firms to spread overhead

Table 2

Distribution of National Income Shares (Percent) at the
Cyclical Peak and Cyclical Trough Dates in
Five Postwar Cycles

	1948 IV P	1949 IV T	1953 III P	1954 II T	1957 III P	1958 II T	1960 II P	1961 I T	1969 IV P	1970 IV T
Employee compensation	63.1	65.4	68.7	68.4	69.9	70.4	70.7	71.5	74.1	75.4
Proprietors' income	17.5	16.4	13.0	13.2	12.1	12.9	11.2	11.5	8.6	8.4
Corporate profits	15.0	13.3	13.2	12.6	12.4	10.5	12.4	10.9	10.4	9.1
Rental income	3.6	4.1	4.2	4.6	4.1	4.3	3.8	3.9	2.8	2.9
Net interest	0.8	0.9	0.9	1.3	1.5	1.8	1.9	2.2	4.0	4.3
Total Shares	100.0	100.0	100.0	100.0	100.0	100.0	100.0	100.0	100.0	100.0

Source: *Business Conditions Digest.*

(i.e. fixed) costs—including the wages of overhead labor as well as rent and interest expenses—over a greater volume of output. Overhead costs per unit of output fall and profit margins rise, thereby enlarging the profits share and diminishing the labor, interest, and rent shares in the value of each unit of output. In recessions, output falls and unit overhead costs rise, thereby squeezing the profits share and enlarging the other shares.

The Wage Lag Hypothesis.   An alternative hypothesis that has been advanced in explanation of the shift in favor of profits' share in the upswing and in favor of labor's share in the downswing is the so-called *wage lag* hypothesis. According to this hypothesis, sticky money wages lag behind price increases during booms and price decreases during slumps. Twenty years ago, economists thought the wage lag was the most important factor accounting for the counter-cyclical behavior of labor's share. Recent empirical work has cast doubt on the strength of this effect, however.

Income Distribution and Its Measurement*

By Thomas M. Humphrey

Part II. Distribution among Families

Summary

This article is the second of a two-part series on the subject of income distribution. The first part discussed the *functional* distribution of income, i.e., the distribution of the national income among the factors of production that combine to produce it. The present article deals with the *size* distribution of income, i.e., the distribution of income among families classified by intervals of income levels.

Key Questions to Consider

■ How was the percentage of total family income divided in 1969 among families when grouped into fifths, that is, the lowest fifth, the next fifth, etc.?

■ What patterns can be detected among blacks and farm residents?

■ What do the terms disperse and skewed mean in the context of family income distribution?

■ What are the three explanations given for income differences?

■ What causes have been given to explain the skewness in income distribution?

■ What are the Lorenz curve and the Gini concentration ratio?

* Excerpt from *Monthly Review,* Federal Reserve Bank of Richmond **57,** No. 10 (October 1971), 2–13. The article appearing here is a considerably abridged version of the original. Reprinted with permission.

Income Distribution and Its Measurement

Part II. Distribution among Families

This article is the second of a two-part series on the subject of income distribution. The first part discussed the *functional* distribution of income, i.e., the distribution of the national income among the factors of production that combine to produce it. The present article deals with the *size* distribution of income, i.e., the distribution of income among families classified by intervals of income levels.

Questions about the relative income positions of the rich and the poor cannot be answered by functional distribution analysis alone. The association of labor income with the poor and capital income with the rich is of doubtful validity. Today, labor income includes the salaries of high-paid corporation executives as well as the wages of unskilled labor, and capital income includes the dividend and interest income received by many persons of modest circumstances as well as by millionaire capitalists.

To determine the extent of equality or inequality in the distribution of income, analysts must examine the size distribution. Information on size distribution suggests the extent to which the benefits of economic growth are shared among various income-size groups in the economy. Study of the size distribution is useful also in evaluating the success of government policies designed to modify the income distribution.

Finally, study of the size distribution helps statisticians to isolate and specify the personal, social, and economic factors contributing to poverty. The paragraphs that follow describe the size distribution of income in the United States and discuss some of the techniques employed in its measurement.

CENSUS INCOME DATA AND DEFINITIONS

The most complete data on income distribution are compiled by the Census Bureau. The data are obtained from answers to a series of questions about income asked in March of each year in connection with the Census Bureau's monthly Current Population Survey (CPS). The CPS consists of scientifically selected samples of approximately 50,000 households drawn from across the nation.

The income concept employed by the Census Bureau is total money income before payment of personal income taxes. Total income includes money earnings, money gifts, and government transfer payments such as unemployment compensation, social security pensions, and welfare payments; it excludes nonmonetary benefits such as free medical care, income in kind, services of owner-occupied houses as well as capital gains and retained corporation profits.

The latter two items augment the wealth of stockholders but are not counted as current income.

The Census Bureau classifies income-receiving units either as *families* or as *unrelated individuals* (sometimes called one-person families). A family is defined as a group of two or more persons living together and related by blood, marriage, or adoption. Unrelated individuals live alone or as boarders in other people's homes. Their number is small relative to the number of people living in family groups and the size distribution of their income differs from that of families. Only the distribution of family incomes is discussed in this article.

INCOME DISTRIBUTION IN 1969 AND 1970

Chart I shows the distribution of total money income among U.S. families in 1969, the latest year for which complete figures are available. The chart indicates the percentage of all families included in each income bracket as well as the percentage of total income received by families in each bracket. For example, the poorest 4.7% of the families—those whose incomes were in the two brackets below $2,000—received about one half of one percent of the income. At the other end of the scale, the 3.6% of all families with

incomes of $25,000 and above received 12.5% of total family income, which averages about $35,786 per family at the upper end of the scale. About 20% of the families had incomes below, and 80% above, the $5,000 level in 1969. Approximately 54% were below the $10,000 income level and slightly less than 20% of the families had incomes above $15,000. Almost 61% of American families received incomes between $5,000 and $15,000.

What was the income of the typical or middle family in 1969? The *median* figure of $9,433 is probably more representative of the income of the typical family than is the *mean* income figure of $10,577. The mean or arithmetic average income is computed by dividing total family income by the number of families. The median figure separates the income recipients into two equal parts, that is, half of the families receive more and half receive less than the median income. When the income distribution is skewed to the right, as is the distribution shown in Chart 1, the mean is disproportionately influenced by the few very high incomes at the upper end of the distribution, and therefore is not as good a measure of the center of the distribution as is the median.

The data in Chart 1 can be condensed by dividing the families into fifths or quintiles and showing the percent of income going to each fifth, as follows.

Chart 1

Distribution of U. S. Families and Total Family Money Income by Income Class, 1969

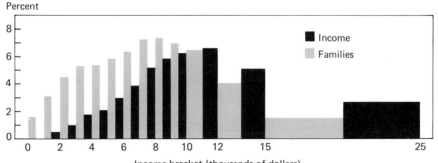

*Less than 0.05 percent.

Source: U. S. Bureau of the Census, *Consumer Income*, Current Population Reports, Series P-60, No. 75.

Income rank	% of total family income
Lowest quintile	5.6
Second quintile	12.3
Third quintile	17.6
Fourth quintile	23.4
Highest quintile	41.0
	100.0
Top five percent	14.7

The 3rd and 4th quintiles, embracing 40% of the families, received 41% of total income. The two lowest quintiles, covering another 40% of the population, received only about 18% of the income. The proportions of income going to the top 20% and top 5% of families, however, were approximately double and triple, respectively, the proportions of families in each of those classifications.

The income distribution of the total of all families shown in Chart 1 conceals diverse distribution patterns of particular subgroups of families comprising the total. Preliminary 1970 data recently released by the Census Bureau show how income was distributed in that year within four of these subgroupings, namely families classified by race and farm-nonfarm residence. This information, presented in Table 1, reveals that the distribution patterns of the incomes of white and nonfarm families differ sharply from those of Negro and farm families.

Farm incomes are almost 30% lower on the average than nonfarm incomes, although the difference in the distribution of economic welfare among farm and nonfarm families is probably not as great as indicated in the table, since farm residents receive real income in the form of goods produced and consumed on the farm but not counted in the income data. The median income of farm families is about $3,230 below that of nonfarm families. The proportion of farm families concentrated in the lower three income brackets is larger and the proportion concentrated in the top two brackets is smaller than is the case with nonfarm families.

The difference between the income distribution of white and black families is even more pronounced than the differential between farm and nonfarm families. The median family income of blacks was only 63% of the median income of white families in 1970. The generally lower level of Negro incomes also shows up in the relative concentration of percentages in the lowest income bracket. In 1970 only 7.5% of white families had incomes below $3,000 whereas 21.1% of black families received incomes less than this figure. At the upper end of the scale the picture is similar. Only 9.5% of black families could claim incomes of $15,000 or more, compared to nearly 24% of white families. The difference between black and white incomes is perhaps most forcefully demonstrated by comparing income classes of greatest concentration. The largest percentage of Negro families is concentrated in the lowest (under $3,000) income class shown in Table 1, whereas the greatest percentage of white families is concentrated in the next to highest ($10,000–$14,999) income category.

Table 1

Distribution Among Income Brackets
of U.S. Families Classified by
Race and Farm-nonfarm Residence, 1971
(In percentages)

Income class	All families	White	Negro	Non-farm	Farm
Under $3,000	8.9	7.5	21.1	8.3	19.9
$ 3,000 – 4,999	10.4	9.5	17.4	10.0	16.3
$ 5,000 – 6,999	11.8	11.3	17.0	11.7	15.9
$ 7,000 – 9,999	19.9	20.1	18.1	20.0	18.5
$14,000 – 14,999	26.8	27.9	16.9	27.2	17.5
$15,000 and over	22.3	23.7	9.5	22.8	12.2
Total	100.0	100.0	100.0	100.0	100.0
Median income	$ 9,867	$10,236	$6,279	$10,006	$6,773
Mean income	$11,106	$11,495	$7,442	$11,254	$7,983

Source: U.S. Bureau of the Census, *Consumer Income*, Current Population Reports, Series P-60, No. 78.

Chart 2

RATIO OF NONWHITE TO WHITE MEDIAN FAMILY INCOME, 1947-1970

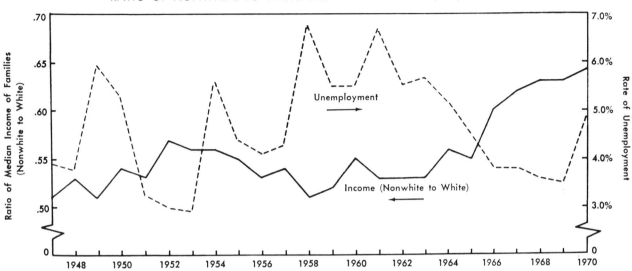

Sources: U. S. Bureau of the Census, **Consumer Income,** Current Population Reports, Series P-60, Nos. 75 and 78;
U. S. Department of Commerce, **Survey of Current Business,** various issues.

The income position of black families relative to white families, although low, has nevertheless improved over the past two decades. Chart 2 indicates that the median income of non-white families has increased from 51% of the median income of white families in 1947 to 64% in 1970.[1] The relative income position of non-white families has not shown steady progress over this period, however. The chart indicates that most of the gains have occurred in years of low or falling unemployment.

Several factors account for the tendency of black incomes to improve relative to white incomes in years of prosperity. First, the black unemployment rate tends to decline more sharply than the white rate in periods of labor market tightness. The unemployment rate of blacks is more sensitive than that of whites to changes in the overall unemployment rate because a greater proportion of black than white workers are unskilled and inexperienced. Since employers tend to concentrate their hiring and firing among the least skilled and least experienced workers, it follows that the Negro unemployment rate is more responsive to a general tightening of the labor market than is the white unemployment rate. Then too, a tight labor market tends to erode discriminatory barriers, thereby enabling blacks to participate in better-paying jobs. Finally, the shortage of skilled workers encourages employers to expand their training programs for the unskilled and the inexperienced and to upgrade employees. This training and occupational upgrading raises the productivity of disadvantaged workers and helps to reduce black-white income differentials.

---

[1] Income data for all *non-white* families was used in computing the series depicted in Chart II because separate data on Negro incomes is not available for years prior to 1964. Negro families account for approximately 90% of all non-white families, the remainder being Indians, Orientals, Mexican-Americans, and others.

DISPERSION OF INCOME

The distributions shown in Chart 1 and Table 1 display two important characteristics. First, the distributions are *disperse*, that is, family incomes are not identical. Second, the distributions are *skewed*, that is, incomes are not symmetrically distributed about the mean. Explanations of the income distribution must account for these two attributes. Specifically, analysts should be able to identify the sources of dispersion and specify the factors that skew the distribution.

Sources of Income Dispersion.   Three main explanations of the source of income differences have been advanced. One explanation holds that disparities arise from the operation of natural forces, such as differences in ability, luck, and other chance factors (illness, accidents, etc.). Supposedly, these natural forces are completely random and outside human control.

A second view claims that income differences are a by-product of rational human choice. According to this view, individuals differ in their preferences for work vs. leisure, risky vs. safe ventures, and immediate vs. deferred money earnings. The economic decisions that individuals make reflect their differing preferences and influence their incomes. Income differences arise because some people choose to work longer hours than others. Then too, income differences among gamblers and risk-takers are much greater than income differences among risk-avoiders. Individuals' rational choices of occupation also result in unequal incomes. Consider an individual choosing among several alternative occupations. The present discounted value of the lifetime earning stream associated with each occupation considered by the individual must be equal at the time he makes his choice. He will exclude from his range of choice income streams with lower present values. Although the present values of all the eligible income streams are identical, their time shapes are dissimilar. Occupations requiring little initial training will yield an immediate stream of low annual earnings. Occupations requiring much initial training will yield high annual earnings beginning at some distant future date. Occupations requiring large initial investments in education must offer higher future incomes than other occupations to compensate the individual for the expense of his education and for income foregone during the years of schooling. Individuals thus choose between a deferred stream of high future earnings and an immediate stream of lower annual earnings. In any given year, the disparities among individual and occupational earnings reflect different levels of training of the various members of the labor force.

A third view holds that income dispersion is an outgrowth of economic, social, and legal institutions. According to this view, the sources of income differences are to be found in: (a) inheritance laws, which permit the transferral of wealth to successive generations of the same families, and (b) barriers to social and economic mobility, such as caste systems, racial discrimination, monopoly power, etc.

Each of these explanations has some validity. Statisticians studying income differences among people classified by age, sex, occupation, location, level of education, etc., have found that chance, choice, and institutional factors all contribute to income disparity.

Causes of Skewness.   Identification of the sources of income differences does not suffice as a complete explanation of the pattern of income distribution. Specification of the causes of income disparity explains only why all incomes are not identical. Complete understanding of the income distribution requires an explanation of the skewness of the distribution, i.e., why income differences are not symmetrically distributed about the average income.

Economists have been less successful in identifying the causes of skewness than in specifying the sources of income disparity. Several possible explanations of skewness have been advanced. One view holds that although income receivers in particular occupations have approximately symmetrical income distributions, the aggregate of these different distributions is asymmetrical. A second, largely tautological, view argues that income-earning abilities, and thus incomes, are not symmetrically distributed. In contrast, a third view holds that abilities *are* symmetrically distributed, but that other factors intervene to distort the link between ability and income. Chief among these distorting factors are inheritance laws, which permit the concentration of wealth, power, and social position among a relatively small number of families. Other factors include differences in parents' willingness to devote time and money in schooling for their children, and credit rationing by leaders who allocate funds only to those with high income-earning abilities, thereby accentuating the initial advantage of a particular group of earners. A fourth explanation is based upon mathematical models of probability in which random proportional changes in individual incomes will generate a skewed income distribution. Much current research is being devoted to the specification of such factors as length of schooling, age, job experience, incidence of chance factors, such as accidents, business failure, lack of job information, etc., which will produce the percentage or proportional differences in incomes required by the probability model.

Appendix

This section describes how some of the measures of income inequality are calculated. For simplicity it is assumed that there are only five families and that their combined money income is $100,000. The distribution of income among the families in this hypothetical example is as follows:

% of families	Income received (thousands of $)	% Income received	Cumulative % of families	Cumulative % of income received	Point on Lorenz curve
0	$ 0	0%	0%	0%	A
Lowest fifth	5	5	20	5	B
Second fifth	10	10	40	15	C
Third fifth	15	15	60	30	D
Fourth fifth	20	20	80	50	E
Highest fifth	50	50	100	100	F

Mean income = $100,000/5 = $20,000.

The data in the table will be used to construct a Lorenz curve and to calculate the Gini concentration ratio and the three most-often used measures of dispersion (the variance, standard deviation, and coefficient of variation of the distribution of incomes).

The Lorenz curve is derived by plotting the data in the last three columns of the table in the accompanying chart. The lowest 20% of the families receive 5% of income (Point B on the chart), the lowest 40% receive 15% of the income (Point C), etc. The charted line ABCDEF is the Lorenz curve. Had there been many more income classes than five, the Lorenz curve would have appeared as a smooth, rounded line instead of the connected line segments.

The Gini concentration ratio is the ratio of the area between the Lorenz curve and the diagonal line to the total area lying below the diagonal. It is computed by (1) calculating the total area beneath the diagonal, (2) calculating the sum of the trapezoidal areas lying beneath the Lorenz curve, (3) subtracting

(2) from (1), and (4) expressing the result as a fraction of the total area enclosed by the diagonal.

1. Total area beneath the diagonal: $\frac{1}{2} \times 100 \times 100 = 5{,}000$
2. Area beneath the Lorenz curve:[1] $50 + 200 + 450 + 800 + 1{,}500 = 3{,}000$
3. Area between diagonal and Lorenz curve: $5{,}000 - 3{,}000 = 2{,}000$
4. Gini concentration ratio: $2{,}000/5{,}000 = .40$

Chart 3

**Construction of Lorenz Curve
and Gini Concentration Ratio**

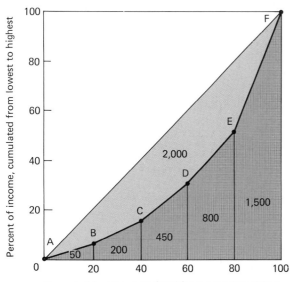

Percent of income, cumulated from lowest to highest

Percent of families, cumulated from poorest to richest

The *variance* of the distribution is found by squaring the deviation of each family income from the mean family income, summing the squared deviations, and dividing this sum by the number of families. Variance = $[(5{-}20)^2 + (10{-}20)^2 + (15{-}20)^2 + (20{-}20)^2 + (50{-}20)^2]/5 = 1{,}150/5 = 230$.

The *standard deviation* of the distribution is merely the square root of the variance. Standard Deviation = Square Root of $230 = 15.17$.

The *coefficient of variation* of the income distribution is simply the standard deviation divided by the mean family income. Coefficient of Variation = $15.17/20 = .76$.

---

[1] The area of each trapezoid is calculated from the formula $A = \frac{1}{2}(h_1 + h_2)b$ where A, b, h_1, h_2 represent, respectively, the area, base, and heights of the left- and right-hand vertical sides of the trapezoid.

Growth of Government Spending*

By Morton B. Millenson

Summary

How governments collect and spend revenues has been a major issue in American politics throughout our history. The nation's independence had its roots in conflicts over raising and spending tax revenues. Our present form of government arose because the Articles of Confederation failed to provide an effective means of raising revenue for national needs.

Government has become our largest industry. Governments generate more income and employ more people than all durable goods industries combined. Nearly one out of every five workers draws a government paycheck.

The impact of government spending on the economy occurs in two ways:

1. Governments make direct demands on the nation's productive resources both in terms of the goods and services they buy and in terms of the share of the labor force they employ.

2. Governments alter the distribution of personal income by taxing some individuals to provide income to others (transfer payments). In addition, the federal government alters spending patterns of state and local governments by transferring taxes raised in some areas to government units elsewhere (grants-in-aid).

The National Income and Product Accounts of the United States begin with 1929 and provide a convenient tool for evaluating the importance of government activity in the total economy. This article traces the growing demands that governments have placed on the economy over the period covered by the National Income and Product Accounts.

Key Questions to Consider

■ How does government spending affect the economy?

■ What is the magnitude of the change in government's role (at all levels) in the economy?

■ What kinds of purchases does government engage in?

■ What share of the labor force is employed in each of the various levels of government? How have these shares changed over time?

■ What comprises total government expenditures? How have they changed over time?

---

* Reprinted with permission from *Business Conditions*, Federal Reserve Bank of Chicago, February 1973, pp. 6–15.

Growth of Government Spending

How governments collect and spend revenues has been a major issue in American politics throughout our history. The nation's independence had its roots in conflicts over raising and spending tax revenues. Our present form of government arose because the Articles of Confederation failed to provide an effective means of raising revenue for national needs.

Despite the importance of taxes and expenditures on the political scene, government spending had little impact on the economy during much of our history. As late as 1900, total purchases of goods and services by all levels of government were less than 7 percent of our total output. This low level of spending reflected the "small government" attitude that pervaded American political thinking through the eighteenth and nineteenth centuries.

Prior to the Depression, spending by state and local governments dwarfed that of the federal government except in time of war. During the 1930s, federal government spending was greatly expanded on a wide variety of programs intended to stimulate the economy and alleviate hardships. The experience of the 1930s dramatically changed the public's expectations of the role of government. At first, these expectations were focused on the federal government, but after World War II this change in outlook extended to state and local governments as well.

Changing expectations were not the only cause of the growing importance of government in the economy over the 44-year period 1929 through 1972. Much of government's influence in today's economy stems from the expansion of activities which had been accepted government functions long before 1929. For instance, the national character of the armed services predates the Constitution. However, the present global scale of U.S. military commitments has increased military costs far beyond the level considered normal prior to World War II. Similarly, public education became a primary responsibility of state and local governments early in our history. But the "baby boom," which began in the late Forties, and the broad expansion of government into higher education have increased costs far beyond anything anticipated in the 1920s and 1930s.

Government activity has been broadened further by vast socially-oriented programs, such as social security, that either were started prior to World War II or were reasonable outgrowths of the trends of the Thirties. Beyond these, government has moved into the space program and atomic energy, areas reserved to science fiction fans before 1940.

Government has become our largest industry. Governments generate more income and employ more people than all durable goods industries combined.

Nearly one out of every five workers draws a government paycheck.

The impact of government spending on the economy occurs in two ways:

1. Governments make direct demands on the nation's productive resources both in terms of the goods and services they buy and in terms of the share of the labor force they employ.

2. Governments alter the distribution of personal income by taxing some individuals to provide income to others (transfer payments). In addition, the federal government alters spending patterns of state and local governments by transferring taxes raised in some areas to government units elsewhere (grants-in-aid).

The National Income and Product Accounts of the United States begin with 1929 and provide a con-venient tool for evaluating the importance of government activity in the total economy. This article traces the growing demands that governments have placed on the economy over the period covered by the National Income and Product Accounts. But before proceeding with a detailed examination of this growth, it is well to fix in mind the total magnitude of the change which has occurred between 1929 and 1972. (See Tables 1 and 2.)

Over the 44-year period, while the total economy grew over 11 times, state and local government purchases of goods and services grew over 20 times. Federal government purchases in 1972 were 81 times larger than in 1929. The federal share of total output was almost eight times as large and the state and local share about twice as large as in 1929. If the relationships of 1929 had been preserved in 1972, state and local purchases of goods and services would have been about $80 billion, instead of the $149 billion actually

Table 1
Comparison of Government Purchases of Goods and Services with Gross National Product

| Year | Gross national product Billion dollars | Government purchase of goods and services | | | | | |
| | | State and local | | Federal | | Total | |
		Billion dollars	Percent of GNP	Billion dollars	Percent of GNP	Billion dollars	Percent of GNP
1929	103.1	7.2	7.0	1.3	1.2	8.5	8.2
1972	1,152.1	148.9	12.9	105.9	9.2	254.8	22.1

Table 2
Comparison of Total Government Expenditures with Gross National Product

| Year | Gross national product Billion dollars | Government expenditures | | | | | |
| | | State and local | | Federal* | | Total | |
		Billion dollars	Percent of GNP	Billion dollars	Percent of GNP	Billion dollars	Percent of GNP
1929	103.1	7.8	7.6	2.5	2.4	10.3	10.0
1972	1,152.1	162.8	14.1	208.5	18.1	371.3	32.0

* Grants-in-aid included in state and local expenditures only to avoid double counting.

spent, and federal purchases would have been a little under $15 billion, instead of the actual figure of $106 billion. The same general picture of very large expansion is also evident where total government expenditures, not just purchases of good and services, are considered.

Purchases of Goods and Services ...

Government expenditures fall into two broad categories: purchase of goods and services and all non-purchase expenditures. Purchases include:

1. items government buys from the private economy;

2. wages and other employment costs;

3. net investment in government-operated enterprises.

Thus, purchases are the direct demands that all levels of government place on the nation's productive capacity. A typical nonpurchase expenditure is the cost of social security benefits, which affects the nation's income distribution pattern but for which the government does not receive any identifiable return. Only the purchase category, therefore, is included when computing gross national product, the total value of the output of the economy.

The growth of government purchases since 1929 reflects the changing patterns of its three major components: federal defense purchases, federal nondefense purchases, and state and local purchases. During the 1929–72 period, state and local spending has dominated, overshadowed only by defense costs during World War II.

Defense purchases, less than $1 billion in 1929, increased slowly during the 1930's, then grew enormously, peaking at $87 billion in 1944, the historic high. Between 1947 and 1951 they were about $10 billion, and then rose to their Korean peak of $49 billion in 1953. The post-Korean decline was small

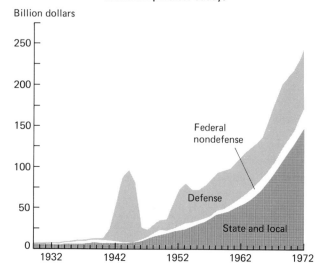

State and local government dominates purchase outlays

Billion dollars

Note: 1972 data are preliminary. Pre-1939 defense spending, not given in National Income Accounts, has been estimated from Treasury data.

and was followed by steady growth which carried defense spending above the Korean high in 1962. The Vietnam peak came in 1969 at $78 billion. After declines in 1970 and 1971, growth began again in 1972.

Federal nondefense purchases rose rapidly from the 1929 level of $500 million to $3.8 billion in 1940. Curtailed during World War II, they recovered quickly as soon as the war ended. By 1949, inflation and general growth of government brought them to almost double the prewar level. During the 1950s, there was a plateau with varying ups and downs, but beginning in 1960 the space program and other expansions of government activity brought on rapid growth interrupted only by a pause in 1969, and they reached $30 billion in 1972.

The pattern for state and local government purchases is quite different than for either category of federal spending. From 1929 to the end of World War II, while federal purchases were growing rapidly, state and local levels hovered around $7 billion.

Once the war was over, state and local purchases began to grow persistently from about $10 billion in 1946 to $149 billion in 1972. New schools to accommodate the baby boom, massive expansion of public college education, highways, and new services for new communities all contributed to the growing costs.

... Command Over 1/5 of GNP

Although the growth in government spending since 1929 has been large, the economy itself was 11 times larger in 1972 than it was in 1929. So, more than dollar levels, it is growth measured as a share of gross national product that delineates the true impact of government on the economy.

World War II, with defense spending consuming almost 42 percent of GNP, dominates the overall picture. After the war, the defense share dropped to around 5 percent of GNP, and remained there until the Korean War. By 1953, the defense share had

Governments' share of GNP
mounted in the postwar era

Percent of GNP

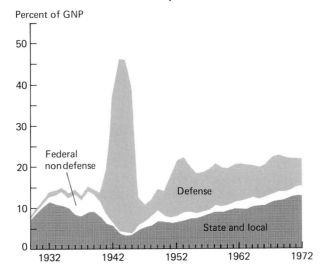

Note: 1972 data are preliminary. Pre-1939 defense spending, not given in National Income Accounts, has been estimated from Treasury data.

nearly tripled and the drop after Korea was small. Since 1959, there has been a steady decline in the relative level of defense purchases, despite the high level of U.S. commitments. Vietnam produced only a minor ripple in this trend, and the 1972 level of 6.6 percent was the lowest since 1950.

The federal nondefense share of GNP rose from less than 1 percent in 1929 to over 4 percent in 1939. Nondefense spending declined during World War II, but after the war there was a sharp climb to just under 3 percent as a result of the first postwar recession, a level never again equaled. From 1950 to 1960, the level hovered around 1.5 percent, with minor ups and downs. Since 1960, there has been a definite upward trend, interrupted briefly by the demands of the Vietnam war. Despite this growth, the 1972 level of 2.6 percent was sharply below the 1939 level.

The dominance of state and local government purchases prior to World War II, and their steady growth since, show up clearly when considered relative to GNP. In 1929, the state and local government share was seven times larger than the federal share. Even after the rapid rise in the federal share in the 1930s while the state and local share was stagnant, the latter was still nearly double the federal level in 1939.

During World War II, massive defense spending by the federal government eclipsed the state and local share, but when the war ended the two shares were about equal. With renewed defense expansion for Korea, federal spending again outpaced state and local spending. After Korea, the steady growth of the state and local sector, and declining defense spending, resulted in again reaching a balance that persisted from 1964 through 1968. Since that time, the total federal share has been declining, while the state and local share has grown. By 1972, it was over one-third larger than the federal share.

Although the impact of government purchases of goods and services on the economy is now substantially higher than the 15 percent share of GNP commanded during the Depression, the share of GNP has remained relatively stable at around 21 percent since 1952. Furthermore, it is the U.S. position in world affairs which created most of the increase.

Manpower Needs of Government . . .

Most discussions of the size of government focus on the federal government, but, in the area of employment, state and local government plays the major role. During the entire 1929–72 period, except during World War II and Korea, state and local government employment has outweighed the combined military and civilian manpower of the federal government.

Both state and local government employment and federal civilian employment quadrupled from 1929 to 1972. Federal civilian employment, always below 1 million prior to World War II, has expanded for each war and retreated to a relatively stable postwar level. However, each postwar level has been higher than the previous postwar level. State and local government employment has grown steadily larger over the entire 1929–72 period.

Employment in the armed forces has expanded far more rapidly in each conflict than has federal civilian employment, and the postwar contraction has been sharper, but the increases for Korea and Vietnam were modest compared to the expansion for World War II. Military employment exceeded federal civilian employment in every year from 1951 until 1972. The differential began dropping after 1968, and by 1972 military employment fell below the civilian level.

Total government employment, including the military, was nearly constant from 1929 to 1935. Since then, a definite growth trend, obscured at times by federal reductions following wartime peaks, has reflected the strong influence of state and local government on the total.

In 1929, total government employment consisted of 600,000 federal civilian employees, armed forces of about 200,000 and 2.5 million state and local government employees. Growth during the 1930s was slow.

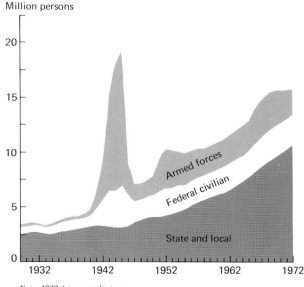

Total government employment has quadrupled since 1929

Million persons

Note: 1972 data are preliminary.

Even with the military preparedness program in 1939, the armed forces that year reached only 400,000, and federal civilian employment reached 900,000 out of total government employment of 4.5 million.

The high point for manpower requirements in World War II was 1945, when the armed forces utilized over 12 million men and federal civilian employment reached 3.8 million. That year, state and local government employment totaled 3.1 million. The peak Korean War year was 1952, when federal civilian employment was 2.4 million, the armed forces reached 3.6 million, and state and local employment was 4.2 million. The Vietnam crest was reached in 1969, when federal civilian employment exceeded 2.8 million, and the armed forces were 3.5 million. By then, state and local government had reached 9.4 million. By 1972, federal civilian employment had declined below 2.7 million, the armed forces were about 2.4 million, and state and local government employment had risen to 10.6 million.

... Take 18 Percent of the Labor Force

The impact of government employment on the manpower resources of the nation is best seen when government employment is examined as a share of the labor force. Most discussions of the labor force concentrate on the civilian labor force because that is the base used by the Labor Department for its statistics on employment, unemployment, and the unemployment rate. However, it is clear that a high proportion of those in the armed forces would seek employment in the civilian economy if they were not in the military. In periods of compulsory military service, the total labor force is larger than normal because some draftees would otherwise be outside the labor force. For purposes of this review, the total labor force, civilian and military, has been used as the measure of the labor supply.

In 1929, all government activities combined employed about 7 percent of the total labor force. This level grew to almost 10 percent of the total by the end of the 1930s. World War II brought on enormous

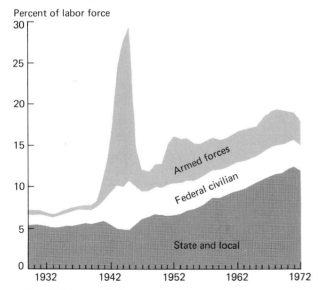

Postwar government employment gains were mainly state and local

Percent of labor force

Armed forces

Federal civilian

State and local

Note: 1972 data are preliminary.

growth, and government employment reached nearly 30 percent of a labor force that had, itself, greatly expanded. In the years between World War II and the Korean War, total government employment was steady at about 12 percent of the total labor force. It jumped to 15 percent during the Korean War and stayed there until 1961. Growth in the early 1960s was slow, but gained speed when the buildup for Vietnam began in 1966. The share soon reached 19 percent, and held constant through most of the Vietnam conflict. However, in 1972, the strong growth of private employment combined with the decline in military activity reduced the level to below 18 percent.

The stability of the federal civilian share of the labor force is particularly remarkable. Since 1947, it has stayed in the range of 3 to 3¼ percent of the supply, except for a small increase above this level during the Korean War, and a still smaller rise for Vietnam.

Since the end of World War II, military manpower demands have been many times larger than before the war. Nevertheless, there has been a persistent downward trend in the military share since the Korean peak in 1952, briefly halted by the Vietnam conflict in 1966–68. By 1972, the military share had declined to its lowest level since 1950.

State and local needs relative to the total supply of manpower have grown steadily since 1947, continuing the trend that began in the early Thirties. While the federal civilian share in 1972 was the lowest since 1941, the state and local share had doubled in that time. In 1972, more than one out of every eight persons in the total labor force was employed by state and local government, and almost one out of five were employed by all government.

Total Government Expenditures ...

While government purchase of goods and services is the direct measure of government's impact on the gross national product, it is total government expenditures that most people associate with the size of government. Total expenditures get primary emphasis in discussions of government budgets, spending, and taxation. This total is the number that determines the level of taxes and borrowing needed to finance government.

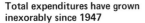

Total expenditures have grown inexorably since 1947

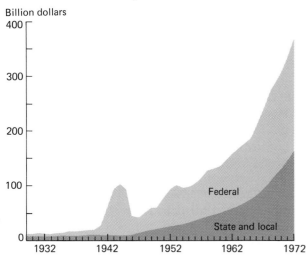

Note: 1972 data are preliminary. Grants-in-aid are included in the state and local sector only to avoid double counting.

Total government expenditures are determined by adding to purchase all of the nonpurchase expenditures for social security, unemployment compensation, welfare payments, subsidies, and other similar expenditures. One of these expenditures by the federal government that requires special consideration is grants-in-aid to state and local governments. These grants are included in the National Accounts as part of federal expenditures, but state and local governments actually spend these funds. Therefore, grants-in-aid must be removed from either state and local expenditures or federal expenditures to avoid double counting. For this article, they have been removed from federal expenditures.

The general pattern of total government expenditures follows that of total government purchase of goods and services. Federal expenditures in the period since World War II have dominated the total, typically being twice as large as all state and local expenditures. The trend toward the increasing importance of federal expenditures had already begun in the Thirties. Federal expenditures of $3.7 billion in 1929 were about one-third the total of $11.5 billion. They grew to $8.0 billion in 1939, almost equal to state and local expenditures of $9.6 billion. Federal expenditures reached their World War II peak level in 1944, when they were almost $95 billion out of total government expenditures of $103 billion. They dropped sharply after World War II before starting to grow again, and did not reach the World War II dollar level again until 1961. They have grown steadily since, reaching $208.5 billion in 1972.

The growth immediately after World War II came from veteran's benefits and foreign aid. Later, social security became a dominant factor, but the space and atomic energy programs, aid to education, and other new programs swelled the total.

State and local expenditures were virtually constant from 1929 to the end of World War II, $7.8 billion in 1929, and $8.4 billion in 1944. Ever since World War II, the growth has been continuous and rapid: $11 billion in 1946, $36 billion in 1956, $84 billion in 1966, and $163 billion in 1972. This growth has been distributed over every area of state and local government activity, but it has been particularly strong in education, public assistance, and public health.

. . . Are 1/3 the Size of GNP

A significantly different pattern from that exhibited by dollar expenditures emerges when the size of expenditures is compared with gross national product. Total expenditures, for all levels of government combined, have shown a persistent upward trend all through the 1929–72 period. Superimposed on this trend are the enormous bulge caused by World War

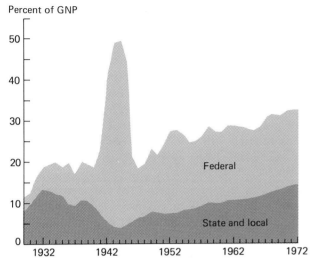

Generally, federal spending is double state and local spending

Percent of GNP

Federal

State and local

1932   1942   1952   1962   1972

Note: 1972 data are preliminary. Grants-in-aid are included in the state and local sector only to avoid double counting.

II and a much smaller bulge caused by Korea. The effect of the Vietnam war is barely noticeable in comparison with that of the two earlier conflicts.

In 1929, total expenditures were 11 percent the size of GNP. They rose to 20 percent in the 1930s, jumped to an all-time high of nearly 50 percent during World War II, then returned to their prewar level of 20 percent immediately after the war. The prewar growth trend resumed in 1947 and persisted through 1972, when the level of total government expenditures was just over 32 percent of GNP. Thus, the increase in the size of expenditures relative to GNP which occurred in the six years 1929–34 was almost as large as the increase during the 34 years 1947–72.

When the purchases of goods and services by the federal government and state and local government were compared, it was seen that the state and local share was the larger through most of the 1929–72 period. However, when the totals of purchase and nonpurchase expenditures of the two sectors are compared, the federal share predominates.

This difference in behavior results from the increasingly important role of federal nonpurchase expenditures, such as social security, in the composition of total federal expenditures. In recent years, nonpurchase expenditures have accounted for about half of all federal spending. Nonpurchase spending of state and local governments is much less important, usually less than 10 percent of expenditures.

The size of state and local government expenditures relative to GNP began to decline in 1933 with the launching of the "New Deal." This downtrend was not reversed until 1945. Although the trend has been rising ever since, expenditures did not climb back to the 1929 level of 7.5 percent of GNP until 1954, and did not exceed the 1932 peak of 13.1 percent until 1970. Nevertheless, since the mid-1950s, growth of state and local expenditures has tended to be the principal source for growth in the relative size of total government expenditures. During the four most recent years, 1969–72, the size of federal expenditures relative to GNP has been declining, while growth of state and local expenditures has accelerated, so that the total level has continued to grow. In 1962, state and local government expenditures were 36 percent of the total. In 1972, they were 44 percent of the total, the highest share since 1940.

Personal Transfer Payments

Except during the World War II period, transfer payments to persons have accounted for the largest portion of nonpurchase expenditures of all governments. They grew from about 50 percent of the total in 1929 to almost 85 percent in 1971. To the extent that transfers are made to different individuals than those taxed to make the payments possible, their primary effect is to shift purchasing power from some individuals to others. This shift in income also occurs with certain other expenditures that are not classed as transfer payments, such as interest payments and subsidies. Because it is not practical to trace the effects of any of these expenditures except transfer payments through to personal income, the actual income redis-

Transfer payments reallocate
more and more personal income

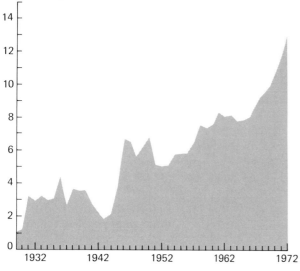

Percent of disposable income

Note: 1972 data are preliminary.

tribution is larger than that resulting from transfer payments alone.

Most, but not all, transfer payments are exempt from income taxes. The impact of transfer payments on the redistribution of purchasing power is, therefore, more accurately measured by comparing the magnitude of transfer payments with disposable personal income rather than with total personal income.

Personal income grew from about $84 billion in 1929 to $795 billion in 1972, more than nine times larger. In 1929, government transfer payments to individuals were less than $1 billion, about 1 percent of total income. In 1972, they reached $104 billion, over 13 percent of the total. In 44 years, transfer payments grew by over 110 times, or 12 times as fast as the growth in disposable income.

The pattern of growth of personal transfer payments as a share of disposable income has involved a complicated series of increases, occurring whenever the scope of benefits was expanded. After each increase peaked, there was a subsequent decline, but never to as low a level as existed prior to the expan-

sion. The legislation of the 1930s raised the transfer payment level from 1 percent of income in 1929 to over 3½ percent before World War II witnessed a decline, reflecting increases in employment and income rather than a lowering of benefits available.

After the war, the level of transfer payments relative to income rose sharply, primarily as a result of GI benefits. Korean War GI benefits and the maturing of the social security system brought subsequent peaks in the years 1950, 1958, and 1961. The decline following the 1961 peak ended in 1964. The level has been rising ever since, as social security benefits have been improved, and medicare was added in 1963. The expansion since 1964 has also reflected growth in direct welfare payments, particularly the "Aid to Families with Dependent Children" program. The increase from just under 12 percent of disposable income in 1971 to over 13 percent in 1972 was the largest year-to-year increase since the end of World War II.

Grants-in-Aid

Transfers of funds from the federal government to state and local units has a long history in the United States. Revenue from sales of public land was turned over to the states in the early 1800s, and other transfers occurred right up to the Depression. However, such transfers were small and unstable, and had little impact on state and local financing or on the federal budget. In 1929, federal grants-in-aid were less than $150 million, provided less than 2 percent of state and local revenues, and were less than 5 percent of federal expenditures.

In the early 1930s, grants-in-aid were used to provide funds for both direct assistance and public work projects. By 1935, they had risen to over $1.7 billion, 20 percent of state and local expenditures and over 26 percent of the federal budget. From then on, they played an important role in state and local finance. Grants dropped substantially in the late 1930s to about $800 million, and remained under $1 billion through the war years. From 1946 through 1957,

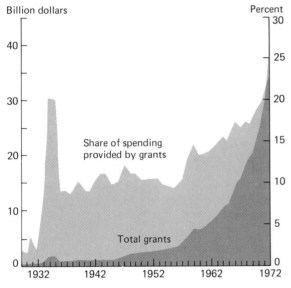

**Federal grants fuel state
and local government growth**

Billion dollars

Percent

Share of spending
provided by grants

Total grants

1932   1942   1952   1962   1972

Note: 1972 data are preliminary.

grants increased at about the same rate as state and local expenditures, providing about 10 percent of state and local government funds.

In 1958, the growth rate of grants-in-aid accelerated, raising the share of state and local spending they funded from 10 to 14 percent. They continued to supply this share until the end of 1965. From then on, they have provided progressively larger shares of state and local expenditures. By 1972, grants-in-aid were just under 24 percent of state and local spending, topping the Depression peak for the first time. Prior to 1957, grants-in-aid never exceeded $3.5 billion. Since then, they have grown every year except 1960, reaching $38.4 billion in 1972.

The share of federal expenditures devoted to grants-in-aid dropped from 26 percent in 1935 to less than 1 percent in 1944. In the immediate postwar period, their share of federal expenditure surged to nearly 6 percent and then settled back to a 4 percent plateau, which lasted through 1956. Since that time, their share of the federal budget has grown steadily. By 1972, grants-in-aid exceeded 15 percent of federal spending, a post-Depression high.

Prior to 1972, most grants-in-aid were earmarked for specific purposes, such as welfare payments, highway construction, and education. In late 1972, revenue sharing began a new era for grants-in-aid. Revenue sharing funds can be used for any legitimate purpose. While currently less than 20 percent of total grants, these funds do represent a new departure in the fiscal relationship between the federal government and states and municipalities. The federal government's role as tax collector for smaller governments seems likely to become increasingly important during the next several years.

Paying for Government Spending*

By Morton B. Millenson

Summary

The combined spending of all levels of government in the United States totaled $382 billion in 1972. This spending level equaled one-third of our gross national product, and was larger than the GNP of Japan, the second largest economy in the free world. All but $16 billion of the total spent was raised by taxes and other charges levied on individuals and businesses.

Government spending and comparable revenue collections on this large scale are modern phenomena. Total government spending in the late nineteenth century was about 8 percent of gross national product. Both spending and revenue were about 30 times larger in 1972 than they were in 1929. Had the growth of government spending merely kept pace with the growth of the economy, revenue requirements would have increased only one-third as much as they actually have. But the lion's share of the growth has gone for activities once considered outside the sphere of governments and for dramatic increases in the scope of activities traditionally assigned to governments.

This article looks at the sources of the revenues collected by governments to pay for their spending.

Key Questions to Consider

■ The change in the size of total government spending has been accomplished by revisions in the way revenues are raised. What changes have occurred in the relative importance of the various kinds of taxes used to raise revenue since 1929?

■ How have government expenditures as a percentage of GNP changed over time?

■ What are the three major tax sources of the federal government today and what percentage of total revenues do they account for?

■ What are the major tax sources state and local governments now rely on, and how have they changed in importance over time?

* Reprinted with permission from *Business Conditions*, Federal Reserve Bank of Chicago, June 1973, pp. 3–12.

Paying for Government Spending

The combined spending of all levels of government in the United States totaled $382 billion in 1972. This spending level equaled one-third of our gross national product, and was larger than the GNP of Japan, the second largest economy in the free world. All but $16 billion of the total spent was raised by taxes and other charges levied on individuals and businesses.

Government spending and comparable revenue collections on this large scale are modern phenomena. Total government spending in the late nineteenth century was about 8 percent of gross national product. This general level of spending persisted through the early part of the twentieth century, except during World War I. In 1929, total government spending was just over $10 billion, 10 percent of gross national product, and was supported by $11 billion in revenue. But beginning with the Depression, the scope of government activities has broadened continuously.

Both spending and revenue were about 30 times larger in 1972 than they were in 1929. Had the growth of government spending merely kept pace with the growth of the economy, revenue requirements would have increased only one-third as much as they actually have. But the lion's share of the growth has gone for activities once considered outside the sphere of governments and for dramatic increases in the scope of activities traditionally assigned to governments.

In 1972, the revenues collected for the social security program alone were nearly as large as the total revenues of all levels of government in 1946. The cost of operating state-supported colleges and universities last year was twice as large as the total revenues of all state governments in 1946. State transfers of funds to local governments—over half for education—were four times the amount local governments collected from all sources in 1946.

Prior to the changes which began with the Depression, government spending meant largely local government spending, and taxes meant payments to local government. In 1929, local governments accounted for almost 60 percent of all government spending, the federal government for just over one-quarter of the total, and state governments for less than 15 percent. In 1972, state governments were still the smallest spenders, although their share had climbed slightly, to 17 percent. The big change was in the relative position of the federal and local governments. Federal spending was well over half the total, while the local share had dropped to about one-quarter.

The changes in the size of total spending were

also accompanied by a drastic revision in ways that revenues were raised. In 1929, when state and local revenues dominated the scene, property taxes were the largest single source of all government revenue by far, raising almost 42 percent of the total. Corporate income taxes were in second place, closely followed by personal income taxes, each contributing about 12 percent of the total. In 1972, reflecting both the dominant position of the federal government and the changes that had occurred in the scope of government activities, the personal income tax was the number one source of revenues, contributing nearly one-third of the total. Contributions for social insurance, which had been number ten on the list in 1929, held second place, contributing about 20 percent of the total. Property taxes had dropped to third place, contributing about 12 percent, and corporate income taxes had dropped to number four.

In the February 1973 issue of *Business Conditions*, the article "Growth of government spending" traced the major patterns of government spending using the data in the National Income and Product Accounts. This article looks at the other side of the coin—the sources of the revenues collected by governments to pay for their spending.

THE GRAND TOTALS

Revenues have been hard-pressed to keep pace with the growth in government spending that has occurred since 1929. When spending is growing, the nature of the legislative process virtually guarantees that enactment of new taxes will lag spending, keeping constant pressures on revenues. Nevertheless, revenues have grown rapidly enough to pay for over 90 percent of total expenditures in the 44-year period. Only during World War II was there a massive shortfall. Although tax increases were very large compared to any previous experience, the expenditures needed for that war were so large that revenues only covered about half the total spending.

The rapid and continuous growth of government revenues has meant that the most recent years have been the biggest contributors to the overall total. From 1929 to 1972, governments collected over $4.5 trillion in revenues. Starting in 1929, it took 26 years to raise the first trillion dollars, but only eight years to collect the next trillion. The most recent trillion dollars was collected in just three years.

While inflation, increased population, and growth of the economy, both in complexity and output, have contributed to increasing government expenditures, hence to growing revenues, it is the increase in demands on government that has been the dominant factor in expenditure growth. By comparing the level of revenues with the size of the gross national product, which also includes the effects of inflation and population and output growth, it is possible to see the extent to which the increased needs for government action have influenced the size of revenues.

Government revenues grew from about 11 per-

Personal Income Taxes are Entrenched as the

Year	Total revenues collected Billion dollars	Personal income tax Percent	Rank	Contributions for social insurance Percent	Rank	Property taxes Percent	Rank	Corporate income tax Percent	Rank	General sales tax Percent	Rank	Miscellaneous taxes Percent	Rank
1929	11	11.7	3	2.2	10	41.2	1	11.9	2	0.0	13	5.7	5
1950	69	26.5	1	10.0	4	10.7	3	25.8	2	2.7	9	8.8	5
1960	140	31.3	1	14.8	4	11.7	3	16.3	2	3.2	7	7.0	5
1972	366	32.4	1	20.2	2	12.2	3	11.3	4	5.3	5	4.5	6

cent the size of GNP in 1929 to about 32 percent in 1972, with only minor deviations punctuating a steady upward trend. Even during the early 1930s, when the dollar level of total revenues was declining, the level relative to GNP grew every year as output fell much more rapidly than tax collections. In fact, the year-to-year rise of revenues relative to GNP in 1932 over 1931 was the second largest in the 1929–72 period. The largest year-to-year increase occurred in 1943, when the impact of wartime tax rates was fully effective for the first time. Despite what were considered massive increases at the time—collections jumped from the prewar level of about 18 percent the size of GNP to just under 25 percent—the levels of the 1942–46 period were low by today's standards. Since 1949, revenues have taken a progressively larger share of GNP, and are now approaching one-third of the total.

SHARING THE PIE

The developments in government activity that have occurred since 1929 completely transformed the historical American relationships between the federal government and state and local governments. Before the Depression, education, health, welfare, highways, and a vast array of other services were provided by state and local governments, particularly local governments. These governments were the dominant factor not only in providing these services but in collecting the revenues to pay for them. The primary function

of the federal government was national defense, and the only federal function which touched the daily lives of all citizens was the postal service.

In 1929, the U.S. armed services employed 255,-000 men, a small number not only by today's standards but also in comparison with the major powers of the time. The federal government's share of total revenues was less than one-third of the total collected that year. Moreover, federal revenues were much more affected by the decline in business activity during the early years of the Depression than were state and local government collections; by 1932 the federal share had dropped to 20 percent of the total.

The advent of the New Deal inaugurated a major change in governmental responsibility. This change was the assumption of the responsibility for public welfare by the federal government. At first, this was accomplished through emergency measures aimed at the specific problems of the Depression. But with the enactment of the social security program, income maintenance became a permanent responsibility of the federal government. Agricultural programs and federal funding of public works programs also date from this period. As a result of these new and shifted responsibilities, federal revenue requirements were nearly 50 percent of the total on the eve of World War II. The increased responsibilities assumed by the federal government in the area of human resources during the 1930s laid the groundwork for the early 1970s, when these expenditures exceeded defense expenditures for the first time.

Number One Revenue Source Of All Governments

Nontax revenue		Gasoline taxes		Liquor taxes		Estate and gift taxes		Tobacco taxes		Motor vehicle licenses		Customs duties		
Percent	Rank	Percent	Rank	Percent	Rank	Percent	Rank	Percent	Rank	Percent	Rank	Percent	Rank	Year
8.7	4	3.7	8	0.1	12	2.0	11	4.0	7	3.0	9	5.3	6	1929
2.3	10	3.3	7	4.2	6	1.2	11	2.6	8	1.1	12	0.8	13	1950
2.7	9	4.1	6	2.8	8	1.6	11	2.1	10	1.1	12	0.8	13	1960
4.0	7	3.1	8	1.9	9	1.8	10	1.4	11	1.0	12	0.9	13	1972

Another change which significantly increased the revenue needs of the federal government was the nation's altered defense posture. With the outbreak of war in Europe in 1939, military expenditures increased sharply, and taxes jumped. Actual U.S. involvement brought still sharper federal tax increases, so that the federal share of total revenue collections reached a peak of 80 percent in 1944. The federal share has been declining slowly but erratically from this abnormally high wartime level. By 1972, the federal share had been lowered to 62 percent of the total.

This gradual swing back toward a larger share of revenues for state and local governments has resulted despite the fact that the defense establishment has been maintained at levels far above the pre–World War II norm. The postwar period has seen explosive growth in the needs for schools, highways, health facilities, and other government services supplied by state and local governments. Throughout the postwar period, and particularly in the past 15 years, spending by state and local governments has risen much more rapidly than have the revenues they collected directly.

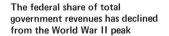

The federal share of total government revenues has declined from the World War II peak

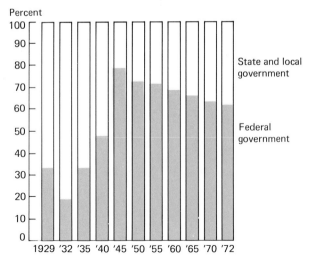

The cost of this added spending has been met by funds collected by the federal government, but transferred to state and local treasuries through numerous special grants ranging from specific programs like the Interstate Highway System to the unrestricted funds of the revenue sharing program. These transfers of funds, known collectively as grants-in-aid, have existed for a long time. They were relatively unimportant prior to the Depression. During the New Deal, grants were used extensively to finance public works projects and direct assistance. From 1939 through 1957, grants-in-aid funded about 10 percent of state and local spending. Since then, they have contributed an ever-growing share, reaching 24 percent in 1972. If state and local governments had collected these taxes directly in 1972, and federal tax collections were reduced by an equivalent amount, the state and local share of total revenue would have been 48 percent, rather than the actual level of 38 percent, very close to the 50–50 situation that existed immediately prior to World War II.

THE FEDERAL TAX BASE

Today, the federal government relies on three tax sources for almost 90 percent of its total revenue. These are, in order of importance, the personal income tax, contributions for social insurance (mainly social security), and the corporate income tax. These three tax sources, combined, have formed the backbone of federal revenues ever since the major World War II increases became fully effective in 1943. The distribution of 1972 receipts by source was:

Source	Percent of total	Percent of total adjusted for overwithholding*
Personal income tax	45.3	43.5
Social insurance	27.7	28.6
Corporate income tax	15.8	16.3
All other receipts	11.2	11.6

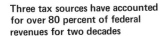

Three tax sources have accounted
for over 80 percent of federal
revenues for two decades

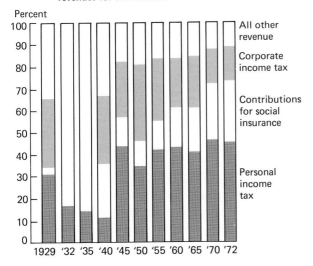

The personal income tax has been an important source of federal revenue during the entire 1929–72 period. The importance of the personal income tax fell sharply during the Depression, not only because of the sharp drop in income, but also because the federal government turned to a host of new taxes during the New Deal period. World War II caused a dramatic turnaround. The personal income tax has been the largest single source of revenue for the federal government since 1943.

Contributions to social insurance first became important in 1937 with the introduction of social security and related payroll taxes. The impact of these new taxes on federal finances was dramatic. For four years, 1937–40, they contributed about one-

fourth of total revenues, and were the largest single contributors in the first three of those years. The imposition of wartime tax changes relegated contributions to third place. Beginning in 1957, changes in the social security program progressively increased the importance of revenue from this source. By 1966, it had grown to be the second largest source, and in 1972 supplied nearly 28 percent of total federal revenue.

The corporate income tax, like the personal income tax, was a well-established major source of federal revenue in 1929. In that year, it was the largest single source, supplying just over 31 percent of the total. Its yield and importance dropped during the 1930s, and then increased sharply with the advent of World War II. It was the second largest federal revenue source from 1943 until 1966. However, its relative importance has been declining steadily since the end of World War II, not only because of the yields of the social security system, but also because the long-term growth in corporate profits has lagged the growth in the economy.

THE PERSONAL INCOME TAX

Students of tax policy generally approve the personal income tax as a revenue measure because of its inherent tendency to relate the tax to the ability to pay and because it has less effect on resource allocation than other taxes. From the standpoint of the federal government, however, it has two advantages which have contributed to making it the most important revenue source. First, it rests on a very large taxable base. Second, the revenue which it can furnish can be changed by very large amounts through minor changes in the rate structure.

The modern income tax was introduced in 1913. Prior to World War II, the revenue-raising potential of the personal income tax went largely untapped. Most people were not touched by it because of the large personal exemptions relative to the income structure. The changes in the tax law necessitated by

◄   * 1972 personal income tax receipts were about $7 billion higher than they would have been if taxpayers had taken full advantage of the right to adjust their withholding closer to their actual tax liabilities. These overpayments will be refunded in 1973, thereby reducing receipts. The adjusted percentages are derived by assuming that the extra withholding in 1972 had not been collected. The adjusted shares show what can be expected from current tax laws in the future.

World War II converted the personal income tax into the broad-based levy it has remained ever since. As a result of this broad application, personal income tax revenues went from $1 billion in 1940 to about $16 billion in 1943. Once the revenue-raising capabilities of this tax were fully revealed, the federal government continued to use it not only as its primary source of revenue, but, through frequent adjustments of rates, as a tool for setting total revenue levels.

CONTRIBUTIONS FOR SOCIAL INSURANCE

Unlike the personal income tax, which was a major revenue source before 1929, contributions for social insurance first became important in 1937, and in 1960 began a trend toward sharply increased importance. Prior to 1937, the only specific elements in this category were payments for the federal employees retirement system and veterans life insurance. Unemployment insurance revenues began in 1936, and social security and railroad retirement programs began supplying revenues in 1937. Since that time, in addition to the gradual expansion of coverage of social security to more classes of wage earners and increases in the wage levels subject to tax, there have been major additions to the total program: railroad unemployment insurance in 1939, coverage of self-employed persons in 1952, and hospital and medical insurance in 1966. In 1972, contributions to social insurance made up nearly 28 percent of total federal revenue.

Recent changes in the social security program which provide for increases in the taxable base income this year and again in 1974, and for further increases in the base in subsequent years, depending on the change in the consumer price index, will raise the share of federal revenue supplied by these contributions above the 30 percent level in the next few years. It should be noted that benefits paid by the various programs in this category have been nearly as large as the revenue collected yearly, but that the difference has contributed toward paying for other programs.

THE CORPORATE INCOME TAX

The corporate income tax has had much the same history as the personal income tax. Both were imposed during the Civil War and then removed for many years. Tax theorists are far less unanimous about the desirability and economic impact of the corporate tax than they are about the consequences of the personal income tax. It is not at all clear whether this tax falls on the buyers of corporate goods and services through higher prices, on workers through lower wages, or on owners through lower rates of return.

Regardless of the actual economic impact of this tax, it has been a substantial contributor to federal revenues throughout the 1929–72 period. In 1929 and again in 1940 through 1942, it was the single largest source of federal revenue, and throughout most of the other years between 1929 and 1966 it was the second largest source of revenue. Nevertheless, its importance has declined steadily since 1965. The corporate tax structure is currently at the lowest level since the period immediately after World War II, but the failure of corporate profits to grow as rapidly as the general economy has been a major factor in the decline. When the temporary surcharge was decreased from the 1969 rate of 10 percent to the 1970 effective rate of 2½ percent, the share of total revenue contributed by the personal income tax actually rose slightly, while the share from corporate income taxes fell.

OTHER TAX SOURCES

Tax sources other than the three major ones have contributed a small but steady share to federal revenue throughout the 1929–72 period. In some instances, these sources made major contributions during part of the period, particularly prior to World War II.

Estate and gift taxes have contributed about 2 percent of total federal revenues since 1929. Rates were raised sharply during the New Deal period, and for a few years they contributed a much larger share, reaching nearly 8 percent of the total in 1936.

Customs duties have been a mainstay of federal revenues. Customs duties contributed 15 to 18 percent of total revenues in the 1929–32 period, but their importance declined steadily thereafter—to less than 1 percent of the total in most years between 1943 and 1964.

Liquor taxes became an important revenue source with the repeal of prohibition. In 1935, they furnished nearly 12 percent of total revenues. However, neither consumption nor rates have increased significantly and they contributed just over 2 percent of the total in 1972.

Excise taxes on a wide variety of other products and services have been used from time to time throughout this 44-year period. During the New Deal, a whole spectrum of excise taxes was introduced and later dropped. These miscellaneous taxes, which made up less than 3 percent of federal revenues in 1929, swelled to nearly 30 percent of the total in 1934 and then faded away. In 1972, the sum of all these other taxes still on the books amounted to less than 4 percent of total federal revenues.

STATE AND LOCAL TAXES—A BROAD-BASED APPROACH

The tax structure of state and local governments has developed on lines almost opposite those followed by the federal tax structure during the 1929–72 period. In the early years of the period, the federal government relied on a wide spectrum of tax sources. By 1972, all but three had faded into relative unimportance, and a single source, the personal income tax, provided nearly half of total federal revenues.

In contrast, over 60 percent of all state and local government revenues in 1929 came from one source, the real estate tax. In 1972, the importance of the real estate tax had shrunk to half its 1929 size, and over

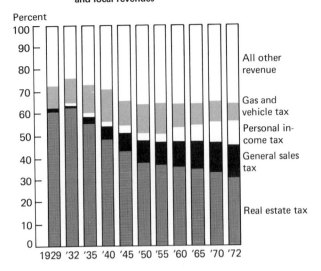

Real estate taxes provide a shrinking share of all state and local revenues

two-thirds of state and local revenues came from a wide array of sources. Federal receipts from the personal income tax in 1972 were 100 times as large as they had been in 1929, but state and local receipts from real estate taxes rose only ten times in the same period.

The growth of state and local revenues that occurred between 1929 and 1972 was much slower in gathering momentum than was the growth in federal revenues. During the Depression, it was virtually impossible for state and local governments to increase their revenues, and yields from existing sources declined appreciably. To economize, many state and local services were cut back. The federal government picked up the responsibility for providing relief to individuals and for public works projects that would have been paid for with local revenues in earlier times.

World War II, following on the heels of the Depression, further deterred expansion of state and local government activities. Military needs absorbed both the fiscal and manpower resources which might otherwise have been devoted to expansion of services by state and local governments. But in the postwar period, the need for state and local government services ballooned. Not only was there a need to make up for the unfilled needs accumulated since 1929, but a host of new demands arose. To meet these needs, state and local governments have continuously raised tax rates and introduced new taxes to supply the necessary revenues. As a result, 1972 receipts were 12 times as large as those of 1945—a growth rate twice that of federal government receipts. Despite this rapid growth, revenues would have fallen far short of requirements had not federal grants-in-aid provided a major supplement to funds raised by state and local governments from their own resources.

It must be borne in mind that aggregate state and local revenues result from the independent taxing actions of thousands of individual jurisdictions. The five states served by the Seventh Federal Reserve District contain over 15,000 taxing units. Thus, when a particular tax grows in importance, more taxing units may be using it, the tax rate may be increasing, or both may be occurring at once.

PROPERTY TAXES

Property taxes were the basic source of state and local financing throughout the nation's early history, and still remain the principal, frequently the only, source of revenue for smaller units of government. While most property tax laws cover a wide scope of property types, difficulties in assessment and collection have resulted in real estate being the only property effectively taxed in most jurisdictions, typically accounting for over 95 percent of property tax revenue. When the nation's economy was primarily rural, the property tax was a rough substitute for an income tax. As the society was transformed into an urban industrial economy, the property tax has become a use tax, particularly on the use of real estate.

No lasting form of taxation has been criticized as severely as the property tax by students of taxation and taxpayers alike. Criticisms range from its inequity

due to the problems of obtaining fair and uniform assessment to the fact that there is often no reasonable relationship between the tax paid and the government services received. Nevertheless, this tax has persisted. It is the only tax source available to many small jurisdictions—other sources have been preempted by the larger units of government, or banned by state constitutional provisions which are difficult to change. Also, local voters appear reluctant to abandon their direct control over the maximum allowable rates of this major tax.

The property tax has largely been abandoned by state governments. State governments received 20 percent of their revenues from property taxes in 1929. By 1971, the most recent year that comparable data are available, property taxes supplied only 2 percent of state collections. Local governments, which were deriving over 75 percent of their revenues from property taxes in 1929, still obtained over 55 percent from that source in 1971. Despite this decline in the importance of property taxes, real estate taxes remain the largest single revenue source for the aggregate of all state and local governments. While the property tax as a share of total revenues collected has declined steadily from 61 percent in 1929 to 31 percent in 1972, the total dollar amount collected under this tax has increased yearly since 1942.

GROWING REVENUE SOURCES

The second largest source of state and local revenues in 1972 was the general sales tax, providing 14.2 percent of the total, almost $20 billion. The general sales tax is relatively modern in origin, and has been used primarily by states, although local use is growing. It was first introduced in 1931, as other revenue sources shrank and state governments actively developed new ones. By 1936, its use was widespread, and by the end of World War II it supplied 7.5 percent of state and local revenues. Sales tax rate increases raised its importance to 10 percent of the total in 1948, a level which remained relatively constant until the early 1960s. Since 1963, as a result of the introduction of local sales taxes as well as some increases in state rates, the sales tax yield has steadily increased.

Another growing revenue source for state and local governments is the personal income tax. Like the sales tax, this tax has been primarily a state tax, but use by local government has been increasing. Only two or three states used the income tax in 1929, and in the aggregate its importance was small. By 1972, 44 states and hundreds of municipalities were using some form of personal income tax, and it contributed 11 percent of total revenues—the third most important tax source to state and local governments.

Contributions for social insurance are another revenue source that has grown steadily over the 1929–72 period. For state and local governments, these contributions do not have the broad base of the federal programs. They are the payments government employees make to retirement and related insurance plans. However, receipts for these programs, which provided less than 2 percent of 1929 revenues, supplied nearly 8 percent in 1972.

THE OLD RELIABLES

The variety of special use, license, excise, and related taxes used by state and local governments to raise revenues is almost endless. Most of these taxes have grown steadily in dollar amounts from 1929 to 1972, but have either just held their own or lost importance as a share of total revenue over the period.

The automobile has created irresistible demands for expenditures for streets and highways, but, at the same time, has provided substantial revenue from licenses and gasoline taxes. In 1929, vehicle license fees supplied 4.5 percent and gasoline taxes 5.5 percent of total revenue. Their combined contribution peaked at about 14 percent in 1949–50. In 1972, the two taxes together supplied about 8 percent of state and local revenues.

Corporate income taxes generally were used by state and local governments before personal income taxes. Corporate taxes made their largest contribution to total revenues, 4.7 percent of the total, right after World War II, then slowly declined in importance until the early 1960s. Since then, state after state has either raised rates or introduced this tax for the first time. In 1972, it contributed just under 4 percent of total revenue.

Liquor, tobacco, death, and gift taxes are all widely used by state and local governments. Small but steady revenue sources, each has accounted for 1 to 2 percent of revenues since 1929. Of the four, only the tobacco tax has not declined in importance over the last ten years.

Miscellaneous license fees, entertainment taxes, resource severance taxes, and pari-mutuel taxes are a few examples of other taxes which are widely employed. Individually, none of these taxes has contributed more than a pittance toward aggregate state and local government revenues, but taken together they supplied nearly 9 percent of the total, about $12 billion, in 1972.

State and local governments also rely on nontax charges for a wide variety of services they provide directly to the public. These range from tuition at public colleges and universities to net income from publicly owned utilities and liquor stores. The sum of these revenues has been a major contributor to total revenue throughout the 1929–72 period. Their total was second only to real property taxes in 1929, when they provided over 12 percent of the total revenue. They remained stagnant in absolute dollar levels and declined as a share of the total through 1947. Then the flood of veterans into colleges and universities set in motion an expansion of state-supported higher education that is still in progress. Not only did enrollment boom, but tuition and other fees have been steadily raised. This increase in revenue from education has been paralleled by increases in charges for a multitude of other services. As a result, nontax revenues supplied nearly 10 percent of the total in 1972.

THE CONTRASTING TRENDS

The difference between the modern revenue patterns of the federal government and of state and local governments is striking. The federal government appears to be moving in the direction of reliance on three tax sources for the lion's share of its revenue. The personal income tax seems locked in at about 45 percent, and contributions for social insurance seem headed for the 30 percent level. These, together with the corporate income tax, have accounted for nearly 90 percent of federal receipts for the last decade.

State and local governments seem headed in the opposite direction. Once completely tied to the real property tax, they have consistently increased the importance of old revenue sources, and expanded their tax base to new sources. Today, the three largest sources combined, property taxes, personal income taxes, and general sales taxes, provide only 57 percent of state and local revenues, less than the property tax alone supplied in 1929.

Grants-in-aid, particularly revenue sharing, and tax increases of the last few years produced a large aggregate surplus for state and local governments in 1972. Furthermore, projections by such groups as the Tax Foundation Inc. suggest that these surpluses will continue for several years. Nevertheless, many individual units of government are facing severe problems in trying to raise adequate revenues. Receipts from their old standby, the real estate tax, are not growing rapidly enough. These governments will have to move toward heavier reliance on more flexible tax sources, such as income taxes, or else exercise ingenuity in devising new revenue sources if they are to meet their growing expenditures.

Much of the 1929–72 period can be viewed as an abnormality in the nation's tax and spending history. Both the Depression and World War II were events that hopefully will not be repeated. The post-war period has witnessed a slow, steady trend toward renewed importance for state and local government expenditures. Today, most taxpayers view the federal government as the primary collector of taxes. However, if current trends continue, and if grants-in-aid are viewed as revenues of state and local governments, the smaller units of government will have first claim on the taxpayer's attention in the years to come.

Reading 20

The Principles of Tax Reform*

By Warren L. Coats, Jr.

Summary

Tax reform has become a motherhood issue. Unfortunately, however, changing the tax laws and improving them are not necessarily synonymous. Citizens pay the tax and, through their political representatives, decide from whom it is to be collected. It is the citizen, therefore, who must ultimately pass judgment on the tax system. This is an important responsibility and not at all an impossible one.

Judgment requires a standard against which to judge. There must be some concept of how things should be ideally in order to judge whether a change is an improvement or not. What follows is the presentation of two criteria of a "good" tax system, an explanation of why most economists favor them, and applications of these criteria to several tax reform controversies, namely, the tax treatment of tax-exempt bonds, capital gains, oil depletion allowances, and tax-exempt foundations.

Key Questions to Consider

■ Explain and give examples of taxes reflecting the two basic principles set forth as criteria in determining a "good" tax system.

■ What activities does the author believe should be financed on the basis of the "benefit received" principle?

■ What are the three bases for an "ability to pay" tax? How do they differ with respect to savings?

■ Why does the author accept income as the appropriate base for an "ability to pay" tax?

■ What are the standards of fairness in taxing income?

■ Why is the author opposed to the existence of tax-exempt bonds, the capital gains tax, and the corporate income tax?

* Reprinted with permission from *Challenge, the Magazine of Economic Affairs,* **16,** No. 6 (January/February 1974) 12–21.

The Principles of Tax Reform

*Judged by criteria of equity and neutrality, the U.S.
tax system is badly in need of a major overhaul.*

---

*Concededly: a good deal of tax law is exceedingly
technical and abstruse. But no on[e] claims that voters
can be magically transformed into tax experts in
several easy lessons. The question rather is whether
they would grasp the basic essential of tax policy if
the issues were adequately presented to them. The
real difficulty, I suspect, is they might understand too
well.*

L. EISENSTEIN
The Ideologies of Taxation (1961)

Tax reform has become a motherhood issue. Unfortunately, however, changing the tax laws and improving them are not necessarily synonymous.
Citizens pay the tax and, through their political representatives, decide from whom it is to be collected.
It is the citizen, therefore, who must ultimately pass
judgment on the tax system. This is an important
responsibility and not at all an impossible one.

Judgment requires a standard against which to
judge. There must be some concept of how things
should be ideally in order to judge whether a change
is an improvement or not. What follows is the presentation of two criteria of a "good" tax system, an
explanation of why most economists favor them, and
applications of these criteria to several tax reform
controversies, namely, the tax treatment of tax-

exempt bonds, capital gains, oil depletion allowances,
and tax-exempt foundations.

This is a treatise not on government, but on the
principles of tax reform. It is important not to con-
fuse tax reform, which is concerned with how taxes
are raised, with tax relief, which is concerned with
the amount of taxes raised. It will be helpful if we
assume that we are given a fixed dollar amount of
taxes that the government must raise and that our
task is to decide how it is to be raised. We are not
discussing tax relief.

The first step is deciding what to tax—choosing
the tax base. The tax to be raised might be spread
evenly among all blue-eyed males or among all people with black hair, or "reasonably" black hair, etc.
These alternatives do not seem reasonable because in
the backs of our minds there are vague notions of
fairness that they violate. If we are to proceed, these
notions must be spelled out and settled upon.

WHICH PRINCIPLE?

Whenever the government collects taxes *someone's*
income is reduced regardless of the intended sources
of the tax. This is as true of corporate taxes, tariffs,
sales taxes, etc., as it is of the personal income tax.

This suggests the individual (or the household) as the reference point in refining our concepts of tax fairness. There are two major camps on this issue which have provided economic literature with a long, flowery and often heated debate. The newer of the two positions asserts that taxes should be levied against individuals in proportion to the benefits they derive from government. The "benefit principle" is a natural outgrowth of social contract philosophy, and was supported by men like Locke, Hume, Hobbes and Rousseau. The other camp asserts that taxes should be divided among individuals according to their respective abilities to pay. The ability-to-pay principle found support from men like Mill, Sismondi, Say, Marshall and Pigou. Support for both positions can be found in Adam Smith.

In my judgment there is a need for each of these principles. In general, free markets assume that people pay for what they get. This is a key factor in determining how the economy's scarce resources are to be employed. Likewise, in taxation, if people pay for the benefits they receive from government (that is, are taxed in accordance with the benefit principle), we can have greater confidence that the government will supply the "right" amount of services. This principle leads to the taxation of gasoline to finance highway construction, to the selling of stamps for postal service (if the word service can possibly be applied here), rather than complete "general fund" financing, and to the taxation of property to finance those municipal services that tend to benefit citizens in relation to the property they own (such as fire and police protection, roads, sidewalks, and waste disposal).

Unfortunately, many necessary government services confer benefits which cannot be attributed to specific individuals or which, by their very nature, should not be paid for by the beneficiaries. National defense is an example of the first type. One person's consumption of it does not reduce its benefits to others. Welfare is an example of the second type. Any program whose very purpose is to transfer income, say from the wealthy to the poor, obviously cannot tax the poor according to the benefit they receive. At this point we must have recourse to the ability-to-pay principle.

Ideally all government activities that can be financed through direct charges or benefit-related taxes should be financed thus. That would still leave us with the problem of financing those government activities, such as national defense, for which no exclusive individual benefit can be established or for which a benefit-related tax would be inappropriate. For such activities, which will be the concern of the rest of this article, I support the ability-to-pay doctrine.

ABILITY TO PAY

This only begins our quest for principles of tax reform, for it does not resolve the problem of how ability to pay is to be determined. However, it does suggest that the search for a fair tax base should be limited to an individual's wealth, income or consumption. These three come down to essentially the same thing except in their treatment of savings. A consumption-based tax is most favorable to savings and a wealth-based tax is least favorable. Although reasonable arguments can be made for each of these tax bases, the most widely supported tax base is income. I am deliberately avoiding a serious discussion of wealth vs. income vs. consumption as the better tax base in order to get on with the discussion of tax reform.

I tentatively accept the majority's preference for income as the base for four reasons. First, the income tax is the backbone of our tax system. It is therefore more likely that we will succeed in amending it than in replacing it altogether with some other tax base. Second, any other tax base (such as wealth or consumption) can always be translated into its impact on income, something I suspect people would have a tendency to do anyway. Third, the techniques of applying the principles of taxation I will soon introduce are essentially the same whether income, wealth or consumption is used as the tax base. As we shall see, these principles suggest the desirability of using as comprehensive a concept as possible of whatever the base is. Fourth, the gains in fairness and efficiency of properly reforming the income tax far outweigh any possible gain that *might* result from a choice of wealth or consumption as the tax base.

EQUAL TREATMENT OF EQUALS

If income, then, is to be the tax base, what is a fair way of taxing incomes in order to raise the required amount of revenue? One of the most widely held standards of tax fairness (or, in economic jargon, tax equity) is the principle of equal treatment of equals. If income is the basic measure of ability to pay, the principle requires that two individuals with the same income should pay the same tax.

A commonsense application of ability to pay suggests only one modification: since we generally tax households (or family units) rather than individuals, an adjustment should be made for the size of the household being supported by the income in question. The first criterion of an ideal tax system can then be restated to say that all households of the same size with the same income should pay the same tax. Bear in mind that this refers to taxes in excess of the benefit-related taxes households may pay.

Capturing the spirit of the above principle requires a proper definition of income. The business concept of net income is instructive. Net income for a firm is total economic gain, regardless of type or source, less all costs incurred in generating it. It is this concept of income as the tax base which, I think, best satisfies most people's sense of fairness in taxation and which is most consistent with the above principle of tax equity. Such a concept of income would constitute a substantial broadening of our current income tax base.

NEUTRALITY

There is a second important criterion of an ideal tax system which is sometimes more difficult for the lay-man to grasp. This is the principle of neutrality. A tax is neutral if it does not alter the relative prices of goods and services—that is, the price of one good relative to the price of another. In a free-enterprise economy prices are the indicators of value. Prices tell firms how badly consumers want one good relative to another. Taking the cost of producing various goods into account, firms are encouraged by profit to produce that collection of goods that in aggregate are most highly valued. A neutral tax does not interfere with the price system's task of directing firms into the provision of the "optimal" quantities of the "right" goods and services. There are a couple of important exceptions, but this is the general rule.

In practice, a neutral tax is one that affects the prices of all goods and services equally, thereby leaving their relative prices unchanged. It may help to point out that an excise tax (a tax on one good or a small number of goods) is anything but a neutral tax. It causes the good to appear artificially expensive relative to other goods to the consumer and artificially unprofitable to the producer, with the result that less of the good will be produced and in its place more of other less valued goods will be produced. In this way an excise tax causes a misallocation of resources; it causes the economy to function inefficiently.

THE TAX BASE

In a very impressive attempt to apply these principles to tax reform in Canada, the Royal Commission on Taxation (generally known as the Carter Commission) recommended that the income tax base be made as comprehensive as is administratively possible, all sources of income being treated alike. As expressed in the Carter Commission's 1967 *Report*:

The proposed tax base must of necessity take into account all of a person's net gains over the year. All gains, after meeting the expenses necessary to generate them, must be reflected in the base. . . . The distinction between wages, interest, dividends, business incomes, gains on shares, bequests, sweepstake winnings, and so on, all would disappear. . . . If economic power is increased it does not matter in principle whether it was earned or unearned, from domestic or foreign sources, in money or in kind, anticipated or unanticipated, intended or inadvertent, recurrent or non-recurrent, realized or unrealized.

Broadening the tax base in this way has the great virtue of raising the same tax revenue with lower tax rates. Such a comprehensive base also measures up well to both our criteria: equity and neutrality. In terms of neutrality it leaves all consumption choices —relative prices—unaffected, save that of leisure. That is, there is no change in economic behavior that will reduce the tax—hence that is caused by the tax—

except the decision about how much to work (there is also some discrimination against saving). This might be a serious tax distortion in resource allocation if it were not for the fact that the personal income tax sets up two opposing forces affecting work effort. The tax reduces the reward for each hour of work and hence acts to reduce the number of hours worked. At the same time, it lowers income and hence acts to increase the number of hours worked in an effort to replace the lost income. Although good evidence is hard to come by, what there is tends to suggest that in the case of current U.S. rates, these two forces more or less offset one another, that the income tax has little or no effect on work effort.

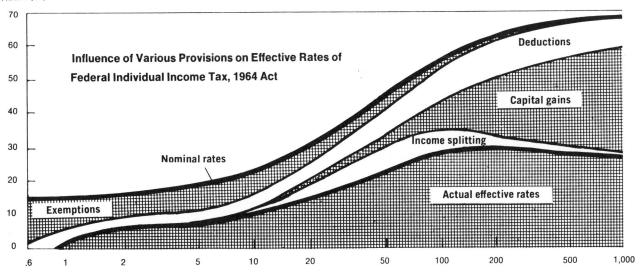

Effective Rates (%)

Influence of Various Provisions on Effective Rates of Federal Individual Income Tax, 1964 Act

Nominal rates

Deductions

Capital gains

Income splitting

Actual effective rates

Exemptions

Total Income (Thousands of Dollars, Ratio Scale)

Source: Special file of about 100,000 Federal Tax Returns for 1962. Chart reprinted from Joseph A. Pechman, "Individual Income Tax Provisions of the Revenue Act of 1964," *Journal of Finance*, Vol. 20 (May 1965). Based on 1962 incomes, with rates applicable beginning Jan. 1, 1965.

TAX-EXEMPT BONDS

In terms of equity, two families of the same size, same general state of health, and same income would pay the same tax. But the existing U.S. income tax clearly

falls short in both equity and neutrality. This can be quickly and clearly illustrated by tax-exempt bonds.

States and municipalities are allowed to issue bonds, paying tax-free interest income to their owners. This practice was initiated to reduce the cost of debt financing for these levels of government. This is achieved because the more desirable, tax-free earnings of these bonds cause their prices to be bid up relative to other bonds (meaning that money can be borrowed at lower interest rates) until their desirability to the marginal investor is equal to that of other bonds. A few numbers will quickly illustrate the point.

A taxpayer in the 50 percent bracket would find himself indifferent to a choice between two equally riskless government bonds if one were a taxable U.S. bond yielding 6 percent and the other a nontaxable state bond yielding 3 percent, because his after-tax income from each would be the same. Such an individual gains no special benefit from tax-exempt bonds. He is the marginal investor referred to above. However, someone in the 70 percent tax bracket would find the tax-exempt bond decidedly advantageous. The 6 percent U.S. bond yields him an $18.00 after-tax income (per $1,000 invested) whereas the 3 percent tax-exempt state bond yields him a $30.00 after-tax income. This means that two people, both with the same 70 percent tax bracket income but different holdings of tax-exempt bonds, would pay different amounts of income tax. This violates our criteria both of equity and of neutrality.

The carefully avoided issue of tax rate progression must be faced at this point. It is often and convincingly argued that marginal tax rates of 60 or 70 percent are unrealistically high and so-called tax loopholes such as tax-exempt bonds are needed to provide necessary relief. In fact, tax-exempt bonds in conjunction with other tax loopholes such as preferential capital gains treatment, income splitting, charitable contributions and some other personal deductions lower the actual average rates paid to below 30 percent. This result is depicted in the chart from Joseph Pechman's *Federal Tax Policy*, and was arrived at as follows:

If the total income reported by taxpayers were subject to the nominal tax rates without any exemptions, deductions, or other special provisions, effective tax rates would begin at 14 percent and rise to almost 70 percent in the very highest brackets. But nobody pays these rates on his entire income. After allowing for all special provisions, the *maximum average effective rate* for any class is less than 30 percent and the tax becomes slightly regressive above $200,000 of income.

The problem with these loopholes is not that they lower the effective tax rate—many economists would agree that these rates should be lowered—but that they are inequitable and non-neutral. In fact, removing the loopholes becomes a way of lowering tax rates without lowering tax revenue. Not every wealthy taxpayer has the same access to the same loopholes, so that people with the same income might pay substantially different taxes. The preferential treatment of one source of income over another also distorts the efficiency with which we use our resources by generating a lot of effort to earn income in lightly taxed forms (capital gains treatment—discussed below—affords a good example of this). The resulting inefficiencies mean that the economy enjoys fewer goods and services from given resources. If marginal tax rates are too high, as in my opinion they certainly are, they should be legislated down directly rather than through the creation of inequitable and distorting tax loopholes (or "foxholes," as Arthur Willis calls them in the American Bar Association's *Studies in Substantive Tax Reform*).

There is still more to the case against tax-exempt bonds. As a means of aiding local financing, tax-exempt bonds are inefficient. The federal government loses more revenue from this device (over half a billion dollars—which must be made up by higher taxes elsewhere) than the states save by it. A more direct subsidy would save everyone money. It would, however, be grossly unfair to begin suddenly taxing the income from such bonds. This is an important point with some slightly delicate aspects well worth pursuing with some care.

The effect of taxing previously tax-exempt bonds would be to cause a fall in their price. To the extent that their tax advantage had been capitalized (i.e., the extent to which their price had risen above other bonds), it would now be uncapitalized, as the advantage would no longer exist. To illustrate: our 50 percent tax bracket marginal investor found the after-tax return on a 3 percent state bond to be the same as on a 6 percent U.S. bond. If we suddenly tax the former along with the latter, its price will fall (as investors, always seeking the highest rate of return for any given risk, move out of the now lower-yielding state bonds into other assets—e.g., U.S. bonds) until its after-tax income of $15.00 per $1,000 bond ($30 less 50 percent income tax) represents the same yield as the $30 after-tax income of a U.S. bond ($60 less 50 percent income tax).

In this hypothetical example, the price of the state bond would be cut in half. It would fall from $1,000 for a $15 per year after-tax income (a 1.5 percent rate of return) to $500 for a $15 per year after-tax income (a 3 percent rate of return), which is the same after-tax yield as that earned on U.S. bonds. This imposes an unfair capital loss on our marginal investor, who was deriving no personal benefit from the nontaxable status of this state bond in the first place.

One solution to the problem is to forbid the issuance of any new tax-exempt bonds while continuing to honor the tax-exempt status of previously issued state and municipal bonds (until all have matured). An alternative solution, one recently proposed by Congress, is to "bribe" local governments to do the same thing—that is, to offer them a cash subsidy for borrowing with taxable rather than nontaxable bonds just sufficient to offset their borrowing advantage with tax-exempt bonds. This approach would stop the issuance of new tax-exempt bonds and phase out the old ones, as in the first case above, while also preserving the revenue advantages of such bonds to state and local government borrowing. Either solution would be an immense improvement over present treatment.

CAPITAL GAINS

Another important area where the current tax law falls far short of the norms of tax equity and neutrality is in the treatment of capital gains. There is no mean-ingful sense in which a $10,000 capital gain affects one's ability to pay taxes any differently than $10,000 acquired in any other way, yet for tax purposes it is treated quite differently. Income derived from a capital gain (such as from the profit—sale price less purchase price—on the sale of a corporate stock) is taxed at one-half the rate of "regular" income or at the rate of 25 percent, whichever is smaller. If the gain is passed on unrealized at death (for example, if a stock is bequeathed unsold), it escapes income taxation altogether.

It is inequitable for a man with a $10,000 wage income to pay at least twice the tax that his neighbor pays with the same—but capital-gain derived—income. This treatment is clearly non-neutral as well. At present, income in capital-gain form is preferable to the same before-tax income in other forms; therefore, much energy goes into classifying income as a capital gain. Corporations tend to retain more of their earnings than otherwise so that the stockholders will receive the profits as an appreciation in the price of the stock—as a capital gain—rather than as a more heavily taxed dividend. This confers a bigger tax saving on high-income people than on low-income people. Collapsible corporations were once a popular way of converting regular income into a capital gain. This technique was popular in Hollywood for lowering taxes on movie profits.

The 25 percent maximum capital gains rate once meant that all taxpayers above the 50 percent tax bracket got a bigger break than the rest. The Tax Reform Act of 1969 removed the 25 percent ceiling on capital gains in excess of $50,000, taxing such capital gains at one-half regular income rates (taxing only half of capital gains income). This was certainly a laudable step in the right direction, but a very modest one indeed. Capital gains should be treated and taxed in full, like any other source of income. The hardship that progressive rates might impose on those realizing capital gains at uneven intervals is better handled by income-averaging provisions.

In any broader tax reform drive, this proposal should be considered in conjunction with the abolition

of the corporate income tax. This tax is at the root of all kinds of inefficient and tax-evasive corporate behavior. It is inequitable as well, leading to double taxation of corporate income, once at a 48 percent rate before distribution and again at the rate applying to the individual stockholder on the remaining 52 percent if distributed. This represents a progressive rate structure of 48–85 percent on this source of income rather than the usual 14–70 percent on other sources of income. The corporate tax could be eliminated with only a negligible loss of revenue and with a substantial gain in equity and neutrality by attributing corporate income to the appropriate individual stockholders and taxing it.

OIL DEPLETION

The treatment of the depletion of mineral reserves (particularly oil) has surely aroused as much emotional reaction on both sides as any tax provision that might be named. Yet the results of applying our standards of equity and neutrality are quite clear. However, the issue has been so long and hotly debated that a careful though cryptic examination is surely needed.

Both corporation and personal income taxes are levied against net income, that is, all costs of producing the income are subtracted from revenue or gross income before arriving at the tax base. This is straightforward except in the treatment of capital such as durable machinery and equipment. Investment in a machine is not a current cost of producing current income, because the machine is only partially used up in the current tax year. It is appropriate to add to current costs only that part of the machine that is actually used up in production: an amount equal to the fall in the value of the investment. This is what we attempt to approximate with depreciation. Thus if the machine is expected to last for ten years we might write off (expense) a tenth of its cost each year.

In the case of oil wells the problem is particularly tricky. The investment, or capital, is the well itself. The *cost* of producing that investment consists of all of the exploration costs leading to its discovery (such as the dry holes) plus development costs at the well needed to turn it into a producing asset. The *value* of this investment (the price for which the producing well could be sold or the capitalized value of the net revenue it is expected to produce), which is what *should* be depreciated, may be greater than, equal to, or less than the cost of producing it. It follows that cost depletion (depreciating the cost of producing the well) does not generally give rise to a correct measure of the actual depreciation of the investment's value. It was in part for this reason that the rough-and-ready alternative of percentage depletion was offered. Percentage depletion allows firms (or individual owners) to deduct 22 percent of the well's gross revenue as a depletion allowance regardless of the amount invested.

For the purchaser of a producing well, percentage depletion usually entails little or no advantage over cost depletion; and as firms may choose which type to use, one method is chosen about as often as the other. Cost depletion in this case *is* based on the true economic value of the investment (the purchase price of the well) and affords no special advantage over normal depreciation of capital in other industries.

The real tax breaks accrue to the discoverer of a productive well, whether he chooses to sell out or operate it himself. If he sells he benefits in two ways. First, the excess of the sale price over the investment cost, called the cost basis, is by definition a capital gain and hence is taxed at the preferential 25 percent rate. Second, the cost basis greatly understates the true investment cost by allowing expensing (immediate deduction of costs against other income) of all exploration costs leading to the discovery and much of the cost of developing the successful well itself. These costs should be treated as part of the cost of the investment (and hence be included in the cost basis used in calculating capital gains) and be depreciated over its lifetime. A hypothetical example may clarify this.

If four unsuccessful wells (dry holes) must be sunk in order to find a successful one, and each well costs $200,000 to drill and $100,000 to bring to a productive state if oil is actually discovered, then the investment in a productive well will be $1,100,000. But $1,000,000 of this can be immediately deducted from other taxable income (that is, expensed, the other $100,000 of development costs becoming the cost basis of the well rather than the full $1,100,000) for a tax savings of $700,000 if we take as our imagined investor a person in the top—70 percent—tax bracket. If the well is then sold for $600,000, the capital gain will be $500,000 (the sale price of $600,000 less the nonexpensible development cost basis of $100,000), which carries a 25 percent capital gains tax liability of $125,000. Our investor will be out $525,000 ($1,000,000 drilling costs, less $700,000 tax refund, plus $100,000 development costs, plus $125,000 capital gains tax on sale of well) but will take in

$600,000 from the sale. This is a profit of $75,000. The economy, however, will have expended $1,100,000 worth of its resources in an investment it valued at only $600,000, which is clearly wasteful. These advantages do not even involve percentage depletion.

If our discoverer decides to hold onto the well and operate it himself, he receives preferential treatment by being allowed to use the 22 percent depletion allowance and to expense the exploration costs as well. This is equivalent to depreciating the investment at least twice. Professor Arnold Harberger of the University of Chicago has estimated the implied subsidy of this tax treatment of the petroleum industry (when the depletion allowance was still 27.5 percent) to be about 35 percent on average for the second example (holding onto the well) and about 50 percent for the first example (selling the well). This compares with a 5 percent subsidy in 1926, when these provisions were first enacted. The difference is due to the much lower personal and corporate income tax rates at that time.

As the petroleum industry is quick to point out, the industry, for all this, does not enjoy exorbitant profits. They are, in fact, quite normal; and it would be quite surprising if they were otherwise. The profit potential of our tax laws has long since attracted enough additional exploration to beat oil's after-tax rate of return down to the average. This, in fact, is the great tragedy of the percentage depletion allowance: it has caused a large and wasteful overinvestment in oil exploration, that is, more than the economy would find profitable in the absence of the special tax treatment. Another way of stating Harberger's findings is "that in order to obtain an equivalent income stream, between 1.36 and 1.95 times as many resources will typically be used in oil exploration by producing companies as in ordinary business investment."

It is sometimes argued that it is in the interest of national defense to subsidize the oil industry. By providing tax inducements for exploration we will make available more domestic oil reserves, so essential for waging modern warfare. This requires two replies: If this argument has merit it would be preferable to make this subsidy openly, as a government disbursement, rather than hide it as an inequitable tax loophole. In that way the sum could be annually reviewed by the Congress and the taxpayers. As Joseph Pechman reported in 1966, "Studies made over the years by the Treasury Department indicate that the annual depletion deductions for oil and gas average out to more than ten times the deduction computed on the basis of the original investment (after allowance for depreciation). . . . The tax benefits of those special provisions are now in excess of $1.5 billion per year."

The defense argument, however, is surely *not* sound. The subsidy will stimulate extra exploration (this is part of the overinvestment waste referred to above), and this will make known more oil reserves than would have been the case. However, in conjunction with totally unwarranted and unreasoned restrictions on the use of foreign oil, the subsidy also stimulates more rapid exhaustion of these reserves, so that unless the national emergency hurries, we will find ourselves with diminished domestic oil reserves. That time may well be upon us.

Although the inequity and non-neutrality of these tax concessions—(*a*) expensing of the investment costs; (*b*) preferential capital gains treatment; and (*c*) depreciating more than original investment value—have been established, it does not follow that Congress should abolish them. Oil companies make the going rate of return on their investments. Suddenly to remove the promised tax subsidy upon which the investment was based would unfairly impose losses on the industry. The problem is the same as with tax-exempt bonds, and so is the solution: deny the subsidy to all future wells while maintaining it for all existing wells for as long as they last.

TAX-EXEMPT FOUNDATIONS

The tax treatment of tax-exempt foundations is another area of considerable controversy. Tax exemption is nothing more than an administratively, and more important, a politically, convenient way to con-fer a government subsidy. A taxpayer in the 50 percent bracket who gives $1,000 to his church realizes that he has actually given up only $500, because deducting $1,000 from his taxable income saves him $500 in taxes. Uncle Sam kicks in the other $500 in lost tax revenue, which must be raised elsewhere. The question then arises: Should foundations, with their multimillion-dollar spending power, enjoy the government subsidies bestowed by their tax exemption? The answer should depend on whether it is foundations per se that we desire social policy to encourage, or the desirable things some foundations do or support. Some critics have argued that much foundation money is spent foolishly or dangerously. The objection here is hopefully not that some foundations spend their money in ways we disapprove of, but that they do so with tax-exempt funds that result in higher taxes for the rest of us. If there are activities that we desire to encourage with government subsidies (charity, research, the arts, etc.), then we can do so more directly than by subsidizing foundations that may or may not spend their money as we wish.

It would be preferable, in my opinion, to enact an equitable tax treatment of foundations without restrictions on how they spend their money. After all, it is not the existence of great wealth or the ways it might be spent that we should object to; it is the fact that it is often gained and maintained with the aid of preferential tax treatment not available to all.

The principles of taxation that have been sketched here will be better understood if we outline some general approaches to foundation tax treatment consistent with them. To do so it is necessary to include some discussion of gift and estate taxation.

It is my position that a man's total income, regardless of sources, should be taxed at the same rate as an equal income of another man in the same general situation. Once this has been achieved, what a person then does with his after-tax income is surely his own affair. It should make no difference if he buys a $4,000 car, $4,000 worth of gratitude from his church, a $4,000 education for his son, or gives $4,000 in cash to his son or to the Socialist Party.

This should be true whether his income is disposed of directly or by the administrator of his estate. There is no place here, in other words, for gift or estate taxation. The more equitable and neutral tax treatment is to include the above $4,000 consistently in the income of whoever receives it (the car salesman, the church, the son's school or the son) and to tax it there. If we choose to subsidize churches or schools, their incomes could be made tax exempt. Exemplifying this very important principle further, it surely seems "fairer" to levy a heavier tax on a man's million-dollar estate when bequeathed to his already rich brother than when divided equally among 100,000 poor families. This is so, not because the one or the other seems a "better" thing to do but because the wealthy brother has greater ability to pay than the 100,000 poor families combined. There should be no tax on estates (they were already taxed when earned) but on inheritances or gifts, which should be taxed as a part of the income of the receiver.

A foundation is often little more than an estate in trust and as such should not be taxed itself; rather, the benefits it bestows should be counted as a part of the income of its recipients and taxed there. In this sense the foundation is much like the corporation, whose income should also be attributed to its owners and taxed there. The foundation, unfortunately, presents more formidable administrative difficulties than the corporation. The major one arises when a foundation or trust exists for the personal benefit of particular individuals, say one's children. A million-dollar estate divided between two children will increase the taxable income of each (ignoring the legitimately deducted expenses incurred in acquiring the money, such as in administering the will) by half a million dollars. If instead the estate goes into a foundation which earns an income which is divided between the two children, their taxable income should nonetheless go up by half a million each plus whatever income the estate subsequently earns. At present they would escape taxes on the million held in trust. This, of course, is the major inducement to the creation of foundations. My example is stretched a bit because

foundations cannot so blatantly exist for personal aggrandizement, but in practice it often comes down to much the same thing. The appropriate course would be to attribute to each child for tax purposes the wealth (as well as its income) from which he receives the income. In the above example that would be easily done by attributing half a million dollars to the rest of each child's taxable income, but in practice it would be more difficult.

I propose the following scheme for consideration. Since it is often difficult to ascertain, and accordingly to tax, the beneficiaries of foundation activities, and since these foundation distributions are often deferred for many years, all foundation income (which would include the initial endowment) should be taxed once at the highest existing personal tax rate (currently 70 percent). Any foundation disbursement to a taxable individual would be "grossed up" and added to that individual's taxable income. The tax already paid by the foundation would then be credited to the individual in question.

An example may help. A foundation is set up with a $100,000 estate. The foundation must then pay a tax of $70,000 (the top personal rate is used to ensure that the foundation is not used by the wealthy for tax avoidance, and, who knows, such a rule may elicit foundation support for lowering the top personal rate). If, for simplicity, it then disburses the entire remaining $30,000 to Mr. Smith, Mr. Smith must "gross up" that $30,000 to $100,000 while simultaneously receiving a tax credit of $70,000. If Mr. Smith previously had a taxable income of $10,000, his taxable income would now be $110,000. At a 60 percent average tax rate his tax liability would be $66,000. He has a tax credit of $70,000 for taxes already paid on his behalf by the foundation, so he receives a refund from the government of $4,000, for a total gift of $34,000.

This seemingly complex procedure simply gives the foundation the job of withholding potential taxes without paying any taxes itself yet taxes all foundation grants to the individual recipient at the tax rate that applies to that individual.

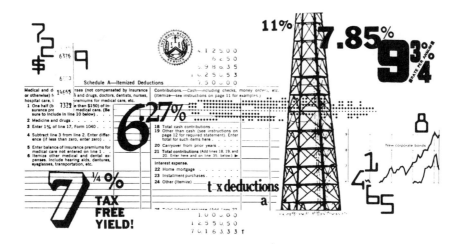

In the event that the foundation gave its $30,000 to an organization which was itself tax exempt (say a church or charity), that organization would receive a full $70,000 tax refund on its $70,000 tax credit, as its tax liability would be zero. Notice that the tax exemption in this scheme is granted to specific groups or activities on the basis of the purposes for which they spend their money rather than to the foundation which distributes the funds to such working organizations. The foundation is not taxed for spending its money any more than the individual, whose estate the foundation represents, would have been.

A third category of disbursement is possible. In addition to taxable individuals and tax-exempt activities there are those not-for-profit operations which neither are tax exempt nor pay taxes. Political parties are in this group—large donations are not deductible. The foundation once again should be treated like an individual. If its $30,000 went to a political party, there would be no accompanying tax credit. In this one instance the foundation would be taxed. It is my belief that such an approach would remove the artificial tax dodge incentive for foundation formation while equitably preserving the just functions of a foundation.

A MAJOR OVERHAUL IS NEEDED

The Tax Reform Act of 1969 was a large patchwork of proposals, occasionally in the right direction and occasionally a bit crude or misdirected. What is really needed, however, is a major and thorough overhaul of the entire tax system along the lines of the impressive Carter Commission proposals for Canada. The Commission recommended, as I have, the adoption of a comprehensive income tax base wherever administratively feasible coupled with the abolition of the corporate income tax and estate and inheritance taxes (by integrating both into the personal income tax base). Pechman estimates that adopting the Carter Commission proposals in the United States would have enabled the government to raise from a personal income tax alone the same tax revenue as was raised from personal and corporate income taxes plus federal estate and inheritance taxes. It could be done, moreover, while reducing the 14–70 percent tax rates to 12–53 percent, with the maximum rate applying to all income over $100,000.

If that does not excite your imagination, consider that the American Bar Association's Special Committee on Substantive Tax Reform, using a substantially

The Principles of Tax Reform   155

broadened but by no means comprehensive income tax base and eliminating the separate corporate income tax, found that the same tax revenue from both corporate and private incomes could be raised by a *flat rate* of 14 percent on personal income alone.

Of course, it is possible to judge each tax and suggested tax reform on the basis of how it affects us personally. Do our tax liabilities go up or down? Such a standard of judgment simply leads to the powerful and influential's achieving their favored loopholes at the tax expense of the rest of us. Until more general standards are adopted and applied, the U.S. income tax will remain in a hopeless mess.

Reading 21

A Primer on Productivity*

By Brian D. Dittenhafer

Summary

One basic economic problem of society, and a primary cause of inflation, is that we try to do more than resources will allow. We want to put a stop to poverty, reduce pollution, increase housing, maintain military defense, and become self-sufficient in energy. We start lofty programs to accomplish these objectives but do not always realize the claims these make on the resources of the economy. Many people do not recognize that the resources available are not limitless but accumulate only gradually. When society's demands on resources grow faster than the resources available, the bidding results in higher prices for goods, or inflation. However, if the volume of goods and services available grows more rapidly, we can raise our demands upon the economy more rapidly. The primary source of growth in resources during the past twenty years has been growth in productivity. This article explains what productivity is all about, and how its growth is related to that of the resources in the economy.

Key Questions to Consider

- What is productivity?

- What factors underlie changes in labor productivity?

- How does real income grow?

----

* Reprinted with permission from *Monthly Review,* Federal Reserve Bank of Atlanta, **LIX,** No. 10 (October 1974), 150–154.

A Primer on Productivity

One basic economic problem of society, and a primary cause of inflation, is that we try to do more than resources will allow. We want to put a stop to poverty, reduce pollution, increase housing, maintain military defense, and become self-sufficient in energy. We start lofty programs to accomplish these objectives but do not always realize the claims these make on the resources of the economy. Many people do not recognize that the resources available are not limitless but accumulate only gradually. When society's demands on resources grow faster than the resources available, the bidding results in higher prices for goods, or inflation. However, if the volume of goods and services available grows more rapidly, we can raise our demands upon the economy more rapidly. The primary source of growth in resources during the past twenty years has been growth in productivity. This article explains what productivity is all about, and how its growth is related to that of the resources in the economy.

WHAT IS PRODUCTIVITY?

To economists, productivity refers to the relationship of output to the labor, materials, and machines (factor inputs) that are used to make the goods and services we consume. The ratio of output to factor inputs is a measure of total factor productivity, or the efficiency with which factor inputs are combined. If we were able to measure exactly how much each factor, such as labor, added to total output, we could calculate the contribution each factor makes to increasing total output. Economists refer to the ratio of total output to a single input as partial factor productivity. Exact measurement of partial factor productivity for the entire economy is impossible, but several economists have estimated the contribution which each factor (and other influences) has made to increasing output. For example, over the years, the amount of capital equipment per worker has increased and this has been a significant source of productivity growth. At the same time, the quality of that capital equipment has improved, and as old machines were removed, more efficient ones took their place. Thus, more machines as well as more efficient ones contributed to productivity growth and helped society produce more goods and services.

According to one estimate,[1] better utilization of men, materials, and machines has caused productivity

---

[1] John W. Kendrick, *Postwar Productivity Trends in the United States, 1948–1969*, National Bureau of Economic Research, New York, 1973, p. 39.

to increase at an average annual rate of 2.3 percent during the postwar period. Estimates such as this are made after detailed and time-consuming study in an attempt to measure the precise contribution of each separate production factor. To obtain more current productivity estimates, a simpler process is used. We simply count the number of man-hours worked and use the total as a substitute, or proxy, for other measures of factor inputs into the economy. Current estimates of total output are also made on a routine basis, so it is relatively easy to estimate labor productivity by forming the ratio of real output to number of man-hours worked. There are technical problems in measuring both the labor input proxy and the total output proxy (see box); but, in general, output per man-hour provides a reasonable estimate of goods produced per hour of labor worked.[2]

WHY DOES LABOR PRODUCTIVITY CHANGE?

The productivity growth rate changes from year to year and even from quarter to quarter. Influences on productivity growth can be classified as either short term (having quick impact on output and productivity) or long term (when more fundamental forces are at work). Short- and long-term forces are at work simultaneously, but the sudden changes in productivity growth rates graphically portrayed in Chart I provide evidence that short-term influences are powerful and can easily overwhelm long-term forces.

SHORT-TERM INFLUENCES

Labor productivity usually declines during a business slowdown and increases during business expansions (see Chart II). In a business slowdown, employment

Charts I and II

Productivity growth rates change quickly, accompanying changes in output,

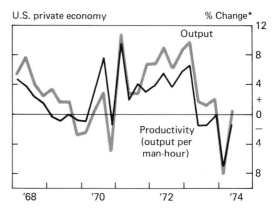

. . . causing a strong cyclical pattern in productivity growth.

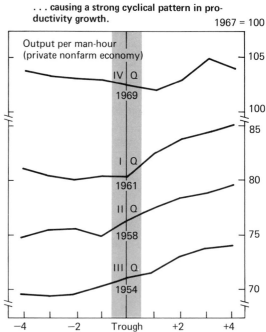

Quarters before and after trough in general business activity

*Change from previous quarter at annual rate.

---

[2] Throughout the rest of this article, unless otherwise stated, the term "productivity" refers to output per man-hour as measured by the U.S. Department of Labor, Bureau of Labor Statistics.

usually declines, but not as much as production. Some workers lose their jobs; but many skilled individuals, who would be difficult or expensive to replace if they were laid off, are retained even when they are not needed for current production. Output declines more than man-hours worked, causing output per man-hour to decline. Partially offsetting this decline is the general tendency of employers to release less efficient workers first and to rehire them last. Therefore, when employment declines, the general quality of the work force increases. Further offsetting the productivity decline during a business downturn is the shortening of the average workweek. Working fewer hours, employees are generally less fatigued and work faster, increasing output per man-hour.

During a business expansion, output grows more rapidly than employment, and man-hours worked are spread over many more units of output. Therefore, as output increases, average productivity also increases. Acting to offset these productivity gains, to some extent, is the hiring of new workers who are relatively inefficient during the training period before they become fully integrated into the work force. Lengthening the work week also increases worker fatigue, reducing productive capacity.

LONG-TERM INFLUENCES

While short-term changes in total productivity over a year or two are generally caused by ups and downs in output and employment, the factors affecting long-term productivity are more basic and occur more slowly. In a general sense, these factors are the amount of equipment that can be used efficiently (capital), the quality of that equipment (technology), the quality of the labor force using that equipment (education and training), and the efficiency with which production factors are combined (resource allocation).

Researchers generally agree that, during the postwar period, more capital has contributed between 20 and 30 percent to growth in total productivity and that improvements in the quality of the labor force, largely the result of education and training, have accounted for another large chunk. Estimates of the contributions of better education and training to total

productivity growth range from 10 to 30 percent. Estimates differ because it is difficult to separate and measure the effects of a larger quantity of a factor input as opposed to a higher quality of that input. For example, it is difficult to isolate the effects of quantity and quality when a growing firm installs one new machine for two of lesser quality. Estimates also vary with the number of sources of economic growth analyzed by the researcher. For example, the greatest contribution to total productivity is generally credited to technology, the result of new discoveries and new techniques for increasing output. However, technology's contribution is usually not measured directly but is estimated as the unexplained growth in production after all other factors are taken into account. Most researchers agree that both improvements in labor force quality and technological advances are dividends on society's investment in education. Increases in research and development expenditures result in inventions of new techniques and more efficient ways of production. (Chart III shows how one prominent researcher has determined the major sources of long-term total productivity gains.)

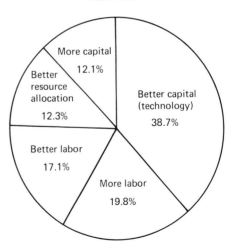

Chart III
Determinants of Productivity Growth, 1929-1969

More capital 12.1%

Better resource allocation 12.3%

Better capital (technology) 38.7%

Better labor 17.1%

More labor 19.8%

Source: Edward Denison, *Accounting for U.S. Economic Growth*, 1927-1969, 1974, Brookings Institution, Table 8.3.

Box   # Some Measurement Problems

On a practical level, the measurement of output per man-hour is more complicated than simply dividing the total of real output by the number of man-hours worked. Only two of the many problems of measuring productivity change are mentioned, but they serve to illustrate the nature of others which exist in measurement of productivity.

The U.S. Department of Labor, Bureau of Labor Statistics (BLS), collects and compiles the output per man-hour data for the national economy. In these measures, output per man-hour is the ratio of the real value of goods and services produced to man-hours of all persons employed, including proprietors and unpaid family workers. The BLS uses man-hours paid rather than man-hours worked as the measure of labor input. The differences between the two concepts is small, but probably widening because of the trend toward more paid vacations, sick leave, and holidays.

Another problem is encountered in calculating output. The measure of output used is the real Gross National Product (GNP) originating in the private economy. Economists identify useful output by observing what people are willing to buy. Accordingly, real GNP is the final market value of goods and services produced in the economy expressed in dollars of constant purchasing power. The market criterion introduces a fundamental bias into productivity calculations, because market price does not measure nonmarket benefits which contribute to society's well-being. A vivid example is available in pollution-control equipment expenditures. These do not result in greater output of marketable goods and, therefore, do not improve productivity. In fact, since they probably lower capital available for directly productive machines, pollution-control expenditures probably lower the long-run output and productivity growth rates. But few would deny that spending for pollution control contributes to real income by improving the quality of life.

Still another factor responsible for productivity growth has been the reduction in hours worked in low efficiency sectors and the increase in hours worked in high efficiency sectors. In the U.S. economy, this effect has been most noticeable in the shift of labor out of farming. The actual amount of output per man-hour is lower in agriculture than it is outside farming, although the growth rate in productivity has been faster on the farm.

MAKING THE PIE BIGGER

Is productivity growth the only thing which increases the total amount of goods and services available in the economy? The answer is "no"; there are several other factors at work generating growth in total output and thus increasing the output pie. For example, variations in the length of the workweek and changes in the proportion of people of working age who are employed can alter total output without affecting output per man-hour. However, increases in productivity have been the largest factor contributing to growth in total output of goods and services. In fact, productivity growth is a prime determinant of the economy's potential output.

WHAT IS "POTENTIAL" OUTPUT?

Potential output is the total of goods and services which could be produced if labor and other resources of the economy were "fully utilized." By fully utilized, we mean the amount of capacity utilization that one could expect to accompany reasonable price stability. To judge future growth in potential output, the President's Council of Economic Advisors made a calculation based on past growth in hours worked and in output per man-hour. The Council currently estimates potential output to be growing at 4 percent annually.[3] This is derived from combining the estimated labor force growth rate of 1.8 percent per year with a 0.3-percent decline in average annual work hours and a 2.5-percent increase in output per man-hour (1.8 − 0.3 + 2.5 = 4.0). Productivity growth is extremely important, then, in increasing potential output and the income pie. Obviously, this is a rather crude calculation, and the results must be used with caution. However, estimating growth in potential output in this way gives a rough idea of how fast total output is growing and serves as a guide to policy. For example, we would expect that if combined government and private demands on the economy were growing at a rate above 4 percent for a sustained period, there would be upward pressures on prices. That is the kind of price increase economists call demand-pull inflation, because it results from society's attempt to use more resources than are actually available.

HOW ARE LABOR PRODUCTIVITY AND PAY RELATED?

Workers know what they get paid per hour or year, and their employers must value labor input in much the same manner. In a competitive economy, no one is hired unless the amount earned from the sale of his output exceeds the wage paid to him.[4] The money

obtained by selling the individual's output ultimately determines his wage. Thus, there should be a direct link between output per man-hour and wages and salaries.

WHY DOES REAL INCOME GROW?

Workers have shared in the benefits of the nation's steadily increasing productivity. Chart IV shows that real income (that is, compensation adjusted for rising prices) has gone up almost steadily and that compensation closely parallels the growth of output per man-hour. This long history of nearly parallel growth in productivity and compensation is no accident. Produc-

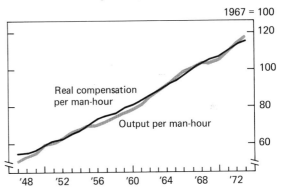

Charts IV and V

Real income grows as productivity grows,

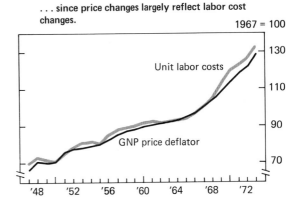

... since price changes largely reflect labor cost changes.

---

[3] "The United States Economy in 1985," *Monthly Labor Review*, Bureau of Labor Statistics, December 1973. Since 1962 when the original estimates were made, the rate of growth in output potential has changed, but the system of estimating it has not. From 1962 through 1965, output potential was estimated by the Council to be growing at a rate of 3.75 percent per year. From the fourth quarter of 1965 to the fourth quarter of 1969, it was estimated to be growing at a rate of 4 percent per year; and from 1969 through 1973, the estimate was a 4.3-percent annual rate of growth.

[4] The use of capital goods is also based on a time concept, and no capital good will be employed unless its expected rate of return exceeds its cost per unit of time. Of course, in marginal productivity theory, any factor input will be employed until the cost of employing it and the revenue derived from employing it are equal.

tivity increases allow more goods to be produced, making possible gains in real income. This increase can occur directly through wage increases or indirectly through governmental programs.

Wage and salary increases larger than productivity gains have resulted in higher prices (see Chart V). Notice how closely prices, measured by the GNP price deflator, follow the trend of unit labor costs. This relationship is not surprising because unit labor costs are calculated by dividing average hourly compensation by output per man-hour. Unit labor costs increase whenever compensation rises faster than productivity. Labor costs are the largest portion of production costs. Therefore, when unit labor costs rise and all else remains unchanged, the price of whatever is produced also rises. This puts upward pressure on the general price level, and the inevitable result is cost-push inflation.[5] For employees who have received pay increases, the impact of higher prices is cushioned by the rise in pay; they may even gain in real income. However, for those who did not gain an increase, the rise in prices causes a decline in real income because their money buys fewer goods and services.

Real income of employees and society in general can increase even if their actual pay does not. There are periods when unit labor costs fall because productivity rises faster than compensation. When this happens, employers have the opportunity to charge lower prices for their products or to raise profits. Thus, in a perfectly competitive economy, productivity gains would be widely shared among many different segments of society. Productivity gains would lower costs, and competition would force goods to be sold at a price equaling the cost of production.

In reality, however, not all wages and prices are set in a competitive market. Many workers and em-

ployers have a degree of monopoly power in their markets, and the gains from productivity are not usually distributed by lowering prices. Instead, workers usually try to increase their wages to the full extent of productivity gains. If they get the better of the bargain, the result usually shows up in higher costs, which employers—if they have enough market power —can recover by raising prices. If workers get the worst of the bargain, productivity gains show up mostly in profits. However, all members of society could benefit if labor and management acted as they would in a perfectly competitive economy and used productivity gains to lower prices rather than raise wages or profits. If all employers and workers did this, prices would fall and, barring other changes, everyone would be able to buy more with the same amount of money. Then even persons on fixed pensions could obtain direct benefits from the education and research to which they had contributed during their working years. Distributing productivity gains in this manner seems more equitable than the current situation, where groups with the greatest economic and political strength make economic gains relative to the rest of the population.

CONCLUSION

Increased efficiency in the use of resources is the ultimate source of increased output per person and the major source of growth in the economy. The most important resource in our economy is labor, and increases in the quality of labor have been an important source of increased output per man-hour worked. But whatever the source of growth in the future, the only path to increased real income and higher living standards for everyone is clearly through increased productivity. A more productive economy allows society to divide a larger pie rather than have different sectors attempting to gain larger slices of the same pie and see the supposed gains vanish in inflation.

---

[5] There are other sources of cost-push inflation, but wages are the source of increases in costs most people think of first. In fact, cost-push inflation can be caused by an increase in the price of any factor used in production.

On Economic Growth*

By Sheldon W. Stahl

Summary

It is noteworthy that throughout much of the world one can perceive a growing sense of concern about the future and what it portends for the world community. In particular, there appears to be an increasing skepticism about the future and the inevitability of worldwide material progress. This shift in attitude from an almost ritualistic optimism on the part of the more well-off countries signifies an erosion in confidence in our ability to shape the future.

To be sure, the notion of some ultimate limit to economic growth should not be viewed as wholly startling in an environment of finite resources and infinite wants. However, with publication of *The Limits To Growth* in 1972—a product of the Club of Rome's Project on the Predicament of Mankind—the issue of the sustainability of growth moved to the foreground of public debate and discussion.

The limits to economic growth are capable of being extended by an intelligent adaptive response by society. Even though growing scarcity of resources and limits on the assimilative capacity of the environment are limiting factors, it should be recognized that a wise stewardship of this planet can extend and expand our habitation on it for many years to come.

Key Questions to Consider

■ What did the Club of Rome conclude in *The Limits To Growth*?

■ What is "exponential growth"?

■ What factors might prevent the collapse suggested in *The Limits To Growth*?

■ What role does economic growth play in an economy?

---

* Reprinted with permission from *Monthly Review*, Federal Reserve Bank of Kansas City, February 1975, pp. 3–9.

On Economic Growth

It is, perhaps, understandable to initially view pressures or problems confronting society from a rather narrow perspective in terms of space and time. Thus, concern is manifested first at the individual level, moving on to higher levels such as the family and community, until ultimately the concern may become global. Similarly, in terms of time, concern over the future typically is subordinated to concern over the present. Thus, it is noteworthy that throughout much of the world, one can perceive a growing sense of concern about the future and what it portends for the world community. In particular, there appears to be an increasing skepticism about the future and the inevitability of worldwide material progress. This shift in attitude from an almost ritualistic optimism on the part of the more well-off countries signifies an erosion in confidence in our ability to shape the future. Leonard Silk, a contemporary commentator on the economic scene, has observed:

The soaring prices of oil and other world commodities, the shortage of food, the heightened tension between the developed and developing countries, the new disease of stagflation—are all these manifestations of a transient crisis or something far deeper and more enduring: the approaching end of the world's explosive population and economic growth?

That is emerging as the basic issue beneath the day-to-day politics and economics of all nations. The world's cardinal objective appears to be shifting from growth to survival.[1]

It is undoubtedly difficult to make such a sweeping assessment and have it apply equally to all of the nations. Certainly, those member states of the Organization of Petroleum Exporting Countries view the future with a decidedly different perspective than do the very poor and energy-deficient developing countries of the Third World. Similarly, although future growth prospects among the industrialized countries are not expected to mirror the achievements of much of the postwar period, it is probably not true that these same nations have come to question their very capacity to survive. Nonetheless, the high degree of complacency about the future exhibited by so many clearly has been jolted by those events to which Leonard Silk has alluded.

To be sure, the notion of some ultimate limit to economic growth should not be viewed as wholly startling in an environment of finite resources and infinite wants. However, with publication of *The Lim-*

---

[1] Leonard Silk, "From Growth to Survival," *New York Times*, November 19, 1974, p. c43.

its *To Growth* in 1972—a product of the Club of Rome's Project on the Predicament of Mankind—the issue of the sustainability of growth moved to the foreground of public debate and discussion. That study, which utilized a computer model of the world, generated the following as one of its conclusions:

If the present growth trends in world population, industrialization, pollution, food production, and resource depletion continue unchanged, the limits to growth on this planet will be reached sometime within the next one hundred years. The most probable result will be a rather sudden and uncontrollable decline in both population and industrial capacity.[2]

This apocalyptic vision of the future contributed to an expanded debate about economic growth—a debate which continues. Although much of the discussion has been addressed to the matter of whether continued economic growth is possible, an increased awareness of certain disamenities which often accompany growth has prompted concern over the necessity or desirability of growth itself. These matters will be explored in the following analysis.

IS GROWTH POSSIBLE?

An important prerequisite to assessing the rather grim conclusion of *The Limits To Growth* is to understand the nature of exponential growth. Exponential growth is characterized by increases which are a constant *percentage* of the whole in a constant time period. Compound interest is a readily familiar illustration of exponential growth. If a sum of money, for example, $1,000, is invested at 7 percent per annum compound interest, at the end of the first year it will cumulate to $1,070. Since the interest for the second year is a percentage of the accumulated amount, the 7 percent return for the second year will exceed that of the first. And in each succeeding year, that same

7 percent rate of return will add successively larger dollar amounts to the total, so that in approximately 10 years, the original sum of $1,000 will have grown to $2,000, or twice the initial investment. At simple interest, or growing linearly, the same 7 percent annual rate of return would require more than 14 years to double the original sum.

Thus, one of the more interesting and significant attributes of exponential growth as compared with linear growth is the relative quickness with which large sums are generated.[3] In fact, the concept of "doubling time"—the time it takes a growing quantity to double in size—is frequently alluded to in discussions of exponential growth. In this regard, it is useful to remember a simple mathematical relationship; the doubling time for any entity is roughly equal to 70 divided by the growth rate. For example, if the rate of growth in world population is assumed to be roughly constant at 2 to 2½ percent per year, then within 30 to 35 years the world population will double. This is a sobering prospect in light of widespread famine and privation affecting many of the world's present inhabitants.

It should be clear that exponential growth, if unchecked, has an explosive quality. It is this quality, particularly as it relates to population and industrial growth, which colors the conclusion of the Club of Rome study. The example of compound interest growth involves a simple and readily predictable system. In a complex system such as that inherent in a

---

[2] D. H. Meadows, et. al., *The Limits To Growth* (New York: Universe Books, 1972), p. 23.

[3] In *The Limits To Growth*, that point is well illustrated by reference to an ancient Persian legend about a clever courtier who gave his king a beautiful chessboard. He asked, in return, that the king give him 1 grain of rice for the first square, 2 grains for the second, 4 grains for the third square, and so forth. In other words, the amount of rice would be doubled with each square right up to the 64th square on the board. The king agreed to the request and ordered rice to be brought from his stores. The fourth square required 8 grains; the tenth took 512 grains; the fifteenth took 16,384; the twenty-first square took more than 1 million grains of rice. By the fortieth square, more than 1 *trillion* grains of rice had to be given the courtier. Long before the sixty-fourth square was reached the king's entire supply of rice was exhausted.

world model with many different quantities that are interrelated, highly dynamic, and growing at different rates, predicting the behavior of the system is much more difficult. Indeed, it is more important to recognize the inherent limitations of the model itself. For the major purpose in constructing the world model, according to the authors of *The Limits To Growth*, was to determine broad behavior modes of the world system—or tendencies of variables within the system to change over time. The authors stress that none of the computer outputs generated is a "prediction," because the model is not extremely detailed or as precise or comprehensive as would be required to generate meaningful predictions. For example, the model considers only one general population which statistically reflects the average characteristics of the world population. In addition, only one generalized resource representing the combined reserves of all nonrenewable resources is plotted on the assumption that each separate resource follows the general pattern, but at its own specific level and rate. The purpose and limitations of such aggregation are explained as follows:

This high level of aggregation is necessary at this point to keep the model understandable. At the same time it limits the information we can expect to gain from the model. Questions of detail cannot be answered because the model simply does not yet contain much detail. National boundaries are not recognized. Distribution inequalities of food, resources, and capital are included implicitly in the data but they are not calculated explicitly nor graphed in the output. World trade balances, migration patterns, climactic determinants, and political processes are not specifically treated.[4]

In assessing behavior modes within a world system, the authors of *The Limits To Growth* conclude that exponential growth of population and capital, followed by collapse, is the basic behavior mode of the world system. However, it is again necessary to note that this represents a statement about the tendencies of certain variables to change over time under certain assumptions. And here, it is important to be aware of the reservations which the authors themselves hold:

. . . We would not expect the real world to behave like the world model in any of the graphs we have shown, especially in the collapse modes. The model contains dynamic statements about only the physical aspects of man's activities. It assumes that social variables—income distribution, attitudes about family size, choices among goods, services, and food—will continue to follow the same patterns they have followed throughout the world in recent history . . .[5]

The shallowness of this latter assumption was clearly acknowledged by the authors in addressing the question of whether the future of the world system was bound to be growth, followed by collapse into a dismal, depleted existence. Such a conclusion would be warranted, they note:

. . . Only if we make the initial assumption that our present way of doing things will not change.

But, they add:

We have ample evidence of mankind's ingenuity and social flexibility. There are, of course, many likely changes in the system, some of which are already taking place.[6]

What are some of the more meaningful changes that are occurring to obviate the notion of world collapse?

If population growth is assumed to proceed exponentially in the future, as in the past, the inexorable pressures of such population growth on the raw materials base, the food supply, and on the carrying capacity of the environment posit eventual collapse of the system. However, there is substantial empirical evidence which demonstrates that with rising affluence, population growth declines. For example, recent data for the United States suggest movement toward a stationary population. Evidence indicates that pres-

---

[4] D. H. Meadows, et. al., pp. 93–94.

[5] *Ibid*, p. 142.
[6] *Ibid*, pp. 127–28.

ent fertility patterns, if continued, will cause the U.S. population to stabilize sometime during the next century. Similarly, in Eastern Europe including Russia and the Ukraine, as well as in northern Italy, the Scandinavian countries, and Japan, the birth rate has come down rapidly during the past three decades or so. And, Tinbergen has noted that in some East Asian countries, birth rates are already declining even though annual per capita income is no more than $300. Since many observers have thought that $1,000 was a sort of per capita annual income threshold to generate a decline in the birth rate, Tinbergen is more optimistic regarding future population trends.[7]

Similarly, technological change or growth helps to forestall or negate the collapse mode generated by the model run. Over the last century in the United States, there is evidence that output per unit of input —technology—has been rising at about an average of 2 percent per year. Additional information for shorter periods of time for Japan and some European countries also shows continued positive growth in technology. Even if one acknowledges that technology is a mixed blessing, technological growth and the increased productivity it engenders are positive elements serving to counter any eventual collapse.

Perhaps one of the most obvious areas of existing flexibility and change involves an adjustment mechanism, particularly with regard to resource depletion. For as certain resources grow increasingly scarce, their values will rise correspondingly and be reflected in higher prices. This may be expected to lead competing producers to seek substitutes that are more readily available and cheaper, or to seek better technology for increasing the efficient utilization of resources. In the absence of such substitutes for the resource in question, the prices of those goods which require that resource will rise relative to the prices of those goods requiring less or none of that particular raw material, and consumers may be expected to shift their purchases away from such goods toward less resource-intensive alternatives. Such effects can be brought about through adjustment mechanisms which not only generate adaptive rather than mechanistic behavior, but which also automatically increase productivity. Reduction in resource requirements per unit of Gross National Product (GNP) is a phenomenon which has been observed over time both in the United States as well as in Western Europe. For, according to Kaysen:

. . . It is not in general true that the share of minerals in the national output or the share of food in the national output, agricultural production, has been rising. Rather it has been falling over the long period. . . . If the MIT thesis were correct, we would expect to see a rising relative share of output in minerals and more resources needed to supply these scarcer and scarcer minerals. We see the opposite, a general decline in the share of output.[8]

And, work by Nordhaus on the limitations to growth posed by a resource constraint leads the author to state that:

The clear evidence is that the future will not be limited by sheer availability of important materials; rather, any drag on economic growth will arise from increases in costs.[9]

One need not agree wholeheartedly with Nordhaus' observation to at least appreciate the fact that adjustments to possible resource depletion are continually being made, and, in the process, the limits to growth may be substantially extended.

Finally, one must reexamine the role of environmental pollution in the scenario described in *The Limits To Growth*. Environmental pollution is viewed as an inescapable concomitant of industrial or economic growth. However, with growth in pollution has also come a growing concern over the environment, and

[7] Jan Tinbergen in *On Growth: The Crisis of Exploding Population and Resource Depletion*, ed. by William L. Oltmans (New York: Capricorn Books, 1974), pp. 16–17.

[8] Carl Kaysen in *On Growth: The Crisis of Exploding Population and Resource Depletion*, p. 68.

[9] William D. Nordhaus, "Resources as a Constraint on Growth," *American Economic Review*, Papers and Proceeding, Vol. 64, No. 2, May 1974, p. 23.

an increased recognition that excessive pollution does not necessarily have to be a by-product of economic growth. If one recognizes those factors which have allowed pollution to increase, it is not at all clear that there is some fixed or immutable limit on the extent to which it may be reduced short of critical levels.

To a very significant degree, excessive pollution occurs because of the absence of any clear-cut property rights to the environment. Because the environment—or more specifically, its assimilative capacity—is owned by all of us in common, this valuable resource had gone unpriced, and had been generally regarded as a free good. Thus, the dumping of wastes into the environment carried no explicit monetary costs for the polluters and their economic activities were priced at less than full cost. But growing concern over environmental pollution has initiated action by society to remedy the problem. Such devices as direct controls regulating the discharge of wastes into the environment are being used with growing frequency. In addition, there are many examples of internalizing or including pollution abatement costs in the cost of production. In these instances, pollution-intensive goods are made more expensive and consumption of them is thereby reduced, and pollution-intensive methods of production are made more costly as well, providing incentives to producers to seek methods of pollution abatement.

Thus, adjustment mechanisms are at work for reducing environmental pollution. To those who would argue that the cost of a healthy environment is prohibitive, Solow suggests:

. . . The annual cost that would be necessary to meet decent pollution-abatement standards by the end of the century is large, but not staggering. One estimate says that in 1970 we spent about $8.5 billion (in 1967 prices), or about 1 percent of GNP, for pollution abatement. An active pollution-abatement policy would cost perhaps $50 billion a year by 2000, which would be about 2 percent of GNP by then. That is a small investment of resources: you can see how small it is when you consider that GNP grows by 4 percent or so every year, on the average. Cleaning up air and water would entail a cost that would be a bit

like losing one-half of one year's growth between now and the year 2000. What stands between us and a decent environment is not the curse of industrialization, not an unbearable burden of cost, but just the need to organize ourselves consciously to do some simple and knowable things. Compared with the possibility of an active abatement policy, the policy of stopping economic growth in order to stop pollution would be incredibly inefficient.[10]

Thus, as the authors themselves suggest, the inevitability of world collapse as seen in *The Limits To Growth* is clearly not a foregone conclusion when one recognizes the model's limitations and some of its more questionable assumptions which underlie the model runs and which generate its results.[11]

IS GROWTH NECESSARY?

In order to maintain an economy reasonably close to full employment, given the historical rate of increase in labor productivity and in labor force growth, the U.S. economy must expand at a rate of between 4 and 5 percent in real terms each year. For this relationship between the rate of economic growth and unemployment to change, either labor force growth or produc-

---

[10] Robert M. Solow, "Is the end of the world at hand?", in *The Economic Growth Controversy,* ed. by Weintraub, Schwartz, and Aronson (New York: International Arts and Sciences Press, Inc., 1973), p. 60.

[11] Recently, the Club of Rome published a second report dealing with the kinds of considerations originally broached in *The Limits To Growth.* Entitled "Mankind at the Turning Point," its authors are Mihajlo Mesarovic, director of Case Western Reserve University's Systems Research Center, in Cleveland, Ohio; and Eduard Pestel, head of Germany's Institute of Mechanics at the Technical University of Hannover. Unlike the earlier highly aggregated world model, their model treats the world as 10 interdependent regions but with their own peculiar social, economic, and geophysical characteristics. Rather than supporting a no-growth philosophy as in the earlier case, the new model promotes the notion of selective growth, with less industrialization in the more affluent countries serving to counterbalance more growth in the poorer nations.

tivity growth rates or both would have to change. If, as noted earlier, zero population growth or a more gradual approach to a steady-state population is achieved in the United States, the rate of economic growth necessary to maintain full employment would decline. Ultimately, with a stable population and new entrants into the labor force equaling those retiring from the labor force, economic growth would only be required to match the rate of gain in labor productivity. If, in addition, current trends toward increased growth in the services sector relative to the goods-producing sector continue, given the generally accepted hypothesis of relatively low productivity growth in that sector, the long-term trend rate of increase in labor productivity may decline, thereby reducing further the rate of annual economic growth consistent with full employment. However, it should be pointed out that even though these trends are evident, it will be some time before they can appreciably reduce the rate of economic growth needed to sustain full employment.

Because the pressure for full employment is one of the most fundamental and persistent pressures throughout the world, any economic policy which leads to unemployment tends to be politically unacceptable. However, those who view growth as undesirable frequently suggest an alternative route to full employment that would obviate the need for economic growth: spreading employment by reducing the number of man-hours worked per year through the use of shorter workweeks, or the like. With a large enough reduction in the average time worked per year, growth in productivity on a per worker year basis would cease as would the growth requirement to sustain full employment. Although such a scheme may have superficial appeal, it lacks economic merit for it promotes deliberate economic inefficiency in order to limit the growth of GNP without adversely affecting employment. In a world plagued by inflation, such a program would be inimical to any long-run solution of that problem. Furthermore, the world is characterized by growing economic interdependency and diminished self-sufficiency, particularly

with respect to material inputs. In such an environment, nations must be capable of earning foreign exchange in order to survive. The present oil situation is starkly illustrative of this point. The ability to compete internationally requires increasing, not decreasing, labor productivity. And, at the same time, the requirements of domestic full employment call for growth rather than its impairment. If these problems plague the more sophisticated and rich industrial nations, they are compounded for the poorer, densely populated, less-developed nations. For the foreseeable future then, economic growth will remain a necessary prerequisite for employment growth.

In addition to employment considerations, economic growth has an important bearing on income distribution. For it is clear that within our own society as well as in others, substantial inequality in the distribution of income has been tolerated largely because of the opportunities for upward mobility afforded by economic growth. Growth has significantly raised the level of income of virtually all classes, including the poorest in this nation. However, a substantial number of poor remain. If, in the future, the reduction of this residual poverty depends more on redistributive efforts—slicing the income pie differently—than as a result of growth *per se*, such efforts are more likely to take place when the total to be shared—the size of the pie—is growing than when it is fixed. And even where the distribution of income proves to be resistant to significant change over time, a given relative distribution will be more attractive if the absolute standard of living at the bottom is being raised through growth, than if the absolute standard remains low or is being reduced. Thus, even if growth cannot guarantee a more equitable distribution of income, the inequities are made somewhat more tolerable.

If one looks at the distribution of income between the developed countries of the world and the underdeveloped nations, the role of economic growth in uplifting them becomes even more apparent. Throughout the post–World War II period, the United States, via the Marshall Plan, Public Law 480, private charities, etc., has made substantial foreign aid contributions to needy nations. As the economic strength of the industrialized nations of the West was restored, they also contributed to foreign aid programs. However, given the enormous concentration of population in the poor countries of Africa, Asia, and Latin America, even if the level of foreign aid were significantly increased, the level of shared income for the inhabitants of these nations would still be very low. And, until a certain minimum level of well-being can be established in these countries, the incentives to stabilize population growth will not exist, and the cycle of poverty will continue unabated.

It is highly unlikely that future aid programs will lead to any significant income redistribution between the affluent and the poor nations. One only need examine our own society to note that charity has never provided a durable basis for a relationship between the poor and those with greater means. Pure give-away programs or even tied give-away programs have become increasingly unpopular, and whenever possible have been replaced by efforts to equalize and expand opportunities both in the economic and political spheres in order to bring about increased participation by the poor. To the extent that this view is correct, continued economic growth would seem to be a vital ingredient in sustaining this process.

A FINAL OBSERVATION

The limits to economic growth are capable of being extended by an intelligent adaptive response by society. Even though growing scarcity of resources and limits on the assimilative capacity of the environment are limiting factors, it should be recognized that a wise stewardship of this planet can extend and expand our habitation on it for many years to come. At the same time, it is becoming increasingly clear that the world has evolved into a place where grinding poverty and affluence share the same stage. Jean-Paul Sartre has said that, "The ultimate evil is man's capacity to make abstract that which is concrete." In a world made small by technological advances in transportation and communications, it becomes increasingly difficult to make abstract the wide disparities in well-being which exist between the haves and the have nots. In this regard, the words of Lester Brown seem particularly appropriate:

In summary, we may now have reached the point in the evolution of global society, in the expansion of economic activity, and in the deteriorating relationship between man and the environment where we must give serious thought to the need to at least attempt to satisfy the basic social needs of all mankind. At first glance this seems terribly ambitious. It may, however, be much less costly than we would at first think if we utilize some of the new technologies and new approaches now available. It may be one of the cheapest ways of insuring our own future well-being.[12]

It would be difficult to envisage the realization of such a laudable goal in a world without growth.

---

[12] Lester Brown, "Rich Countries and Poor," *Daedalus*, V. 102: #4 (Fall 1973), p. 164.

Reading 23

Growth and Antigrowth: What Are the Issues?*

By E. J. Mishan

Summary

Debate on the growth-antigrowth theme has become a fashionable pastime over the past five years. There are two aspects to the debate: first, whether continued economic growth is physically possible and, second, whether such growth is desirable. Both questions are linked together in any policy conclusion, but they can be treated separately.

If it is conceded that, once subsistence levels have been passed, the sources of man's most enduring satisfactions spring from mutual trust and affection, from sharing joy and sorrow, from giving and accepting love, and from open-hearted companionship and laughter; if it is further conceded that in a civilized society the joy of living comes from the sense of wonder inspired by the unfolding of nature, from the perception of beauty inspired by great art, from the renewal of faith and hope inspired by the heroic and the good—if this much is conceded, then is it possible to believe that unremitting attempts to harness the greater part of man's energies and ingenuity to the task of amassing an ever greater assortment of material possessions can add much to people's happiness? Can it add more than it subtracts? Can it add anything?

Recognizing the darker side of economic growth, we must conclude that the game is not worth the candle. And the answer to the question of whether continued economic growth in the West brings us any closer to the good life cannot be other than a resounding No.

Key Questions to Consider

■ Mishan concludes that were there to be no technological innovation in the future, we would not be able to grow indefinitely. What is the basis for this conclusion?

■ What arguments has Mishan cited which are used in the debate as to whether economic growth is desirable?

■ Mishan states, "The incidence of a single spillover alone—be it foul air, endless traffic bedlam, noise, or fear of criminal violence—can be enough to counter all of the alleged gains of economic prosperity." Does he, or can you, provide an economic basis for this statement, or is it simply impressionistic?

* Reprinted with permission from *Challenge, the Magazine of Economic Affairs* **16,** No. 2 (May/June 1973), 26–31.

Growth and Antigrowth: What Are the Issues?

Is growth possible? Is it desirable? Here are some reasons for taking it easy.

Debate on the growth-antigrowth theme has become a fashionable pastime over the past five years. And since its continued enjoyment must depend to a large extent on its inconclusiveness, it would be boorish as well as presumptuous to propose that we try to reach a settled conclusion.

But the present enjoyment in the continual conflicts of opinion may become marred by a growing sense of frustration from repeated failure to organize our thoughts and to acquire perspective on the subject. The time has come to steer the debate away from rhetorical appeals and toward more direct confrontation—less bark and more bite are called for. I propose, therefore, that we define the issues more carefully and lay down ground rules for a more searching investigation.

There are two aspects to the debate: first, whether continued economic growth is physically possible and, second, whether such growth is desirable. Both questions are linked together in any policy conclusion, but they can be treated separately.

THE PHYSICAL POSSIBILITY OF SUSTAINED GROWTH

Let us first consider the physical possibility of growth. To ask whether the world *can* continue to maintain a 2–3 percent growth rate is to pose a question about technological possibilities. It might well be that GNP, as conventionally measured, could grow at this rate *provided* all resources were properly allocated. This means that all productive services would have to be correctly priced. *Uneconomic* pollution of air, water, etc., would have to be prevented. Indeed, an ideal allocation might require that all, or nearly all, productivity gains be utilized to increase leisure, which would imply that "real" goods per capita would not grow, or would grow very little. This "constant-physical product" economic growth obviously would be very much easier to maintain over time than the conventional "increasing-physical product" growth.

172

But is it realistic to expect such allocative wisdom to prevail under existing economic and political institutions? To ask about the actual prospects of growth, we must also speculate about the changes, if any, in political and economic institutions that are likely to be brought about by changes in public attitudes. At the same time, we must abstract from certain present dangers that threaten human survival itself—the danger of ecological catastrophe from ruthless interference in the biosphere, the danger of genetic calamity from increased radiation or new chemicals, the danger of nuclear Armageddon. Each of these threats has arisen from economic and technological growth, and each will be further aggravated by such growth in the future.

Suppose, however, that we can reasonably anticipate a stable world population in the foreseeable future and that the question we have to face is whether, irrespective of the distribution of future world product, an average rate of growth per capita of *physical* product, comparable to that "enjoyed" in the postwar period, can be maintained for the next few centuries. What should we have to know in order to tackle such a question?

Knowledge of existing reserves of materials used in modern industry is clearly not enough. We already have rough estimates of the remaining reserves of coal, oil, and a large number of metals. And even if they turn out to be underestimates by as much as a factor of two or three, it will make little difference in the number of years required to exhaust them at current rates of depletion. If, for example, world oil consumption continues to increase at a rate of about 10 percent per annum, known reserves (including projected future discoveries) should be exhausted in about two decades. Even if reserves turn out to be as much as 4 times as large as currently estimated, we could keep going only for another 14 years; and if they were 8 times as large (which is hardly possible), we could keep going for another 2 decades. There is, I think, general agreement that we cannot continue to mine a wide range of primary materials *at current rates* for much longer than the end of the century.

Knowledge of economics is not enough either. Economists continue to remind us (unnecessarily perhaps) that as a resource becomes more scarce, its price rises and it is used less intensively. True, the rise in the price of a depleting resource is also expected to induce enterprises to switch to substitutes. These substitutes are unfailingly on tap in the textbooks, but in the world we live in we cannot be so sure that our luck will continue to hold. Indeed, it may be an unreasonable expectation. At current rates of usage, all known reserves of silver, gold, copper, lead, platinum, tin, and zinc will be used up within 20 years. There is no historical experience of finding substitutes simultaneously for so large a group of important materials.

We may reasonably conclude, therefore, that *were there to be no technological innovation in the future*, we simply would not be able to continue to grow indefinitely. The earth and its resources are all too finite, and our continued absorption of them on an ever larger scale must eventually exhaust them. The only question would be when.

The crucial variable in all optimistic forecasts, and in all declarations of faith, is technological innovation. Living in a world that is today being transformed before our eyes by new applications of science, we have an almost irresistible presumption in favor of scientific capability. If it merely sounds possible, the layman is ready to believe it will happen.

Thus we are ready to accept the idea of a vast proliferation of nuclear power plants over the earth, with problems of space solved and with radiation and heat hazards all kept well under control. And we are ready to imagine also that technology will discover increasingly more efficient and inexpensive ways of recycling materials. As for food supplies, the optimistic view is that the problem can be solved by intensive monoculture which utilizes large tracts of land and large amounts of chemical fertilizers and pesticides—the methods of the so-called green revolution. We are to ignore the social consequences of such agrotechnology on the economy of the hundreds of thousands of Asian villages, and the urban problems that follow the disruption of traditional ways of life.

I do not want to sound too cynical. It may all be wonderfully possible—or we may all be wonderfully lucky. I would simply affirm that there is room for legitimate doubt. The advance of technology in the West over the past 200 years might well be attributable to especially favorable circumstances. Up to the present there was no problem of limits to the assimilative capacity of the biosphere, or of the availability of cheap fossil fuels. As for scientific progress, we may be running into diminishing returns to the scale of research—partly because of an incipient breakdown in communications among an expanding array of narrowly focused specialists.

Perhaps there are no solutions to a number of problems that scientists are working on. It may be that what we want to do just cannot, in the nature of things, ever be done—though it may take us decades to realize this. Finally, it is possible—alas, more than possible—that should we succeed in wrestling some of nature's closest secrets from her breast, we shall live to wish we had not.

A sustained per capita growth rate of 3 percent per annum implies that the average income in 150 years will be about 100 times as large as the average income today, and 10,000 times as large in another 150 years. Just contemplate the amounts of energy and materials required to meet such fantastic standards. Just what shape will expenditures of this magnitude take? And how on earth (literally) will a person manage to absorb them?

THE DESIRABILITY OF SUSTAINED ECONOMIC GROWTH

Assuming that per capita growth could be maintained indefinitely at current rates, we must still ask whether such growth is desirable. Has economic growth promoted social welfare in the recent past, and is it likely to do so in the future? An odd assortment of arguments come up in this debate, a number of which are definitely "nonstarters." We can save time and

heat by recognizing some of them before going any farther.

First, there is the frequent statement that technology—the main force behind current economic growth—is itself neutral. One cannot associate it with good or evil attributes and "it all depends on how man uses it." But the *potential* of science and technology is not the issue. Their *actual* effects are. Intelligent conjecture about the future presupposes some knowledge of the reach of modern science and also some idea of the probable scientific developments over the foreseeable future. From this we can speculate about some of the more likely consequences on our lives, bearing in mind the limitations of men and the driving forces of modern institutions, economic and political.

A related response, the invocation of a "challenge" to man to "face the future" or to "be worthy of his destiny," must also go off the board. Otherwise we shall find ourselves with a two-headed penny. For wherever science and technology can be seen to have created problems, the technocrats exclaim "challenge" and perceive an immediate need for more technology. We must be alert to the possibility that some of the problems inflicted upon us by the advance of technology can also be solved by using less of the existing technology.

Nor is it, for similar reasons, legitimate to argue that we should seek the "optimal," or just-right, rate of growth. One can imagine some distillation of economic growth, some essence purified of all harmful external effects, which cannot fail to result in ideal human progress. But such flights of inspiration offer no plausible picture of the future and no guide to action. Economists all know that a narrow range of adverse spillovers—such as air and water pollution, noise, congestion and tourist blight—can be reduced given some political effort. Yet in judging the quality of life over the last two decades, we obviously cannot abstract from the brute facts of expanding pollution. So, also, in debating the foreseeable future, it is not the potential ideal that is at issue, but the political likelihood of realizing significant reductions in each of the familiar forms of pollution.

The "need" to maintain the momentum of economic growth in order to enable us to do good deeds like helping the poor, promoting high culture, or expanding higher education is also not on the agenda. This argument might win ethical support even if it were agreed that economic growth actually entailed a decline in social welfare for the majority of people. But the fact is that such worthy objectives can all be realized *without* sustained economic growth. In the United States, so much is produced which is trivial, inane, if not inimical, that we already have more than enough to transfer resources for these more meritorious purposes.

It is convenient for the professional economist to interpret people's economic behavior as reflecting their mature judgment about what is most conducive to their happiness. But I hope that he is not such a fool as really to believe it. It is also convenient for the economist to champion the right of the citizen to spend his money as he wishes. For my part, I have no objection if he prefers to sleep on a mattress stuffed with breakfast cereal. For I am not questioning his right to choose; I am questioning the consequences of his choice. We can sharpen the debate by focusing not on motivation, but only on the consequences.

Having, hopefully, cleared away some of the verbal undergrowth that tends to impede the progress of this debate, we are better able to perceive the issues that can be decisive. The issues can be divided, arbitrarily perhaps, into two categories:

1. In the first are the conventional array of adverse spillovers—air pollution, water pollution, solid waste pollution, noise, uglification of town and country—all of which have increased alarmingly since the war. The question is whether they have more than offset the "normal" expectations of welfare gains from economic growth.

2. In the second category are the remaining consequences of economic growth. How much weight is to be given to those pervasive repercussions that are less tangible and more complex than the familiar external diseconomies? Unwittingly, through the pro-

cess of continually and unquestioningly adapting our style and pace of life to technological and commercial possibilities, we may be losing irrevocably traditional sources of comfort and gratification.

It is difficult to draw a balance sheet summarizing the net welfare effects of the increased output of goods and the concomitant spillovers in the last few years. Even if we had all the physical data—from the hazards of chemical pesticides to rising levels of noise, from oil-fouled beaches the world over, to forest-cropping and earth-stripping—we should, in a closely interdependent economic system, be faced with the almost impossible task of evaluation. My inclination is to describe what has been happening on the advancing pollution front in impressionistic terms, taking it for granted that the balance of the argument will be restored by the unremitting efforts of commercial advertising, establishment politicians, company chairmen, and the spate of articles in our newspapers and magazines that speak loudly of the goodies we have and of goodies yet to come.

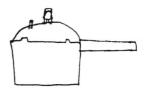

The incidence of a single spillover alone—be it foul air, endless traffic bedlam, noise, or fear of criminal violence—can be enough to counter all of the alleged gains of economic prosperity. Let a family have five television sets, four refrigerators, three cars, two yachts, a private plane, a swimming pool, and half a million dollars' worth of securities. What enjoyment is left if it fears to stroll out of an evening, if it must take elaborate precautions against burglary, if it lives in continuous anxiety lest one or another, parent or child, be kidnapped, mutilated or murdered? A fat bag of consumer goods, an impressive list of technical achievements, can hardly compensate for any one of such perils that have come to blight the lives of millions of Americans.

The old-fashioned notion of diminishing marginal utility of goods and the increasing marginal disutility of "bads" can also bear more emphasis. For one thing, choosing from an increasing variety of goods can be a tense and time-consuming process. For another, as Stefan Linder observes in his admirable and amusing *Harried Leisure Classes*, Americans cannot find time to make use of all the gadgets and sports gear they feel impelled to buy.

In addition, the "relative income hypothesis" (or, more facetiously, the "Jones effect") argues strongly against continued economic growth, if only because it is a predicament for which the economists can propose no remedy consistent with such growth. In an affluent society, people's satisfactions, as Thorstein Veblen observed, depend not only on the innate or perceived utility of the goods they buy but also on the status value of such goods. Thus to a person in a high consumption society, it is not only his absolute income that counts but also his *relative* income, his position in the structure of incomes. In its extreme form—and as affluence rises we draw closer to it— only relative income matters. A man would then prefer a 5 percent reduction in his own income accompanied by a 10 percent reduction in the incomes of others to a 25 percent increase in both his income and the incomes of others.

The more this attitude prevails—and the ethos of our society actively promotes it—the more futile is the objective of economic growth for society as a whole. For it is obvious that over time everybody cannot become relatively better off. The economist can, of course, continue to spin his optimal equations even in these conditions, but he has no means of measuring the loss in terms of utter futility. Since the extent of these wealth-dissipative effects are never measured, estimates over the last few years of increments of "real" income (or "measured economic welfare") must be rejected as wholly misleading.

Reflecting on the unmeasurable consequence of economic growth, Gilbert and Sullivan's dictum "Things are never what they seem" is a proper leitmotif.

Consider first the motive force behind economic growth. Bernard Shaw once remarked that "discontent is the mainspring of progress." The secret of how to keep people running is to widen the gap between their material condition and their material expectations. That gap is a fair measure of their discontent, and it was never wider than it is today. It is institutionalized by the agencies of Madison Avenue and hallowed by our system of higher education.

If continued discontent with what they have is required to keep people buying the increasing output of industry, and continued discontent with their status is necessary to keep them operating the machine, can we really believe that people are nonetheless happier as they absorb more goods? Does not the consequent struggle for status in an increasingly anonymous society become so obsessive as to cut a person off from enjoyment of the largeness of life? Does not this "virtue" of motivation act to shrivel a person's generous impulses, to make him use other people as a means to advancement, corrupting his character and his capacity for friendship?

Next, let us look at the "knowledge industry," whose products fuel the engine of economic growth. In a society that pays ritual homage to our great secular cathedrals of knowledge, the words "scientific research" are holy and scholarship is almost synonymous with saintliness. But the social consequences of the disinterested pursuit of knowledge are not all beyond dispute. The harrowing degree of specialization that results from the attempt to advance the expanding boundary of any discipline can crush the capacity of men for instinctual pleasure and can make communication between scientists, even those working in the same field, increasingly difficult.

The advance of scientific knowledge enhances the secular to the detriment of the sacred. One wonders if the loss of the great myths, the loss of belief in a benevolent deity, in reunion after death, has not contributed to a sense of desolation. One wonders also if a code of morality can be widely accepted in a society without belief in any god or in any hereafter.

As decisions are increasingly influenced by experts, democracy becomes more vulnerable. As historical knowledge grows, and hawk-eyed scholars find a vocation in debunking national heroes and popular legend, the pride of peoples in their common past is eroded and, along with it, their morale as well.

We might also want to ponder briefly some of the unexpected repercussions of a number of much-heralded inventions. Consumer innovations over the recent past and foreseeable future appear to be largely labor-saving—inventions that reduce dependence on others, or, rather, transfer dependence to a machine. Given that the machine is incomparably more efficient, can its efficiency in yielding services compensate for the inevitable loss of authentic human experience? Packaged and precooked foods save time for the busy housewife. Personal contacts necessarily decline with the spread of more efficient labor-saving devices. They have already declined with the spread of supermarkets, cafeterias, and vending machines. And they will continue to decline with the trend toward computerization in offices and factories, toward patient monitoring machines and computer-diagnoses in hospitals, toward closed-circuit television instruction, automated libraries and teaching machines.

Thus the compulsive search for efficiency, directed in the main toward innovations that save effort and time, must continue to produce for us yet more elegant instruments for our mutual estrangement. We might ask if the things commonly associated with the good life—a more settled way of natural beauty and architectural dignity, a rehabilitation of norms of propriety and taste—can ever be realized by affluent societies straining eternally to woo the consumer with ever more outlandish and expendable gadgetry and seeking eternally for faster economic growth.

If it is conceded that, once subsistence levels have been passed, the sources of man's most enduring satisfactions spring from mutual trust and affection, from sharing joy and sorrow, from giving and accepting love, from open-hearted companionship and laughter; if it is further conceded that in a civilized society the joy of living comes from the sense of wonder inspired by the unfolding of nature, from the perception of beauty inspired by great art, from the renewal of faith and hope inspired by the heroic and the good—if this much is conceded, then is it possible to believe that unremitting attempts to harness the greater part of man's energies and ingenuity to the task of amassing an ever greater assortment of material possessions can add much to people's happiness? Can it add more than it subtracts? Can it add anything?

Recognizing the darker side of economic growth, we must conclude that the game is not worth the candle. And the answer to the question of whether continued economic growth in the West brings us any closer to the good life cannot be other than a resounding No.

The Limits to Growth: A Critique*

By Mahbub ul Haq

Summary

The Limits to Growth—the study sponsored by the Club of Rome† and conducted by a team led by Professor Dennis Meadows at the Massachusetts Institute of Technology—was published in March 1972. Its main conclusion—that man is faced by ecological catastrophe unless zero growth rates in population and industrial production are attained by 1975—attracted great attention and controversy. Here a World Bank economist offers his views.

The basic thesis in the *Limits* is a simple one—and for that very reason it has a powerful appeal. It derives its conviction from the simple notion that infinite growth is impossible on a finite planet. It lends an air of frightening urgency to this notion by contending that the limits to growth are already being reached and that mankind is destined for catastrophe during the next 100 years unless this growth is stopped right away.

The basic weakness of the *Limits to Growth* thesis is not so much that it is alarmist but that it is complacent. It is alarmist about the physical limits which may in practice be extended by continued technological progress, but complacent about the social and political problems which its own prescriptions would only exacerbate. Yet it is just such problems which are probably the most serious obstacles in the way of enjoyment of the earth's resources by all its population. The industrialized countries may be able to accept a target of zero growth as a disagreeable, yet perhaps morally bracing, regime for their own citizens. For the developing world, however, zero growth offers only a prospect of despair and world income redistribution is merely a wistful dream.

Key Questions to Consider

- What are the major themes of the *Limits to Growth* model?

- What are the assumptions underlying the model?

- What criticisms does the author of the article make about each of the assumptions?

- What problems stem from the highly aggregative nature of the model?

- What are the policy implications of the model?

---

* Reprinted with permission from *Finance and Development*, **9**, No. 4 (December 1972), 2–8.

† The Club of Rome is a loose-knit group of about 75 men from 25 nations that includes eminent scientists, industrialists, economists, sociologists, and educators. Despite lack of formal budget or organizational structure, it aims to spur action on major world problems through research projects.

The Limits to Growth: A Critique[1]

The basic thesis in the *Limits* is a simple one—and for that very reason it has a powerful appeal. It derives its conviction from the simple notion that infinite growth is impossible on a finite planet. It lends an air of frightening urgency to this notion by contending that the limits to growth are already being reached and that mankind is destined for catastrophe during the next 100 years unless this growth is stopped right away.

The basic thesis of the *Limits to Growth* model breaks down into the following major themes:

1. Many critical variables in our global society—particularly population and industrial production—have been growing at a constant percentage rate so that, by now, the absolute increase each year is extremely large. Such increases will become increasingly unmanageable unless deliberate action is taken to prevent such exponential growth.

2. However, physical resources—particularly cultivable land and nonrenewable minerals—and the earth's capacity to "absorb" pollution are finite. Sooner or later the exponential growth in population and industrial production will bump into this physical ceiling and, instead of staying at the ceiling, will then plunge downward with a sudden and uncontrollable decline in both population and industrial capacity.

3. Since technological progress cannot expand all physical resources indefinitely, it would be better to establish conscious limits on our future growth rather than to let nature establish them for us in catastrophic fashion.

The authors concede that more optimistic alternative assumptions can be built into the model but they contend that this merely postpones the problem by a few decades so that it would be better to err on the side of action now rather than later. They are also conscious of some of the problems that zero growth rates may raise for the world. They hint at policies of income redistribution between the rich and the poor nations as well as within these nations; and they plead for a change in the composition of production away from industrial output and toward the social services. Unfortunately, many of the redeeming qualifications that the authors mention are not pursued by them and are generally lost in their anxiety to make their predictions as dramatic as possible.

[1] This article is based on a World Bank analysis of *The Limits to Growth*, undertaken by a team of which the author was chairman. The author is grateful to Messrs. Nicholas Carter, Edward Hawkins, Douglas Keare, Bension Varon, Charles Weiss, and Kunniparampil Zachariah for their help.

THE BASIC ASSUMPTIONS

Any study of the *Limits* model clearly must start with a critical examination of the assumptions that went into the model of the world economy on which it is based; it is a truism that a model is just as good as the assumptions built into it. Our investigations showed that many assumptions in the model were not scientifically established and that the use of data was often careless and casual. This was particularly true of the assumptions regarding nonrenewable resources and pollution. We also found that, contrary to the protestations of the authors, the model was fairly sensitive to the choice of these assumptions, and that reasonable adjustments in the assumptions regarding population, nonrenewable resources, and pollution could postpone the predicted catastrophe by another 100 to 200 years even if one accepted the general methodology of the model. And in this context an additional 100 years might be as vital as an additional second might be to a car driver in a traffic emergency —it could transform the whole situation.

Population

The *Limits* model is right in postulating that world population has been growing exponentially in the last century and that, if the present rate of growth continues, today's population of 3.6 billion will double in the next 35 years. However, while such medium-term assumptions are fairly sound, the model does not do justice to a number of demographic factors that are likely to come into play in the long run, and which may even be significant in the short run.

To begin with, some of the recent demographic trends indicate that fertility has already started to decline in a number of countries. Of the 66 countries for which accurate data are available, as many as 56 show a decline. Most demographers are agreed by now that the 1970s will see the population growth rate reach a plateau so that by 1980 population growth rates will tend to decline, slowly at first and rapidly thereafter.

Furthermore, one of the major features in the population model of the *Limits* is that fertility and mortality levels are determined largely by economic factors, such as the level of industrial production and the output of services. Population growth in the *Limits* model can only be reduced by increasing per capita industrial production. This in turn increases the output of services, including education, which both permits the growth of family planning services and creates the climate for their use to be effective. Little attention is given to the possibility—considered realistic by many demographers—that population growth may be checked by family planning even at low levels of income.

No one will deny that continued population growth at the present rate is a serious matter which should engage the urgent attention of humanity. The question is not whether population growth can continue unchecked forever; it simply cannot. The real issue is how to arrest it through deliberate policies of population planning, and through technological breakthroughs in population control methods suitable for use in the poor nations.

We should not, however, play down the population problem as presented in the *Limits* model. Even if population control efforts are successful, the world will still be left with a substantial population problem in both absolute numbers and scope for future growth. The long time lags involved in demographic change ensure that population growth would continue for several generations after balance had been achieved between mortality and fertility. Any prognostication about the future, therefore, must take into account the inevitability of a world population several times larger than the present 3.6 billion.

Nonrenewable Resources

A number of assumptions have been made about nonrenewable resources which turn out, on close examination, to be characterized by the same rather dramatic gloom with which *Limits* views population. The figures on reserves of nonrenewable resources generally come from the U.S. Bureau of Mines, but the Bureau warns that 80 percent of their reserve estimates have a confidence level of less than 65 percent; *Limits* ignores this important reservation. Moreover, some of the reserve estimates—particularly for the communist countries—are extremely old or incomplete; some estimates for Mainland China, for example, go back to 1913! Again, reserve estimates have been revised frequently over time and are likely to change again in our own lifetime; between 1954 and 1966, the reserve estimates for one of the largest resources, iron ore, rose by about five times. It is estimated by the Bureau of Mines that even these reserves can be doubled at a price 30 to 40 percent higher than the current price. Similarly, the reserve estimates for copper today are 3.5 times their level in 1935 and it is estimated that they could be more than doubled again if the price were three times higher. The *Limits* authors allow for such contingencies by assuming that reserves could increase by five times over the next 100 years. This assumption has appeared generous to many who have been alarmed by the sweeping prognostications of *Limits* but it is in fact extremely—and many experts would say almost irrationally—conservative.

It can, of course, be objected that reliance on such illustrations of how the world's resource base has expanded shows an unjustified and adventuresome confidence in history. However, this can no more be faulted than the use of history in the *Limits* study which only looks at the story of irrationality, waste, and neglect.

The pessimism of the assumptions on nonrenewable resources becomes even more evident if one considers that the concept of resources itself is a dynamic one: many things *become* resources over time. The expansion of the last 100 years could not have been sustained without the new resources of petroleum, aluminum, and atomic energy. What are tomorrow's possibilities?

As an immediate example, there exists the imminent potential for exploiting resources on the seabed. Reserves of nodular materials—the most promising underwater source of minerals—distributed over the ocean floor are estimated at levels sufficient to sustain a mining rate of 400 million tons a year for virtually an unlimited period of time. If only 100 million tons of nodules are recovered every year—a target which appears to be within reach in the next 10 to 20 years—it would add to the annual production of copper, nickel, manganese, and cobalt to the extent of roughly one fourth, three times, six times, and twelve times, respectively, compared to the current free world production levels. And the present production cost estimates are a fraction of current prices—$\frac{1}{5}$ for copper, $\frac{1}{13}$ for nickel, $\frac{1}{24}$ for cobalt. These estimates—like all such estimates—are very tentative; but there is a good deal of evidence that exploitation of seabed resources is fast becoming a real possibility.

If certain resources are likely to become scarcer—or, to use the jargon of the economists, if supply inelasticities are likely to develop—it is a scientific and intellectual service to humanity to draw attention to those resources and to the time period over which they may vanish, given current usage and the present state of knowledge. Research into these areas is, therefore, both useful and vital. But it is quite another thing to argue that no amount of research, no technological breakthroughs, will extend the lifetime of these resources indefinitely or to pretend that supply inelasticities will afflict all natural resources in the same manner and at the same time in an aggregate model. While identification of specific supply inelasticities in advance of time is a definite service, sweeping generalizations about complete disappearance of all nonrenewable resources at a particular point of time in the future is mere intellectual fantasy.

It should also be remembered that the waste of natural resources is a function of both their seeming abundance and of public attitudes. It is quite possible—and indeed probable—that with either of the above factors changing, resources can be conserved without undue pain. For the major flaw of today's pattern of consumption is not really that we consume too many final goods and services, but that we use our resource inputs extremely inefficiently. If certain resources become more scarce and their relative price increases, there will be a powerful incentive for their more efficient use—a factor that *Limits* completely ignores, as it ignores similarly potent positive factors throughout. For instance, energy can be much more economically used. There is scope for smaller cars with weaker engines, public rather than private transport, increasing efficiency in burning fuels and in generating and distributing electricity, and improved design of aircraft engines and bodies.

Looking at the problem, as *Limits to Growth* has done, in terms of quantifying the life expectancy of resources as presently constituted, we conclude that these are sufficient to last very much longer than stipulated. It is not a question of expecting natural resources to accommodate forever our current patterns of growth, production, and consumption; clearly, they will not. But we are confident that natural resources will last long enough to allow us time to make deliberate adjustments in the way we use them so that resource needs can be met indefinitely. We have seen no convincing evidence to suggest that mankind faces a final curtain about 100 years from now through depletion of nonrenewable resources.

Pollution

The assumptions regarding pollution are the weakest part of the model of world economic activity on which *Limits* is based. In many instances they are not established on any scientific basis. We still know so little about the generation and absorption of pollution, and about the effects of pollution, that definite functions are very hard to establish.

Our examination of the relationships between pollution and economic growth began with a study of the model developed in the book *World Dynamics*.[2] We did this because the *Limits* model was not available to us at that time. This indirect examination was justified because the *Limits* model treats pollution in much the same way that *World Dynamics* does. The main differences are that *Limits* allows for a time lag between the generation of pollution and its effects and also for pollution resulting from agricultural development. However, these differences are hardly important for the main argument of the *Limits* model.

Although little is known about the generation of pollution, it is simply claimed in the *World Dynamics* model that it rises at the same speed as the growth in capital stock per capita. As natural resources are used, progressively more capital must be applied to extract a given amount of final output—because of the necessity of using increasing amounts of energy in production as resources are either consumed or disposed of. Hence pollution grows to increasingly higher levels. In fact, the prediction of a pollution catastrophe depends on the value of the ratio assumed in the model between the pollution level and capital stock per capita. It appears from our study, however, that if the assumed value could be reduced by $\frac{5}{8}$—an adjustment well within the error range of the data—the prediction of catastrophe would be completely erased. Since data on actual relationships between pollution and capital stock are sparse, there is no particular reason to favor one value for the ratio rather than another.

Again, in discussing the earth's capacity to absorb pollutants, the *World Dynamics* model assumes, entirely arbitrarily, that the world's overall capacity to absorb pollution is four times the present annual level and that pollution levels beyond certain limits will start affecting human mortality. While it may be true that accumulating pollution levels may destroy present concepts of living during the next 100 years, there is little evidence that life itself will be destroyed.

Furthermore, the authors do not fully consider that higher levels of industrial development will allow societies to devote additional resources to taking care of the pollution problem without sacrificing continued economic growth. It has been estimated, for example, that the United States could spend $16 billion a year, or about one third the annual increase in its gross national product, and achieve a substantial reduction

---

[2] Jay W. Forrester, *World Dynamics* (Cambridge, Massachusetts, U.S.A., 1971), Wright-Allen Press.

in pollution over the next six years. Despite this, the United States could still increase its per capita consumption by another $900 over this period. Similarly, it has been calculated that about 80–90 percent of present pollution can be removed at a relatively low cost: the cost increases would be about 5 percent for industrial waste; 2 percent for thermal electricity; and 10 percent for automobiles.

Despite such objections to the *Limits* model, it should not be thought that pollution is of little global concern or that it is unrelated to economic growth. It is simply that information of the kind given above —which is extremely pertinent to the *Limits* projections—illustrates that pollution build-up and world collapse is *not necessarily inevitable even with continued economic growth.*

In general, however, the assumptions of the model regarding population, depletion of nonrenewable resources, and pollution generation and absorption should not be taken lightly. However, more study and research is needed to establish more reasonable parameters for these three critical variables in a long-term model.

NATURE OF THE MODEL

From an analysis of the basic assumptions of the model, we turned to its essential nature and methodology. Here we found that our analysis was handicapped by the extreme aggregation found in the model. The whole world is treated as one and homogenous even when it is clear that the real world is characterized by vast differences in income and consumption patterns: for instance, the per capita income levels in developed countries are 14 times those in the developing countries; and the style of development, the patterns of growth, and the composition of consumption demand vary widely in different parts of the world.

The highly aggregate nature of the model raises a number of difficulties in analysis. For one thing, it is not clear how seriously one can take averages of various variables which are widely dissimilar. For another, it makes any plausible interpretation of the model very difficult. There is only one aggregate natural resource or one aggregate pollutant, keeping one guessing as to how representative its behavior is of the real world which is marked by much greater diversity, complexity, and substitutability.

More important, it is not possible to get any useful policy guidance from such an aggregate view of the world. The real world is divided politically into a number of nation states and economically into developed and developing countries. They do not all behave similarly nor are they affected in the same manner. Thus, if natural resources are being progressively depleted, this may raise their price and benefit the producing countries which are mostly in the developing world. The transfer of resources from the rich to the poor nations in such a situation may well alter the overall pattern of growth rates. Such natural checks and balances arise in the real world but they are not allowed for in the *Limits* aggregate world model which moves only in one direction—toward disaster.

Before we can arrive at any useful or relevant conclusion, a minimum condition is to construct at least a "two-world" model, distinguishing between the developed and the developing world. Without a greater degree of disaggregation there is a great danger that the model may become a caricature of the real world rather than a mere abstraction.

The methodology used in the model further helps us along the road to disaster. It does not allow for economic costs and prices nor for conscious choices made by society; there are no real corrective mechanisms—only physical engineering relationships. The world keeps on proceeding in its merry way—frittering away its resources, populating itself endlessly, accumulating pollution—until one fine morning it hits disaster.

Is this a realistic abstraction from the world as we know it? In the real world, there is not one nonrenewable resource but many. They do not suddenly disappear collectively but become more and more scarce individually. As each resource becomes more scarce, price signals flash and alarm bells ring all over the world. This directs technological research into them; possibilities of substitution are explored; conscious choices are made by society to economize on them, to do without them, or to enlarge their exploitation by using marginal reserves or by recycling at a higher price. In other words, corrective mechanisms start working. Similarly, it is hard to believe that a pollution crisis can sneak upon humanity as insidiously as the model implies. Even a modest level of pollution would mean that even though the world average of persistent pollutants were still quite low and not yet obnoxious to human health, some particular localities would be suffering to a point at which corrective action would have to be taken—London, for example, introduced legislation to help purify its air and eliminate the deadly "peasoup" fogs.

Humanity faces these problems one by one, every year in every era, and keeps making its quiet adjustments. It does not keep accumulating them indefinitely until they make catastrophe inevitable. One does not have to believe in the invisible hand to subscribe to such a view of society. One has merely to believe in human sanity and its instinct for self-preservation. While the model itself contains hardly any mention of conscious corrective mechanisms, in a larger sense its very appearance can be regarded as part of the corrective mechanism which societies devise in response to major problems.

One of the most curious parts of the model is its treatment of the role of technology. In an age of the most dramatic technological progress, the authors contend that there cannot be a continuation of such rapid progress in the future. And this is merely an assumption, not a proven thesis. The model *assumes* that certain things in this world—population, capital stock, pollution—will grow at exponential rates; but it *assumes* that certain other things—specifically technology to enlarge the resource base and to fight pollution—will not grow exponentially. Any such model is inherently unstable and we should not be surprised if it leads to disaster.

The authors' assumptions are, however, scarcely realistic since man so far has continuously proved his ability to extend the physical limits of this planet through constant innovations and technological progress. There is no reason to think that technological innovations in conserving, recycling, and discovering new resources, and in combating pollution will stop simply because by their very nature we cannot predict them in advance.

Policy Implications of the Model

The policy implications which flow from the *Limits* model are the least stressed and the least developed part of the book. Yet, it is these policy implications that have attracted the greatest attention since the book has appeared. The major policy conclusion from the model is the prescription of a zero growth rate, both in population and in material production. But that prescription is not logically derived from the model. Even if one accepts some of the premises of the authors about certain physical limits to further unchecked growth, it is not clear from their work why the world must immediately move in 1975 to zero growth rates. Since the model is excessively aggregated, the authors are in no position to discuss various alternative choices which are still open to society even if physical limits to growth are conceded.

There is first the choice between development and defense. Presently, about $200 billion is being spent on defense, which is one of the major users of world resources and generators of pollution. If society is really concerned about resource constraints, could it not consciously choose to devote less resources to defense and more to development? Again, there is the choice of patterns of growth. If natural resources become more scarce, could society not decide to have a different pattern of consumption—based on more services and leisure—which is less resource-consuming? Finally, if the rich nations were to stop growing, the growth of the developing world could well proceed without putting major pressures on global physical limits, whatever these may be. These are some of the real choices that humanity faces at present and a good deal of debate is centering on them. But these choices can hardly be considered in the context of the *Limits* model which is sweeping in its overall policy prescriptions.

Another area of policy concern is world income distribution. If we were to accept, as the authors do, the thesis that the world cannot be "saved" except through zero growth rates, we must also demonstrate that world income redistribution on a massive scale is possible. Otherwise, freezing the present world income distribution would not "save" the world; it would only bring about a confrontation between the haves and the have-nots. The *Limits* recognizes this but skips the issue rather lightly as if it were a mere irritant. It does not address itself to the basic issue; how is such a redistribution to be brought about in a stagnant world? Through negative growth rates in the developed world and positive growth rates in the developing countries? Through a mass immigration of the populations of the developing countries into the developed world? Through a massive transfer of resources under a world income tax? And what is the realism of all this in a world that is rather reluctant to transfer even 1 percent of its gross national product in the form of development assistance? While income redistribution is a desirable objective and must be pursued with full vigor, we must recognize that it is going to be even more difficult to achieve—both within and between nations—if there is no prospect of future growth and various groups fight to keep their share in a stagnant world.

The basic weakness of the *Limits to Growth* thesis is not so much that it is alarmist but that it is complacent. It is alarmist about the physical limits which may in practice be extended by continued technological progress, but complacent about the social and political problems which its own prescriptions would only exacerbate. Yet it is such problems which are probably the most serious obstacles in the way of enjoyment of the earth's resources by all its population. The industrialized countries may be able to accept a target of zero growth as a disagreeable, yet perhaps morally bracing, regime for their own citizens. For the developing world, however, zero growth offers only a prospect of despair and world income redistribution is merely a wistful dream.

The shock waves generated by the *Limits* will do good if they start some serious academic work on the long-range issues of global survival. To the extent that they divert effort from the grave but probably soluble problems of our own day to plans for dealing with specters in the future, they can only do harm.

Reading 25

GNP and Economic Welfare*

By Frederick Strobel

Summary

The Sixties were an unprecedented period of sustained economic growth, despite the minor recession early in the decade. Real output, adjusted for price increases, rose at an annual average of over 5 percent and unemployment fell steadily. However, this economic growth was accompanied by a renewed questioning of its net benefits. Rapid growth was attacked for its undesirable side effects, such as pollution and wasteful land use. Criticism was eventually directed at the concept of Gross National Product, the chief measure of economic growth.

Initially Gross National Product was conceived as a means of measuring a nation's economic activity. However, since increased economic activity is usually associated with rising standards of living or economic well-being, GNP growth has often been linked with increased economic welfare. This article examines the general concept and definition of GNP as currently computed and assesses its effectiveness as an indicator of economic welfare. It also examines two other concepts which, while abstracting from the GNP calculations, try to measure economic welfare rather than economic activity.

Key Questions to Consider

- What is GNP?

- What are the shortcomings of GNP as a welfare indicator?

- What is MEW? How does it differ from GNP?

* Reprinted with permission from *Monthly Review*, Federal Reserve Bank of Atlanta, **LIX,** No. 6 (June 1974), 74–79.

GNP and Economic Welfare

The Sixties were an unprecedented period of sustained economic growth, despite the minor recession early in the decade. Real output, adjusted for price increases, rose at an annual average of over 5 percent and unemployment fell steadily. However, this economic growth was accompanied by a renewed questioning of its net benefits. Rapid growth was attacked for its undesirable side effects such as pollution and wasteful land use. Criticism was eventually directed at the concept of Gross National Product, the chief measure of economic growth.

Initially Gross National Product was conceived as a means of measuring a nation's economic activity. However, since increased economic activity is usually associated with rising standards of living or economic well-being, GNP growth has often been linked with increased economic welfare. This article examines the general concept and definition of GNP as currently computed and assesses its effectiveness as an indicator of economic welfare. It also examines two other concepts which, while abstracting from the GNP calculations, try to measure economic welfare rather than economic activity.

WHAT IS GNP?

GNP has become part of most vocabularies as the final market value of goods and services an economy produces annually. GNP for 1972 and 1973, using the spending approach, is shown in Table 1. Under this form of GNP accounting, the value of goods produced closely approximates spending on final goods and services.[1] Estimates of four major categories—personal consumption expenditures, gross private domestic investment, net exports, and government purchases of goods and services—are summed to equal total GNP. To remove price effects, GNP can be divided by the Implicit Price Deflator to yield GNP in 1958 or "constant" dollars. Constant dollar or "real" GNP in 1973 grew 5.9 percent; in other words, the real growth rate was 5.9 percent.

Items included in GNP are generally measurable by market transactions since they yield a market price or a wage. Home-produced services, for example, are not counted in GNP. But if a homeowner pays a painter $700 for labor and $50 for paint, the full $750 is included under personal consumption in the GNP accounts. If he paints the house himself, only the price of the paint—$50—is included. Moreover, GNP accounting makes no distinction between "more desirable" or "less desirable" goods and services (provided they are legal). Pondering whether to spend $8

---

[1] The exception to this equality will be the net change in inventories.

on a bottle of Tennessee whiskey or on a book on child rearing, the consumer need not worry what effect his purchase has on GNP. Consumer sovereignty reigns; either purchase will raise GNP by $8. Published quarterly at annual rates, GNP and the GNP accounts are probably the most widely used set of statistics in current economic analysis.

Because the production of goods and services creates income, GNP can also be estimated using the income approach. This involves summing payments to producers of goods and services (factors of production). Totaling wages, proprietors' income, rent, corporate profits, interest, indirect business taxes, and depreciation will then approximate Gross National Product as presented in Table 1. Using this approach, the $700 payment to the painter mentioned before is usually counted as proprietors' income. The income approach to computing GNP not only provides a statistical check on the accuracy of the GNP total calculated through the spending method but also supplies additional information for economic analysis.

The use of GNP accounts in economic analysis was further expanded during the Sixties by the development of econometric models. Today, many of the well-known models produce a computerized forecast of the GNP accounts in detail.[2] These models, some incorporating as many as several hundred equations, often project GNP using both spending and income approaches. In addition, they relate GNP projections to those of other economic variables.

GNP AS A WELFARE INDICATOR

Encompassing so many different areas of economic activity, GNP is often used as a measure of economic welfare. For example, one study shows that between

[2] See "Econometric Models—What They Are and What They Say for 1971," F. R. Strobel and W. D. Toal, *Monthly Review*, Federal Reserve Bank of Atlanta, March 1971.

Table 1

U.S. Gross National Product
(Spending approach)

	$ Billions	
	1972	1973
Personal consumption expenditures	726.5	804.0
Durable goods	117.4	130.8
Nondurable goods	299.9	335.9
Services	309.2	337.3
Gross private domestic investment	178.3	202.1
Fixed investment	172.3	194.2
Nonresidential	118.2	136.2
Structures	41.7	48.4
Producers' durable equipment	76.5	87.8
Residential structures	54.0	58.0
Nonfarm	53.5	57.4
Farm	.6	.6
Change in business inventories	6.0	8.0
Nonfarm	5.6	7.3
Farm	.4	.6
Net exports of goods and services	-4.6	5.8
Exports	73.5	102.0
Imports	78.1	96.2
Government purchases of goods and services	255.0	277.1
Federal	104.4	106.6
National defense	74.4	73.9
Other	30.1	32.7
State and local	150.5	170.5
Gross National Product (GNP)	1,155.2	1,289.1
GNP implicit price deflator, 1958 = 100	146.1	153.9
GNP in 1958 "constant" dollars	786.1	831.8
Real growth (percent change in constant dollar GNP)	6.1	5.9

Source: U.S. Department of Commerce.

1953 and 1963, real GNP growth of about 3½ percent was necessary to keep the unemployment rate from rising.[3] If the same relationships were to hold true today, a growth rate of less than 3½ percent would not create enough jobs to absorb a labor force which expands with population. In other words, the unemployment rate would increase. Linking GNP growth rates to unemployment rates is one way GNP is used as a welfare indicator. By the same token, intolerable inflation frequently accompanies extremely rapid real economic growth, causing a loss in economic welfare.

Since output creates income, we can also draw welfare implications from the income side of the GNP accounts. A rise in per capita income is often considered desirable. But per capita income figures alone say nothing about how that income is distributed, which has implications for economic welfare.

SHORTCOMINGS OF GNP AS A WELFARE INDICATOR

Even the effectiveness of GNP's prime function, which is designed to measure economic activity, has been questioned. The construction of GNP figures involves difficult estimating procedures and value judgments. These criticisms can also be applied to its service as a welfare indicator.

GNP is further criticized for not allowing for "externalities," i.e., items that fall outside the price system. For example, the pollution given off by an industrial plant is a cost to society. Yet, if the offending company were made to produce in a nonpolluting way, it might conceivably be forced out of business, the product discontinued, and GNP reduced. But general welfare may be increased. One can think of many similar examples. The benefits enjoyed by users of a city-operated park may far exceed the dollar cost of building and operating it. Yet only the money spent by the local government on it is included in GNP; benefits to users are not measured or included.

More indirect exclusions from GNP, loosely classified as externalities, are such tenuous concepts as leisure and happiness. A rising GNP does not necessarily mean increased leisure time for the average American. GNP does not measure the cost to economic welfare of such items as additional commuting time, hours worked, and the increasing necessity for two-job families. More people owning second homes, camping vehicles, boats, etc., may indicate more leisure for some Americans, but the GNP does not indicate who is buying these goods or who in society is producing these leisure-time products.

Another criticism of the GNP computation is the exclusion of home-produced services. For example, a housewife's services are not included in the GNP. But if she gets a job and hires a maid, both the maid's and her services are then counted. Defenders of the present computation method counter that most of these exclusions are difficult to calculate. However, critics reply that if the rental value of home-owner occupied houses can be estimated and included in GNP, a housewife's services should also be computed.[4]

Criticized for its exclusions, GNP is also taken to task for what it includes, for example, the so-called "defensive" expenditures: police and law enforcement, personal security expenses, pollution control, and national defense. Critics charge that GNP should not include government expenditures to fight rising crime since these reflect a deterioration in the quality of life. A similar argument might be made for burglar alarm systems in private homes—practically non-

---

[3] Arthur M. Okun, "The Gap Between Actual and Potential Output," *The Battle Against Unemployment*, W. W. Norton and Company, New York, 1965, p. 17.

[4] Much of the difficulty with this argument involves the use of the term "services of a housewife." Perhaps the argument should revolve around the cost of keeping a house clean, which is the primary function of a maid; the services of a housewife extend far beyond merely cleaning house. Nordhaus and Tobin use the term "housekeeping."

existent years ago but increasingly common today. Spending for pollution control is similarly questioned, since in part this money is spent to correct previous unwise business or government practices, thus tending to overstate gains in output.

Arguments against including national defense spending in the GNP accounts, similar to those made against including police and law enforcement, purport that a growing GNP boosted by heavy military spending increases the danger of global war and reduces the quality of life. Proponents of including defense expenditures claim defense deters wars and averts the disruptions of a wartime economy.

Defense spending is a large item in the total Federal budget included in GNP accounts, totaling $73.9 billion in 1973, or 69 percent of total Federal purchases of goods and services (see Table 1).

OTHER MEASURES OF WELL-BEING

Although the United States has the highest per capita income in the world, its quality of health is allegedly poorer than that of some less wealthy nations. Spending more on health care services relative to the GNP than any other country, one might expect the U.S. to have one of the lowest infant mortality rates; however, it ranks only eleventh among the countries listed in Table 2. Similarly, while Sweden leads with an average life expectancy of 74.19 years, the United States ranks eighth, at 71.10 years, behind such nations as Japan, Canada, and France. In this way, GNP dollar amounts spent on medical care might be misleading as to the quality of health in the United States.

Many other such economic and social indicators are available, though none command the attention of the single aggregate GNP. The Department of Health, Education, and Welfare in 1969 published the results of an exploratory effort to develop a set of social indicators. Entitled "Toward a Social Report," [5] it begins:

---

[5] *Toward a Social Report*, p. 7.

Table 2

Infant Mortality and Fertility Rates
(Nations with per capita income
greater than $1,000)
1971

	Infant mortality rate (Deaths per 1,000 births)	Birth rate (Per 1,000 female population age 10–49)
Sweden	11.1	54.4
The Netherlands	11.1	67.6
Finland	11.8	47.5
Japan	12.4	59.9
Norway	12.7	65.0
Denmark	14.2	53.2
France	14.4	60.5
New Zealand	16.5	80.4
United Kingdom	17.9	62.0
Canada	18.8	58.7
United States	19.2	59.3
Ireland	19.6	87.2
Belgium	19.8	64.0
Luxembourg	22.5	47.9
Germany (Federal Republic of)	23.2	55.4
Austria	26.1	56.9
Italy	28.3	58.9
Kuwait	39.4	190.0

Source: *Statistical Yearbook 1972*, Statistical Office of the United Nations.

"The nation has no comprehensive set of statistics reflecting social progress or retrogression. There is no government procedure for periodic stock-taking of the social health of the nation. The Government makes no social report." Citing several deficient areas such as health, social mobility, physical environment, poverty, public order, and safety, the report recommends a set of social indicators be developed, not merely as a by-product of administrative accounting procedures, but for public policy use. It recognizes the value of GNP statistics because they provide an aggregate measure and meaningful detail. But as for social statistics, "the trouble is that the weights needed for aggregated indexes of other social statistics are not available except within particular limited areas."

More recently, the government released *Social Indicators, 1973.*[6] A 245-page statistical volume describing U.S. social conditions and trends, it is the first of its kind published by the Federal Government. Covering health, income, and education, the report represents a start toward a more extensive social indicator system.[7] Data are restricted to objective conditions, are not weighted toward any single index of economic and/or social welfare, and contain no international comparisons. Nonetheless, it is an important effort since it gathers many welfare-related statistics into one volume.

THE "MEASURE OF ECONOMIC WELFARE"

To help overcome the shortcomings of GNP as a welfare indicator, William Nordhaus and James Tobin of Yale University have constructed a welfare index based on national income accounts but aimed at measuring economic welfare.[8] One obvious defect of GNP, according to the two authors, is that it is an index of production and not consumption, which in their opinion is the goal of economic activity. With this in mind they have rearranged, reclassified, and imputed terms to design an index better reflecting consumption rather than production but utilizing the GNP framework.

In computing the Measure of Economic Welfare (MEW), they begin with personal consumption

spending from the national income and product (GNP) accounts. They then reclassify several GNP expenditures to fit their consumption (welfare) theory. Capital goods such as automobiles and housing are counted in GNP in the year in which they are purchased. Nordhaus and Tobin initially leave out these purchases, instead including them in a separate wealth formation estimate.[9] Into wealth formation they also add education and health expenditures as capital investments. Government durable goods purchases such as public buildings are treated similarly. They then add to personal consumption the services drawn from this net stock of wealth, based upon the time such assets will yield services.[10]

A second major adjustment is the exclusion of "instrumental expenses." These are defined as activities that are not directly sources of utility, such as police services, sanitation, road maintenance, and national defense. While Nordhaus and Tobin admit these expenditures are "among the necessary overhead costs of a complex industrial nation," they have no *direct* bearing on consumption. Without denying that "given the unfavorable circumstances that prompt these expenditures, consumers will ultimately be better off with them than without them . . . the only judgment we make is that these expenditures yield no direct satisfaction."

A third major category of adjustments is the imputation of values for items measuring the quality of life and nonmarket productive activities (such as housekeeping services) which are estimated and added into the MEW.

A final major adjustment subtracts what Nordhaus and Tobin term the "disamenities of urbanization." Although acknowledging that economic growth delivers much in the way of new products and higher living standards, they recognize such growth increases

[6] Executive Office of the President: Office of Management and Budget, *Social Indicators, 1973*, U.S. Government Printing Office, Washington, D.C., 1973.

[7] The areas covered are: health, public safety, education, employment, income, housing, leisure and recreation, and population.

[8] William Nordhaus and James Tobin, "Is Growth Obsolete," *Economic Growth*, National Bureau of Economic Research, New York, 1972, pp. 1–80.

[9] Estimates of wealth are those developed earlier by Goldsmith, Kendrick, T. Schultz, and Machlup. Estimates of services from wealth are based on the work of Juster. For full references, see "Is Growth Obsolete," pp. 30–31.

[10] Thus a refrigerator with an expected ten-year life would count 10 percent of the purchase price in annual consumption.

urbanization. This brings increased costs of traffic congestion; air, water, and noise pollution; higher crime rates; and similar externalities common to urban life. To compensate for these urban disamenities, they subtract from the MEW total estimates of income differentials necessary to hold people in areas of denser population, since urban incomes are significantly higher than nonurban ones.

These computations and an adjustment for capital formation discussed below produce what Nordhaus and Tobin label a sustainable measure of economic welfare. From 1929 to 1965, when Net National Product grew on average 3.1 percent annually, the Measure of Economic Welfare grew at a somewhat slower pace, 2.3 percent. On a per capita basis, NNP rose by 1.7 percent annually and the MEW by 1.0 percent. Thus Nordhaus and Tobin conclude that while the U.S. standard of living has increased both in the aggregate and on a per capita basis over that period, it did not increase as much as the output of goods and services.

THE NET NATIONAL WELFARE INDEX

The Economic Planning Agency of the Japanese Government has recently produced an interim report on the conceptual framework of a Net National Welfare (NNW) Index similar to the Nordhaus-Tobin MEW.[11] Its expressed purpose is to provide a policy goal complementary to the GNP accounts.

As in the MEW, consumption is the key welfare indicator in the NNW Index with, however, some differences. For example, the NNW groups educational, health, and medical expenses under the current year's government consumption; the MEW includes these in capital formation. Similar to the MEW, though, judicial and police, general administrative, and defense expenditures are excluded from government spending. Durable goods purchases, commuting,

and personal business expenses are excluded from personal consumption, and, like Nordhaus and Tobin, the Japanese add back services from personal durable goods on an accrual basis. Also, services from government durable goods purchases are prorated over time, based on these assets' useful lives. Value of leisure time [12] is an additional item in the NNW; nonmarket activities such as housekeeping are also added in. This estimate is based on the average female worker's wage.

The major minus items are, first, environmental maintenance costs, which include normal government expenses such as water and sewage treatment. A second major adjustment is for environmental pollution damages, the estimated cost of damage not presently being corrected (automobile exhausts, industrial pollution, etc.). When the government does spend the funds necessary to correct such damages, this expense is also excluded from NNW but under environmental maintenance costs.

A third major adjustment is for losses related to urbanization. Here, where Nordhaus and Tobin calculate income differentials under the broader category of "disamenities of urbanization," the Japanese exclude two smaller categories. First, they adjust for losses attributable to the deterioration of commuting environment, based on the premise that commuting more than 60 minutes daily results in "physical fatigue and mental pain." Commuting hours exceeding 60 minutes per day are multiplied by the average wage, and the resulting value is subtracted from the NNW total. Also subtracted is an estimated dollar value loss caused by traffic accidents, based on compensation paid for personal injuries. (The basic approaches of the Japanese NNW Index and the Nordhaus-Tobin MEW Index are shown in Table 3.)

The results of the Japanese NNW Index are similar to the MEW: namely, the growth in national welfare as measured by each index has trailed the output of goods and services. While Japanese growth

---

[11] "An Interim Report of the N.N.W. Development Committee," Economic Planning Agency, Tokyo, January 19, 1973.

[12] This is computed by multiplying leisure hours by an average wage.

Table 3

Similar Approaches To Computing
A Welfare Indicator

Nordhaus-Tobin and the Japanese Economic Planning Agency
Add:
Personal consumption
Government consumption
Services of consumer capital goods
Services of government capital goods
Value of leisure time
Value of nonmarket productive activity
(1) Total plus items

Nordhaus-Tobin subtract from (1):	The Economic Planning Agency subtracts from (1):
Private instrumental expenditures	Durable goods purchases
Durable goods purchases	Maintenance cost of environment
Other household investments	Environmental contamination
Costs of urban disamenities	Losses caused by urbanization
To form a Measure of Economic Welfare (MEW)	To form a Net National Welfare (NNW) Index

Note: All computations are in constant dollars/yen.

rates have been nothing short of spectacular, the ratio of NNW to NDP [13] has fallen in recent years. From a high of 1.15 in 1955, this ratio fell to 1.01 in 1965 and plummeted to .92 in 1970. A major reason for this has been environmental pollution, which reduced NNW by 0.2 percent in 1955, 11.6 in 1965, and 13.8 in 1970.

THE SUSTAINABLE GROWTH INVESTMENT REQUIREMENT

The Japanese Government follows an investment addition approach patterned on a concept developed by Nordhaus and Tobin. Basically, there is a computation for the amount of growth in gross investment which would permit per capita consumption to grow at the rate of technological progress. If the amount of investment growth required to achieve this end is less than actual investment, a factor called

Net Investment is added to the NNW (or MEW). If, however, the investment growth requirement exceeds the actual amount of investment in the economy, the difference is subtracted, thus reducing NNW.

A WELFARE DEFLATOR

A third approach to measuring economic and social welfare from the GNP accounts is that proposed by Robert Lekachman.[14] He suggests a welfare deflator similar to a price index. In contrast to the MEW and NNW methodology, this approach would deflate total GNP in the way GNP is adjusted for price changes. The deflator would be a composite measure of welfare improvement or deterioration. Rather than yielding a

---

[13] Net National Product minus capital formation equals NDP.

[14] Robert Lekachman, "The Income Accounts of Tomorrow," *Survey of Current Business: Fiftieth Anniversary Issue*, U.S. Department of Commerce, July 1971, pp. 119–123. This fiftieth anniversary issue of the *Survey* contains a number of interesting articles commenting on the GNP accounts, their current construction, and suggestions for future improvements.

GNP in constant dollars, the results would yield an index in real welfare terms. The final results would show an index sensitive on the upside to favorable indicators such as reduced crime and, on the downside, to unfavorable indicators such as greater air pollution.

EVALUATION OF WELFARE MEASUREMENTS

Many benefits stem from constructing a national welfare index. Perhaps the most obvious are those derived from a systematic approach to measuring economic welfare in an aggregative or total sense. Second, in the attempt to measure economic welfare, statistics from subareas are produced. Measuring nonmarket activities should yield new techniques of economic and social analysis. While these may be in their elementary stages, further research should refine them, bringing more realistic measures and results.

However, one problem accompanying a welfare index is that its construction, as that of the GNP accounts, requires value judgments. While there may not be any more of them, the fact that many are new, as opposed to the GNP accounts, might hinder acceptance of such an index.

Still another, not unrelated problem, is a definitional one. In the Nordhaus-Tobin formulation, economic welfare is primarily a function of consumption. Defense and police expenditures, for example, are excluded, since they do not *directly* improve consumer well-being. Yet one may argue that such expenditures indirectly contribute to economic well-being and that such a measure should take this into account. However, an obvious problem would be one of assigning weights to these contributions.

The problem of value judgments and definitions in computing such an index raises another major question. If an index is to be computed for policy purposes, who should perform the computation? Should it be a government agency, a university, or a private business under contract with the Federal Government? Such an index might differ materially depending upon the viewpoint of the organization constructing it. The Japanese have chosen to follow a government design.

This leads to a further question. Would it be possible, using such an index, to set national goals for improving economic welfare through legislation? Setting such goals is not unprecedented, as witnessed by the Employment Act of 1946. This act made it the continuing policy and responsibility of the Federal Government to foster conditions which will promote maximum employment, production, and purchasing power.

The key to the question of legislated economic welfare goals lies in the simple fact of acceptance. Such an index would have to be developed with the general backing of Congress and the business and academic communities. Any disagreements could be handled by an appreciation of what the index means and what it includes or excludes. For example, if defense expenditures were excluded, then during a wartime or other period of national emergency, welfare growth targets might have to be modified. During a peacetime or "normal" period, growth targets could be set higher. In general, the many problems of developing and using an index of economic welfare do not seem insurmountable. Such an index should not replace the GNP accounts but could lend an important dimension to economic policymaking.

How Reliable Are Those Price and Employment Measures?*

By David B. Thomas

Summary

Striking an acceptable balance between inflation and unemployment has become, in recent years, a herculean task for policymakers who must ride herd on the American economy. With the public clamoring for slower inflation and lower unemployment, furrow-browed officials in Washington complain that conventional policy instruments can't seem to handle both problems simultaneously. Recent experience bears this out. Unemployment has responded only sluggishly to the stimulative economic policies of the last two years, while at the same time inflationary pressures have continued to plague the economy.

Curing this malady would be difficult even with perfect statistics. The problem is compounded by the fact that our most commonly used measures of inflation and unemployment—the Consumer Price Index (CPI) and the unemployment rate—may not be infallible. Unemployment occasionally charts a substantially different course than the official rate suggests. And the Consumer Price Index, built into many wage settlements, may significantly overstate the level of inflation.

Key Questions to Consider

■ What are the shortcomings of the unemployment rate as an economic indicator?

■ Do the movements normally reported in the unemployment rate from month to month really indicate that something is changing in the economy?

■ What are the major problems with the Consumer Price Index (CPI)?

■ Given the shortcomings of the unemployment rate and the CPI, why do policymakers continue to use them?

* Reprinted with permission from *Business Review*, Federal Reserve Bank of Philadelphia, April 1973, pp. 17–22.

How Reliable Are Those Price and Employment Measures?

"Price Index Is Up Sharply on Record Grocery Rise," *New York Times*, February 23, 1973

"Unemployment Rate Dips to 5%, Best in 2½ Years," *Philadelphia Inquirer*, February 3, 1973

"Consumer Price Increase Narrowed 0.3%," *Wall Street Journal*, November 22, 1972

"Prices Rise 0.4%; Increase Biggest in Last 5 Months," *New York Times*, August 23, 1972

Striking an acceptable balance between inflation and unemployment has become, in recent years, a herculean task for policymakers who must ride herd on the American economy. With the public clamoring for slower inflation and lower unemployment, furrow-browed officials in Washington complain that conventional policy instruments can't seem to handle both problems simultaneously. Recent experience bears this out. Unemployment has responded only sluggishly to the stimulative economic policies of the last two years, while at the same time inflationary pressures have continued to plague the economy.

Curing this malady would be difficult even with perfect statistics. The problem is compounded by the fact that our most commonly used measures of inflation and unemployment—the Consumer Price Index (CPI) and the unemployment rate—may not be infallible. Unemployment occasionally charts a sub-

stantially different course than the official rate suggests. And the Consumer Price Index, built into many wage settlements, may significantly overstate the level of inflation.

UNEMPLOYMENT RATE: A PROBLEM OF SAMPLES AND SEASONS

The unemployment rate, which shows what portion of the labor force is out of work at any given time, is one of the most widely used and closely watched barometers of economic conditions. Policymakers, concerned with providing jobs for all those willing, able, and wanting to work, use it in determining and evaluating programs geared toward this goal. The jobless rate also is often used to gauge the utilization of productive capacity. As such it acts as a thermostat by signaling when the economy is either straining or operating beneath its productive capacity. While the unemployment rate (see Box 1) can be useful in assessing the state of the economy, it has many shortcomings.

The Sampling Scheme. If Bureau of Labor Statistics measurements indicate the unemployment rate dropped from 5.5 to 5.3 percent last month, this

Box 1   # Employed or Unemployed? Conflicting Conceptions

Employment figures are culled from the largest monthly sampling in the world, the Current Population Survey. Conducted for the Bureau of Labor Statistics (BLS) by the Bureau of Census, this survey gathers data concerning the employment status of some 105,000 people, 16 years or older, across the country. During 1971 some 145 million Americans fitted this description. Thus, each person in the survey represents about 1,350 in the total population.

The Bureau of Labor Statistics is responsible for defining what is meant by "employed" and "unemployed" *:

Job Holders. Employed are persons 16 years or older who, during the week previous to the monthly Current Population Survey, either

- did any work at all for pay or profit, or
- worked a minimum of 15 hours without pay for a family business, or
- have a job but are temporarily out of work because of such factors as strikes, vacations, bad weather, or illness.

---

* Source: U.S. Department of Labor, Bureau of Labor Statistics; *BLS Handbook of Methods*, Bulletin 1711.

Job Seekers. To be classified as unemployed, a person must

- be 16 years or older, and
- be currently available for work, and
- have engaged in some specific job-seeking activity during the previous four weeks, and
- not have worked at all for pay during the week previous to the survey.

Many critics claim that BLS requirements for being classified as unemployed are stringent. Because of this, they state, there's a small army of the "disguised" or "hidden" unemployed—those who would like to work but have had such bad luck finding jobs in the past that they have given up pounding the pavement.

According to the BLS classification scheme, discouraged workers such as these would not be counted as members of the labor force, since they have not engaged in a specific job-seeking activity within the last month. Some believe that because of this, the official unemployment rate tends to understate the actual jobless rate.

---

would be heralded by the news media and public as proof that labor market conditions are improving. In such a case, however, it is possible that the percentage of unemployed didn't change a bit—it may even have risen!

Such potential discrepancies between the measured and actual unemployment rates arise because jobless figures are derived from only a sample of the population. These sample results may differ from the figures that a full census would produce.

For example, to be certain that any measured change in the unemployment rate isn't only the result of variations inherent in the sampling process, it must change by .2 percent or more between the consecutive

months.[1] Movements in the jobless rate of less than this amount can reasonably be attributed to sampling errors. And even though a .2 percent decline is significant "statistically," it doesn't necessarily indicate a large decrease in the percentage of the labor force out of work.[2]

---

[1] John E. Bregger, "Unemployment Statistics and What They Mean," *Monthly Labor Review*, November 1971, p. 24.

[2] The chances are nine out of ten that the true change in the unemployment rate will be within .2 percent of the measured change. Thus, when the measured rate declines by .2 percent between two consecutive months, the true decline could be any value between zero (since .2 − .2 = zero) and .4 (since .2 + .2 = .4).

Predictable Patterns?   Because factors such as school opening and closing dates, crop seasons, production schedules, and holidays cause employment to fluctuate regularly from month to month, published unemployment figures are most often seasonally adjusted. The fluctuation which usually occurs during a particular month is removed in the adjusted rate, making it easier to discern how the jobless picture has changed relative to previous months.

Additional error may creep into monthly unemployment figures, almost gremlinlike, through the seasonal adjustment process. This is because the method used relies mainly upon seasonal patterns observed in past years and cannot pick up any new pattern before it actually occurs. Variations in weather conditions, holidays, production schedules, and school openings and closings insure that seasonal patterns will never be constant. To the extent that such events occur, the adjustment process may compound the error already present.

Predicting the size of this "seasonal adjustment" error for any particular month is impossible. After one or two years, however, when any new seasonal patterns have been identified, the official rate is revised. Over the past few years these revisions have averaged about .1 percent—a reasonable approximation of the error caused by the adjustment process.

Unemployment Figures in Perspective.   The total error for BLS monthly estimates of changes in the unemployment rate might be as high as .3 percent—about .2 percent from sampling error and .1 percent from seasonal adjustment error. To be absolutely certain that the job scene differs between two consecutive months, then, the unemployment rate must change by at least this much (for example, fall from 5.8 to 5.5 percent). Yet, during the past year it varied by this amount during only two months.

Does this make movements like those reported for the remaining ten months completely meaningless? Perhaps. If the measured unemployment rate fluctuates by small amounts around a particular level

for several months in a row, chances are that these changes are only the result of measurement error. If it shows small movements in the same direction for several consecutive months, however, then the jobless picture is *actually* changing. Trends in the rate give a better reflection of what is happening in the job market than the change for a single month (even if none of the month-to-month movements forming the trend are "statistically" significant in themselves).

Finally, inasmuch as the amount of sampling error decreases when the size of a sample increases, quarterly figures for unemployment, which are derived from samples three times the size of the monthly samples, are much more reliable than monthly ones. If the official rate falls from 5.9 to 5.7 percent between two quarters, as it did during 1972, for example, the chances are greater than 19 out of 20 that the jobless rate actually decreased.

GAUGING INFLATION WITH THE CPI

Coming to grips with slippery unemployment figures is just one aspect of the problem economists and policymakers face in analyzing the tradeoff between rising prices and joblessness. The other side of the problem is that of measuring inflation. The Consumer Price Index is the yardstick commonly used.[3] The "cost of living" index, the CPI's popular name, suggests the rationale undergirding this choice. Of all price indices, this one best gauges the effect of rising prices on the workers' purchasing power. Thus, it reflects many of the headaches and hassles caused by inflation.

Although calculation of the CPI is a relatively straightforward task (see Box 2), the index may not accurately reflect inflationary pressures in the econ-

---

[3] The CPI is officially called "The Consumer Price Index for Urban Wage Earners and Clerical Workers."

omy. Errors infiltrate the CPI just as they do jobless figures. However, sampling errors and the seasonal adjustment process account for only a small portion of the potential inaccuracies in the CPI.[4] Two major problems with the CPI are caused by improved goods and services and by changes in the buying habits of consumers.

Quantifying Quality. Technological progress improves the quality of many goods and services. A color TV made in 1973 is quite different from one built ten years earlier: It has a wider screen, clearer reception, sharper color, and hopefully will last longer. Some consumer advocates, notwithstanding, there are few people who would trade a '73 color set for an unused '63 model.

If the CPI is to measure changes in purchasing power accurately, the prices of goods and services included in the market basket must be adjusted to represent such quality changes. Suppose the price of a particular color model rose by 20 percent since 1963. To some consumers this might indicate a 20 percent inflation in the price of color TVs during this period. But the '73 model offers the consumer more quality and satisfaction than the '63 one. The price of color TVs may not have risen at all, if price increases reflect the changes in quality.

The BLS is confronted with the need, in such a case, to decide what part of a price increase is the result of quality improvement and what part is purely inflationary. Methods have been developed to do this. But assigning a dollar and cents value to things such as TV set durability or better color reception is a tricky business.

Many economists claim that BLS methods of adjusting the prices of goods for quality changes have failed to capture the full effects of quality improvements. This shortcoming, they maintain, causes the CPI to overstate the rate of inflation by .5 to 1.5 percent annually.[5]

Changing Consumption Patterns. Additional upward bias in the CPI is caused by the relative inflexibility of the "market basket" used in its calculation (see Box 2). The current weight structure of the expenditure classes is based upon the results of the 1960–61 Consumer Expenditure Survey. According to the index, then, consumers today have the same basic spending patterns as they did more than a decade ago.

The "fixed" construction of the CPI's market basket ignores the tendency of consumers to substitute relatively low-priced goods for relatively high-priced ones. Since the early 1960s, for example, families might have budgeted a higher percentage of their

---

[4] Seasonal adjustment isn't as significant a problem in the all-items CPI, so the index isn't presented in the adjusted form. The prices of goods included in the market basket have different seasonal variation patterns which largely cancel each other. To the extent that this is true, the adjusted numbers would provide no new information.

It is inevitable that a certain amount of sampling error be present in the CPI, because the index is constructed from monthly samples of retail outlets. Fortunately, however, the amount of error originating here is insignificantly small. The chances are 19 out of 20 that sampling error will not exceed .08 percent for any particular month. When the "rounding-off" of the price figures is taken into consideration, this makes a .2 percent change in the CPI between two consecutive months statistically significant. For example, if BLS measurements indicate the CPI rose from 100.0 to 100.2 during some months, we can be 95 percent confident that prices actually did rise.

[5] The argument that unaccounted-for improvements in quality cause an upward bias in the CPI is by no means universal. Some economists, although probably less than the majority, believe the reverse is true—that unaccounted-for deterioration of quality causes the CPI to understate the actual rate of inflation.

For a more thorough analysis of the upward bias in the CPI resulting from quality changes, see William H. Wallace, "Measuring Price Changes," *Monthly Review* of the Federal Reserve Bank of Richmond, November 1970; and Richard Ruggles, "Measuring the Cost of Quality," *Challenge*, November 1961. A fuller discussion of possible downward bias in the CPI appears in Jack E. Triplett, "Quality Bias in Price Indexes and New Methods of Quality Measurement," Zvi Griliches, ed., *Prices Indexes and Quality Change: Studies in New Methods of Measurement* (Cambridge, Mass.: Harvard University Press, 1971), pp. 180–214.

Box 2   **The "Base Period Market Basket": How the BLS Keeps Tabs on Prices**

The method used by the Bureau of Labor Statistics to measure changes in the price level of consumer goods and services involves two basic steps. First, about once every ten years a large sample of consumers falling into the category of "urban wage earners and clerical workers" are interviewed concerning their spending habits.* (The most recent survey was undertaken in 1960–61.) From the results of this Consumer Expenditure Survey, the BLS is able to construct the index's "base period market basket." For the sake of simplicity, consider the market basket as representing a single budget that shows how Norman Normal, the typical consumer, spent his income of $10,000 during the base year.

About 400 different goods and services are included in the market basket—everything from apples to washing machines. These items are divided into 52 expenditure classes of similar products or services. A fixed weight is assigned to each class on the basis of how Norman Normal divided his income among the

classes. For example, if he budgeted 5 percent of his income for fresh vegetables, this expenditure class would receive a weight of .05. Weights are assigned to products within each class on the same basis, with these weights showing how Mr. Normal budgeted his money among the products included in a particular class.

After the "base period market basket" has been constructed, the second step, that of monitoring prices, is relatively easy. Each month the BLS sends surveyors to selected retail outlets in major cities across the country to collect data concerning current prices of goods and services included in the market basket. When this information has been gathered, the BLS calculates exactly how much it would now cost to purchase the same set of goods and services (the market basket) that Norman Normal bought in the base period with his $10,000 income.

The level of the CPI is calculated by dividing the market basket's current cost by its base period cost and multiplying this figure by 100. Suppose we find that it now costs $11,000 to buy Mr. Normal's market basket. The new level of the index, then, is [($11,000/ $10,000) × 100] or 110. This indicates that the prices of goods and services purchased by consumers have risen, on the average, by 10 percent since the base period.

---

* Some people critically point out that this group represents only about 40 percent of the total population. In recent years, however, this occupational classification has lost most of its significance, as the spending habits of this group have become similar to those of the rest of the population. Thus, although the index does not claim to represent all consumers, it probably represents a large majority of them.

---

income for chicken and a lower percentage for pork, because the price of chicken has risen less than the price of pork.

Overlooking such "substitution effects" gives too much weight to goods and services with rapidly rising prices. This, in turn, causes the index to overstate the rate of inflation. Judging by the experience gained from past revisions of the market basket, the amount of upward bias coming from this source is in the neighborhood of .5 percent annually.[6]

---

[6] See "Needed: A New Dimension for the CPI," *Monthly*

A Relatively Accurate Index.   In the final analysis, the CPI, like most other economic indicators, has its strong and weak points. The index's strength lies in its ability to measure *relative* changes in the rate of inflation on a month-to-month basis. For example, when the CPI rises by .8 percent in July and .4 during August, the rate of inflation has dropped by about half during August. However, inadequate adjustment for quality changes and new consumption patterns

---

Economic Letter, First National City Bank of New York, November 1970.

may cause the index to overstate *absolute* changes in the level of consumer prices by as much as 1 to 2 percent a year. Thus, although the rate of inflation fell by about half in the example, it is much less certain that prices increased by .8 percent in July and .4 percent in August. And this is the CPI's basic weakness.

BETTER CAUTIOUS THAN CONFIDENT

Policymakers continue to base their decisions on changes in the Consumer Price Index and the unemployment rate, even with the awareness that these indicators may not be totally accurate. There is little choice, for even if the two measures are less than perfect, they are among the best we have at present. Given these circumstances, the indices' limitations, with respect to accuracy, must be recognized and considered when basing policy decisions on their movements. Overreacting to small month-to-month changes in unemployment figures, as the news media and public often do, could lead to perverse policy decisions. The same should be said of relying too heavily on changes in the price level as measured by the CPI. Finally, it should be remembered that monthly price and unemployment figures are only rough gauges of economic trends and, as such, do not lend themselves to "fine tuning" the economy.

Reading 27

What Is Money?*

Summary

To the man in the street, money is the paper currency in his wallet and the coins in his pocket. On a moment's further reflection, he names the balance in his checking account also; checks drawn on it work as well as currency or coin when he has payments to make. What about the savings account he keeps at his bank, or a certificate of deposit that he holds? For that matter, how about the savings account he maintains at the savings and loan? Are these money, too? This is a harder question.

Perhaps the best answer to this question is that there may be no one best place to draw the line. Thus the monthly *Federal Reserve Bulletin* carries a tabulation entitled "Measures of the Money Stock," in which three such measures are presented.

The first of these measures, M_1, defines money quite narrowly; indeed, M_1 is often termed narrow money. Broad money usually refers to M_2, which includes an asset category, time deposits, that is slightly less moneylike than M_1. Similarly, M_3 extends the definition a little further still—further away from the purest of moneyness.

Defining money, then, is a tricky business. But it is a necessary first step that has to be taken before any serious study can be made of money's role in economic affairs. With a definition in hand, whichever one it may be, the analyst may proceed to measure the size of the money supply and to monitor changes in it that take place over time.

Key Questions to Consider

- What do the three measures of the money stock tabulated by the Federal Reserve Board include?

- What factors would determine which definition an analyst would use?

- What is the connection between money and economic activity?

* Reprinted with permission from *Business Conditions*, Federal Reserve Bank of Chicago, June 1971, pp. 9–15.

What Is Money?

To the man in the street, money is the paper currency in his wallet and the coins in his pocket. On a moment's further reflection, he names the balance in his checking account also; checks drawn on it work as well as currency or coin when he has payments to make. What about the savings account he keeps at his bank, or a certificate of deposit that he holds? For that matter, how about the savings account he maintains at the savings and loan? Are these money, too? This is a harder question.

FROM MONEY TO NEAR-MONEY

Unlike the more "obvious" forms of money, savings accounts or certificates cannot be immediately and directly used to make payments. First, they have to be converted into one of the kinds of money that can be directly spent. Still, in another sense, they seem to be all but indistinguishable from money. While checks cannot be written on savings accounts, sums on deposit are almost as readily accessible as checking account balances. Withdrawals in practice can be made at any time and without advance notice to the bank or the savings association. Certificates are somewhat less easy to turn into cash, as they carry specific maturity dates. Yet even these instruments can be cashed on the holder's demand, with some sacrifice in interest yield. Savings deposits and certificates, therefore, are less "liquid" than demand deposits (checking accounts), or coins and currency, but not much. The distinction is slight. And the interest yield that savings or other time accounts produce may more than compensate for their lesser relative liquidity. Obviously, it does—or depositors would refuse to keep funds in such forms. Clearly, savings accounts and other time deposits at banks and thrift institutions look a lot like money and may well deserve to be encompassed by the definition of money.

Nor does this end the matter. What about credit union shares? U.S. savings bonds? Treasury bills and notes? Corporate bonds and stocks? Is the list endless? Clearly it cannot be if the definition of money is to be a useful one. The recitation of asset forms that need to be considered for inclusion in the definition of money serves to suggest that "moneyness" is a matter of degree. If this is so, if assets of all kinds—and even "nonfinancial" assets—may be thought of as having moneyness or liquidity to some extent, it still seems important to draw a line that will separate money from all other assets. But where should this line be drawn?

THREE DEFINITIONS

Perhaps the best answer to this question is that there may be no one best place to draw the line. Thus, the monthly *Federal Reserve Bulletin* carries a tabulation entitled "Measures of the Money Stock," in which three such measures are presented. These are separately labeled and defined as follows:

M_1: currency (including coin) and demand deposits (checking accounts).

M_2: M_1 plus savings and other time deposits of commercial banks, excepting negotiable certificates of deposit of $100,000 and more at major commercial banks.

M_3: M_2 plus deposits of mutual savings banks and accounts at savings and loan associations.

The first of these measures, M_1, defines money quite narrowly; indeed, M_1 is often termed narrow money. Broad money usually refers to M_2, which includes an asset category, time deposits, that is slightly less moneylike than M_1. Similarly, M_3 extends the definition a little further still—further away from the purest of moneyness.

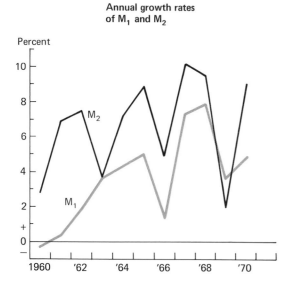

Annual growth rates of M_1 and M_2

It may be noted that the *Bulletin* tabulation labels no one of these as *the* money stock or money supply. The three are simply offered as alternative possible measures. The user or the analyst may take his pick. Or, he may wish to devise a definition of his own, offering it not necessarily as a definition of money as such, but rather as the definition of a financial or monetary magnitude he deems to be significant. Commercial bank reserves and the monetary base—two measures of the foundation that bank deposits and bank credit rest upon—are regarded by some as more useful than any of the money concepts above. Other analysts, however, prefer to move out the other way, to a measure even broader than M_3, to which they add such other financial asset forms as credit union shares, Treasury bills, and so on.[1]

MONEY IN THE MARKETPLACE

An analyst who views money primarily in terms of its role as a medium of exchange usually will be most comfortable with the narrow M_1 definition of money, including as it does those financial assets that may be used directly in the marketplace. Coin, currency, and checks drawn on demand deposits all fit this description. Although certain other holdings may be so used —a negotiable certificate of deposit or travelers' check might be an example—their importance as media of exchange is negligible, and little harm is done if only those assets encompassed by the M_1 definition are treated as bona fide exchange media.

MONEY AS LIQUIDITY

Money is more than a medium of exchange, though, as the textbooks point out. Beyond its usefulness as a

---

[1] Some of the technicalities involved in the derivation of money supply measures are dealt with in the accompanying boxed statement, which also illustrates the interrelations among alternative definitions of money.

unit of account or standard of deferred payments is its asset role. As the ultimate in liquid assets, money is ideal to hold for protection against contingencies, such as unexpected interruptions in income or needs to cover emergency outlays. In addition, money balances enable holders to move quickly to take advantage of investment or speculative opportunities. In short, every economic entity is motivated to hold money not only in order to carry on its routine activities in the marketplace, but also to afford it some leeway in the management of its earning assets and to provide it a cushion against unforeseeable occurrences.

The analyst who assigns priority to the financial-asset role of money in the economy is apt to prefer a broader to a narrower definition of money. In good part, this reflects uncertainty over just where the line around money is to be drawn. Thus, the difference between currency and demand deposits, both of which are within *any* definition of money, may appear greater than the difference between, say, savings and loan accounts, which are components of M_3 and Treasury bills, which are not. Yet the exclusion of bills may not be bothersome if they tend to behave much as the elements within the money measure. But in any event, the money-as-asset analyst regards money as something considerably more than only the coins and pieces of paper that people use to pay their bills and settle their debts.

WHAT'S IN A DEFINITION?

Defining money, then, is a tricky business. But it is a necessary first step that has to be taken before any serious study can be made of money's role in economic affairs. With a definition in hand, whichever one it may be, the analyst may proceed to measure the size of the money supply and to monitor changes in it that take place over time.

Professional opinion remains divided on the nature of the connection between money and economic activity, and particularly on the direction of causation.

This is despite the close attention that economists and others have devoted to monetary matters over the past 150 years and the voluminous masses of empirical evidence that they have examined. One view (the monetarist) emphasizes the importance of money in determining economic activity and contends that changes in the existing stock of money motivates changes in spending and income, given the pattern of money use.

Critics assert that this view assumes away the problem by positing an unchanged pattern of money use. The critics believe that any given change in the money supply—as by a Federal Reserve System move inducing banks to increase loans and deposits—often will be offset by a change in velocity. Many among this group, indeed, question the efficacy of monetary actions in general, contending instead that fiscal policy measures, such as changes in the rate of federal spending or changes in tax rates that affect the level of disposable income, have far greater impact on economic activity than do monetary policy actions. Holders of this view are quick to agree that monetary policy is not wholly impotent, conceding that changes in the money supply affect interest rates, which, in turn, influence business investment spending—and even consumer spending through their impact on capital values or "wealth."

Despite major differences on the importance of monetary matters and the relationship between money and economic activity, there is all but universal agreement that some sort of connection exists and, moreover, that some influence runs from money *to* economic activity. (Unless this were so, there would be little for monetary policy, and central banks, to do!) But how strong this relationship is, and how it compares with influences on activity from other quarters—and influences running from activity to money—are questions that have yet to be fully answered.

Now, granted that money matters, what concept or definition of the money supply provides the best measure of monetary influences upon economic activity? Opinion on this, not surprisingly, is divided. At least three points of view may be identified.

Box   # Money Supply Measures and Their Derivation

The accompanying table illustrates relationships among three widely used measures of the money supply, as well as showing the several adjustments that must first be made in the important demand deposit component. The estimates given are averages for four weeks ending January 27, 1971.

	Billions of dollars
Gross demand deposits at all commercial banks	$ 242.9
—Cash items in process of collection	− 31.6
—Interbank deposits	− 28.6
—U.S. Government deposits	− 6.5
—Federal Reserve float	− 3.8
+Foreign deposits at Federal Reserve banks ...	+ 0.4
=Demand deposits in money supply	$ 172.9
+Currency in hands of the public	+ 49.2
=M_1	$ 222.1
+Commercial bank time deposits (excluding CDs of $100,000 and more at major banks) ...	+207.2
=M_2	$ 429.3
+Deposits at nonbank thrift institutions (mutual savings banks, savings and loan associations)	+217.9
=M_3	$ 647.2

Source: *Federal Reserve Bulletin* and Federal Reserve System data.

The adjustments made in gross demand deposits may be explained as follows:

Interbank deposits are liabilities owed by one bank to another. They are excluded from the money supply because the computation of total demand deposits requires consolidating balance sheets of the individual banks. Such aggregation results in the canceling out of all deposits owed by one commercial bank to another. Not included in the interbank category are deposits at mutual savings banks and foreign commercial banks, and M_1-type deposits at Edge Act corporations and branches and agencies of foreign banks.

Cash items in the process of collection (CIPC) and Federal Reserve float—often combined as "bank float"—are accounts that have much in common. Both are temporary accounts measuring the double-counting of demand deposits arising from inherent lags in the check clearing process. If check clearing were instantaneous, these accounts would be unnecessary.

Cash items in the process of collection accounts for checks that the bank has collected but for which it has not yet received credit from the Federal Reserve bank. Federal Reserve float occurs when two banks are given credit for the same reserves.

For example, assume a father sends a check for $100 drawn on a Springfield bank to his son in Chicago. When his son deposits the check in his Chicago bank, the bank credits his deposit and debits CIPC. Thus, the Chicago bank registers an increase in demand deposits. But no corresponding reduction has taken place yet in the Springfield bank's deposits. This temporary double-counting of the $100 is called "float," which the deduction of CIPC from gross demand deposits is designed to eliminate.

When the Chicago bank forwards the check to the Federal Reserve bank, the Fed makes the proper bookkeeping entries and then sends the check to the Springfield bank. The Chicago bank must wait a certain time (corresponding to the interval judged necessary for the Springfield bank to notify the Fed that it has received the check) before it is credited with the reserves. When this period passes, the Chicago bank records an increase of $100 in reserves and a reduction of $100 in CIPC.

If processing the check between the Fed and the Springfield bank is delayed, the Springfield bank will not have drawn down its reserves and deposits at the end of the prearranged period. As a result, both banks will be credited with the reserves corresponding to the check. This type of double-counting of reserves is called Federal Reserve float. To correct the money supply for such double-counting, it is necessary to subtract Federal Reserve float from gross demand deposits. When the Springfield bank eventually does notify the Fed of receipt of the check, its deposits and reserves are drawn down, eliminating float.

The rationale for excluding U.S. Government deposits from the money supply is that such deposits probably have little influence upon government expenditures. Nevertheless, some economists, believing that these deposits should be included, argue that U.S. Government deposits are qualitatively no different than state and local government deposits, which are included.*

The inclusion of foreign deposits at Federal Reserve banks also has been questioned. It has been

argued that they are primarily for foreign exchange transactions rather than for the purchases of U.S. goods and services and, therefore, should be excluded from the money supply.

Recently, adjustments have been made in the money supply to correct a considerable understatement, resulting from the rapid increase in Eurodollar transactions. Eurodollar transactions often have resulted in checks being deposited with U.S. commercial banks from their foreign branches, thereby increasing U.S. bank assets (CIPC) and liabilities (demand deposits).

As mentioned previously, the purpose of the CIPC account is to prevent double-counting. Yet, until quite recently, foreign agency demand deposits have not been included as a component of demand deposits. Therefore, the subtraction of CIPC from gross demand deposits would result in an understatement of the money supply. This error has become more serious in recent years as the volume of Eurodollar transactions has increased.

To correct for this, the demand deposit component in money supply measures now includes those deposits associated with Eurodollar transactions.

Inclusion of these deposits offsets the CIPC items associated with Eurodollars, thereby eliminating the understatement in the money supply.

---

* See Paul S. Anderson and Frank E. Morris, "Defining the Money Supply: The Case of Government Deposits," *New England Economic Review*, March/April 1969, pp. 21–31. For the official view, see Board of Governors of the Federal Reserve System, *Supplement to Money and Monetary Statistics, Section I, Banks and the Monetary System*, October 1962, p. 7.

Note: For a more thorough discussion, see Irving Auerbach, "International Banking Institutions and the Understatement of the Money Supply," *Monthly Review*, Federal Reserve Bank of New York, May 1971, pp. 109–18. Also, see Joseph G. Kvasnicka, "Eurodollars—An Important Source of Funds for American Banks," *Business Conditions*, Federal Reserve Bank of Chicago, June 1969, pp. 9–20.

THE CLAIM FOR NARROW MONEY

On one hand is the belief that it is money in the narrowest sense, or M_1, that has the most analytical usefulness. This follows from the notion that M_1 is made up solely of monies that are directly spendable. Spending, which is just another way of looking at income, entails the transfer of money (M_1-type money) from buyers to sellers; therefore, it seems to follow that changes in M_1 play an important role in determining expenditures. This definition or *a priori* approach sidesteps the necessity for any empirical testing.

THE OPPOSITE EXTREME

Those critical of the monetarist doctrine believe that what really matters is the economy's total liquidity or moneyness. According to this view, the oncoming course of economic activity is foreshadowed by today's liquidity position of consumers, businesses, and governmental agencies. Holdings of M_1-type money constitute a part of an aspect of liquidity—a rather nebulous and slippery term—but no more than that. But clearly, non-M_1 moneylike assets, such as time deposits, savings certificates, credit union shares, readily saleable securities, and perhaps also certain

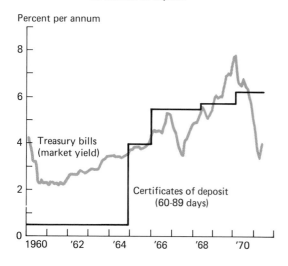

Treasury bill rates and
maximum rates payable on
certificates of deposit

Percent per annum

Treasury bills
(market yield)

Certificates of deposit
(60-89 days)

1960   '62   '64   '66   '68   '70

financial assets that are not readily saleable, also need to be taken into account. Furthermore, a significant further aspect of liquidity is the readiness with which funds may be realized by borrowing, the "availability" (and price) of credit. Liquidity to those who subscribe to this position appears to be little less than the *potential* behind spending and, therefore, interest rates are believed to provide a better reading of monetary conditions than any of the definitions of the money supply. Money, even by the broadest definition, may be a big part of total liquidity, but there are other components, further into the spectrum of financial assets (and credit), that enter also. Adherents to this view often define money as the sum of those financial assets found through empirical research to be the closest substitutes for M_1 and M_2. Hence, if Treasury bills were found to be close substitutes for M_1, money would be defined to include them.

MONEY IS WHAT MONEY DOES

Finally, there is the stand among those who emphasize the importance of monetary actions that money is ap-

propriately defined as that magnitude whose behavior best predicts the course of economic activity. If, in the past, changes in M_1 have been a better indicator of contemporaneous or subsequent changes in, say, total income (GNP) than have M_2 or M_3 (or other measures), then M_1 defines money. The task of defining money, therefore, reduces itself to an exercise in regression analysis, by which the measure that best explains changes in economic activity is identified.

Work that has been done on the problem appears to suggest that M_1 and M_2 fit about equally well, so that either, or an average of the two, could serve satisfactorily as *the* definition of money. But the correspondence of these two measures has been severely strained at times.

M_1, M_2, AND REGULATION Q

In much of past experience, M_1 and M_2 have grown at comparable rates and thus provided similar readings of monetary conditions. But recently, the aggregates have grown at distinctly different rates. In 1968 and 1969, market interest rates rose above the maximum rates payable on bank deposits as established by Regulation Q. This induced investors to withdraw their funds from time deposits and to purchase high-yielding securities. The decline of time deposits caused M_2 to grow at a much slower rate than M_1. Since 1970, however, falling rates in the market have reversed the flow, and funds have moved back into time deposits from securities. In this time, therefore, M_2 has grown at a considerably faster rate than M_1, and the two measures continue to give considerably different impressions of monetary conditions.[2]

The effects of Regulation Q, therefore, appear to illustrate the point that the appropriateness of a

---

[2] Professor Milton Friedman, the U.S.'s foremost monetarist, has argued that neither measure is reliable when M_1 and M_2 diverge and that the answer lies somewhere in between. His solution would be to eliminate the cause of the divergence; i.e., abolish Regulation Q.

definition of money depends on the use to which it is to be put. Thus, determining what constitutes money is a challenging task that is heavily dependent upon both economic theory and empirical research and, until economists resolve their differences on how money influences economic activity, this issue promises to remain a controversial one.

Controlling Money with Bank Reserves*

By William N. Cox, III

Summary

"The Fed *somehow* does *something* to bank reserves, which *somehow* makes the banks to *something* to bank deposits, which *somehow* have *something* to do with the money stock."

A vague statement. But an accurate statement, perhaps, of the vagueness with which many citizens view the mechanics of Federal Reserve operations. Yet the mechanics of what happens and why are important, because no one can really understand or criticize Fed policy unless he has a common-sense grasp of how it operates.

The purpose of this article, therefore, is expository: to see, first, how the Federal Reserve's operations on bank reserves serve to control the total of deposits held at commercial banks, and to see, second, how control of those total deposits relates to control of the money stock. Our purpose is to fill in those "somethings" and "somehows."

Key Questions to Consider

■ How can the Fed limit the total of bank deposits?

■ How is it that by buying literally anything, the Fed can increase the supply of reserves?

■ What is the Fed funds market and what purpose does it serve?

■ Briefly describe the four complications encountered by the Fed in its operations to control total bank deposits.

■ With the focusing of the Fed's policymakers on the money stock rather than total deposits, a new concept has emerged, "reserves available to support private deposits" (RPD's). How is this concept used?

* Reprinted with permission from *Monthly Review*, Federal Reserve Bank of Atlanta, **LVIII,** No. 4 (April 1973), 55–59.

Controlling Money with Bank Reserves

"The Fed *somehow* does *something* to bank reserves, which *somehow* makes the banks do *something* to bank deposits, which *somehow* have *something* to do with the money stock."

A vague statement. But an accurate statement, perhaps, of the vagueness with which many citizens view the mechanics of Federal Reserve operations. Yet the mechanics of what happens and why are important, because no one can really understand or criticize Fed policy unless he has a common-sense grasp of how it operates.

The purpose of this article, therefore, is expository: to see, first, how the Federal Reserve's operations on bank reserves serve to control the total of deposits held at commercial banks, and to see, second, how control of those total deposits relates to control of the money stock. Our purpose is to fill in those "somethings" and "somehows."

CONTROLLING "WIDGET" PRODUCTION

To understand what sort of system the Fed uses to control total bank deposits, let's use a hypothetical product and call it a widget. All we have to imagine about widgets is that thousands of widgetmakers pro-duce and sell millions of them every year and make a profit doing it.

Suppose, now, that for some reason the Federal government wanted to control widget production at a rate of 500,000 per month. Quite aside from whether this would be a good idea or not, how could such control be accomplished? There are lots of ways, perhaps, but our interest is in one that would work like this: First, the government would print Widget Production Permits. Each would say:

This permit entitles the holder to produce five widgets per month. Production of widgets without this permission is expressly prohibited.

Then the government would distribute 100,000 permits among widget producers. If each permit allowed the production of five widgets a month, then the 100,000 permits would impose a monthly production ceiling of 500,000 widgets.

Would the permit system work to control widget production? Three conditions would have to be satisfied. First, nobody but the government could issue the permits. (Successful counterfeiting, for instance, would beat the system.) Second, the government would have to be able to enforce the 5-to-1 ratio between widgets produced and permits held. (If a widgetmaker were able to produce without permits, the scheme would limit authorized production but leave actual production unaffected.)

Third, the government would have to depend on competition for profits among the widgetmakers to ensure that actual production did not fall short of the 500,000 ceiling. (If widgetmakers found it profitable to produce only 200,000 widgets a month, then the permit system would merely impose a meaningless ceiling on production without *controlling* it.)

Apparently, then, such a permit system would work to control total widget production only if the government could control the number of permits, only if the prescribed ratio between permits and production could be enforced, and only if competition for profits impelled widgetmakers to produce up to the permit-set ceiling.

The widget-control scheme parallels the system employed by the Federal Reserve to control total bank deposits. Bank deposits are our widgets, commercial banks are our widgetmakers, and bank reserves are our Widget Production Permits. We can verify that the system should work by checking the banking analogies of the three requirements for effective control.

Bank reserves themselves, for the most part, are checking-account balances held *by* commercial banks *at* their regional Federal Reserve Banks. Since the Fed keeps the books, there is no way to counterfeit our "permits." So for now, at least, we can assume the first requirement is satisfied. The second requirement for workability, enforcement of the ratio between the reserves held by the banks and the deposits their customers hold with them, is assured by traditional surveillance and examination of banks' activities. Since these first two conditions are met, the Fed's system should impose a ceiling on the total amount of bank deposits. In fact, it does.[1]

As to the third question, whether limiting the total of deposits is tantamount to controlling that total, it does appear that competition for profits among commercial banks operates to keep the actual deposit total very close to its limit. In practice then, setting a ceiling on total deposits operates to control the total.[2]

Basically, then, the Fed can limit the total of bank deposits (1) by limiting the amount of customer deposits an individual bank can hold for each dollar of reserves held by the bank, and (2) by controlling the total amount of reserves available to banks for permitting the deposits. Competition among the banks themselves normally keeps total deposits close to the reserve-set limit, so that the power to limit is, in practice, the power to control the national deposit level.

SEVEN IMPORTANT FEATURES

Now let us abandon the widget and extend our discussion to several important features of the deposit-control system. The seven features described below have been selected to flesh out our description of the tools and framework through which Fed policy exerts its influence.

First, notice that the system we described permits the Fed virtually no control over the distribution of deposits *among* commercial banks. Reserves only serve to control the total. Banks compete with each

---

[1] Until the 1930's reserves were not viewed as a deposit-control tool. When the Federal Reserve was established in 1914, reserve balances at the Fed were intended to provide

each bank with a backup stock of funds. Much like the savings an individual might put aside for a rainy day, deposits at the Fed were "reserved" for unforeseen contingencies.

[2] Commercial banks add to the overall amount of bank deposits when they make loans, which they do by accepting a borrower's promise to repay and simultaneously crediting additional funds to the borrower's checking account. Normally, a bank will continue to make additional loans and add to the overall level of deposits as long as the interest the borrower pays on the loan exceeds the bank's costs in making it. Costs would include whatever interest the bank itself would have to pay for funds it borrows, plus allowances for administrative overhead and for assuming the risks of lending.

other, subject to supervisory ground rules, to divide the total among themselves.

Second, we can see that the reserve system, by enabling the Fed to control the level of total deposits, automatically empowers the Fed to *change* that level as an act of policy. The Fed can move to increase or decrease the deposit limits on the banking system by acting to increase or diminish the reserve account balances commercial banks hold at the Fed. (The process is trickier than it looks, however, as we shall shortly see.) To decide what policy actions to take and what changes to make in the amount of reserves available, top Fed officials meet each month as the Federal Open Market Committee, the Fed's forum for monetary policy.

Third, let us ask just *how* the Fed acts to increase or decrease the supply of reserves available to commercial banks. Reserves, remember, are deposit balances held by commercial banks at the 12 regional Federal Reserve Banks. To increase the total amount of these reserve balances, all the Fed has to do is . . . buy something. Buy anything, in fact, as long as payment is made with a check drawn on a Federal Reserve Bank. What happens, in effect, is that the seller deposits the Fed's check with his commercial bank, and his bank deposits it with the Fed for credit to its reserve account. To decrease the reserve total, on the other hand, all the Fed has to do is sell something, as long as the Fed takes payment for what it sells by reducing its reserve account obligation to a commercial bank.

Buy what? Sell what? Anything, in theory, just as long as the payment is eventually credited to or deducted from a commercial bank's reserve account at the Fed. When the Fed buys a computer or pays an economist, for example, total bank reserves increase. More realistically, though, the only market large and efficient enough to handle the Fed's purchases and sales is the "open market" for government securities.[3]

A fourth feature is that the limitation on total deposits can also be changed without open-market purchases or sales by the Fed. Instead of changing the amount of reserves available to the banks, the Fed can simply change the amount of deposits each dollar of reserves will permit. This is what happens when the Fed changes reserve requirement ratios. If the ratio is initially 6-to-1, then each dollar of reserve balances permits the issue of six dollars in deposits. But if the ratio is changed to 7-to-1, each reserve dollar permits seven deposit dollars, thereby raising the total deposit limit to seven-sixths of the former level.[4] In practice, the Fed does not change reserve-to-deposit ratios very often, preferring the alternative of changing the amount of reserves with open market operations.

A fifth feature of the reserve-control system is that banks can borrow reserves directly and temporarily from the Fed. This takes place through the so-called discount window. Banks whose applications are approved pay the discount rate, a Fed-set interest rate which has also come to be viewed by the public as a gauge of the Fed's determination to hold down or encourage up bank deposit levels.[5]

Another means of giving banks temporary flexibility in meeting their reserve requirements was inaugurated in 1968: Since then banks have been allowed to carry forward up to 2 percent of their reserve excesses or deficiencies into the subsequent reserve-computation period.

Sixth, we can note that banks normally try to hold a few extra reserves at the Fed in excess of the

[3] The open market is where already-issued government securities are traded by investors, hence the term "open market operations." See "What Are Open Market Operations?", Harry

Brandt, this *Review*, May 1960 (revised March 1972). Reprinted in *Federal Reserve Policymaking and Its Problems*, 2nd ed., Number VII (Readings in Southern Finance, Atlanta, Federal Reserve Bank of Atlanta, November 1972), p. 30.

[4] The ratios are often expressed, equivalently, as percentage reserve requirements. A 10-to-1 ratio implies a 10-percent reserve requirement; a 5-to-1 ratio implies a 20-percent reserve requirement, etc.

[5] See "The Discount Rate: Problems and Remedies," this *Review*, June 1972. Also, "Member Bank Borrowing: Process and Experience," Arnold A. Dill, this *Review*, April 1973.

amounts required by the deposit levels they report. Banks often lend their excess balances to other banks overnight in the market for Federal Reserve balances —the Fed funds market, for short. Banks looking for reserves bid among each other for use of other banks' excess reserve balances, and the interest rate that emerges from each day's bidding is called the Federal funds rate. This rate is a sensitive reflection of how much pressure, if any, there is between the banks' determination to expand their deposits and profits, on the one hand, and the Fed's determination to limit such expansion, on the other.

Seventh and finally, it is important to realize that banks use reserve balances to settle debts among themselves. Traffic is heavy, since commercial banks are constantly taking credit for checks deposited with them and crediting other banks for checks written by their own customers. Banks also consummate their Federal funds transactions by asking the Fed to transfer reserves. A commercial bank's reserve balance is almost continuously changing in reflection of debits and credits resulting from thousands of banking transactions. This complicates the bankers' job of keeping enough reserve balances at the Fed to permit the deposits held at his bank and explains why the discount window and the Fed funds market are often useful.

SOME FRUSTRATING COMPLICATIONS

The Fed's system for using bank reserves to control total bank deposits, though simple in concept, encounters some frustrating complications in practice. This section discusses four of them.

The first follows from the facts that all bank deposits are not the same and that all deposits do not carry the same deposit-to-reserve ratio. Commercial banks issue deposits with diverse characteristics: checking-account balances available on demand and paying no interest, interest-bearing savings account balances, and fixed-maturity certificates of deposit, for example. All of these deposit forms are bank liabili-

ties and each, as it happens, is subject to a numerically different deposit-to-reserve ratio. Current regulations, moreover, require larger banks to hold more reserves per dollar of deposits than smaller banks.[6] So all deposits are not the same, and the same reserve ratio does not apply to all deposits.

This proliferation of deposit types and reserve-to-deposit ratios complicates the reserve-control system. If the Fed wants the banks to issue more demand deposits and decides to supply additional reserve balances through open market operations to permit the additional demand deposits, for example, then Fed policymakers have to guess how many of the additional reserves will be used by the banks for additional demand deposits, and how many will be used for additions of other deposit types. (We shall return to this example in the next section.)

A second, somewhat different complication is that various hard-to-predict events operate on their own to increase or decrease the total amount of reserves available. It is almost as if a tribe of gremlins were capriciously stealing and replacing each bank's stock of reserves, shifting the reserve total up and down in the process.

One reason this happens is that banks can count the currency and coin they hold in their vaults as reserves. Putting the details aside, the result is that total reserves change every time a bank customer deposits currency or cashes a check at a teller's window. Essentially the same result occurs every time the U.S. Treasury or a foreign central bank shifts deposits between a commercial bank and a Federal Reserve Bank.

The biggest gremlin of all, though, arises from what bankers call Fed float. Banks use the Fed to clear checks, as we said, crediting the reserve account of a bank which submits a check with a delay estimated to equal the time it will take to collect the check (by deducting reserves from another bank).

---

[6] To further complicate matters, there are other "non-deposit liabilities" of banks which must also be backed by reserves, as, for example, Eurodollar liabilities.

When the estimate is poor, so that the deduction and the credit fail to coincide, Fed float results. This Fed float varies from day to day, as when a snowstorm delays the physical shipment of checks from a major city, thereby delaying the collection of those checks in other cities. As it varies, so does the total of reserves available.

We call gremlins like these market factors. The Fed works hard to predict how these factors will shift and tries to offset their effects by buying or selling government securities. (This, in fact, is what impels the Fed to engage in a large dollar volume of open market operations almost every day. If the problem were simply to add a few reserves every month to allow for gradual growth in the economy's need for deposits, then the Fed could probably get by with a single security purchase each week.)

A third operational complication surfaces when one considers that thousands of banks hold reserve balances at the Fed. It is a big job just to add up how many deposits each bank holds in each reserve-ratio category. With the banks' cooperation, an elaborate deposit tabulation and accounting system has been built and is constantly being improved. Even with this, though, a bank itself is often unsure of its deposit totals until the following day or thereafter. This is perhaps the main reason why reserve balances and deposit totals are matched up on a weekly average basis rather than daily.[7]

A final complication, here at least, is that only four out of ten commercial banks are members of the Federal Reserve System. Only about 40 percent of U.S. banks, therefore, are subject to the direct influence of the Fed's reserve system. (Nonmember banks must conform to alternative reserve requirements established by state laws.) Fortunately, however, member banks account for about 80 percent of U.S. bank deposits.

These are some of the headaches—there are many others—which the Fed encounters as it tries to use the bank reserve system to limit total bank deposits. Although the scheme is conceptually so simple it seems as though it would have to work, perhaps in practice the surprising thing is that it works at all.

BANK RESERVES, THE MONEY STOCK, AND RPD's

With some complications, then, the reserve system we have discussed enables Fed policymakers to exert control over total bank deposits. Increasingly in the 1970's, however, Fed attention has focused not on total deposits but instead on the money stock.[8] As a result, the Fed has experimented with various methods of tailoring the existing reserve system to its new problem of controlling the stock of money.

The money stock, in each of several definitions, includes some types of bank deposits but not others. Demand deposits of private customers are always included in the money stock, for example; negotiable certificates of deposit are never included. Looking at the other side of the same coin, this means that the total of deposits, the total subject to reserve control, includes some types of deposits not included in the money stock.[9]

The basic problem is how to use reserves to control a particular part of total deposits (i.e., those classified as money) while ignoring the remainder of total deposits (i.e., those not classified as money).

---

[7] The reserve statement period is a seven-day week, Thursday through Wednesday, over which banks must hold enough reserve balances, on average, to meet the requirements implied by their deposit levels reported two weeks previously.

[8] The main objective of Fed policy is economic stabilization. The Federal Open Market Committee has increasingly adopted the view that appropriate control of the money stock is the best way to pursue that objective. For a discussion of the issues involved, see "The Money Supply Controversy," this *Review*, June 1969.

[9] The money stock also includes one nondeposit item: currency and coin in the hands of the nonbank public. In practice, this currency component of money is much smaller and less volatile than the deposit components, so that the problem of controlling money is largely the problem of controlling the deposit components of money.

We alluded to this problem in an earlier example: If the Fed decides to supply additional reserve balances with the intent of permitting growth in money-type deposits, there is nothing to prevent the banks from using the reserves to increase nonmoney-type deposits. Conversely, if deposits of the nonmoney type increase, banks must find reserves to permit the increase, perhaps even at the expense of an undesired decline in money deposits.

The situation resembles a family which classifies its expenses as either necessity expenditures or luxury expenditures. If the family's total expenditures stay at their limit of spendable income, then an increase (or decrease) in necessity expenditures must be accompanied by a decrease (or increase) in luxury expenditures. We could say that the spendable income limit resembles the limit imposed by the quantity of reserves available to the banks, luxury expenditures correspond to the money-type deposits whose levels the Fed wants to control, and necessity expenditures correspond to the other nonmoney deposits. (There is nothing necessitous or luxurious about either group of deposits, however.)

The Fed has an advantage the family may not have: The spendable income in its case (i.e., available reserve balances) can be adjusted through open market operations. If the family enjoyed this advantage and if, like the Fed, it wished to control its luxury expenditures while taking care of whatever necessities came along, then the family would be able to adjust its income to control the "income available to support luxury expenditures." If the family wished to hold this latter component of income constant, for instance, it would have to make total spendable income adjustments exactly in tandem with movements in necessity expenditures, thereby maintaining a constant sub-budget for luxuries.[10]

Just as the family might focus on "income available to support luxury expenditures," the Fed focuses on "reserves available to support private deposits," or RPD's. The Fed subtracts, from the total of reserves available to the banks, those reserves required to permit (nonmoney) deposits of the Treasury and the (nonmoney) interbank deposits banks hold with each other, along with an allowance for excess or unused reserves. The reserves these nonmoney deposits use up correspond to the family's necessity expenditures. RPD's, then, are essentially what reserves remain to support money deposits after the reserves being used for other purposes have been subtracted.

By focusing their attention on RPD's, Fed policymakers try to push aside the other reserve-bearing bank liabilities and focus their attention on the private demand deposit component of the money stock at member banks. RPD's provide one way of tailoring the Fed's control over bank reserves to control those deposits defined as money for the purpose of generating desirable behavior in the overall money stock. This procedure is basically the one adopted on an experimental basis in 1972. Conceptually, we can see how it ought to work. Whether it works in practice is still a matter for debate.

The importance of RPD's, in any case, should not be exaggerated. Their use is only experimental. It is a means of trying to regulate the money stock but not an end in itself. The money stock, furthermore, is far from being the sole objective of monetary policy. RPD's do not equal Federal Reserve policy, but they do reflect an ingenious new approach to an important aspect of policy.

A BRIEF SUMMARY

The reader who has stuck with us should now have a feel for how reserves are used as the basic tool of monetary policy. We have seen how reserves can effectively limit total deposits. We have seen how this limitation approximates control but says nothing about the distribution of deposits among banks. We have seen how the Fed's open market operations and

---

[10] This might be realistic where a family sent a son or daughter to college and agreed to pay for rent, tuition, and books plus a fixed allowance for incidentals.

reserve requirement changes work and how the Federal funds market and the discount window fit into the larger scheme. We have also explored the nature of some of the practical complications faced by the Fed as it attempts to employ the basic deposit-limitation scheme. Finally, we tried to bridge the gap between the money stock and reserves, explaining why the concept of RPD's has emerged in the 1970's.

Reading 29

The Workings of the Federal Open Market Committee*

By Harry Brandt

Summary

Almost every fourth Tuesday, the Federal Open Market Committee meets in Washington to decide whether to place its influence on the side of loosening or tightening credit. This body is an important part of the policy-making machinery of the Federal Reserve System, and its decisions affect our entire economic system. Yet, despite the vital function it performs, the workings of the Committee are not too familiar to the general public.

Open market operations refer to the buying and selling of bankers' acceptances, foreign currencies, and, most important, U.S. Government securities. Purchases of Government securities directly bring about an increase in bank reserves, thus banks are able to lend more money. Sales of Government securities by the System have the opposite effect. The Federal Open Market Committee sets open market policy, which is the most important monetary policy instrument.

Key Questions to Consider

■ How is the amount of money banks are able to lend changed by open market operations?

■ What is the role of the Federal Open Market Committee (FOMC)? Who belongs to it?

■ How are issues peculiar to certain regions of the nation considered in the FOMC meetings?

■ How are policies agreed upon at the FOMC meeting actually implemented?

* Reprinted with permission from *Monthly Review,* Federal Reserve Bank of Atlanta, **LVII,** No. 7 (July 1962. Revised, December 1971) 73–76.

The Workings of the Federal Open Market Committee

Almost every fourth Tuesday, the Federal Open Market Committee meets in Washington to decide whether to place its influence on the side of loosening or tightening credit. This body is an important part of the policy-making machinery of the Federal Reserve System, and its decisions affect our entire economic system. Yet, despite the vital function it performs, the workings of the Committee are not too familiar to the general public.

OBJECTIVES OF THE FEDERAL RESERVE SYSTEM

Certainly, the activities of the Federal Reserve System as a whole are more widely understood than the work of the Open Market Committee. The Reserve System's job relates to counteracting sharp swings in the economy and to helping achieve a higher standard of living and a stable dollar. In an economy as complex as ours, one can obviously not expect the System to attain these goals single-handedly. The Federal Reserve's contribution comes by way of regulating the amount of money and bank credit in the economy. When the economy's total capacity to produce goods and services runs well ahead of total demand and unemployment is great, the System encourages spend-ing with borrowed money. In such a situation, it eases credit by means of an expansion in bank reserves. But when total demand threatens to exceed productive capacity and endangers price stability, the System discourages spending by tightening credit.

Federal Reserve officials are confronted continuously with this problem of deciding whether to lean in the direction of easing or tightening credit. To arrive at the proper decision, policy makers must assess the economic and credit scene, a task requiring constant study and analysis.

Policy makers not only must decide what action to take, but also must choose among the available policy instruments. Statutory authority for the exercise of these instruments is divided among the Board of Governors, the twelve Federal Reserve Banks, and the Federal Open Market Committee. The tools include the power to engage in open market operations, to alter reserve requirements of member banks and stock market margin requirements, and to change the discount rate—the rate at which Reserve Banks lend to member banks.

Open market operations refer to the buying and selling of bankers' acceptances, foreign currencies, and, most important, U.S. Government securities. Purchases of Government securities directly bring about an increase in bank reserves, thus banks are able to lend more money. Sales of Government securities by the System have the opposite effect.

The Board of Governors of the Reserve System has the authority to set reserve requirements and stock market margin requirements. Discount rates are established by individual Reserve Banks but are subject to review and determination by the Board of Governors. The Federal Open Market Committee sets open market policy, which is the most important monetary policy instrument.

ROLE OF THE OPEN MARKET COMMITTEE

Meetings of the Open Market Committee provide the coordination made necessary by this diffusion of responsibility. Policy makers often take advantage of Committee meetings to discuss possible changes in discount rates and reserve requirements as well as to decide upon open market policy.

Actual membership on the Open Market Committee is limited to the Board of Governors, plus the presidents of five Reserve Banks. The President of the Federal Reserve Bank of New York, which actually conducts open market operations for the Committee, is a permanent member, while the other presidents rotate in designated order. Since 1955, when the executive committee of the Open Market Committee was disbanded, those presidents not serving on the Committee have been invited to attend the meetings. They do not have the right to vote but may participate freely in the discussions.

Not only the size of the group but the frequency of the meetings influences the process of policy formulation by the Open Market Committee. Prior to 1955, meetings were held quarterly, but since then they have generally been held every three or four weeks. This permits frequent review of the economy and allows for quick shifts in policy. In emergencies, telephone conferences can be arranged. These procedures support the view that monetary policy is a flexible tool of public policy.

The frequent meetings also help in the proper timing of policy changes to conform to seasonal and extraordinary needs as well as Treasury financing operations. For example, whenever the Treasury is involved in a large financing operation, the Committee customarily makes no major policy change, for it does not wish to interfere or give special aid to the Treasury. Still, there are advantages to meeting even when an immediate policy change is ruled out since a tentative decision as to later action may be reached.

ECONOMIC INTELLIGENCE

The research departments at each Reserve Bank and at the Board of Governors conduct long-range studies of various problems relating to monetary policy, and they continually study short-run business and financial developments and the effects of policy actions already taken. Analysis of the current data is most intensive in the immediate days before the Open Market Committee meets.

Policy makers prepare for these meetings in different ways, but many rely heavily on discussions with senior advisers and on briefing sessions with their economic staffs. Shortly before each Open Market meeting, the Board of Governors confers with its advisers and economists; many Reserve Bank presidents do likewise.

The arrangement followed at the Federal Reserve Bank of Atlanta is probably typical. The President meets on the Friday or Monday before the Open Market meeting with his research officers and economists. The topics discussed at these sessions vary, but generally each economist reviews an important aspect of the business and financial situation that is of particular importance at the time. District as well as national trends are scrutinized. The discussion ends with an expression of views as to what policy should be.

In addition, the economists prepare several written reports. The reports cover a variety of subjects, such as employment, production, construction, farming, international developments, bank credit, bank reserves, money supply, interest rates, and recent policy effects. These experts also provide the President from time to time with special reports on mortgage credit, leading business indicators, savings flows, and other significant topics.

The President has help not only from his own staff but from the staffs of the Board of Governors and the New York Bank as well. For example, he receives a report covering open market operations every week, a supplemental report covering operations through the close of business of the day preceding the Committee meeting, and detailed written reports on the economy, the balance of payments, and financial conditions. For information from the "grass roots," the President of each Bank relies upon his Board of Directors and upon those at the branches. Much time at the various Directors' meetings is devoted to economic reports from different geographic areas within the district. This process of taking the economic pulse and considering appropriate policy is duplicated to some degree or other throughout the Federal Reserve System.

THE COMMITTEE MEETS

To see just how the Open Market Committee decides what to do, let us sit in on a hypothetical Committee meeting. The Committee meets in the building of the Board of Governors in Washington. We have already noted which policy members take part. Also present are various economists and other advisers.

The Chairman of the Board of Governors is also Chairman of the Federal Open Market Committee. He ordinarily calls the meeting to order at 9:30 a.m. The first order of business is the adoption of the minutes from the previous meeting. Then, the Chairman calls on the official responsible for the System's foreign currency operations. Next, the Director of the Division of International Finance discusses foreign developments, with an emphasis on this country's balance of payments. After this, the Director of the Division of Research and Statistics evaluates current business conditions. Next, one of the advisers to the Board reviews domestic financial conditions. Instead of oral reports, the Board staff at times presents a visual economic presentation covering domestic and international developments. And, when appropriate, System officials report on international conferences that they have attended. Then, the Chairman calls on the official responsible for executing the Committee's open market decisions. That official supervises the actual buying and selling of U.S. Government securities at the New York Federal Reserve Bank and is called the Manager of the System Open Market Account. Typically, he summarizes the operations undertaken since the last meeting and discusses problems, if any, that he has encountered in trying to carry out the Committee's intentions. He alerts the group to any special developments that have taken place in the financial markets, such as speculation in Government securities. He makes a special point of calling the policy makers' attention to dates of forthcoming Treasury financing operations that, as already noted, may affect the timing of policy action.

After these contributions, the Chairman throws the floor open to each member of the Board and each of the twelve presidents for comments on economic developments. The President of the Federal Reserve Bank of New York, who is also Vice Chairman of the Committee, usually talks of business and credit developments in national terms because the New York Bank is located in the country's financial center. He further addresses himself to international developments and open market and other Federal Reserve policies that seem appropriate in the light of these conditions.

The members of the Board of Governors also discuss developments in national terms. Some individual presidents, however, occasionally include comments about conditions in their particular districts. These comments serve the purpose of calling attention to developments that are peculiar to certain parts of the country and are not apparent from national statistical aggregates. (Other district comments are transmitted in writing by each Federal Reserve Bank president to the Open Market Committee participants in advance of the meeting.) Monetary policy, though, can be applied only in broad strokes. This is particularly true for the open market instrument. Open market transactions initially affect the reserve position of a limited number of banks, but subsequently the reserves are diffused throughout the banking system. Thus, there is no assurance, for example, that only banks located in distressed areas would benefit from increases in Federal Reserve holdings of Government obligations—that is, open market purchases. Since open market transactions cannot be adjusted to regional or area peculiarities, the district reports can do no more than be one of several important elements going into the final Committee decision.

CONDUCTING A "GO-AROUND"

The procedure whereby each policy maker gives his views and recommends policy is called the "go-around." Picture 19 well-informed people participating in the "go-around" and you can well imagine that often there is some difference of opinion. Some might believe that reserve pressures should be tightened; others might think reserve pressures should be eased; and still others, that policy be left unchanged.

The Chairman has the job of synthesizing the various opinions. Before he does, he expresses his point of view. Normally speaking at the end of the "go-around," he has the benefit of the views already expressed. He then states what he considers to be the consensus or majority policy position expressed around the table. It should be pointed out that in deriving the consensus only the position of the voting Committee members is considered.

If the consensus or majority position in favor of some particular policy is clear, no formal vote is taken. Indeed, the differences in views are often rather small and turn around slight variations in degree of ease or restraint. However, if the Committee is divided, the Chairman may call for further discussion or another "go-around" in order to get a clearer view, after which a formal vote is taken.

If you are curious as to what the consensus has been at any meeting during the past year, merely refer to the *Annual Report of the Board of Governors*. The 1970 *Report*, for example, states that the consensus of a meeting in August 1970 was that some easing of conditions in credit markets and somewhat greater growth in money should be promoted. Usually, most Committee members are in broad agreement as to the appropriate credit policy, so that formal dissents are relatively few; however, the number of formal dissents has increased in recent years. The consensus becomes part of the Committee's instructions to the Manager.

The Committee has often expressed its intentions to the Manager in qualitative terms such as "ease" or "restraint." The terms "ease" or "restraint" are not precise. Some persons, for example, may associate ease or tightness with short-term interest rates; others, with a certain level of total reserves or a combination of various indicators. Therefore, some persons hold the view that the Committee should set forth its policy in precise quantitative terms.

Some Committee members have, indeed, experimented with framing instructions in terms of some quantitatively definable figure. The Committee, though, has not used precise quantitative targets, partly because no single measure is completely reliable or meaningful. Conditions in money and credit markets change rapidly. And while some indicators are more useful guides in interpreting credit conditions than others, no single measure is always satisfactory.

To aid in implementing policy, the Committee, however, informs the Manager as to what it considers an appropriate range for key money market interest rates and reserves. And since January 1970, the Committee has placed growing emphasis on the growth of the money supply and other monetary aggregates in implementing policy.

FORMAL DIRECTIVE TO THE NEW YORK BANK

After the Committee has agreed upon a policy consensus, its job is almost finished. Left to the end are the voting on a formal policy instruction or directive to the New York Reserve Bank and other special agenda matters. The directive contains a reference to the Committee's assessment of the current economic situation and sets forth the broad objective that the Committee wants to attain. The New York Reserve Bank also operates under a set of technical authorizations, which the Committee can modify at any time, governing the conduct of open market operations.

For the actual operations, the scene shifts to the Federal Reserve Bank of New York. There a plan is usually drawn up by 11:00 each morning as to what action, if any, should be taken that day. It is then discussed in a telephone call made by the Manager to one of the presidents currently serving on the Open Market Committee and to a representative of the Board of Governors. This daily conference call is one of several techniques by which the policy-making body—the Federal Open Market Committee—keeps in close contact with the executor of the policy—the Federal Reserve Bank of New York.

Reading 30

The Myth of Fiscal Policy: The Monetarist View*

By Ira Kaminow

Summary

Times are changing. What is obvious today was obviously wrong yesterday; this is as true of questions involving economic issues as any others. Many of us, for example, believe in the efficacy of fiscal policy—in the Government's power to influence the level of national income by its own spending and taxing policies. Indeed, the expenditure-income chain explanation of the operation of fiscal policy is part of today's conventional wisdom. The Government spends more or spurs private spending by taxing less, and so creates more jobs and higher profits. The new income so created generates additional demand and private spending, creating even more income.

All this is Keynesian economics—the so-called New Economics. But it wasn't long ago that the Keynesian Revolution was rejected by most laymen, and not long before that, that it was rejected by most economists. Today, with victory in hand, the New Economics is facing a counter-revolution which may again change the economic thinking of the nation. There is a small but highly vocal group of economists who are suspicious of Keynesian economics in general and of fiscal policy in particular. The members of the group are sometimes called Monetarists.

Monetarists view the controversy over economic theories as being like a law suit. As judges, they rule that the New Economists have presented no acceptable historical evidence in support of the income-expenditure theory. Monetarists do not claim that the income-expenditure chain is erroneous in principle—merely that history tells us it is too weak or unpredictable to be of much use for economic policy.

Key Questions to Consider

- What are the key points of Monetarist and Keynesian economics?

- According to the Monetarists, what happens if the economy has more money than it requires?

- Why, according to the Monetarists, will fiscal policy, e.g., an increase in government expenditure, serve to raise national income?

- Why is "constant relative money balances" so vital to the Monetarist explanation?

- How do the Monetarists and the Keynesians differ as to the factors affecting the demand for money?

* Reprinted with permission from *Business Review*, Federal Reserve Bank of Philadelphia, December 1969, pp. 10–18.

The Myth of Fiscal Policy: The Monetarist View

Times are changing. What is obvious today was obviously wrong yesterday; this is as true of questions involving economic issues as any others. Many of us, for example, believe in the efficacy of fiscal policy—in the Government's power to influence the level of national income by its own spending and taxing policies. Indeed, the expenditure-income chain explanation of the operation of fiscal policy is part of today's conventional wisdom. The Government spends more or spurs private spending by taxing less, and so creates more jobs and higher profits. The new income so created generates additional demand and private spending, creating even more income.

All this is Keynesian economics—the so-called New Economics. But it wasn't long ago that the Keynesian Revolution was rejected by most laymen, and not long before that, that it was rejected by most economists. Today, with victory in hand, the New Economics is facing a counter-revolution which may again change the economic thinking of the nation. There is a small but highly vocal group of economists who are suspicious of Keynesian economics in general and of fiscal policy in particular. The members of the group are sometimes called Monetarists.[1]

Monetarists view the controversy over economic theories as being like a law suit. As judges, they rule that the New Economists have presented no acceptable historical evidence in support of the income-expenditure theory. As litigants, they present the following case: (1) over the years, the major movements in national income have been associated with major movements in the money supply and *vice versa*; (2) no equally strong or systematic relation can be found to support the Keynesian view of the operation of fiscal policy; (3) therefore, monetary forces have played a much more important and/or more stable role in determining national income than fiscal forces. Monetarists do not claim that the income-expenditure chain is erroneous in principle—merely that history tells us it is too weak or unpredictable to be of much use for economic policy.

A SIMPLE EXPLANATION OF THE MONETARIST VIEW

How do the Monetarists reconcile their view of history with the apparently powerful logic of the

[1] Strictly speaking, the Monetarist view involves more than mere suspicion of the efficacy of fiscal policy. Indeed, one can be a Monetarist and still agree that fiscal policy has a powerful and systematic influence on the economy. Nevertheless, the popular press identifies Monetarist with those who believe that monetary policy is much more important than fiscal policy, and this usage of the term is adopted here.

income-expenditure chain?[2] The heart of the Monetarist view is the supply of and demand for money—a dramatic shift from the usual emphasis. Because of the near total victory of the New Economics (at least in introductory textbooks on economics) in the fifties and sixties, the spotlight of popular policy discussions has been firmly set on the pivot point of Keynesian economics—the demand for goods.

A look at the economy from the perspective of the money side of things (or the goods side, for that matter) will reveal only a partial and perhaps slightly distorted picture of the economy. Nevertheless, anyone who has been to the circus knows how difficult it is to look at all three rings at once and that there is something to be gained from looking at only one at a time.

Although not all economists agree on the defini-

tion of money, we will not break too much with tradition if we use the term to mean all assets that are generally accepted as a means of payment (see box). More concretely, we can define money as the sum of coins, paper currency, and checking account deposits.

An easy way to illustrate the Monetarist view is to suppose that a certain quantity of money is required to support any particular level of income. When national economic activity (as measured by income) rises, more money is required to carry on conveniently day-to-day transactions; when economic activity declines, households and businesses find that they engage in fewer transactions, and hence, need less money. More specifically, we can assume that the demand for money balances *relative* to the level of income (what economists call desired *relative* money balances) is fixed. By way of illustration, we can imagine that institutional arrangements—like the availability of credit cards and the length of the average pay period—lead the public to desire money balances equal in value to 10 percent of national income. If annual national income is $800 billion, then desired balances would be $80 billion.

What happens if the economy has more money than it requires? Say, for the sake of argument, that

---

[2] A completely accurate answer to this question is extremely complex. There is no reason, however, why the complexities and nuances should keep us from the essence of the Monetarist argument. A look at the simplest version of the theory (a version not seriously proposed by anyone) will reveal more than an investigation of one which requires endless digressions and footnotes and which reflects the particular views of only one or two Monetarists.

Box   # Let's Be Sure That We're Talking About the Same Thing

It is always a good idea to be sure of our definitions. One word that means different things to different people is money. The great variety of usages has contributed to numerous misunderstandings by economists and laymen. A selected list of what economists DON'T mean by money will be helpful in understanding what they do mean by the word. Economists rarely use the word money in the following contexts:

1. "How much money (income) did you earn last year?"
2. "Most of his money (wealth) is tied up in bonds."
3. "It's almost impossible to get mortgage money (credit) in today's market."
4. "This country does not have enough money (resources) to fight the war in Vietnam and the war on poverty."

When economists use the word money, they usually mean assets (cash and checking account balances at banks) that are generally accepted as a means of payments—for example, "If I didn't keep some money on hand, I'd be running to the savings bank every time I wanted to buy a candy bar."

the actual stock of money in the previous example is $90 billion, or $10 billion more than is required. Since money yields no pecuniary return, households and businesses will attempt to exchange money for other assets—assets that yield satisfaction directly (like television sets) and assets that yield a pecuniary return (like stocks and bonds). The increased demand for goods and services will stimulate greater output and perhaps will boost prices as markets respond to the new demand. At the same time, the increased demand for financial assets like stocks and bonds will drive interest rates down. The decline in interest rates will further encourage the demand for goods by making credit cheaper. This will induce still higher prices and output. The pace of economic activity will quicken. Economic activity will continue to increase until income is pushed up to a level consistent with the $90 billion money stock—that is, to $900 billion.

The rigid relationship between the demand for money and national income makes this environment inhospitable to fiscal policy. If the national goal is to raise income, it can be achieved only by raising the money stock. An increase in Government expenditures won't work except for a very short time. As soon as income rises a bit, the money stock will be inadequate. There will be a general scramble for money, and the private demand for goods will decline as businesses and households try to increase their holdings of money. Consequently, income and output will be pulled back down by the limited money stock.

Stated somewhat differently, any increase in Government expenditures (not accompanied by an appropriate increase in the money stock) will be matched by an equal decline in private expenditures; any decrease in Government expenditures (not accompanied by an appropriate decline in the money stock) will be matched by an equal increase in private expenditures.

The key that allowed monetary policy to work in the simple world just described is the constancy of desired *relative* money balances. In order to achieve an equilibrium, annual national income will always adjust so that it is ten times the stock of money. If

we can control the money supply, we can control national income. The key that locked fiscal policy out is that Government taxing and spending policies have no effect on desired relative money balances. No matter what fiscal policies are followed, annual national income will always tend to be ten times higher than the stock of money. In these two keys are the germs of the Monetarist position: (1) Although demand for relative money balances is not fixed, it is the most stable and predictable variable on which we can count for economic policy. (2) Although fiscal policies may have some influence on desired relative money balances, they do not have a strong, predictable influence; therefore, fiscal policies are of relatively little or no use.

A LOOK AT THE NEW ECONOMICS FROM THE MONEY SIDE

Advocates of the New Economics do not agree that income is the only variable that exerts a strong, predictable influence on the demand for money. They argue that a typical family might find it very convenient at some given level of income to go about its daily business with an average checking account balance of $100. But convenience must be balanced against cost. One hundred dollars in the checking account is not earning interest. When the interest rate on savings accounts is very low, the household may indeed hold a $100 checking account balance. But let the interest rate rise substantially and the household may decide that it can get by with only $75 or $50 worth of money. The lower money balance might mean more bother—more accurate balancing of the checkbook, more trips to the bank—but the bother is compensated by the greater interest income. In short, the New Economists argue that both the level of income and the interest rate determine the desired stock of money. By adding this additional ingredient—interest rates—the New Economist can salvage the argument for the expenditure-income chain.

Keynesians expect roughly the same kind of

initial response to fiscal policy as do the Monetarists. An increase in Government expenditures drives income up, and the existing stock of money becomes inadequate to handle the additional income. In an effort to acquire more money, people try to sell nonmonetary financial assets such as bonds. As the supply of these assets rises relative to demand, interest rates begin to rise to make them more attractive to buyers. This hike in interest rates is the key that is supposed to let fiscal policy back in. Higher interest rates mean that the economy will be able to support a higher level of income with the given stock of money. With higher interest rates, households and businesses find it advantageous to economize on the use of money—to make the existing stock "go farther." The economy will, after the initial shock of added Government expenditures, come to rest at a higher level of national income—and higher interest rates. The higher interest rates are necessary; otherwise, the public could not be induced to hold the same quantity of money at the higher level of activity. Put in slightly different terms, the ratio of desired money balances to income will decline because interest rates have risen.

An extreme version of the Keynesian view gives rise to the so-called liquidity trap. Imagine what would happen if the public were willing to hold whatever money balances were offered at the prevailing interest rate. The public would make no attempt to convert new money balances into other assets, regardless of how much money the authorities pumped into the economy. Any new money that was placed in the economy would be willingly held at the existing interest rate and income. Monetary policy is completely frustrated if and when we get into the trap because then the public's actions are unaffected by changes in the money supply.

In contrast, recall that in the simple Monetarist case the demand for *relative* money balances doesn't change. Individual members of the public never will be willing to hold unlimited quantities of money. If new money is added to the economy, the public will have "too much" money and will try to get rid of the

excess. This process will drive income up to a new equilibrium.

DOES IT MATTER IF THE INTEREST RATE MATTERS?

The single most revealing element in the encounter between Monetarists and New Economists is that they cannot agree on the relevance of the interest rate. The Monetarist Milton Friedman wrote:

... in my opinion no 'fundamental issues' in either monetary theory or monetary policy hinge on whether [the demand for money depends on interest rates].[3]

The Keynesian Paul Samuelson wrote:

... the minute you believe that [the demand for money depends on interest rates], you have moved to ... the post-Keynesian position.[4]

Keynesians insist that the interest rate is the added gear in the mechanism that allows fiscal policy to work. For them, fiscal policy (viewed from the money side of the economy) gives authorities control over the interest rate and, through the interest rate, control over desired *relative* money balances. The Monetarists insist that this control must be inconsequential because they see no evidence that it has worked in the past (New Economists, of course, dispute the charge of lack of evidence). For the Monetarists there are two possibilities: (1) fiscal policy has had an erratic, unsystematic effect on the interest rate

---

[3] Milton Friedman "Interest Rates and the Demand for Money" *Journal of Law and Economics*, October 1966, p. 85. For some technical reasons, not all Monetarists would agree 100 percent with this quotation. For our purposes, however, it seems to reflect adequately the Monetarist view.

[4] Paul Samuelson "The Role of Money in National Economic Policy," *Controlling Monetary Aggregates* (Boston: The Federal Reserve Bank of Boston, 1969), p. 12.

and, hence, an unobservable effect on national income, or (2) fiscal policies have been so mild as to have only a small effect on interest rates.

The issue (regarding the demand for money) that is of primary importance to the Monetarist is the stability and predictability of desired relative money balances. Evidence of a highly unstable and unpredictable ratio of money balances to national income would directly contradict the efficacy of monetary policy. In terms of the Keynesian theory, the instability would arise if we fell into a liquidity trap. The Monetarists are therefore considerably more interested in whether a trap exists than in whether the demand for money is sensitive to the interest rate.

HISTORICAL EVIDENCE I: THE DEMAND FOR MONEY

It is time to fish or cut bait. A number of issues have been raised and questions asked about the demand for money. What kinds of answers does history provide? To make things manageable, we can concentrate on three key questions: (1) Does the demand for money depend on income? (2) Is the demand for money sensitive to interest rates? (3) Have we ever been caught in a liquidity trap?

Question One: What Role for Income? Virtually every empirical study undertaken has shown that the demand for money depends on the level of income. Sometimes the relationship is based on a linkage between current income and money demand through the level of transactions of the sort we discussed earlier. Sometimes the relationship is based on more subtle arguments.

These more subtle discussions generally presume that economic well-being is a more important determinant of the demand for money than is the volume of transactions. The discussions take as their point of departure the notion that improved economic status for a nation (or an individual) means a greater de-

mand for most assets, including money. In fact, at least one economist believes that money is a luxury in the sense that the demand for it rises very rapidly as a nation (or individual) moves up the economic ladder.

The two measures of economic well-being that have been used to explain the demand for money are wealth and permanent income. Everyone is familiar with the notion of wealth, and there should be no dispute that it is one measure of economic well-being. The meaning of permanent income, however, is not widely known.

Permanent income is most simply described as expected average lifetime income. It is a good measure of economic well-being because it is adjusted for temporary ups and downs. A day laborer who happens to be working his way through medical school has a higher *permanent* income than his co-worker whose actual or *measured* income is the same but whose ambitions and income expectations are more modest.

Economists who take the permanent income approach do not deny the importance of measured income. They argue that current and past levels of measured income are the most important influences on permanent income. They claim that expectations are largely formulated on the basis of past experience.

Question Two: How Important is the Interest Rate? Historically, the interest rate has influenced the demand for money.[5] This much we know with virtual certainty—that is, if unanimity of opinion implies certainty of knowledge. There is some disagreement, however, on just how important the interest rate has been. Some economists, like Milton Friedman and Maurice Allais, take the view that the interest rate is so unimportant in determining the demand for money that little is lost if it is ignored. Other investigators,

---
[5] There are, of course, many interest rates. We shall ignore here the important question of selecting the appropriate one.

however, have presented evidence that the demand for money is highly sensitive to changes in the rate of interest. Perhaps the most sensitive relationship was found by Allan Meltzer who estimated on one occasion that any given percentage change in long-term interest rates would be matched by an equal percentage change (in the opposite direction) in the demand for money.

The disagreement over the importance of the interest does not follow "party lines." As it turns out, all three of the economists mentioned in the last paragraph are Monetarists. Estimates of the interest sensitivity by Keynesians are greater than zero but less than Meltzer's.

A major reason for all this disagreement about the importance of the interest rate is that it is often difficult to untangle the influence of interest rates from other influences on the demand for money. Interest rates vary in a more or less systematic way over the business cycle—they generally go up during expansions and down during economic contractions.

Other variables that are likely to influence the demand for money also behave more or less predictably over the cycle. This raises the possibility that an investigator will wrongly attribute the influence of some other variable to interest rates, or the influence of interest rates to other variables.

Milton Friedman and Anna J. Schwartz, in particular, argue that an uncritical reading of history has led to an overemphasis on the role of the interest rate in determining the demand for money.

It is well known that relative money balances (the ratio of money balances to income) fall during expansions and rise during contractions. Generally speaking, therefore, relative money balances are high when interest rates are low (during slumps), and are low when interest rates are high (during booms). The interest rate seems to do a good job in explaining movements in the demand for relative money balances.

Friedman and Schwartz argue that there is another factor to explain movements in relative money balances over the cycle. It is based on the idea

of permanent income (expected average lifetime income) mentioned earlier. During economic downturns, people anticipate that things will get better; so permanent income is higher than measured income. During periods of prosperity, people guess that incomes are unusually high; so permanent income is lower than measured income. Over the cycle, permanent income fluctuates much less than measured income because people recognize that a good deal of income fluctuations are transitory. If the demand for money depends on permanent income, it will fluctuate relatively little over the business cycle because permanent income is relatively stable over the cycle. Therefore, during periods of recovery, the demand for money will rise more slowly than measured income, so relative money balances (the ratio of money balances to measured national income) will fall. During periods of contraction, the demand for money will fall more slowly than measured income, and relative money balances will rise.

Friedman and Schwartz offer some evidence in support of their views in their famous study *A Monetary History of the United States*. For example, they point to the period, 1932–1937, during which both interest rates and relative money balances fell. This pattern is clearly inconsistent with the interest-rate explanation of movements in the demand for money. The 1932–1937 experience is very easily explained by the permanent income concept. In the mid-1930's, the economy started to climb out of the depths of the Great Depression. Income was rising. Nevertheless, vivid memories of 1929, 1930, and 1931 lingered. People were not so sure that the recovery was going to be sustained. Permanent income rose, but not so fast as measured income. Desired money balances, which respond to permanent income, grew more slowly than measured income. So, the ratio of money balances to measured income fell.

Not all economists agree that the Friedman and Schwartz evidence is convincing. A number of studies have shown that the interest rate has had a strong influence even if one accepts the permanent income hypothesis. In fact, Friedman and Schwartz seem to have retreated slightly on this point. In 1966, Friedman wrote "most estimates [of the interest rate sensitivity], including some we have obtained in our own subsequent work are higher ... than the estimate Anna J. Schwartz and I used in *A Monetary History*." [6]

Question Three: Have We Ever Been Trapped?   The answer to this question can be stated very succinctly: The great weight of historical evidence indicates that we have never been in a liquidity trap. A number of studies have attempted to find periods in American history when the public was willing to hold whatever quantity of money balances was made available. Over the periods investigated, the public has always made attempts to unload excess money balances in exchange for other assets.

A Summary.   Studies of the demand for money can be thought of as the first round in the debate over the efficacy of monetary and fiscal policy. The nice thing about the first round is that each side can go back to its corner confident that it took the round on points. Monetarists smell victory because of the absence of any evidence of the existence of a trap. To them this is the crucial issue. Keynesians are delighted with the outcome because of the overwhelming evidence of the interest sensitivity of the demand for money.

HISTORICAL EVIDENCE II: THE MONETARISTS' GRAND EXPERIMENTS

The second round in the debate brings us back to the beginning—to the Monetarist claim that (1) the major movements in national income have been associated with major movements in the money supply and *vice versa,* and (2) no equally strong or systematic relationship can be found to support the Keynesian theories. For the Monetarist, none of the evidence on in-

terest rates and the demand for money can change these facts. For Keynesians, these "facts" are highly debatable.

Without getting involved in the technical arguments, we can briefly indicate the debate on this evidence.

Keynesian Objection 1:   Mere association does not imply causation. The close relationship between money and national income could reflect a causal influence running from money to income; from income to money (if, for example, the monetary authorities tried to provide enough money to meet the needs of trade); a dependence of both money and income on some third variable; or, as is most likely, a little bit of all three. There is, in short, no way to determine the strength or predictability of the causal link from money to national income using the Monetarist's tools.

Monetarist Response: We agree that mere association does not imply causation. Indeed, we even agree that there has been some influence running from income to money. Our point is that a major cause of the observed coincidence of movement is the effect of monetary forces on national income. There is no need to debate this on a conjectural level, however, because history is not totally silent on this point. There is some opportunity to examine situations in which it is unlikely that the direction of causation went from income to money. One illustration includes those times in history when the money supply has increased because of gold inflows or for other reasons unrelated to income. During these periods, income has risen after the rise in the money supply.

Keynesian Objection 2:   The Monetarist's tools may be too crude to pick up the strong influences of fiscal policies. It is a mistake to presume such influences do not exist simply because the impact of fiscal policies cannot be measured by the somewhat naive techniques of the Monetarist. The workings of fiscal and monetary policies on the economy are very complex.

[6] Milton Friedman, "The Interest Rate and the Demand for Money," *op. cit.* pp. 72 and 73.

There is no shortcut to the very hard work of learning about complex and subtle interrelations in the economy.

Monetarist Response: We could not agree more. The economy is certainly complex, and we know very little about it. In fact, this is what we have been saying right along. We conclude that on the grounds of our ignorance, we ought to go with what we've got, and what we've got is this relationship between the supply of money and national income. If more complicated tests show how fiscal policy works, then it will be time to use them. Right now we cannot unlock the code.

Keynesian Objection 3:   Your tests are not as conclusive as you think. The definition of monetary and fiscal variables is open to question. We have come up with definitions different from yours that show a strong correlation between fiscal policy and national income.

Monetarist Response: We believe that our measures of fiscal and monetary forces are superior to the Keynesians' measures. We frequently get the impression that the Keynesians choose their measures more because they give good results than because they seem reasonable from an economic standpoint.

A SUMMING UP

It is easy to be pessimistic over the state of the art of economic policy. One can find competent econo-mists at every point on the spectrum between "only money matters" and "money doesn't matter at all." To be sure, the great majority take more moderate positions, but even the moderate range is wide and offers rather diverse policy prescriptions. It would be safe to say that the economics profession could under no conceivable set of circumstances offer anything like a "standard" policy prescription. The point is frequently made that the only thing on which most economists will agree is that policy was wrong. But there is rarely any agreement on what correct policy would have been or even what the actual policy was.

The gloominess of the state of affairs, however, is broken by occasional rays of hope. We are currently devoting more resources than ever before toward finding out how the economy works. Millions of dollars have been spent on large-scale econometric models of the United States. Builders of these models claim that they have made long strides in the past decades. It is in these models and in other attempts to interpret economic history that the real hope lies.

There has been a market shift in the great economic debate since the initial victories of the New Economics. In the late 1940's and early 1950's, it was generally believed by Keynesians that money didn't matter at all. By the early and mid 1960's, the Monetarists had made sufficient headway to shift the question from "does money matter?" to "does fiscal policy matter?" The New Economists have largely recognized the importance of money, but not its dominance. The Monetarists, however, continue to question the empirical relevance of fiscal policy.

Reading 31

The Money Supply Controversy*

By William N. Cox, III

Summary

The present controversy over the importance of money and monetary policy is by no means unprecedented—economists have pondered and argued about money for decades. There is nevertheless a new element in the current controversy over the money supply: The debate has heated up substantially enough to move from the professional economic journals into the popular press. Fundamentally at issue is the influence of money on spending, prices, employment, and economic growth—matters that certainly concern us all.

This article cannot pretend to describe the money supply debate comprehensively, since the arguments involved are numerous, extensive, and in some cases quite technical. Fortunately, however, the basic positions in the debate are straightforward enough to permit a simplified description that captures the flavor of the controversy between the "Keynesians" and the "Monetarists."

Key Questions to Consider

- How does the Keynesian view of money differ from the view of the predepression economists?

- What is the current Monetarist view?

* Reprinted with permission from *Monthly Review,* Federal Reserve Bank of Atlanta, **LIV,** No. 6 (June 1969), 70–75.

The Money Supply Controversy

The present controversy over the importance of money and monetary policy is by no means unprecedented—economists have pondered and argued about money for decades. There is nevertheless a new element in the current controversy over the money supply: The debate has heated up substantially enough to move from the professional economic journals into the popular press. Fundamentally at issue is the influence of money on spending, prices, employment, and economic growth—matters that certainly concern us all.

This article cannot pretend to describe the money supply debate comprehensively, since the arguments involved are numerous, extensive, and in some cases quite technical. Fortunately, however, the basic positions in the debate are straightforward enough to permit a simplified description that captures the flavor of the controversy between the "Keynesians" and the "Monetarists." The following synopsis presents an idea of what the money supply controversy is all about.

HISTORICAL PERSPECTIVE

Some notion of history will help us place the current money dispute in perspective, and the period just before the Depression is a good place to begin. At that time, many economists thought the quantity of money (currency plus private demand deposits) had a strong impact on prices, but had little or no influence on jobs or business activity. In its crudest form, the pre-Depression theory was simple: The amount of money, in relation to the supply of goods and services produced, determined prices. An increase in the money supply encouraged spending and raised prices; a decrease in the money supply lowered prices. A crude form of the quantity-of-money theory predicted that a 50-percent increase in the money supply would raise prices by 50 percent as long as there were no changes in the physical quantity of goods available. The amount of goods produced and number of jobs available, on the other hand, were expected to be untouched by changes in the quantity of money since the economy's productive resources—labor and nonlabor alike—were assumed to be fully employed, guided by the unseen hand of market forces.

In the more refined versions of pre-Depression quantity-of-money theory, the velocity, or turnover of money (the speed at which money circulates through the economy), was also recognized as an important determinant of the price level. But velocity, like the physical amount of goods produced, was thought to be relatively stable, so these more refined theories also concluded that changes in the quantity of money were primarily a cause of price changes, and of little else.

This is not to say that every economist writing before the Depression looked at the world in quite this way. But our generalizations still form a reasonably accurate description of pre-Depression economic views: automatic full employment together with a price level set by the quantity of money. Not too surprisingly, this approach produced few debates about what the Federal Reserve System should do to stabilize spending and production, for the economy was expected to take care of itself automatically.

THE KEYNESIAN VIEW

Then came the Depression, bringing serious questions about the prevailing economic doctrines and shaking the pre-Depression assumption of automatic full employment. Controversy flared as millions of people remained out of work and output fell far below the economy's capacity to produce. Something obviously was wrong, but pre-Depression economic theory was unable to explain what it was.

Keynesian Economics.   The basic difficulty of the Depression was obvious: Why were people eager to work and spend but unable to find jobs when businessmen were eager to produce but unable to find customers? The English economist John Maynard Keynes offered both an explanation and a remedy. The problem, he said, was that the amount of goods and services demanded by consumers, investors, and the Government was not sufficient to keep the economy producing at full capacity. Businessmen could not be expected to produce what they could not sell. If private demand was not strong enough to pull the economy out of depression, then the Government should step in and stimulate spending enough to provide buyers for the nation's full-capacity output. This was the essence of the "Keynesian" prescription, and the beginning of the broad concept of Government responsibility for economic stabilization which was eventually written into the Employment Act of 1946.

Fiscal Policy.   Most Keynesians believed that fiscal policy—the use of the Government's power to spend and tax—offered the best way to bridge the gap between insufficient spending and full-capacity output. The Government, by increasing its own spending, could contribute directly to the total demand for goods and services. Alternatively, it could reduce taxes, giving the private sector more disposable income to spend. Although Keynesians disagreed on the dosage of fiscal policy and on the details of how it should be operated, their confidence in fiscal action was virtually universal.

Many Keynesians, recommending the use of fiscal policy, doubted whether monetary policy could do much by itself to stimulate spending and economic activity. Still, monetary action did occupy a prominent place in the Keynesian theoretical scheme, which described how an increase in the money supply might lower interest rates and thereby induce businessmen to spend more for plant and equipment. Unlike the pre-Depression economists, then, the Keynesians did think monetary action might affect employment and production as well as prices. But in practice they were afraid that bank reserves pumped into the economy by the Federal Reserve System would pile up unused instead of generating new spending. A favorite homily of the forties and early fifties, "You can't push on a string," succinctly captured the prevalent scepticism about the effectiveness of monetary policy.

By the late 1950's, the Keynesian fiscal policy prescription had won the acceptance of most economists, and of many policymakers as well. Congress enacted a tax cut in 1964 for the specific purpose of stimulating the economy, and subsequently passed the tax increase of 1968 with a restrictive objective in mind. Although the effectiveness of these fiscal actions is still in dispute, their existence illustrates how much the Keynesian view has been accepted.

Monetary Policy Becomes More Appealing.   But even as fiscal policy came to be deliberately administered in the sixties, fresh controversy arose about its superiority over monetary policy as a tool of economic stabilization. Monetary policy began to look increasingly appealing. One reason is that enactment of fiscal legislation takes time—it took 18 months to pass the 1968 tax surcharge. Monetary policy decisions can be implemented much more quickly.

A changed economic environment also helped to bring monetary policy back into favor. Monetary economics is a pragmatic business, one where researchers are prone to concentrate on current policy problems. In the thirties and forties, when the main problem of unemployment clearly called for stimulative action, theorists focused on the problem of economic stimulation. But the 1950's brought an additional headache—inflation—and the 1960's brought unprecedented difficulties in our balance of payments. These new problems both called for policy measures that were restrictive, not expansionary. Consequently, many Keynesians who had said "you can't *push* on a string" began to take the position that monetary policy could indeed *pull* on the string—could pull down total spending. Monetary policy offered a method of restricting spending that was easy to implement, even if it could not stimulate spending.

Policy Mix.   For these and other reasons, most Keynesians today believe stabilization of the economy requires an appropriate "mix" of both fiscal and monetary actions. The recommended policy mix is likely to be one in which flexible monetary actions by the Federal Reserve are combined with occasional but more massive shifts in fiscal policy.

Keynesian economists still disagree on exactly how the Federal Reserve exerts its influence on aggregate spending. Generally speaking, they say changes in bank reserves initiated by the Federal Reserve affect the prices (interest rates) of diverse financial assets such as money market instruments and bonds. These price changes then produce adjustments in financial portfolios and changes in spending. Elaborate statistical models are now being used to trace responses to monetary actions through specific financial markets. The basic thesis underlying these studies is that Federal Reserve actions operate through the cost and availability of credit.

THE MONETARIST VIEW

While Keynesians stress the importance of both fiscal and monetary policy, other modern economists take a quite different position. These so-called Monetarists believe that changes in the money supply are the crucial determinants not only of prices, but also of spending, production, and employment. They downgrade the importance of Keynesian fiscal policy and are decidedly unsympathetic to the notion of "fine-tuning" the economy.

Just as Keynesian economics is associated with Keynes, Monetarist economics is often linked to Professor Milton Friedman of the University of Chicago. The contemporary money supply controversy now raging in the popular press is essentially a debate between the Keynesians and the Monetarists.

Though the Monetarists are not of one mind, they agree that money exercises a dominant influence on business activity, and they go on to draw definite policy recommendations from this thesis. Monetarists feel the economy is inherently stable, tending toward full employment and sustainable growth. In these circumstances, the best thing the Government can do to help the economy realize its full-employment potential is to allow the money supply to grow at the same rate as the economy's capacity to produce (roughly 3 to 5 percent annually). This is the "money supply rule."

The Federal reserve has the power to stabilize the economy, or at least to let the economy stabilize itself, through its ability to control bank reserves and the money supply. Unfortunately, say the Monetarists, this power has been misused. They feel Keynesians have intensified rather than mitigated business fluctuations with their well-meaning attempts to manage the economy. Money supply growth, as a consequence of discretionary efforts to stabilize the economy, has fluctuated. A boom has followed whenever the Federal Reserve System has quickened the rate of money growth. Recessions, they allege, have resulted when money growth has slowed.

Empirical Support.   Considerable empirical work has been presented to support the Monetarist opinion. Most prominent is a study by Milton Friedman and Anna Schwartz, in which they analyzed data on the behavior of money in the United States all the way back to the Civil War.[1] Changes in money supply growth have been very closely associated with changes in income, economic activity, and prices, they found. From their analysis, they and other Monetarists conclude that changes in the money supply *cause* swings in the business cycle.

Monetarist Theory.   Monetarists base their arguments on theory as well as history, describing the way in which they think changes in the money supply produce adjustments affecting output, employment, and prices. The amount of money people wish to have is tied closely to the level of income, they say. If the supply of money expands faster than the amount people wish to have, they will try to spend away the unwanted portion of their money balances. Inflation results. If the money supply expands more slowly than income, rising less rapidly than the amount of money people want to have, people will try to build up their money balances by cutting back their spending. In this case, the result is unemployment, according to the Monetarist theory.

We should point out that the Monetarists do not regard the cause-and-effect relationship between money and income as absolutely tight. Monetarists recognize, just as Keynesians do, that the economy will always be subject to unexpected shocks from changes in expectations and from adjustments to im-

perfections and structural changes in our economy. They also realize that the Federal Reserve's control over the money supply is not perfect. Monetarists do not argue that adherence to the money supply rule would produce perfect economic stabilization; they simply say that it would yield much better results than the flexible policy mix approach now in vogue.

Monetarists, incidentally, take a non-Keynesian view of interest rates, doubting that they exert much influence on total spending and business activity. Monetarists are inclined to feel instead that interest rate changes result from the allocation of funds by market forces. Changes in both spending and interest rates, they feel, are mutual responses to changes in the money supply.

SHORTCOMINGS

The Monetarists offer a persuasive case for their prescription, and efforts to promote their view have won varying degrees of support. The money supply controversy received extensive hearings before the Joint Economic Committee of Congress last year. The hearings culminated in a recommendation by the JEC that the Monetarist prescription of the steady money supply growth be followed—with qualifications.

Yet, a great many economists still have reservations about the Monetarist scheme. These reservations involve fundamental disagreements about monetary theory. Whereas Monetarists think the influence of money supply on economic activity is important enough to neglect virtually everything else, other economists feel such neglect would be unwarranted and dangerous.

Is Money All That Matters?   The issue is whether money is nearly all that matters, or merely one of many things that matter, as far as stabilization policy is concerned. Spending, and hence production and incomes, may change when businessmen alter their expenditures for plant and equipment because of infla-

---

[1] *A Monetary History of the United States, 1867–1960.* National Bureau of Economic Research, Princeton, N.J.: Princeton University Press, 1963.

tionary expectations. Consumers may decide to cut back their spending and increase their saving for reasons unrelated to the money supply—such as in anticipation of higher taxes. Shifts in Government spending may affect total spending. Strikes may interrupt the course of business activity. Such things may be equally important as changes in the money supply, or even more important.

Do changes in money *cause* changes in income and production? Probably. But the causal influence may run the other way too. An increase in spending and business activity may itself stimulate additional demands for money which, if accommodated by the Federal Reserve, result in an increased money supply. An increase in spending calls for greater amounts of money for use in the channels of trade. When this happens, a change in the money supply is a response to, rather than a cause of, a change in business activity. To the extent that this happens, the Monetarists have the tail wagging the dog.

Velocity.   Another unresolved aspect of the controversy is the question of velocity. Velocity, the ratio of income to money, describes the speed with which money changes hands as it flows through the economy. Increases in velocity may affect spending decisions, because spenders then have more money available than they want to hold—not because there is more of it, but because it is circulating faster. Although Monetarists think velocity is relatively stable, this remains an unsettled question. If velocity is not stable, then a reduction in the money supply would not reduce spending, since the money already in the economy would change hands more quickly. The decrease in money might be offset substantially by an increase in velocity. Whether this happens or not is an open question.

What Is Money?   Generally rising interest rates in the postwar period have made interest-bearing financial assets, such as certificates of deposit, more attractive than they used to be relative to money. Corporations in particular have economized on their money balances, substituting interest-bearing assets for demand deposits. As these kinds of substitutes for conventionally defined money have become more and more appealing, considerable controversy has developed about the proper definition of "money."

Professor Friedman, for instance, prefers to include time deposits at commercial banks in his definition, along with currency and private demand deposits. His historical investigation mentioned earlier suggested to him that changes in time deposits have much the same influence on income as do changes in demand deposits and currency. Yet the period Friedman examined in his study preceded the evolution of the large denomination certificate of deposit, a unique financial instrument that now comprises an important part of time deposit balances. Today's time deposits, in other words, are different from the time deposits Friedman studied. For this and other reasons, Friedman himself agrees that this is not an ideal measure of money since there is actually a spectrum of financial assets possessing varying degrees of "money-ness."

The basic problem is that the significance of changes in any particular group of financial assets can be deceptive. Movements may simply represent investor substitution between, say, time deposits and marketable securities such as Treasury bills. Many other financial assets, such as accounts at savings and loan associations, may be close substitutes for demand deposits. Is it proper to include one kind of financial asset in the all-important definition of money while excluding other close substitutes? This definitional question has not been satisfactorily resolved.

Problems of Aggregation.   One further important shortcoming of the Monetarist view deserves our attention. Monetarists are prone to take an aggregated view of the economy, and to leave the distribution of money and income to competitive forces. Such an aggregated approach seems unsatisfactory, partly because it neglects the disproportionate impact of monetary actions. A case in point is the homebuilding industry where market imperfections have at times impeded the flow of funds through savings institutions into home mortgages. Monetary policy must recognize and adapt to situations like this.

CONCLUDING COMMENTS

It would be nice if we could project ourselves 20 years into the future and look back to see how the money supply controversy had been resolved. Perhaps we could also see what new controversies had moved into the spotlight by that time. But since this is impossible, we shall conclude instead with several comments on the present status of the money supply debate.

The arguments are heated, but the fervor of the parties involved should not obscure the substantial amount of agreement that exists. Almost all economists today share the goals of high employment, orderly economic growth, stable price levels, and long-run balance in our international payments. They generally agree, too, that the Government should do what it can to influence total spending in such a way as to achieve these goals. The basic question is not *if*, but *how*, these things can best be accomplished.

At first glance, the Monetarists argue persuasively that money is the crucial determinant of economic activity. But as we have examined the Monetarist scheme more closely, we have noted a number of serious shortcomings.

Even aside from these, the Monetarist theme, by attaching so much importance to the behavior of a single economic variable, tends to downgrade the complexity of our economy. Monetarists are less inclined to appreciate the consequences of this complexity, partly because they have assumed them away in their theorizing. But acceptance of the Monetarist arguments, in the sense of basing policy on them, re-

quires a reasonable acceptance of the assumptions on which their arguments are based. This is a strong requirement. Our economy's wages, prices, and interest rates, for instance, do not allocate labor services, products, and credit nearly as neatly as the Monetarists hope they do and, therefore, may be incapable of acceptably providing "automatic" economic stability. Whether balance of payments problems might be solved by allowing the exchange rates between currencies to move freely, as the Monetarists suggest, is debatable.

Is a simple monetary rule the final answer? Economists have long sought to find such a simple answer. Some, for example, thought fiscal policy was a panacea, but disillusion followed. We have to be prepared to admit that a simple answer does not exist. But even if a simple rule could be found, discretionary policy would still offer an important advantage that could not be matched by rigid adherence to a rule. Flexible policy permits learning from mistakes, offering a built-in capability for improving the efficiency of policy actions. Policy performance can continue to adapt and improve by preserving its flexibility.

Judging from the way in which other economic controversies have been resolved in the past, we can expect a synthesis to emerge. Indeed, there are already some signs of this. Monetarist attacks have caused Keynesians to pay much more attention than they previously did to the behavior of money. Monetarists, on the other side, are increasingly recognizing that the economy deviates from their theoretical assumptions, and are consequently qualifying the rigidity of their money supply rule. When we look back on the money supply controversy 20 years from now, we shall probably find that these synthesizing tendencies have produced considerably more agreement than now exists in the controversy over the money supply.

The Role of the Money Supply in the Conduct of Monetary Policy*

By Arthur F. Burns

Summary

During the past two years the American economy has experienced a substantial measure of prosperity. Real output has increased sharply, jobs have been created for millions of additional workers, and total personal income—both in dollars and in terms of real purchasing power—has risen to the highest levels ever reached.

Yet the prosperity has been a troubled one. Price increases have been large and widespread. For a time, the unemployment rate remained unduly high. Interest rates have risen sharply since the spring of 1972. Mortgage money has recently become difficult to obtain in many communities. And confidence in the dollar at home and abroad has at times wavered.

The present inflation is the most serious economic problem facing our country, and it poses great difficulties for economic stabilization policies. We must recognize that it will take some time for the forces of inflation, which now engulf our economy and others around the world, to burn themselves out. In today's environment, controls on wages and prices cannot be expected to yield the benefits they did in 1971 and 1972, when economic conditions were much different. Primary reliance in dealing with inflation—both in the near future and over the longer term—will have to be placed on fiscal and monetary policies.

Key Questions to Consider

■ What is the role of monetary policy according to Chairman Burns?

■ What responses does Chairman Burns give to the two questions of Senator Proxmire?

■ What factors caused the extraordinary price rises of 1973?

■ What role should fiscal policy play according to Chairman Burns?

---

* A letter written by Dr. Arthur F. Burns, Chairman, Board of Governors, Federal Reserve System, Washington, D.C., to Senator William Proxmire, November 6, 1973. Reprinted with permission of the author. The letter appeared in *Business Review*, Federal Reserve Bank of Dallas, December 1973.

The Role of the Money Supply in the Conduct of Monetary Policy

November 6, 1973

The Honorable William Proxmire
United States Senate
Washington, D.C.

Dear Senator Proxmire:

I am writing in further response to your letter of September 17, 1973, which requested comments on certain criticisms of monetary policy over the past year.

As stated in your letter, the criticisms are: (1) "that there was too much variation from time to time in the rate of increase in the money supply, that monetary policy was too erratic, too much characterized by stops and starts"; and (2) "that the money supply had increased much too much last year, in fact that the increase would have been too much even if we had been in the depths of a recession instead of enjoying a fairly vigorous economic expansion."

These criticisms involve basic issues with regard to the role of money in the economy, and the role that the money supply should play in the formulation and execution of monetary policy. These issues, along with the specific points you raise, require careful examination.

CRITICISM OF OUR PUBLIC POLICIES

During the past two years the American economy has experienced a substantial measure of prosperity. Real output has increased sharply, jobs have been created for millions of additional workers, and total personal income—both in dollars and in terms of real purchasing power—has risen to the highest levels ever reached.

Yet the prosperity has been a troubled one. Price increases have been large and widespread. For a time, the unemployment rate remained unduly high. Interest rates have risen sharply since the spring of 1972. Mortgage money has recently become difficult to obtain in many communities. And confidence in the dollar at home and abroad has at times wavered.

Many observers have blamed these difficulties on the management of public economic policies. Certainly, the Federal budget—despite vigorous efforts to hold expenditures down—continued in substantial deficit. There has also been an enormous growth in the activities of Federally-sponsored agencies which, although technically outside the budget, must still be financed. The results of efforts to control wages and prices during the past year have been disappointing. Partial decontrol in early 1973 and the subsequent freeze failed to bring the results that were hoped for.

Monetary policy has been criticized on somewhat contradictory counts—for being inflationary, or for permitting too high a level of interest rates, or for failing to bring the economy back to full employment, or for permitting excessive short-term variations in the growth of the money supply, and so on.

One indication of dissatisfaction with our public policies was provided by a report, to which you refer in your letter, on a questionnaire survey conducted by the National Association of Business Economists. Of the respondents, 38 percent rated fiscal policy "over the past year" as "poor"; 41 percent rated monetary policy "over the past year" as "poor"; only 14 percent felt that the wage-price controls under Phase IV were "about right." If this sampling is at all indicative, the public policies on which we have relied are being widely questioned. Many members of the above group, in fact, went on record for a significant change in fiscal policy. In response to a question whether they favored a variable investment tax credit, 46.5 percent said "yes," 40 percent said "no," and 13.5 percent expressed "no opinion."

Let me turn now to the questions raised in your letter and in some other recent discussions about monetary policy. I shall discuss, in particular, the role of money supply in the conduct of monetary policy; the extent and significance of variability in the growth of the money supply; and the actual behavior of the money supply during 1972–73.

ROLE OF MONEY SUPPLY

For many years economists have debated the role of the money supply in the performance of economic systems. One school of thought, often termed "monetarist," claims that changes in the money supply influence very importantly, perhaps even decisively, the pace of economic activity and the level of prices. Monetarists contend that the monetary authorities should pay principal attention to the money supply, rather than to other financial variables such as interest

rates, in the conduct of monetary policy. They also contend that fiscal policy has only a small independent impact on the economy.

Another school of thought places less emphasis on the money supply and assigns more importance to the expenditure and tax policies of the Federal Government as factors influencing real economic activity and the level of prices. This school emphasizes the need for monetary policy to be concerned with interest rates and with conditions in the money and capital markets. Some economic activities, particularly residential building and State and local government construction, depend heavily on borrowed funds, and are therefore influenced greatly by changes in the cost and availability of credit. In other categories of spending—such as business investment in fixed capital and inventories, and consumer purchases of durable goods —credit conditions play a less decisive role, but they are nonetheless important.

Monetarists recognize that monetary policy affects private spending in part through its impact on interest rates and other credit terms. But they believe that primary attention to the growth of the money supply will result in a more appropriate monetary policy than would attention to conditions in the credit markets.

Needless to say, monetary policy is—and has long been—a controversial subject. Even the monetarists do not speak with one voice on monetary policy. Some influential monetarists believe that monetary policy should aim strictly at maintaining a constant rate of growth of the money supply. However, what that constant should be, or how broadly the money supply should be defined, are matters on which monetarists still differ. And there are also monetarists who would allow some—but infrequent—changes in the rate of growth of the money supply, in accordance with changing economic conditions.

It seems self-evident that adherence to a rigid growth rate rule, or even one that is changed infrequently, would practically prevent monetary policy from playing an active role in economic stabilization.

Monetarists recognize this. They believe that most economic disturbances tend to be self-correcting, and they therefore argue that a constant or nearly constant rate of growth of the money supply would result in reasonably satisfactory economic performance.

But neither historical evidence, nor the thrust of explorations in business-cycle theory over a long century, give support to the notion that our economy is inherently stable. On the contrary, experience has demonstrated repeatedly that blind reliance on the self-correcting properties of our economic system can lead to serious trouble. Discretionary economic policy, while it has at times led to mistakes, has more often proved reasonably successful. The disappearance of business depressions, which in earlier times spelled mass unemployment for workers and mass bankruptcies for businesmen, is largely attributable to the stabilization policies of the last thirty years.

The fact is that the internal workings of a market economy tend of themselves to generate business fluctuations, and most modern economists recognize this. For example, improved prospects for profits often spur unsustainable bursts of investment spending. The flow of personal income in an age of affluence allows ample latitude for changes in discretionary expenditures and in savings rates. During a business-cycle expansion various imbalances tend to develop within the economy—between aggregate inventories and sales, or between aggregate business investment in fixed capital and consumer outlays, or between average unit costs of production and prices. Such imbalances give rise to cyclical movements in the economy. Flexible fiscal and monetary policies, therefore, are often needed to cope with undesirable economic developments, and this need is not diminished by the fact that our available tools of economic stabilization leaves something to be desired.

There is general agreement among economists that, as a rule, the effects of stabilization policies occur gradually over time, and that economic forecasts are an essential tool of policy making. However, no economist—or school of economics—has a monopoly on accurate forecasting. At times, forecasts based largely on the money supply have turned out to be satisfactory. At other times, such forecasts have been quite poor, mainly because of unanticipated changes in the intensity with which the existing money stock is used by business firms and consumers.

Changes in the rate of turnover of money have historically played a large role in economic fluctuations, and they continue to do so. For example, the narrowly-defined money stock—that is, demand deposits plus currency in public circulation—grew by 5.7 percent between the fourth quarter of 1969 and the fourth quarter of 1970. But the turnover of money declined during that year, and the dollar value of GNP rose only 4.5 percent. In the following year, the growth rate of the money supply increased to 6.9 percent, but the turnover of money picked up briskly and the dollar value of GNP accelerated to 9.3 percent. The movement out of recession in 1970 into recovery in 1971 was thus closely related to the greater intensity in the use of money. Occurrences such as this are very common because the willingness to use the existing stock of money, expressed in its rate of turnover, is a highly dynamic force in economic life.

For this as well as other reasons, the Federal Reserve uses a blend of forecasting techniques. The behavior of the money supply and other financial variables is accorded careful attention. So also are the results of the most recent surveys on plant and equipment spending, consumer attitudes, and inventory plans. Recent trends in key producing and spending sectors are analyzed. The opinions of businessmen and outside economic analysts are canvassed, in part through the nationwide contacts of Federal Reserve Banks. And an assessment is made of the probable course of fiscal policy, also of labor-market and agricultural policies, and their effects on the economy.

Evidence from all these sources is weighed. Efforts are also made to assess economic developments through the use of large-scale econometric models. An eclectic approach is thus taken by the Federal Reserve, in recognition of the fact that the state of economic knowledge does not justify reliance on any single forecasting technique. As economic research has cumulated, it has become increasingly clear that money does indeed matter. But other financial variables also matter.

In recent years, the Federal Reserve has placed somewhat more emphasis on achieving desired growth rates of the monetary aggregates, including the narrowly-defined money supply, in its conduct of monetary policy. But we have continued to give careful attention to other financial indicators, among them the level of interest rates on mortgages and other loans and the liquidity position of financial institutions and the general public. This is necessary because the economic implications of any given monetary growth rate depend on the state of liquidity, the attitudes of businessmen, investors, and consumers toward liquidity, the cost and availability of borrowed funds, and other factors. Also, as the nation's central bank, the Federal Reserve can never lose sight of its role as a lender of last resort, so that financial crises and panics will be averted.

I recognize that one advantage of maintaining a relatively stable growth rate of the money supply is that a partial offset is thereby provided to unexpected and undesired shifts in the aggregate demand for goods and services. There is always some uncertainty as to the emerging strength of aggregate demand. If money growth is maintained at a rather stable rate, and aggregate demand turns out to be weaker than is consistent with the nation's economic objectives, interest rates will tend to decline and the easing of credit markets should help to moderate the undesired weakness in demand. Similarly, if the demand for goods and services threatens to outrun productive capacity, a rather stable rate of monetary growth will provide a restraining influence on the supply of credit and thus tend to restrain excessive spending.

However, it would be unwise for monetary policy to aim at all times at a constant or nearly constant rate of growth of money balances. The money growth rate that can contribute most to national objectives will vary with economic conditions. For example, if

the aggregate demand for goods and services is unusually weak, or if the demand for liquidity is unusually strong, a rate of increase in the money supply well above the desirable long-term trend may be needed for a time. Again, when the economy is experiencing severe cost-push inflation, a monetary growth rate that is relatively high by a historical yardstick may have to be tolerated for a time. If money growth were severely constrained in order to combat the element of inflation resulting from such a cause, it might well have seriously adverse effects on production and employment. In short, what growth rate of the money supply is appropriate at any given time cannot be determined simply by extrapolating past trends or by some preconceived arithmetical standard.

Moreover, for purposes of conducting monetary policy, it is never safe to rely on just one concept of money—even if that concept happens to be fashionable. A variety of plausible concepts merit careful attention, because a number of financial assets serve as a convenient, safe, and liquid store of purchasing power.

The Federal Reserve publishes data corresponding to three definitions of money, and takes all of them into account in determining policy. The three measures are: (a) the narrowly-defined money stock (M_1), which encompasses currency and demand deposits held by the nonbank public; (b) a more broadly-defined money stock (M_2), which also includes time and savings deposits at commercial banks (other than large negotiable time certificates of deposit); (c) a still broader definition (M_3), which includes savings deposits at mutual savings banks and savings and loan associations. A definition embracing other liquid assets could also be justified—for example, one that would include large-denomination negotiable time certificates of deposit, U.S. savings bonds and Treasury bills, commercial paper, and other short-term money market instruments.

There are many assets closely related to cash, and the public can switch readily among these assets. However money may be defined, the task of determining the amount of money needed to maintain high employment and reasonable stability of the general price level is complicated by shifting preferences of the public for cash and other financial assets.

VARIABILITY OF MONEY SUPPLY GROWTH

In the short-run, the rate of change in the observed money supply is quite erratic, and cannot be trusted as an indicator of the course of monetary policy. This would be so even if there were no errors of measurement.

The record of hearings held by the Joint Economic Committee on June 27, 1973 includes a memorandum which I submitted on problems encountered in controlling the money supply. As indicated there, week-to-week, month-to-month, and even quarter-to-quarter fluctuations in the rate of change of money balances are frequently influenced by international flows of funds, changes in the level of U.S. Government deposits, and sudden changes in the public's attitude towards liquidity. Some of these variations appear to be essentially random—a product of the enormous ebb and flow of funds in our modern economy.

Because the demands of the public for money are subject to rather wide short-term variations, efforts by the Federal Reserve to maintain a constant growth rate of the money supply could lead to sharp short-run swings in interest rates and risk damage to financial markets and the economy. Uncertainties about financing costs could reduce the fluidity of markets and increase the costs of financing to borrowers. In addition, wide and erratic movements of interest rates and financial conditions could have undesirable effects on business and consumer spending. These adverse effects may not be of major dimensions, but it is better to avoid them.

In any event, for a variety of reasons explained in the memorandum for the Joint Economic Committee, to which I have previously referred, the Federal Reserve does not have precise control over the money supply. To give one example, a significant part of the money supply consists of deposits lodged in nonmember banks that are not subject to the reserve requirements set by the Federal Reserve. As a result there is some slippage in monetary control. Furthermore, since deposits at nonmember banks have been reported for only two to four days in a year, in contrast to daily statistics for member banks, the data on the money supply—which we regularly present on a weekly, monthly, and quarterly basis—are estimates rather than precise measurements. When the infrequent reports from nonmember banks become available, they often necessitate considerable revisions of the money supply figures. In the past two years, the revisions were upward, and this may happen again this year.

Some indication of the extent of short-term variations in the recorded money supply is provided below. Table 1 shows the average and maximum deviations (without regard to sign) of M_1 from its average annual growth rate over a three and a half year period. As would be expected, the degree of variation diminishes as the time unit lengthens; it is much larger for monthly than for quarterly data, and is also larger for quarterly than for semi-annual data.

In our judgment, there need be little reason for concern about the short-run variations that occur in the rate of change in the money stock. Such variations

Table 1

Deviations in M_1 from Its Average Rate of Growth, 1970 Through Mid-1973

Form of data	Annual rates of change, in percent	
	Average deviation	Maximum deviation
Monthly	3.8	8.8
Quarterly	2.4	5.5
Semi-annual	1.8	4.1

have minimal effects on the real economy. For one thing, the outstanding supply of money is very large. It is also quite stable, even when the short-run rate of change is unstable. This October the average outstanding supply of M_1, seasonally adjusted, was about $264 billion. On this base, a monthly rise or fall in the money stock of even $2½ billion would amount to only a 1 percent change. But when such a temporary change is expressed as an annual rate, as is now commonly done, it comes out as about 12 percent and attracts attention far beyond its real significance.

The Federal Reserve research staff has investigated carefully the economic implications of variability in M_1 growth. The experience of the past two decades suggests that even an abnormally large or abnormally small rate of growth of the money stock over a period up to six months or so has a negligible influence on the course of the economy—provided it is subsequently offset. Such short-run variations in the rate of change in the money supply may not at all reflect Federal Reserve policy, and they do not justify the attention they often receive from financial analysts.

The thrust of monetary policy and its probable effects on economic activity can only be determined by observing the course of the money supply and of other monetary aggregates over periods lasting six months or so. Even then, care must be taken to measure the growth of money balances in ways that temper the influence of short-term variations. For example, the growth of money balances over a quarter can be measured from the amount outstanding in the last month of the preceding quarter to the last month of the current quarter, or from the average amount outstanding during the preceding quarter to the average in the current quarter. The first measure captures the latest tendencies in the money supply, but may be distorted by random changes that have no lasting significance. The second measure tends to average out temporary fluctuations and is comparable to the data provided on a wide range of non-monetary economic variables, such as the gross national product and related measures.

Table 2

Growth Rates of Money Supply on Two Bases

		Annual rate of change, in percent	
		M	Q
1972	I	9.2	5.3
	II	6.1	8.4
	III	8.2	8.0
	IV	8.6	7.1
1973	I	1.7	4.7
	II	10.3	6.9
	III	0.3	5.1

A comparison of these two ways of measuring the rate of growth in M_1 is shown in Table 2 for successive quarters in 1972 and 1973. The first column, labeled M, shows annual rates calculated from end-months of quarters; the second column, labeled Q, shows annual rates calculated from quarterly averages.

As may be seen, the quarterly averages disclose much more clearly the developing trend of monetary restraint—which, in fact, began in the second quarter of 1972. Also, the growth of M_1, which on a month-end basis appears very erratic in the first three quarters of 1973, is much more stable on a quarterly average basis. For example, while the level of M_1 did not expand significantly between June and September, the quarterly average figures indicate further sizable growth in the third quarter. For purposes of economic analysis, it is an advantage to recognize that the money available for use was appreciably larger in the third quarter than in the second quarter.

EXPERIENCE OF 1972–73

During 1972, it was the responsibility of the Federal Reserve to encourage a rate of economic expansion adequate to reduce unemployment to acceptable levels. At the same time, despite the dampening effects of the wage-price control program, inflationary pressures were gathering. Monetary policy, therefore, had to balance the twin objectives of containing inflationary pressures and encouraging economic growth. These objectives were to some extent conflicting, and monetary policy alone could not be expected to cope with both problems. Continuation of an effective wage-price program and a firmer policy of fiscal restraint were urgently needed.

The narrowly-defined money stock increased 7.4 percent during 1972 (measured from the fourth quarter of 1971 to the fourth quarter of 1972). Between the third quarter of 1972 and the third quarter of 1973, the growth rate was 6.1 percent. By the first half of 1973, the annual growth rate had declined to 5.8 percent, and a further slowing occurred in the third quarter.

Evaluation of the appropriateness of these growth rates would require full analysis of the economic and financial objectives, conditions, and policies during the past two years, if not longer. Such an analysis cannot be undertaken here. Some perspective on monetary developments during 1972–73 may be gained, however, from comparisons with the experience of other industrial countries, and by recalling briefly how domestic economic conditions evolved during this period.

Table 3 compares the growth of M_1 in the United States with that of other industrial countries in 1972 and the first half of 1973. The definitions of M_1 differ somewhat from country to country, but are as nearly comparable as statistical sources permit. It goes without saying that each country faced its own set of economic conditions and problems. Yet it is useful to note that monetary growth in the United States was much lower than in other major industrial countries, and that it also was steadier than in the other countries.

The next table shows, in summary fashion, the rates of change in the money supply of the United States, in its total production, and in the consumer price level during 1972 and 1973. The table is based on the latest data. It may be noted, in passing, that, according to data available as late as January 1973, the rate of growth of M_1 during 1972 was 7.2%, not 7.4%; and that the rate of increase in real GNP was 7.7%, not 7.0%. In other words, on the basis of the data available during 1972, the rate of growth of M_1 was below the rate of growth of the physical volume of over-all production.

The table indicates that growth in M_1 during 1972 and 1973 approximately matched the growth of real output, but was far below the expansion in the dollar value of the nation's output. Although monetary policy limited the availability of money relative to the growth of transactions demands, it still encouraged a substantial expansion in economic activity; real output rose by about 7 percent in 1972. Even so, unemployment remained unsatisfactorily high throughout the greater part of the year. It was not until November that the unemployment rate dropped

Table 3

Annual Percent Rates of Growth in Money Supply

	4th quarter 1971 to 4th quarter 1972	4th quarter 1972 to 2nd quarter 1973
United States	7.4	5.8
United Kingdom	14.1	10.0
Germany	14.3	4.2
France	15.4	8.7
Japan	23.1	28.2

Table 4

Money Supply, GNP, and Prices in the U.S.

(Percent change at annual rates)

	4th quarter 1971 to 4th quarter 1972	4th quarter 1972 to	
		2nd quarter of 1973	3rd quarter of 1973
Money supply (M₁)	7.4	5.8	5.6
Gross National Product			
Current dollars	10.6	12.1	11.7
Constant dollars	7.0	5.4	4.8
Prices			
Consumer price index (CPI)	3.4	7.1	7.8
CPI excluding food ...	3.0	4.0	4.1

below 5½ percent. For the year as a whole, the unemployment rate averaged 5.6 percent. It may be of interest to recall that unemployment averaged 5.5 percent in 1954 and 1960, which are commonly regarded as recession years.

Since the expansion of M_1 in 1972 was low relative to the demands for money and credit, it was accompanied by rising short-term interest rates. Long-term interest rates showed little net change last year, as credit demands were satisfied mainly in the short-term markets.

In 1973, the growth of M_1 moderated while the transactions demands for cash and the turnover of money accelerated. GNP in current dollars rose at a 12 percent annual rate as prices rose more rapidly. In credit markets, short-term interest rates rose sharply further, while long-term interest rates also moved up, though by substantially less than short-term rates.

The extraordinary upsurge of the price level this year reflects a variety of special influences. First, there has been a world-wide economic boom superimposed on the boom in the United States. Second, we have encountered critical shortages of basic materials. The expansion in industrial capacity needed to produce these materials had not been put in place

earlier because of the abnormally low level of profits between 1966 and 1971 and also because of numerous impediments to new investment on ecological grounds. Third, farm product prices escalated sharply as a result of crop failures in many countries last year. Fourth, fuel prices spurted upward, reflecting the developing shortages in the energy field. And fifth, the depreciation of the dollar in foreign exchange markets has served to boost prices of imported goods and to add to the demands pressing on our productive resources.

In view of these powerful special factors, and the cyclical expansion of our economy, a sharp advance in our price level would have been practically inevitable in 1973. The upsurge of the price level this year hardly represents either the basic trend of prices or the response of prices to previous monetary or fiscal policies—whatever their shortcomings may have been. In particular, as the above table shows, the explosion of food prices that occurred this year is in large part responsible for the accelerated rise in the over-all consumer price level.

The severe rate of inflation that we have experienced in 1973 cannot responsibly be attributed to monetary management or to public policies more generally. In retrospect, it may well be that monetary policy should have been a little less expansive in 1972. But a markedly more restrictive policy would have led to a still sharper rise in interest rates and risked a premature ending of the business expansion, without limiting to any significant degree this year's upsurge of the price level.

CONCLUDING OBSERVATIONS

The present inflation is the most serious economic problem facing our country, and it poses great difficulties for economic stabilization policies. We must recognize, I believe, that it will take some time for the forces of inflation, which now engulf our economy and others around the world, to burn themselves out. In today's environment, controls on wages and prices cannot be expected to yield the benefits they did in 1971 and 1972, when economic conditions were much different. Primary reliance in dealing with inflation—both in the near future and over the longer term—will have to be placed on fiscal and monetary policies.

The prospects for regaining price stability would be enhanced by improvements in our monetary and fiscal instruments. The conduct of monetary policy could be improved if steps were taken to increase the precision with which the money supply can be controlled by the Federal Reserve. Part of the present control problem stems from statistical inadequacies—chiefly the paucity of data on deposits at nonmember banks. Also, however, control over the money supply and other monetary aggregates is less precise than it can or should be because non-member banks are not subject to the same reserve requirements as are Federal Reserve members.

I hope that the Congress will support efforts to rectify these deficiencies. For its part, the Federal Reserve Board is even now carrying on discussions with the Federal Deposit Insurance Corporation about the need for better statistics on the nation's money supply. The Board also expects shortly to recommend to the Congress legislation that will put demand deposits at commercial banks on a uniform basis from the standpoint of reserve requirements.

Improvements in our fiscal policies are also needed. It is important for the Congress to put an end to fragmented consideration of expenditures, to place a firm ceiling on total Federal expenditures, and to relate these expenditures to prospective revenues and the nation's economic needs. Fortunately, there is now widespread recognition by members of the Congress of the need to reform budgetary procedures along these broad lines.

It also is high time for fiscal policy to become a more versatile tool of economic stabilization. Particularly appropriate would be fiscal instruments that could be adapted quickly, under special legislative rules, to changing economic conditions—such as a variable tax credit for business investment in fixed capital. Once again I would urge the Congress to give serious consideration to this urgently needed reform.

We must strive also for better understanding of the effects of economic stabilization policies on economic activity and prices. Our knowledge in this area is greater now than it was five or ten years ago, thanks to extensive research undertaken by economists in academic institutions, at the Federal Reserve, and elsewhere. The keen interest of the Joint Economic Committee in improving economic stabilization policies has, I believe, been an influence of great importance in stimulating this widespread research effort.

I look forward to continued cooperation with the Committee in an effort to achieve the kind of economic performance our citizens expect and deserve.

Sincerely yours,

ARTHUR F. BURNS

Reading 33

Letter on Monetary Policy*

By Milton Friedman

Summary

For more than a decade, monetary growth has been accelerating. It has been higher in the past three years than in any other three-year period since the end of World War II. Inflation has also accelerated over the past decade. It, too, has been higher in the past three years than in any other three-year period since 1947. Economic theory and empirical evidence combine to establish a strong presumption that the acceleration in monetary growth is largely responsible for the acceleration in inflation.

I recognize, of course, that there are now, and have been in the past, strong political pressures on the Fed to continue rapid monetary growth. Once inflation has proceeded as far as it already has, it will take time to eliminate it. Moreover, there is literally no way to end inflation that will not involve a temporary, though perhaps fairly protracted, period of low economic growth and relatively high unemployment. Avoidance of the earlier excessive monetary growth would have had far less costly consequences for the community than cutting monetary growth down to an appropriate level will now have. But the damage has been done. The longer we wait, the harder it will be. And there is no other way to stop inflation. The only justification for the Fed's vaunted independence is to enable it to take measures that are wise for the long run even if not popular in the short run.

Key Questions to Consider

- Professor Friedman claims that the Fed is responsible for the rate of inflation experienced by the United States in 1973. What empirical evidence does he cite to support his argument? Does he provide a theoretical basis for the inflation?

- How does Professor Friedman believe the Fed can achieve more precise control over the conduct of monetary policy?

---

* Reprinted with permission from the author. The letter appeared in *Review*, Federal Reserve Bank of St. Louis, **56,** No. 3 (March 1974), 20–23.

Letter on Monetary Policy

The Honorable William Proxmire
Joint Economic Committee
United States Senate
Washington, D.C. 20510

Dear Senator Proxmire:

On September 17, 1973, you asked the Chairman of the Board of Governors of the Federal Reserve System to comment on certain published criticisms of monetary policy. On November 6, 1973, the Chairman replied on behalf of the System. This Reply has been widely publicized by the Federal Reserve System. It was reprinted in the *Federal Reserve Bulletin* (November 1973) and in at least five of the separate Federal Reserve Bank *Reviews.*

The Reply makes many valid points. Yet, taken as a whole, it evades rather than answers the criticisms. It appears to exonerate the Federal Reserve System from any appreciable responsibility for the current inflation, yet a close reading reveals that it does not do so, and other evidence, to which the Reply does not refer, establishes a strong case that the Fed has contributed to inflation. The Reply appears to attribute admitted errors in monetary policy to forces outside the Fed, yet the difficulties in controlling and

measuring the money supply are largely of the Fed's own making.

The essence of the System's answer to the criticisms is contained in three sentences, one dealing with the Fed's responsibility for the 1973 inflation; the other two, with the problem of controlling and measuring the money supply. I shall discuss each in turn.

RESPONSIBILITY FOR INFLATION

The severe rate of inflation that we have experienced in 1973 cannot responsibly be attributed to monetary management (italics added).

As written, this sentence is unexceptionable. Delete the word "severe," and the sentence is indefensible.

The Reply correctly cites a number of special factors that made the inflation in 1973 more severe than could have been expected from prior monetary growth alone—the world-wide economic boom, ecological impediments to investment, escalating farm prices, energy shortages. These factors may well explain why consumer prices rose by 8 percent in 1973 (fourth quarter 1972 to fourth quarter 1973) instead of, say, by 6 percent. But they do not explain why inflation in 1973 would have been as high as 6 percent in their absence. They do not explain why consumer prices rose more than 25 percent in the five years from 1968 to 1973.

The Reply recognizes that "the effects of stabilization policies occur gradually over time" and that "it is never safe to rely on just one concept of money." Yet, the Reply presents statistical data on the growth of money or income or prices for only 1972 and 1973, and for only one of the three monetary concepts it refers to, namely, M_1 (currency plus demand deposits), the one that had the lowest rate of growth. On the basis of the evidence in the Reply, there is no way to evaluate the longer-term policies of the Fed, or to compare current monetary policy with earlier policy, or one concept of money with another.

From calendar year 1970 to calendar year 1973, M_1 grew at the annual rate of 6.9 percent; in the preceding decade, from 1960 to 1970, at 4.2 percent. More striking yet, the rate of growth from 1970 to 1973 was higher than for any other three-year period since the end of World War II.

The other monetary concepts tell the same story. From 1970 to 1973, M_2 (M_1 plus commercial bank time deposits other than large CDs) grew at the annual rate of 10.5 percent; from 1960 to 1970, at 6.7 percent. From 1970 to 1973, M_3 (M_2 plus deposits at nonbank thrift institutions) grew at the annual rate of 12.0 percent; from 1960 to 1970, at 7.2 percent. For both M_2 and M_3, the rates of growth from 1970 to 1973 are higher than for any other three-year period since World War II.

As the accompanying chart demonstrates, prices show the same pattern as monetary growth except for the Korean War inflation. In the early 1960s, consumer prices rose at a rate of 1 to 2 percent per year; from 1970 to 1973, at an average rate of 4.6 percent; currently, they are rising at a rate of not far from 10 percent. The accelerated rise in the quantity of money has clearly been reflected, after some delay, in a similar accelerated rise in prices.

However limited may be the Fed's ability to con-

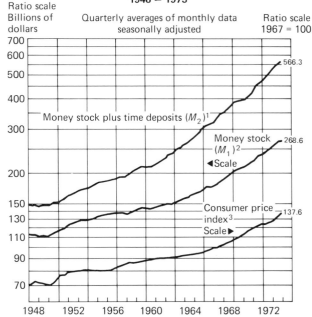

Movements in Money and Prices
1948 – 1973

Ratio scale
Billions of dollars

Quarterly averages of monthly data
seasonally adjusted

Ratio scale
1967 = 100

[1] Defined as money stock plus saving deposits, time deposits, open account, and time certificates other than negotiable CDs of $1000,00 of large weekly reporting banks.
[2] Defined as (1) demand deposits of commercial banks other than domestic interbank and U.S. Government, less cash items in process of collection and F.R. float; (2) foreign demand balances at F.R. Banks; and (3) currency outside the Treasury, F.R. Banks, and vaults of commercial banks.
[3] Consumer Price Index, All Items.

Latest data plotted: 4th quarter, 1973

trol monetary aggregates from quarter to quarter or even year to year, the monetary acceleration depicted in the chart, which extended over more than a decade, could not have occurred without the Fed's acquiescence—to put it mildly. And however loose may be the year-to-year relation between monetary growth and inflation, the acceleration in the rate of inflation over the past decade could not have occurred without the prior monetary acceleration.

Whatever therefore may be the verdict on the short-run relations to which the Reply restricts itself, the Fed's long-run policies have played a major role in producing our present inflation.

There is much evidence on the shorter-term as well as the longer-term relations. Studies for the

United States and many other countries reveal highly consistent patterns. A substantial change in the rate of monetary growth which is sustained for more than a few months tends to be followed some six or nine months later by a change in the same direction in the rate of growth of total dollar spending. To begin with, most of the change in spending is reflected in output and employment. Typically, though not always, it takes another year to 18 months before the change in monetary growth is reflected in prices. On the average, therefore, it takes something like two years for a higher or lower rate of monetary growth to be reflected in a higher or lower rate of inflation.

Table I illustrates this relation between monetary growth and prices. It shows rates of change for three monetary aggregates and for consumer prices over two-year spans measured from the first quarter of the corresponding years. The average delay in the effect of monetary change on prices is allowed for by matching each biennium for prices with the prior biennium for money. Clearly, on the average, prices reflect the behavior of money two years earlier.

To avoid misunderstanding, let me stress that, as the table illustrates, this is an *average* relationship, not a precise relationship that can be expected to hold in exactly the same way in every month or year or even decade. As the Reply properly stresses, many factors affect the course of prices other than changes in the quantity of money. Over short periods, they may sometimes be more important. But the Federal Reserve, and the Federal Reserve alone, has the responsibility for the quantity of money; it does not have the responsibility, and certainly not sole responsibility, for the other factors that affect inflation. And the record is unmistakably clear that, over the past three years taken as a whole, the Federal Reserve System has exercised that responsibility in a way that has exacerbated inflation.

This conclusion holds not only for the three years as a whole but also for each year separately, as Table II shows. The one encouraging feature is the slightly lower rate of growth of M_2 and M_3 from 1972 to 1973 than in the earlier two years. But the tapering off is mild and it is not clear that it is continuing. More important, even these lower rates are far too high. Steady growth of M_2 at 9 or 10 percent would lead to an inflation of about 6 or 7 percent per year. To bring inflation down to 3 percent, let alone to zero, the rate of growth of M_2 must be reduced to something like 5 to 7 percent.

Table I

Money and Prices
(Annual rates of change, first quarter to first quarter)

| | Monetary measures | | | Consumer prices | |
	M_1	M_2	M_3		
1959–61	0.8%	2.5%	4.6%	1.1%	1961–63
1961–63	2.4	5.9	7.6	1.3	1963–65
1963–65	4.1	6.9	8.3	2.7	1965–67
1965–67	3.7	7.2	6.7	4.2	1967–69
1967–69	7.3	9.4	8.8	5.5	1969–71
1969–71	4.8	6.3	6.3	3.9	1971–73
1971–73	7.2	10.4	12.6	9.1*	1973–

* First quarter 1973 to fourth quarter 1973.

Table II

Recent Monetary Growth Rates
(Percent change, annual data)

	M_1	M_2	M_3
1970–71	7.0%	11.8%	12.8%
1971–72	6.4	10.2	12.5
1972–73	7.4	9.5	10.7

CONTROLLING AND MEASURING THE MONEY SUPPLY

The conduct of monetary policy could be improved if steps were taken to increase the precision with which the money supply can be controlled by the Federal Reserve. Part of the present control problem stems from statistical inadequacies (italics added).

Again these sentences from the Reply are literally correct, but they give not the slightest indication that the difficulties of controlling and measuring the money supply are predominantly of the Fed's own making. The only specific problems that the Reply mentions are the "paucity of data on deposits at nonmember banks" and the fact that "nonmember banks are not subject to the same reserve requirements as are Federal Reserve members."

Nonmember deposits do raise problems in measuring and controlling the money supply, but they are minor compared to other factors. The Reply's emphasis on them is understandable on other grounds. Almost since it was established in 1914, the Fed has been anxious to bring all commercial banks into the System, and has been worried about the defection of banks from member to nonmember status. It has therefore seized every occasion, such as the Reply provides, to stress the desirability of requiring all banks to be members of the System, or at least subject to the same reserve requirements as member banks.

Control

Nonmember banks raise a minor problem with respect to control. Their reserve ratios do differ from those of member banks. But nonmember banks hold only one-quarter of all deposits. This fraction tends to change rather predictably, and changes in it can be monitored and offset by open market operations.

A far more important problem with respect to control is the lagged reserve requirement that was introduced by the Fed in 1968. This change has not worked as it was expected to. Instead, by introducing additional delay between Federal Reserve open market operations and the money supply, it has appreciably reduced "the precision with which the money supply can be controlled by the Federal Reserve." Other measures taken by the Fed have had the same effect. In an article on this subject published recently, George Kaufman, long an economist with the Federal Reserve System, concluded, "by increasing the complexity of the money multiplier, proliferating rate

ceilings on different types of deposits, and encouraging banks, albeit unintentionally, to search out nondeposit sources of funds, the Federal Reserve has increased its own difficulty in controlling the stock of money. . . . To the extent the increased difficulty supports the long voiced contention of some Federal Reserve officials that they are unable to control the stock of money even if they so wished, the actions truly represent a self-fulfilling prophecy."

Even more basic is the procedure used by the Open Market Desk of the New York Federal Reserve Bank in carrying out the directives of the Open Market Committee. These directives have increasingly been stated in terms of desired changes in monetary aggregates rather than in money market conditions. However, the Desk has not adapted its procedure to the new objective. Instead, it tries to use money market conditions (that is, interest rates) as an indirect device to control monetary aggregates. Many students of the subject believe that this technique is inefficient. Money market conditions are affected by many forces other than the Fed's operations. As a result, the Desk cannot control money market conditions very accurately and cannot predict accurately what changes in money market conditions are required to produce the desired change in monetary aggregates.

An alternative procedure would be to operate directly on high-powered money, which the Fed can control to a high degree of precision. Many of us believe that the changes in high-powered money required to produce the desired change in monetary aggregates can be estimated tolerably closely, even now. They could be estimated with still greater precision if the Fed were to rationalize the structure of reserve requirements.

Measurement

Repeatedly, in the past few years, the Fed's statisticians have retrospectively revised estimates of monetary aggregates, and sometimes, as in December 1972, by very substantial amounts.

The one source of measurement error mentioned

in the Reply is the unavailability of data on nonmember banks. This is a source of error because nonmember banks report deposit data on only two, or sometimes four, dates a year. The resulting error in estimates for intervening or subsequent dates has sometimes been sizable, but mostly it has accounted for a minor part of the statistical revisions. In any event, this source of error can be reduced drastically by sampling and other devices which the Fed could undertake on its own without additional legislation.

More important sources of error are seasonal adjustment procedures and the estimation and treatment of cash items, nondeposit liabilities, and foreign held deposits.

It has long seemed to me little short of scandalous that the money supply figures should require such substantial and frequent revision. The Fed is itself the primary source of data required to measure the money supply; it can get additional data it may need; it has a large and highly qualified research staff. Yet for years it has failed to undertake the research effort necessary to correct known defects in its money supply series.[1]

CONCLUSION

For more than a decade, monetary growth has been accelerating. It has been higher in the past three years than in any other three-year period since the end of World War II. Inflation has also accelerated over the past decade. It too has been higher in the past three years than in any other three-year period since 1947.

---

[1] On January 31, 1974, after this comment had been drafted, the Board of Governors of the Federal Reserve System announced "the formation of a special committee of prominent academic experts to review concepts, procedures and methodology involved in estimating the money supply and other monetary aggregates." I have agreed to serve as a member of this committee.

Economic theory and empirical evidence combine to establish a strong presumption that the acceleration in monetary growth is largely responsible for the acceleration in inflation. Nothing in the Reply of the Chairman of the Federal Reserve System to your letter contradicts or even questions that conclusion. And nothing in that Reply denies that the Federal Reserve System had the power to prevent the sharp acceleration in monetary growth.

I recognize, of course, that there are now, and have been in the past, strong political pressures on the Fed to continue rapid monetary growth. Once inflation has proceeded as far as it already has, it will, as the Reply says, take some time to eliminate it. Moreover, there is literally no way to end inflation that will not involve a temporary, though perhaps fairly protracted, period of low economic growth and relatively high unemployment. Avoidance of the earlier excessive monetary growth would have had far less costly consequences for the community than cutting monetary growth down to an appropriate level will now have. But the damage has been done. The longer we wait, the harder it will be. And there is no other way to stop inflation.

The only justification for the Fed's vaunted independence is to enable it to take measures that are wise for the long run even if not popular in the short run. That is why it is so discouraging to have the Reply consist almost entirely of a denial of responsibility for inflation and an attempt to place the blame elsewhere.

If the Fed does not explain to the public the nature of our problem and the costs involved in ending inflation; if it does not take the lead in imposing the temporarily unpopular measures required, who will?

Sincerely yours,
MILTON FRIEDMAN
Professor of Economics

Inflation and Economic Policy*

By David P. Eastburn

Summary

This article deals with four closely related problems: causes of inflation; what to do about inflation; the role of interest rates; and evening out the burdens of fighting inflation.

Key Questions to Consider

■ What causes inflation?

■ What can be done about inflation?

■ What is the role of interest rates in dealing with inflation?

———————

* Reprinted with permission from *Business Review*, Federal Reserve Bank of Philadelphia, September 1974, pp. 3–6.

Inflation and Economic Policy

This article deals with four closely related problems: causes of inflation; what to do about inflation; the role of interest rates; and evening out the burdens of fighting inflation.

CAUSES OF INFLATION

If we could somehow create an economic discomfort index the way weathermen combine temperature and humidity, I suspect we would find ourselves about as uncomfortable as at any time in recent years. Prices are soaring, the unemployment rate is creeping up, and interest rates are at record levels.

Without minimizing any of the difficulties we face, I believe the major problem is inflation. We are in perhaps the worst peacetime inflation in our history. Unless we begin to unwind inflation, I am fearful of the consequences not only for the economy but for our entire social fabric.

Our current inflation has many causes, but it is helpful to divide them into two main aspects. One aspect involves extraordinary events such as crop failures, oil embargoes, and dollar devaluations. They come and go and often not much can be done about them. Beef prices skyrocket then taper off; wheat supplies diminish then expand; anchovies disappear from the coast of Peru and then reappear. If we are lucky, these phenomena occur at different times. In the last couple of years we have been unlucky; many extraordinary events have occurred together.

A second aspect is monetary. Whatever immediate events may cause prices to rise—including shortages and higher wage costs—a higher price level cannot be sustained without sufficient money. In retrospect it would have been better if money had not grown so rapidly over much of the past decade. The reasons for this growth go to a large extent to considerations other than inflation which the Federal Reserve has believed to be important. Throughout much of the period there are primary concerns about the disadvantaged—those unemployed, living in dilapidated housing and attending crowded schools. Ample growth in money was necessary to meet these economic and social problems. In more recent periods, the Federal Reserve, partly reflecting views of Congress, has been concerned about the effects of high and rising interest rates. Still more recently, concerns for the stability of financial institutions have come to the fore.

Whatever the reasons, the consequence of this history is that we find ourselves with rapid increases in both prices and money. The question is how to deal with them.

WHAT TO DO ABOUT INFLATION

There are no quick or painless answers. Inflation has taken nearly a decade to build up and will take considerable time and discipline to unwind. There are, I believe, four essential requirements for dampening inflation.

First, we have to become more realistic about our capacity to fulfill our wants. There has been a tendency in recent years to pass over a hard fact of life—scarcity of resources. We simply cannot fulfill all desires, for all people, all at once, although we may earnestly wish to do so. Scarcity is still with us even in an affluent society.

A second requirement for fighting inflation is a firm handle on fiscal policy. In this regard, Congress is to be congratulated for passing the recent budget reform bill. This legislation can give Congress the kind of control that is long overdue.

Third, I believe there is a limited role for an incomes policy. We've just been through 32 months and four phases of controls, and the economy has just plain had it with controls for awhile. But there could still be a useful role for monitoring and publicizing key wage and price decisions.

Finally, we need to keep a firm grip on money and credit. History teaches two lessons about the impact of monetary policy. One is that inflation cannot continue without the money to finance it. Therefore, if inflation is to be moderated, growth in money must also be moderated. A second lesson is that growth in money must be moderated slowly to avoid sending the economy into a serious recession.

Translated into current policy, these lessons mean that the recent 7 percent growth in money (the narrow money supply or M₁) must be moderated over a period of time, and the time could be quite long. I believe it is important, therefore, for the Federal Open Market Committee to set long-run targets for moderating growth and then diligently pursue hitting these targets. In fact, the FOMC has been attempting such a procedure for over two years now. I'm hopeful that

with experience and resolve we'll be able to improve the accuracy of our aim.

ROLE OF INTEREST RATES

What would such a policy mean for interest rates? I am uncomfortable with high interest rates, especially with the record levels we are currently experiencing. But we should be clear about two things: one is what is necessary to bring interest rates down; the other is the role which interest rates play in combating inflation.

The Federal Reserve could try to lower interest rates by supplying money and credit more generously than it has. A faster growth rate for money would likely lower short-term interest rates temporarily, but only temporarily. Opening the money spigot further would add still more fuel to the fires of inflation. This in turn would add to inflationary expectations, and interest rates would rise as lenders protect themselves by building in larger inflation premiums. So, a looser monetary policy aimed at lowering interest rates now would eventually lead to higher rates.

The surer way to lower interest rates is by reducing inflation. In order to do this, the Federal Reserve has to be less generous in supplying money and credit. Cutting back on the flow of money and credit into the economy itself will push up interest rates temporarily. In time, however, slower monetary growth will lead to less inflation and lower interest rates. So, a restrictive monetary policy now aimed at slowing the rate of inflation will lead in time to lower interest rates, not higher ones.

In the meantime, we should recognize that interest rates are playing an important role in combatting inflation. I say this despite the fact that the effect of interest rates has long been debated. I believe, however, that rising interest rates do choke off some demand for credit and therefore do help to bring total demand for goods and services into better balance with the ability of the economy to meet these demands.

A final question remains, however: What is the impact of credit restraint and high interest rates on various sectors of our economy and society?

EVENING OUT THE BURDENS OF FIGHTING INFLATION

One of the burdens of combating inflation will be a higher unemployment rate than we would like. I believe the benefits of moderating inflation will be widely distributed and therefore the burden of fighting inflation should be as widely distributed as possible. Liberalized unemployment benefits, public service jobs, welfare reform, training and education programs are all ways of dealing with problems of those hit hardest by slack in the job market.

The financial burdens of a restrictive monetary policy are also not distributed evenly across the economy. High interest rates, for example, impact heavily on housing and some public projects. A logical question, therefore, is whether we could allocate credit in such a way as to smooth out the burdens or even favor some high-priority sectors at the expense of lower-priority ones. In other words, should the Federal Reserve *allocate* credit as well as *create* credit?

I approach this question with considerable sympathy. Forces at work in our society, especially over the past decade, confront us with aspects of the distribution of burdens and benefits with an urgency that we have never felt before. They will not go away. There is a good reason for the Fed to consider the matter of the allocation of credit with great care and concern.

A few years ago I explored the question as thoroughly as I knew how in an article which I should be happy to submit for the record.[1] I asked our research staff to undertake further studies of selective credit

controls, their history and their efficacy. The first volume of these studies will appear shortly after the turn of the year. I should like now simply to make five points in summary.

First, selective credit controls are less necessary when markets are working well. One reason credit does not flow into markets such as housing is that artificial limitations are placed on interest rates and lenders. The point is that action to eliminate usury ceilings and other such restraints would make selective credit controls less necessary.

Second, the Fed's experience in attempting to direct credit into "productive" and away from "nonproductive" uses has not been good. The reason is that it becomes virtually impossible in practice to determine which uses are really productive and which are nonproductive. I agree with those who believe that a basic solution to inflation is to enlarge the economy's ability to produce. My point is that selective credit controls offer little practical promise of directing funds in ways that will accomplish this. If, in fact, it should be part of policy to direct funds into capital investment, this is being done quite effectively by today's tight capital market.

Third, the idea that positive incentives might be helpful in directing funds in certain ways has a great deal of appeal. We in Philadelphia have done considerable analysis, for example, of the proposal that variable reserve requirements be placed on various kinds of bank assets. A lower requirement could be placed on high-priority loans and a higher requirement on lower-priority loans. Our research indicates a major problem: credit is extremely mobile and people are ingenious in substituting one kind of credit for another. If, for example, reserve requirements were to favor home mortgages over business loans, it seems inevitable that businessmen would simply by-pass banks to go to other lenders or the open market. An effective program of credit allocation would have to apply across the board. The workability of such a program seems questionable, to say the least. The costs could be enormous.

---

[1] "Federal Reserve Policy and Social Priorities," *Business Review* of the Federal Reserve Bank of Philadelphia, November 1970, pp. 2–8.

Fourth, if, in spite of these difficulties, Congress were to decide that credit should be controlled in accordance with certain social priorities, I believe that determination of these priorities is properly a matter for Congress, not the Federal Reserve.

Fifth, the goal of stimulating certain sectors of the economy and restraining others might in some cases better be approached through fiscal rather than credit action. The variable investment tax credit is one possibility. Direct provision of funds for the mortgage market is already being employed. Other possibilities should be explored.

I conclude from all this that, over time, the question of allocating credit should be studied further. Our analysis to date, however, suggests serious problems. Perhaps the most important point is that if we can avoid inflation through general monetary and fiscal policy, we have less reason to be concerned with the allocation of credit. A program of credit allocation is no substitute for responsible policy in dealing with the overall supply of money and credit.

A Perspective on Stagflation*

By John J. Seater

Summary

Conventional economic wisdom holds that inflation and unemployment aren't supposed to increase at the same time. We're supposed to face a tradeoff—more of one and less of the other. Yet with both unemployment and inflation rising in 1974, there appeared to be no tradeoff, only the worst of both worlds. This phenomenon—dubbed stagflation—is frustrating everyone. We're stuck with stagflation and economists have trouble explaining it, let alone knowing how to cure it.

An increasingly popular school of thought, however, holds that stagflation is neither inexplicable nor uncontrollable. This band of economists argues that stagflation is based on the old standbys of rational economic behavior—supply and demand, and monetary and fiscal policies. Hence, its cure must have the same foundations.

Key Questions to Consider

- What kinds of unemployment are there?
- How is the existence of stagflation explained?
- What are the cures for stagflation?

_____

* Reprinted with permission from *Business Review*, Federal Reserve Bank of Philadelphia, May 1975, pp. 19–30.

A Perspective on Stagflation

Downgrading economics has become chic. The profession is in a shambles, many claim, because the "old-time religion" doesn't work anymore, and no new Moses is on the horizon to lead us from the economic wilderness.

Conventional economic wisdom holds that inflation and unemployment aren't supposed to increase at the same time. We're supposed to face a tradeoff—more of one and less of the other. Yet with both unemployment and inflation rising in 1974, there appeared to be no tradeoff, only the worst of both worlds. This phenomenon—dubbed stagflation—is frustrating everyone. We're stuck with stagflation and economists have trouble explaining it, let alone knowing how to cure it.

An increasingly popular school of thought, however, holds that stagflation is neither inexplicable nor uncontrollable. This band of economists argues that stagflation is based on the old standbys of rational economic behavior—supply and demand, and monetary and fiscal policies. Hence, its cure must have the same foundations.

THE TYPES OF UNEMPLOYMENT

Getting to the whys and wherefores of stagflation requires an understanding of the three types of unemployment.

Even in the best of times, there are the voluntarily unemployed—people who have just entered the labor force or have quit their jobs to look for something better. These people, who choose to pass up low-paying or distasteful jobs in order to search for higher-paying or more enjoyable jobs, are said to be *frictionally unemployed*.

Another group of unemployed consists of those who have been fired because of structural changes in the economy. For example, consumers may decide to buy fewer books and more TV sets. This means that some editors will be thrown out of work, and more electrical workers will be hired. Such structural changes occur continually, and it takes time for the newly unemployed to find jobs. These people are the *structurally unemployed*.

When the number of frictionally and structurally unemployed equals the number of job vacancies in the economy, unemployment can be said to be at its "natural rate," and the economy can be said to be at full employment.[1] There are enough jobs around for the unemployed; the unemployed just don't fit the jobs. By this definition, full employment does not

---

[1] Full employment often is defined as that state in which all expectations are realized. The two definitions seem to be equivalent, however.

mean no unemployment; it means no unemployment *in excess of (or below!)* the natural rate.

A third type of unemployment, which we can call *excess unemployment*, arises when the total demand for the economy's goods and services (aggregate demand) falls below the sum of everything business wishes to produce (aggregate supply). For example, consumers decide to save more and spend less; in particular, suppose they decide to buy fewer automobiles. Then automobile producers, finding their cars unsold, will lay off workers. Unlike structural unemployment, excess unemployment is not matched by increases in vacancies because demand is not merely shifting from one market to another; it is decreasing in the total of all markets. So when aggregate demand falls below aggregate supply, the number of unemployed exceeds the number of vacancies.

Government can eliminate excess unemployment by applying monetary and fiscal policies that stimulate total demand—increasing the money supply, increasing Government spending, and reducing taxes. As demand increases, producers hire idle labor. However, once unemployment reaches its natural rate, the Federal Government cannot permanently reduce it further with just monetary and fiscal policies. When this is attempted, unemployment dips temporarily, then bounces back to its natural rate. The rate of inflation, however, rises to a new level and stays there.

HISTORICAL PERSPECTIVE

What is the current natural rate of unemployment for the U.S. economy? No one knows for sure. Although the data on unemployment are very good, data on vacancies are not, partly because they have been collected only for about five years. Meaningful comparisons of unemployment and vacancies are thus impossible. One way around the problem, though, is to estimate the natural rate of unemployment by finding the average rate of unemployment over a long period. The idea is that cyclical fluctuations will cancel out over a long period so that the average rate will approximate the natural rate. For the period

1900–29, the average rate of unemployment is 4.8 percent. Remarkably, the average rate for the period 1948–73 is also 4.8 percent.[2] For the sake of argument, then, let's assume the natural rate of unemployment is 4.8 percent.[3]

In 1970, about when the current criticisms of economics and talk of stagflation began, the unemployment rate averaged 4.9 percent, almost equal to the assumed natural rate, but up from the low 3.5 percent rate of 1969. In 1974 the average unemployment rate was 5.6 percent. However, since 1913 there have been nine years outside the Great Depression which had unemployment rates higher than 1974's rate. (These years are listed in Table 1.)

Inflation last year proceeded at a rate of 12.2 percent. This is unusually high, but it has been exceeded four times since 1913, as shown in Table 2. The extraordinary development of 1974 was not so much that the rates of unemployment and inflation were high, but rather that they rose simultaneously. Actually, this situation was not unprecedented; it has occurred six times before in this century. Table 3 lists the pairs of years in which both the rate of unemployment and of inflation rose from one year to the next. What does seem to be unprecedented in 1974, though, are the magnitudes by which these rates rose. Only 1946 and perhaps 1915 offer anything comparable.

---

[2] The World War I, Great Depression, and World War II years have been ignored because they were clearly unusual periods.

[3] Although there is currently no consensus on the actual value of the natural rate of unemployment, most estimates place it between 4.5 and 5.5 percent. The present explanation of stagflation is compatible with any of these values. Some people who believe that 5 percent unemployment is too high might favor a reduction in the natural rate of unemployment itself. Economists do not fully understand how the natural rate is determined, but many believe that the natural rate cannot be changed by countercyclical stabilization policies—that is, by monetary and fiscal policies. Apparently, other kinds of policies, such as education, retraining, and information programs, would be needed.

Table 1

Unemployment Has Exceeded 1974's Rate
Nine Times Since 1913

Year	Annual average rate of unemployment*
1914	8.0%
1915	9.7
1921	11.9
1922	7.6
1949	5.9
1958	6.8
1961	6.7
1963	5.7
1971	5.9
1974	5.6

* Unemployment comprises roughly those people not working but looking for a job.
Source: U.S. Department of Labor, Bureau of Labor Statistics.

Table 2

1974's Rate of Inflation Has Been Exceeded
Four Times Since 1913

Year	Annual rate of inflation (December to December)
1916	18.7%
1917	20.7
1918	14.6
1946	18.1
1974	12.2

Source: U.S. Department of Labor, Bureau of Labor Statistics.

AN EXPLANATION OF STAGFLATION

One explanation of stagflation that has gained favor among economists, though it is not universally accepted, holds that there are two parts to the stagflaion story—unemployment and its relation to what

Table 3

Stagflation Has Occurred Before

Year	Annual rate of inflation	Annual average rate of unemployment
1914	0.9%	8.0%
1915	2.1	9.7
1927	− 1.9	4.1
1928	− 1.1	4.4
1932	−10.3	23.6
1933	0.5	24.9
1945	2.2	1.9
1946	18.1	3.9
1956	2.9	4.1
1957	3.0	4.3
1962	1.2	5.5
1963	1.6	5.7
1973	8.8	4.9
1974	12.2	5.6

Source: U.S. Department of Labor, Bureau of Labor Statistics.

business wants to produce (or, aggregate supply), and inflation expectations and their relation to what people want to buy (or, aggregate demand).

Unemployment. Let's begin with unemployment. Unemployment rises above its natural rate when, because of some shock to the economy, aggregate supply exceeds aggregate demand. "Too much" is being produced or, as economists say, there is "excess aggregate supply." Whenever producers face excess aggregate supply, they lay off workers and curtail production, thereby tending to eliminate the oversupply of goods. However, the laid-off workers, suddenly finding their incomes reduced, curtail their spending. These cutbacks in turn reduce aggregate demand, so that producers still find they are producing "too much," which sets off another round of layoffs. Eventually, because of what economists call the multiplier (see the Appendix), this process stops with the economy left in a state of lower output and higher unemployment.[4] Recession has set in.

During or after a recession, prices eventually fall, or at least rise more slowly than before it. For example, in 1929, prices fell by 2.5 percent, in 1930 by 8.8, in 1931 by 10.3, and in 1954 by 0.5. In 1958, 1961, and 1971—all terminal years of recessions— prices did not fall but their rate of increase dropped considerably.[5]

That prices may rise rather than fall during a recession—as in 1958, 1961, 1971, and 1974—needs explanation. Indeed, these bouts of stagflation seem to contradict basic economic theory. Recessions are characterized by too much production relative to demand, and the textbook response to excess supply is a drop in prices. So, how can prices rise during a recession? The answer to this question seems to lie in people's *expectations* about future prices.

Expectations.   People learn from experience. If they observe that prices have been rising at a constant rate for a long time they will come to believe that prices will continue to rise at that rate in the future—in other words, people will anticipate the inflation. Let's see how this relates to their economic behavior. Let's suppose that people change their expectations so that they suddenly anticipate higher inflation in the future. For example, suppose people were previously anticipating no inflation but now become convinced that a 10-percent price rise is more likely. They then figure their money will be worth less in the future than it is today. Since it will buy more today than it will tomorrow, they are better off spending their money now. If the economy is near full employment, this

attempt to accelerate buying will jack up demand and drive up prices today. Changes in expectations about *future* prices therefore affect *today's* prices. (See Box 1 for a more detailed discussion of the interaction between expected and actual price behavior.)

At the outset of inflation, however, people are unlikely to change their outlook for future price increases very rapidly. The reason is they cannot be sure at first that the price changes are permanent rather than temporary. If inflation persists, however, people will build more and more of it into their expectations, and in time they will completely adjust to it. At that point, when people fully anticipate inflation, the rate of inflation tends to level off. (Again, see Box 1.)

A Theory of Stagflation.   Stagflation gets underway as people revise their expectations about inflation and try to take additional steps to protect themselves from it. One way they can protect themselves is to try to buy today what will cost more tomorrow. But with everybody playing the same game, more buying pressure is put on the economy and today's prices turn out to be higher than they otherwise would be.

Unemployment increases for a slightly different and more complicated reason, however. At first, people are "fooled" by increased inflation and take jobs they wouldn't ordinarily take in a less inflationary economy. But after a while, they catch on to their "errors" and revert to their old behavior.

Let's see how that can happen by taking a simple example of Sam Searcher, diligent job seeker. Sam lives in an environment where prices have been increasing at about 2 percent a year for sometime, so that everyone expects that this rate is likely to continue into the future. The unemployment rate is 4.8 percent (the presumed natural rate), and unfortunately Sam is one of the frictionally unemployed. Suppose that the Government pursues expansionary monetary and fiscal policies to bring unemployment to 3 percent— well below the natural rate. Since there is no "slack" in the economy, the effect of these stimulative policies must be a general rise in prices, say, on the order of 10 percent. Most of the increase in prices will be

---

[4] This state will not last forever, according to economic theory. Eventually, prices and wages will fall. The falling prices lead to an increase in aggregate demand, and the falling wages lead to an increase in employment. Ultimately, the economy returns to full employment.

[5] In 1971, the drop occurred even before wage-price controls were instituted.

Box 1   # Expectations and Economic Activity Interact

Suppose the economy has been in the happy state of full employment with no inflation for a long time. Suddenly, prices begin to rise by 10 percent a year. At first, people will feel that, because prices have been constant for so long, the current increases are a quirk and soon will stop. However, if the inflation continues at the rate of 10 percent, eventually people will change their minds about the temporary nature of the inflation. They will come to believe that 10 percent inflation is here to stay. As people decide that inflation has become permanent, however, they alter their buying behavior. They reason that if prices go up tomorrow, their money will be worth less than it is today. Therefore, better to spend the money today rather than tomorrow when it will buy less. So in anticipating inflation, people attempt to accelerate their purchases and increase their demand for goods. Unfortunately, because the economy is at full employment, more goods cannot be provided to meet the higher demand. Instead, prices must rise by even more than the 10 percent rate to throttle this extra demand. Consequently, the expectation of inflation, by raising aggregate demand, has increased inflation itself. More

inflation heightens expectations, spurring yet another round of inflation, and so on up the spiral.

What stops prices from soaring through the roof? As prices rise faster than expected, the *real* (or price-adjusted) value of that part of people's wealth in assets with fixed dollar values such as cash begins to fall. For example, if someone has a $100 bill in his wallet and prices suddenly double, the $100 becomes worth only half as much as before—it can buy only half as many goods. As the value of peoples' wealth falls, they channel less of their income into consumption and more into saving to restore at least part of their lost real wealth. So, the reduced value of wealth reduces consumption, which in turn relieves pressure on prices.

In summary, as inflation proceeds and price expectations rise, people tend to increase their consumption; however, simultaneously, the inflation eats into peoples' real wealth and this tends to reduce consumption. Eventually, these two forces come into balance. Once this happens, inflation stops rising and continues at a constant rate. There are no further forces to change the actual rate at which prices rise.

unanticipated, because people are expecting a 2-percent inflation based on past experience. What effect will this have on unemployment? Let's see what Sam Searcher is doing.

On April 1, Sam contacts the XYZ Corporation and learns of a vacancy at $10 an hour. He tells them he is unwilling to work for less than $11 an hour and goes back to searching. On April 2, inflation begins because of the Government's stimulative policies, and XYZ starts getting higher prices for its products. On April 3, XYZ decides to raise the wage associated with its vacancy to $11 an hour to attract more workers. They call Sam and tell him they are now willing to pay $11 an hour. Delighted, Searcher accepts and becomes employed. Multiply this situation across the country, and unemployment falls below its natural

rate. Consequently, it seems that lower unemployment has been bought by higher inflation. However, by the time, say, April Fools' Day 1976 has rolled around, Sam Searcher and others like him have learned that inflation has been galloping along at 10 percent and that as a result *all* wages and prices, not just their own, have risen. In fact, they discover that their current wages of $11 an hour are worth no more now than the $10-an-hour wage was worth on April 1, 1975. Because they were not willing to work at $10 an hour at the old prices, they are not willing to work at $11 an hour now at the new prices; for they recognize that relative wages and prices have not changed. They quit work and once again become unemployed. Unemployment returns to its natural rate. However, inflation continues at the rate of 10 percent.

Stagflation has set in. Inflation has increased from 2 to 10 percent as a result of overly stimulative policies, whereas after a temporary decline, unemployment has risen back to the natural rate. When people perceive that all prices have risen simultaneously and build this into their expectations, their behavior is no longer affected by inflation; so that even though inflation may be higher, unemployment after a period of economic adjustment will end up back at its natural rate. (See Box 2 for a demonstration that anticipated inflation does not affect economic behavior.)

Box 2   Fully Anticipated Inflation Does Not Affect Economic Behavior

Let's look closely at the situation where prices are rising at a constant and fully anticipated rate. How are people behaving? Consumers, expecting higher prices in the future, demand wage contracts that allow for future wage increases to match the anticipated price increases. Employers, expecting to sell their goods for higher prices, are willing to grant such contracts. Everybody is happy, and the inflation affects neither employment nor output.

Interest rates also reflect the expected rate of inflation. Lenders, expecting prices to rise, demand that an inflation premium equal to the expected rate of inflation be tacked onto the interest rate charged for loans. For example, if lenders would charge 5 percent interest, compounded continuously, on loans when there is no inflation, then if they come to expect a rate of inflation of 10 percent, they will up their interest rate to 15 percent. Borrowers, in contrast, are willing to pay the inflation premium because they, expecting a rate of inflation of 10 percent, figure they will be able to earn the extra 10 percent with the borrowed money. Again, everybody is happy, with inflation affecting neither savings nor investment.

Inflation, then, *once fully anticipated*, has no effect on the unemployment rate. The reason for this startling conclusion is that once everyone anticipates inflation fully and adjusts to this anticipation, the inflation will not affect *relative prices*. (The real rate of return on money balances is an exception; it is reduced by an increase in inflation. However, the effects of this change are small for the moderate rates of inflation experienced by the U.S. and can be ignored.)

Economic activity depends not on the absolute levels of wages, prices, and assets, but on their relative values. For example, when the price of, say, butter rises relative to margarine, people reduce their consumption of the former and buy the latter. However, when *all* wages, prices, and asset values rise by the same proportion (and this change is correctly perceived by the public), there are no changes in anyone's economic behavior. Because prices have doubled, people must spend twice as many dollars for every item they buy. But because wages and asset values also have doubled, people have twice as many dollars to spend. Their "real income" and "real assets" are unchanged, and they will continue to buy exactly the same basket of goods as before prices, wages, and asset values doubled. Therefore, if inflation proceeds at a rate of 10 percent and if everybody expects it to proceed at this rate, then all wages, prices, and asset values will rise at a rate of 10 percent. In short, their relative values will not change and economic activity will be unaffected by the inflation.

The following example may be helpful. Mr. Chubby lives for three days—today, tomorrow, and the day after tomorrow. He currently has a job at which he works an hour a day and earns 15 cents an hour. He plans to work today and tomorrow and then retire the day after tomorrow. He only consumes 10-cent candy bars. Chubby, having foresight, plans to spend 10 cents today and 10 cents tomorrow, saving 5 cents each day toward his retirement, when he will spend his savings on one last candy bar. Chubby's life plan is summarized in the following table: (cont.)

Box 2 (Cont.)

	Today	Tomorrow	Day after tomorrow
Hours worked	1	1	0
Earnings	15¢	15¢	0¢
Candy bars consumed	1	1	1
Expenditure	10¢	10¢	10¢
Stock of savings at start of day	0¢	5¢	10¢
Addition to stock of savings	5¢	5¢	−10¢

Suppose that everything goes according to plan today, so that Chubby earns his 15 cents, buys one candy bar, and saves 5 cents. At the end of the day, his assets total 5 cents. Suppose, however, that at the end of today the Government announces it will double all wages, prices, and asset holdings before tomorrow. Then Chubby can anticipate an increase in the price of candy bars to 20 cents apiece, and an increase in

his current asset holdings to 10 cents. As we can see from the following table, Chubby can stick to his plan of working one hour tomorrow, retiring the day after tomorrow, and consuming one candy bar each day:

	Tomorrow	Day after tomorrow
Hours worked	1	0
Earnings	30¢	0¢
Candy bars consumed	1	1
Expenditure	20¢	20¢
Stock of savings at start of day	10¢	20¢
Addition to stock of savings	10¢	−20¢

The doubling of all wages, prices, and asset values has no effect on Chubby's economic behavior.

FROM THEORY TO REALITY

Economists who subscribe to the natural rate view say that it explains events in the U.S. economy since the middle '60s. In 1964, inflation was proceeding at the low rate of 1.2 percent, and unemployment was 5.2 percent. As the Vietnam War heated up, inflation rose to 6.1 percent in 1969, and unemployment fell below the natural rate to 3.5 percent. Subsequently, however, unemployment began to rise back toward the natural rate but inflation remained high, as the natural rate theory would predict. Unemployment continued to rise (except during 1973, when it fell somewhat following the highly stimulative monetary policy of 1972) above the assumed natural rate until in 1975 it reached the 8–9 percent range.

Why did unemployment rise far beyond the natural rate even though people were beginning to anticipate increased rates of inflation? The answer seems to be that the Government believed that inflation was "too" high and had to be reduced. Consequently, restrictive monetary and fiscal policies were

implemented. Total demand fell below the amount that businesses wanted to produce. As unwanted inventories began to pile up, firms cut back production and layoffs began, touching off a period of sharp contraction of economic activity. With the sharp slackening in demand the pace of inflation has slowed, but because double-digit inflation remains fresh in the minds of the people, inflationary expectations still plague the economy. As a result, prices are still rising at a fast clip by historical standards. But as people revise downward their inflation expectations and curtail further their attempt to "beat inflation," a further easing of price pressures is in the cards, according to the natural rate view.

In short, the process that brought the economy to a high rate of inflation is being reversed. Eventually both the actual and expected rates of inflation will fall to a more acceptable level, and unemployment will return to its natural rate. The economy will end up back in a state of full employment with little or no inflation. (See Box 3 for a graphical depiction of this whole process.) How rapidly the economy returns to

Box 3   # How the Natural Rate Process Works

The economy starts at point A, where inflation is 0 and unemployment is at the natural rate N. As inflation begins to rise, unemployment falls at first because people are fooled into thinking their wages have risen relative to prices and therefore accept employment more readily. Unemployment reaches its low point at B. As people begin to learn of inflation, unemployment begins to rise because people find that their wages in fact have not increased relative to prices by as much as they had thought, and they therefore leave employment more readily. Once everybody fully anticipates the inflation, the economy ends up at C, with inflation proceeding at 10 percent but employment back at its natural rate. If at this point inflation were to rise to 20 percent, the process would be repeated and the economy would move from C to D to E.

Graph 1

**How Increasing the Rate of Inflation
Can Lower the Rate of Unemployment
Temporarily But Not Permanently**

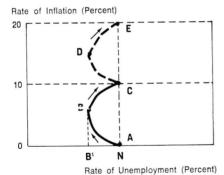

Graph 2

How to Get Back to a Zero Rate of Inflation

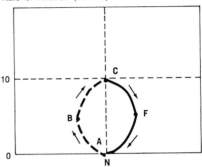

point A to point C. The economy moves from C back to A via F. At point A, both the expected and actual rates of inflation are back down to 0 percent, and unemployment is at its natural rate. The economy is back in a state of full employment with no inflation.

Graph 3 shows the recent path of the U.S. economy.

Graph 3

The Recent Experience of the U.S. Economy

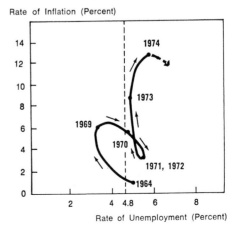

How can the economy be moved back from C to A? Suppose the economy is at C in Graph 2, which corresponds to C in Graph 1. The expected rate of inflation equals the actual rate. Suppose Uncle Sam ends the stimulative policies that brought the economy from A to C. Then aggregate demand falls below aggregate supply. This takes pressure off prices and reverses the process that brought the economy from this happy state depends on the policies pursued. The natural rate approach presents policymakers with a Hobson's choice—eliminating inflation *requires* some increase in unemployment. How much unemployment is chosen determines how quickly the inflation is eliminated.

POLICY CHOICES: HOW FAST TO GO AND WHO GETS HURT?

The natural rate approach suggests that the higher the unemployment rate now, the faster inflation will be eliminated, and the sooner the natural rate of unemployment can be restored. The more restrictive the Government makes its policies, the more demand declines. Hence, the rate of inflation subsides more rapidly, and people quickly revise down their expectations about inflation. However, more restrictive policies also mean more unemployment. Consequently, a clear tradeoff emerges. The faster the economy is forced to return to price stability and full employment, the higher is the unemployment that must be endured in the meantime. Conversely, the lower the rate of unemployment is kept, the longer the economy will take to return to price stability and full employment.

Why isn't it possible to employ restrictive policies to fight inflation but keep unemployment down by starting a program like the WPA of the 1930s? That's possible, but here the Government must be careful. The purpose of Government-sponsored job programs is to spread the burden of fighting inflation more equitably across the population. There are two ways to finance a job program—by increasing deficit spending or by increasing taxes. Any simple increase in deficit spending would tend to offset the original restrictive policy that was instituted to fight inflation. The anti-inflationary thrust of the total program would be less. However, if the Government is going to employ deficit spending to finance job programs and still salvage some anti-inflationary benefits from its policies, it must pay the workers something less

than their original salaries. The less the Government pays the workers it hires, the more rapidly inflation will be eliminated, but the larger will be the burden of the anti-inflation struggle.

The other possibility is to finance the job programs by taxes instead of by deficit spending. Under this scheme, the job programs themselves would have little, if any, net effect on aggregate demand, no matter what their size. Every dollar given to unemployed Paul simply would be taxed away from employed Peter. This is merely a transfer of income and has no effect on the total amount of income there is to be spent. However, it would spread the burden of the inflation fight in a way many people consider more equitable.

Following this logic, the Government can use WPA-style programs to fight unemployment while it is fighting inflation. However, if total policy is to remain anti-inflationary, *someone still must get hurt temporarily.* Either the people rehired by the jobs program must be paid less than their original salaries, or the people still employed must pay higher taxes to finance the jobs program, or both.[a]

There are, then, two policy tradeoffs. First, there is a speed tradeoff. The faster society wants to reduce the rate of inflation, the greater the unemployment burden it must bear during the process of price reduction—but, the sooner it can return to normal conditions. Second, there is a distribution tradeoff. Whatever speed tradeoff society chooses, it must decide how to distribute the ensuing burden. It can adopt a

---

[a] Why couldn't the Government apply stimulative policies to reduce unemployment and institute wage-price controls to prevent inflation? The debate over controls is complex and beyond the scope of this article. What is pertinent here is that controls do *not* eliminate the cause of inflation—excess demand; they merely force the demand pressures to manifest themselves in different ways. For example, if prices cannot rise to clear the market, people may have to spend more time waiting in lines to make their purchases, which means that although it costs fewer dollars to buy goods, it costs more time. Controls do not cure the disease of inflation; they only affect the symptoms.

"hands-off" policy, in which the unemployed bears a disproportionate share of the burden of reducing inflation, or it can attempt to alleviate unemployment through Government assistance, in which case some of the burden of reducing inflation is shifted to others.

Rx FOR STAGFLATION?

The natural rate view appears to have some merit in explaining the current predicament of the U.S. economy. The basic idea is that stabilization policy has been used in an attempt to keep unemployment below its natural rate. As unemployment returned to its natural rate, stagflation resulted. In an attempt to combat the resulting inflation, unemployment was permitted to rise to its currently high levels. Relief on the inflation front has finally begun to appear.

Within this framework of analysis, the "old-time religion" offers a cure for our ills. In a nutshell, the cure is to bear a temporary burden of higher unemployment, lower incomes, and/or higher taxes until inflationary expectations are eliminated. Granted, this cure is painful. But, unfortunately, if the natural rate approach is correct, there seems to be no other remedy. What choices there are revolve around how fast the economy should take the inflationary cure and how the burden should be distributed.

Appendix: The Multiplier Effect

Let's look at a very simple example to see the main points involved. Assume that the only factor of production is labor and that producers are all philanthropists who pass on all their profits to workers. Then each worker is paid exactly the value of what he produces. Suppose all workers are alike and earn $10,000. Suppose all workers always devote four-fifths of their income to consumption and one-fifth to saving.

Imagine that the Federal Government suddenly cuts its purchase of consumption goods by $10,000. Producers react by cutting production goods by $10,000 and fire one worker. This fired worker, having lost his income, reduces his consumption. He was earning $10,000, of which he spent four-fifths, or $8000. For simplicity, suppose that when he is fired, he stops consuming altogether so that total spending drops by another $8000 over and above the Government's original reduction of $10,000. Producers now must cut production by $8000. They do this by firing four-fifths of a worker, that is, by reducing the number of hours that one worker is employed by four-fifths (for example, if workers normally work an eight-hour day, one of them now would work $8 - 4/5$

$\times 8 = 1.6$ hours) and reducing his pay by $8000. He must reduce his consumption by $4/5 \times \$8000 = \$6400$. This causes producers to reduce output again and reduce another worker's pay and so on. The total reduction in pay turns out to be

$$\$10,000 \times \frac{1}{1 - 4/5} = \$50,000.$$

The total number of man-hours eliminated is

$$\frac{8 \frac{\text{hours}}{\text{worker}}}{\$10,000 \frac{\text{output}}{\text{worker}}} \cdot 10,000 \frac{1}{1 - \frac{4}{5}} = 40,$$

which is equivalent to firing five workers. The fraction

$$\frac{1}{1 - 4/5} = 5$$

is called "the multiplier." There are two important things to notice in this example. (1) Because of the multiplier, the decrease in Government spending caused a contraction in the economy that was larger than the original decrease in spending itself. (2) This contraction did not continue indefinitely so as to wipe out the entire economy but stopped at a point determined by the multiplier.

This simple example overstates the multiplier; there are many "leakages" in the economic system which reduce the multiplier from the pure, theoretical value used above. Adjustments in interest rates, the existence of unemployment compensation, and the automatic reduction in tax receipts that occurs as incomes fall are examples of such leakages. However, for simplicity's sake, these complications are ignored.

Changing Views
of Comparative Advantage*

By Thomas M. Humphrey

Summary

Economists' views of the sources and nature of comparative advantage have undergone significant change since Ricardo's time. Originally thought to be based on international differences in labor productivity and later on relative endowments of factor proportions, the comparative advantages enjoyed by developed countries such as the U.S. are now seen as emanating largely from human skills, knowledge, and technology.

Recent developments in the world economy—including the increasing international mobility of capital, the faster dissemination of technology, and the narrowing differential between the economic capability of the U.S. and her trading partners—have also altered economists' conceptions of the pattern of this country's comparative advantage. The structure of comparative advantage, once thought to be stable and enduring, is now seen as shifting rapidly and frequently, thereby raising the risks of specialization and the costs of adjustment. Protectionists, claiming that these adjustment costs are unduly high, hold that the doctrine of comparative advantage is no longer valid. But free traders still contend, as did Ricardo, that the principle of comparative advantage provides the best guide for the optimal allocation of any nation's resources and the maximization of world welfare. In short, free traders argue convincingly that the benefits of unrestricted commerce outweigh the costs. Most economists would probably agree that the basic conclusion of the comparative advantage doctrine—that free trade is mutually beneficial—remains as cogent today as it was in Ricardo's time.

Key Questions to Consider

- What is the importance of the concept of comparative advantage?

- Why has attention been focused on the concept of comparative advantage in recent years?

- What developments strengthened economists' suspicions that structural changes in U.S. comparative advantages were occurring?

- What does the Factor-Proportions Theory explain?

- What were Wassily Leontief's findings? How have his paradoxical findings been explained in light of the Factor-Proportions Theory?

- How does the "New View" integrate previous theories and new empirical evidence?

- Why do protectionists feel that the doctrine of comparative advantage is obsolete?

- How does the "free trade school" answer the protectionists' arguments?

* Reprinted with permission from *Monthly Review*, Federal Reserve Bank of Richmond, **58,** No. 7 (July 1972), 9–15.

Changing Views
of Comparative Advantage

International trade theory is based on the fundamental concepts of comparative advantage. This concept refers to the relative cost or productivity advantage one country enjoys over others in the production of certain commodities. Since the early nineteenth century, economists have employed the concept to explain why nations trade, to demonstrate the gains from trade, and to predict the commodity composition and geographical pattern of trade flows.

Events, empirical research, and policy debates have all combined in recent years to focus attention once again on the subject of comparative advantage. Chief among the events has been the sharp deterioration of the U.S. merchandise trade balance since 1964, culminating in the $2.9 billion deficit in 1971—the first deficit since 1935. This experience has convinced many observers that there has been an adverse structural shift in the sources of U.S. comparative advantage, an interpretation that is relatively new. Up to 1970, short-run, cyclical influences rather than long-run structural factors were cited as the principal cause of the dwindling trade balance. That is, domestic inflation accompanying a sharp business upswing, associated in part with the Vietnam War, was thought to be the chief factor contributing to a strong surge in U.S. imports and to declining price competitiveness of U.S. exports. Specifically, analysts attributed the trade balance deterioration to such factors as excess aggregate demand, slowing productivity growth, escalating wage rates, and rising unit labor costs—all characteristics of the inflationary boom of the late 1960's. By 1971, however, the inflation interpretation seemed inadequate. For instance, excess demand had been eliminated in the recession of 1970. It is true that cost-push inflation had not disappeared, but its effect on the trade balance should have been partly neutralized by price movements abroad. In 1971, many of this country's trade competitors were experiencing rates of inflation, rises in unit labor costs, and increases in export prices that outstripped those here. Despite this relative improvement on the inflation front, however, the U.S. trade balance deterioration persisted. But if cyclical changes in relative rates of inflation could not explain all of the trade balance decay, what additional explanations might there be? Some economists began to suspect that long-run forces were altering the basic determinants (technological superiority, factor proportions, resource availability) of the pattern of U.S. comparative advantage.

Suspicions of an adverse structural shift in U.S. comparative advantages were strengthened by other developments, including: (1) the phenomenal rise in the economic capability of such leading U.S. trade partners as Japan and Germany; (2) the trend toward increased economic integration within regional trade blocs, which has resulted in intra-bloc trade creation and extra-bloc trade diversion; and (3) the growth of the multinational corporation, which has provided a major channel for the international transmission of technology, capital, and managerial skills. These developments have forced policymakers and businessmen to reassess longer-run U.S. trade prospects.

The resurgence of discussion on the topic of comparative advantage has not resulted solely from developments on the world trade scene, however. Statistical research, too, has played a role. Recent empirical studies have severely challenged some long-established notions about the nature and sources of U.S. comparative advantage. For example, as recently as the mid-1950's it was widely believed that the superior competitive position of U.S. products in world markets stemmed from the large stock of tangible capital with which American labor worked. Moreover, the structure of U.S. comparative advantage was thought in some quarters to be stable and enduring. Within the past decade, however, researchers have found evidence indicating that U.S. comparative advantage emanates from skills, knowledge, and technology rather than from a high capital/labor ratio, and that the structure of comparative costs is continually being altered by the generation and diffusion of technical knowledge.

The subject of comparative advantage has also surfaced in current debates over trade policy. Modern protectionists claim that the comparative-cost doctrine has little contemporary validity, while free-traders maintain that it is still a valid policy guide.

These recent events, empirical studies, and policy debates have had a substantial impact on international trade theory. Current explanations of comparative advantage differ markedly from older, traditional explanations. This article indicates how economists' conceptions of the nature and sources of comparative advantage have been altered by recent empirical research and by the changing position of the United States in world trade.

The Classical Doctrine of Comparative Advantage. A nation is said to have a comparative advantage in the production of a good when its efficiency in producing that good compared to its efficiency in producing another good is higher than that of other nations. The first clear statement of this concept dates back to the early nineteenth century when David Ricardo formulated his celebrated England-Portugal, cloth-wine example. Suppose that in England it takes 10 labor hours to produce a unit of cloth and 12 labor hours to produce a unit of wine. That is, the productivity of an hour of English labor is 1/10 unit of cloth or 1/12 unit of wine. In Portugal, however, the labor requirements per unit of output are nine and eight, respectively, in cloth and wine. That is, the productivity of an hour of Portuguese labor is 1/9 unit of cloth or 1/8 unit of wine. Then the ratio of labor productivity (output per labor hour) in cloth production to that in wine production is higher for England than for Portugal (12/10 vs. 8/9). England, in this example, although absolutely less efficient than Portugal in the production of both commodities, nevertheless clearly has a comparative advantage in cloth. Portugal, conversely, has a comparative advantage in wine.

Ricardo's chief objective in using his illustration was to demonstrate the *mutual profitability* of international specialization and free trade, i.e., that the gains from trade would accrue to all nations. Ricardo explained that each nation, by specializing in the production and export of its comparative advantage good, could obtain the other good with a smaller sacrifice of its export good than if it endeavored to produce the import good itself with labor transferred from the export industry. If England, for example, sought to be self-sufficient in wine, the production of each unit of that commodity would require the release from cloth production of labor-hours sufficient to produce 12/10 units of cloth. The cloth cost, therefore, of each wine unit in England (12/10) is much higher than its cost in Portugal (8/9). Similarly, the wine sacrifice per unit of cloth in a self-sufficient Portugal (9/8) would be higher than in England (10/12). Clearly, Englishmen could obtain wine more cheaply by producing cloth and trading it to Portugal, where a unit of wine costs less than one unit of cloth, than by producing it at home at a cost of more than one unit of cloth. Likewise, Portuguese could get cloth more cheaply by producing wine and trading it to England, where cloth costs less than one unit of wine, than by producing it domestically at a cost of more than one wine unit. In short, by specializing and engaging in free trade, England could obtain wine from Portugal at a smaller sacrifice of English cloth, and Portugal could obtain cloth from England at a smaller sacrifice of Portuguese wine. Each nation, therefore, could obtain via specialization and trade more of both goods from the same amount of labor input or, alternatively, obtain the same amount of goods with less expenditure of labor, than if it endeavored to be self-sufficient. As Ricardo emphasized, these gains from trade in no way depended on absolute levels of productivity. For instance, one country might be *absolutely* more efficient than its trading partners in the production of all commodities; yet that country would still find trade beneficial as long as its *relative* costs, or productivity ratios, differed from those in other countries.

Taking their cue from Ricardo, other nineteenth century classical economists attributed comparative advantages solely to national differences in relative labor productivity, i.e., ratios of output per man hour for pairs of commodities. No explicit recognition was given, in the classical analysis, to the productivity of other factor inputs, such as capital and land, nor was it explained why the labor productivity ratios differed among countries.

The Factor-Proportions Theory.   Later, in the 1920's and 1930's, economists added a second factor of production, capital, to the model and attempted to link comparative advantages to nations' relative endowments of capital and labor. According to the factor-proportions theory, a country with a relatively high capital/labor ratio would export capital-intensive commodities and import labor-intensive ones. The former commodities tend to be relatively inexpensive in the capital-rich country, because they use intensively the country's relatively abundant (hence relatively cheap) resource, capital. Labor-intensive commodities, however, tend to be comparatively dear since they embody large amounts of the country's relatively scarce and expensive resource, labor. Conversely, a country with a relatively high labor/capital ratio would export labor-intensive goods and import capital-intensive ones. Each country has a comparative advantage in producing goods that use intensively the country's relatively plentiful resource. In short, each country's product-mix, as well as the commodity composition and geographical pattern of its trade, would be determined by international differences in factor proportions.

Leontief's Test.   Although relatively simple, the factor proportions theory seemed to exhibit considerable explanatory power, thereby accounting for its almost universal acceptance prior to the early 1950's when its validity was finally challenged by empirical research. The factor-proportions theory predicted that the U.S., certainly the most capital-abundant country in the world, would export capital-intensive goods and import labor-intensive ones. But a 1953 study by Harvard University's Wassily Leontief revealed that, contrary to the theory, U.S. exports were actually *less* capital-intensive than U.S. imports. Evidently, the U.S. had a comparative advantage in relatively labor-intensive goods and a comparative disadvantage in relatively capital-intensive ones, despite the relative scarcity of labor and the relative abundance of capital in this country.

Leontief's paradoxical findings created much consternation among adherents of the factor proportions theory. Leontief himself attempted to reconcile his findings with the theory by suggesting that U.S. labor is three times more efficient than foreign labor, the difference being due to "entrepreneurship and superior organization" rather than to a high capital/

labor ratio. In other words, U.S. labor measured in terms of efficiency units (i.e., units of equivalent foreign labor) is three times more plentiful than when conventionally measured (i.e., U.S. man years). Thus, because of the efficiency factor, or labor-quality differential, of three, the U.S. is actually a labor-abundant country. Consequently, the measured factor composition of U.S. trading patterns conforms to the factor proportions explanation. Leontief's conjecture, however, was an unsatisfactory resolution of the paradox, because it did not adequately identify the factors augmenting labor's efficiency. Subsequent research has focused on the precise specification of these factors. In contrast to Leontief, however, recent researchers have tended to treat these efficiency-augmenting factors as types of capital instead of as additional units of labor.

Sources of U.S. Comparative Advantage. If U.S. comparative advantage is not based on the large amount of tangible capital per worker in this country, then what *is* its basis? Several possible sources of comparative advantage have been studied, including, among others: (1) the large amounts of *human capital* embodied in the labor force, i.e., high labor skills stemming from education and training; (2) technological superiority based on research and development (R and D) expenditures; (3) economies of scale resulting from the large domestic market, which enables goods to be produced at lower costs in the U.S. than abroad; (4) greater availability of entrepreneurial talent and innovativeness in the U.S. than abroad; (5) the domestic availability of certain raw materials combined with their nonexistence abroad; and (6) tariff structures that bias U.S. production and export toward labor-intensive commodities.

Empirical Findings. Of the possible determinants of U.S. comparative advantage, the most important, according to recent empirical studies, appear to be human capital (skills) and R and D activity. Recent studies indicate that inputs of human capital—measured either by the capitalized value of the differential between the annual wages of skilled and unskilled labor, or by the ratio of highly skilled workers to total workers—tend to be significantly higher in U.S. industries with strong net export positions than in those industries having weak export positions. Moreover, comparisons of representative bundles of U.S. export and import-competing goods (the latter being a proxy for foreign-produced imports) show the former to have a higher skill content than the latter. In fact, when estimates of human capital are combined with estimates of tangible capital in a measure of total capital input, U.S. exports become more total-capital-intensive than the products of U.S. import-competing industries. Researchers have also found fairly strong positive correlations between various measures of industry R and D activity (e.g., R and D spending as a percentage of total sales, or the ratio of scientists and engineers to total employment) and alternative indices of export performance (e.g., gross and net exports as a percent of total sales, or U.S. share of total exports of major industrial countries).

These studies, of course, are not without shortcomings, and should be interpreted with some skepticism. For example, the assumption that wage differentials (a measure of skill differences) stem solely from disparities in education, training, and other types of human investment, seems unwarranted. Also, in view of the probable close correlation between skill intensity and R and D activity in given industries, one could question whether skills and R and D activity are mutually exclusive determinants of comparative advantage. Despite these shortcomings, however, recent evidence is sufficient to suggest that the chief determinants of our comparative advantage are (1) human capital and (2) technological superiority, as represented by R and D activity.

The importance of the technology factor is illustrated in Chart 1, which contrasts the strong trade surplus in technology-intensive manufactured products with the increasing trade deficit in nontechnology-intensive products. High-technology products account for more than one-half of U.S. total exports and about one-third of total imports. Low-technology

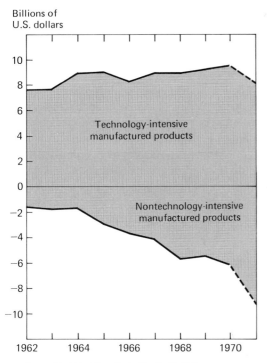

Chart 1

**U. S. Trade Balance Trends in
High-Technology and Low-Technology
Manufactured Products**

Billions of
U.S. dollars

Technology-intensive
manufactured products

Nontechnology-intensive
manufactured products

Source: *The United States in the Changing World Economy,*
Volume II: *Background Material,* December 1971,
U. S. Government Printing Office, Washington, D. C.

capital broadly defined, advocates of the factor-proportions theory can still maintain that U.S. exports are indeed capital intensive, as the theory predicts.

Many economists, however, prefer a newer interpretation, which states that labor skills and technology indirectly promote the development of temporary trade advantages by fostering the new product or process innovations that generate those advantages. This interpretation of the role of skills and technology in the creation of comparative advantages is a component of a new theory of international trade.

The New View.   The new view integrates a number of previously mentioned determinants of comparative advantage into a dynamic, "technology gap" explanation of international trade. According to this theory, the availability of entrepreneurial, scientific, and engineering talent enables domestic firms to generate continually the sophisticated new products increasingly demanded by consumers in the affluent U.S. After its introduction in the domestic market, a new good is usually exported to profitable foreign markets. The knowledge, technical capabilities, and special managerial skills required for the successful introduction of the innovation provides the U.S. producer with an initial advantage in world markets. In other words, U.S. competitiveness is based on a "technology gap."

The technological advantage enjoyed by the U.S. producer is transitory, however. The technology gap is continually narrowing for particular products as knowledge of the innovation spreads abroad and foreign producers adopt it. Eventually the transfer of technology is completed, and the technological lead of the U.S. in this product vanishes. Production of the good may eventually pass almost entirely from the U.S. to foreign countries, which then export it to the U.S.

Note, however, that while this country's technological advantages in some products are disappearing, others are constantly being created. The entire structure of trade advantages, in fact, is continually being

products, too, compose roughly one-third of U.S. total imports but constitute only one-eighth of U.S. exports.

Factor-Proportions or Technology Gap?   The finding that U.S. exports are skill-intensive and technology oriented is consistent with both the old factor-proportions interpretation of comparative advantage and a newer interpretation based on the concept of a "technology gap." As mentioned previously, the older interpretation is still valid provided one extends the concept of capital to include labor skills (human capital) and capital-embodied technology as well as tangible capital (plant and equipment). That is, with modified by the simultaneous destruction and generation of technology gaps. It is this dynamic conception of comparative advantage, which views individual advantages as transient components of an evolving structure, that distinguishes the new view from the older interpretations.

Faster Diffusion of Technology. An important implication of the new view is that U.S. producers systematically must generate innovations as rapidly as knowledge of the old technology is disseminated abroad, if the U.S. is to maintain its traditionally strong foreign trade position in manufactured goods. Pessimists fear that it is becoming more difficult for U.S. producers to maintain the required pace of innovation.

For one thing, the required pace may be increasing. Foreign producers seem to adopt new methods more quickly now than they formerly did. The international diffusion of technical knowledge is much faster than it used to be. Trade in research-intensive new products, international licensing and sale of patents, foreign travel by scientists and professionals, private direct investment, and, of course, faster means of transportation and communication all serve as vehicles for the rapid transmission of technical knowledge. The more rapid spread of technology, of course, shrinks the average lead-time that U.S. producers have to profitably exploit foreign markets. In short, acceleration in the rate of transfer of technology may have increased the required rate of innovative activity while simultaneously reducing the potential profitability of any given innovation and thus the incentive of U.S. producers to undertake it.

The Multinational Firm. A major factor contributing to the more rapid propagation of U.S. technology has been the phenomenal growth in direct investment by U.S. firms in manufacturing facilities abroad. Such investment, the outstanding value of which increased from $32 billion in 1960 to $71 billion in 1970, promotes the transfer of technology in two ways. First, investment is often accompanied by direct transfer of a "package" of capital, production techniques, skills, and managerial methods to foreign subsidiaries. Skilled personnel are often considered as indispensable complementary inputs to be used in combination with physical capital facilities. Therefore, managerial and technical people are frequently dispatched abroad by the parent firm to tend the equipment as well as to advise and train the employees of its subsidiaries. Second, the increased competition provided by U.S. subsidiaries stimulates local producers to adopt the latest technology and spurs them to undertake innovative activity of their own.

Pessimists also fear that our research lead is being eroded by the willingness of other industrial powers to devote a greater proportion of their resources to productive research than we do. Although R and D spending in the United States is almost triple that of Western Europe and eight times that of Japan, too much of this spending, it is claimed, is for sterile defense purposes. Our civilian research effort—measured by civilian R and D expenditures as a percent of GNP or by the proportion of the population engaged in civilian R and D work—was surpassed by that of Japan and Western Europe in the 1960's.

The pessimists' case is by no means proved, however. It is too early to determine whether the U.S. has suffered a permanent reduction in its technological lead. A longer run perspective is useful here. One need only remember that as recently as five years ago spokesmen for the nations of Western Europe were raising the specter of inevitable domination of European markets by U.S. owned firms (the so-called "American Challenge" thesis of French journalist J. J. Servan-Schreiber). These same people were also predicting a growing technology gap, with Europe receding progressively behind the U.S. position of technological superiority. Moreover, these people were lamenting the loss of scientists and other skilled professionals to the U.S. via emigration (the so-called "brain drain"). Just as the tide has turned for Western Europe, so it may also turn for the U.S. In contrast to the pessimists, some observers are confident that U.S. producers can continue to generate innovations at an expanded rate. Moreover, the optimists point out that the transfer of technology is two-way, i.e., U.S. producers have benefitted from the reverse transfer of foreign innovations, capital, and skilled personnel. Finally, contrary to the "sterility" contention of the pessimists, defense related research expenditure may ultimately have a high commercial pay-off, although admittedly the rate of technological advance may be less than it would be if the same research effort were allocated by the private sector according to economic instead of military criteria.

Is the Comparative Advantage Principle Obsolete?

Does the doctrine of comparative advantage provide a useful and valid guide for trade policy in the modern world? Should the U.S. continue to press for freer trade according to the dictates of this doctrine, even though foreign goods are becoming increasingly competitive with ours? Should the U.S. adhere to the doctrine and discontinue producing goods that can be obtained at lower opportunity cost via importation than via domestic production? These questions form the heart of much of the current controversy surrounding U.S. foreign economic policy.

Protectionists, convinced that freer external trade and investment would result in the export of U.S. jobs and the loss of U.S. technological supremacy, argue that the comparative advantage doctrine has little contemporary validity, although admittedly the doctrine might apply in a static world. In a stationary world, capital and labor would be fixed in quantity and immobile internationally. Moreover, technological change would be absent, thereby freezing international differences in technology at their initial levels. In such a world each nation would have a well-defined, enduring set of comparative advantages based either on factor proportions or on technological superiority. There would be no problem of sudden shifts in the ranking of comparative cost differences with consequent disruption in the industrial composition of the world's major economies. The stability and durability of the pattern of compar-

ative advantages would insure the virtual absence of risks of specialization.

In the real world, however, these conditions are violated. The real world is dynamic, not stationary. Change is the rule; static conditions the exception. Factors of production are mobile internationally; and technological leadership waxes and wanes, contrary to the assumptions underlying the classical free trade model. Protectionists contend that the international mobility of capital and managerial resources can quickly alter factor proportions. For example, a domestic U.S. industry could exhibit a high ratio of capital and entrepreneurial skill relative to labor and natural resources in one decade, but a low one in the next, as U.S. capital and management go abroad to combine with foreign labor and natural resources. Similarly, the rapid dissemination of knowledge may eliminate and even reverse a nation's technological lead. In short, in the modern world, there is no stable, lasting basis for comparative advantages. The list of rankings is constantly shifting. Protectionists maintain that the rapidly shifting list of comparative advantages requires an unattainable degree of adaptability in the economy. Lacking infinite flexibility, the economy cannot alter its product-mix or reallocate its resources swiftly enough to keep up with changing comparative cost conditions. Consequently, free trade must lead to structural maladjustment, resource unemployment, and periodic deficits in the merchandise trade balance.

Thus, according to the protectionist argument, a free-trade policy is harmful to a country confronted with shifting comparative advantages and constrained by an imperfectly flexible industrial structure. This very line of reasoning has been employed by labor leaders and businessmen who advocate controls on U.S. trade and direct foreign investment.

The free trade school disagrees with the protectionists. While not denying that comparative advantages change more rapidly today than in Ricardo's time, free traders think that the economy has sufficient flexibility to adjust to such changes. Free traders do not necessarily believe that the declining merchandise trade balance is indicative of a fundamental incapacity of the economy to adjust. Instead, they see it as a perfectly normal adaptation to changing comparative advantages, in which our net exports of merchandise have been supplanted by net exports of capital, technology, and skills. In fact, some free traders are predicting persistent deficits in the U.S. merchandise trade accounts over the next several decades. This prospect does not alarm them, however. They think the merchandise trade deficits can be offset by earnings from net exports of services together with the dividend earnings of U.S. capital located abroad, thereby maintaining overall equilibrium of our total balance of payments. That is, the earnings of new U.S. comparative advantage activities—supplying the rest of the world with advanced services, skills, and technology either embodied in capital or complementary to it—would compensate for the deficit incurred in this country's former comparative advantage activity, merchandise trade. If the U.S. reaches a position characterized by a persistent trade deficit offset by net exports of services and return on foreign investment, it will have attained the same "mature creditor" stage in the development of its balance of payments that Great Britain reached in the nineteenth century. Great Britain, although confronted with a chronic excess of imports over exports, experienced little difficulty up to World War I in balancing its international accounts. That country simply covered its import surplus with the interest and dividend yield from its accumulated foreign investments.

In answer to protectionist claims that trade restrictions are needed because the economy is not sufficiently adaptable to changing comparative advantages, free traders point out that trade restrictions would actually reduce adaptability. By shielding domestic producers from foreign competition, protection would permit them to be more sluggish in adapting to technological change initiated abroad. Finally, free traders point out that comparative advantages *within*

the U.S. are continually being altered by changes in tastes, technology, and the geographical location of resources. Yet, protectionists do not advocate restrictions on domestic trade or on the domestic migration of labor and capital.

Free traders, of course, are not unaware of the dislocations incidental to rapid change. But they emphasize that such dislocations are better alleviated by tax-financed adjustment assistance (job retraining, employment counseling, relocation subsidies, etc.) than by departure from the principle of comparative advantage. Financed by the beneficiaries of change, adjustment assistance would permit a more equitable sharing of the costs of change while simultaneously redirecting dislocated resources into the new lines of comparative advantage.

In short, free traders point out that the doctrine of comparative advantage is still the blueprint for the most efficient allocation of resources. They argue convincingly that policies that combine the precepts of this doctrine with adjustment assistance to groups dislocated by change will do more to promote overall welfare than will protectionist policies.

Summary. Economists' views of the sources and nature of comparative advantage have undergone significant change since Ricardo's time. Originally thought to be based on international differences in labor productivity and later on relative endowments of factor proportions, the comparative advantages enjoyed by developed countries such as the U.S. are now seen as emanating largely from human skills, knowledge, and technology.

Recent developments in the world economy—including the increasing international mobility of capital, the faster dissemination of technology, and the narrowing differential between the economic capability of the U.S. and her trading partners—have also altered economists' conceptions of the pattern of this country's comparative advantage. The structure of comparative advantage, once thought to be stable and enduring, is now seen as shifting rapidly and frequently, thereby raising the risks of specialization and the costs of adjustment. Protectionists, claiming that these adjustment costs are unduly high, hold that the doctrine of comparative advantage is no longer valid. But free traders still contend, as did Ricardo, that the principle of comparative advantage provides the best guide for the optimal allocation of any nation's resources and the maximization of world welfare. In short, free traders argue convincingly that the benefits of unrestricted commerce outweigh the costs. In concordance with this latter view, most economists would probably agree that the basic conclusion of the comparative advantage doctrine—that free trade is mutually beneficial—remains as cogent today as it was in Ricardo's time.

Bibliography

Baldwin, Robert E. "Determinants of the Commodity Structure of U.S. Trade," *American Economic Review*, 61 (March 1971).

Branson, William H. and Junz, Helen B. "Trends in U.S. Trade and Comparative Advantage," *Brookings Papers on Economic Activity* (2:1971).

Geiger, Theodore. "A Note on U.S. Comparative Advantages, Productivity and Price Competitiveness," *U.S. Foreign Economic Policy for the 1970's: A New Approach to New Realities*. Planning Pamphlet No. 130. Washington: National Planning Association, 1971.

Goldfinger, Nat. "A Labor View of Foreign Investment and Trade Issues," *United States International Economic Policy in an Interdependent World*, Vol. 1. Papers submitted to the President's Commission on International Trade and Investment Policy. Washington: Government Printing Office, 1971.

Hufbauer, G. C. "The Impact of National Characteristics and Technology on the Commodity Composition of Trade in Manufactured Goods," *The Technology Factor in International Trade*, Raymon Vernon (ed.). New York: National Bureau of Economic Research, 1970.

Johnson, Harry G. "International Trade: Theory," *International Encyclopedia of the Social Sciences*, Vol. 8. New York: Macmillan and Free Press, 1968.

_____ . *Comparative Cost and Commercial Policy Theory for a Developing World Economy*. Wicksell Lectures, 1968. Stockholm: Almqvist and Wiksell, 1968.

Keesing, Donald B. "Labor Skills and the Structure of Trade in Manufacturers" and "The Impact of Research and Development on United States Trade," *The Open Economy: Essays on International Trade and Finance*, P. B. Kenen and R. Lawrence (eds.). New York: Columbia University Press, 1968.

Kenen, Peter B. "Skills, Human Capital and Comparative Advantage," *Education, Income, and Human Capital*, W. Lee Hansen (ed.). New York: National Bureau of Economic Research, 1970.

Vernon, Raymond. "The Economic Consequences of U.S. Foreign Direct Investment," *United States International Economic Policy in an Interdependent World*, Vol. 1. Papers submitted to the President's Commission on International Trade and Investment Policy. Washington: Government Printing Office, 1971.

Yudin, Elinor B. "Americans Abroad: A Transfer of Capital," *The Open Economy: Essays on International Trade and Finance*, P. B. Kenen and R. B. Lawrence (eds.). New York: Columbia University Press, 1968.

Updating the World of Trade*

By Stanley H. Ruttenberg

Summary

The trouble with trade today—or at least with any serious discussion of the problems the United States faces as a major participant in world trade—is that some people are "hung up" with outmoded, outdated concepts which may have been true 30, 20, or even 10 years ago, but which no longer fit the realities of today's world.

The world has changed since the current conventional wisdom became conventional. If the United States is to have a foreign trade policy which is relevant to today and more especially which is consistent with U.S. goals, a whole new conceptual framework on which to hang that policy must be developed. This framework must recognize the newly emerging economic and political institutions, keep pace with swift changes in the developing world technocracy, and enable the United States to continue to be on the leading edge of social advance.

All of this adds up to saying that a new, fresh, and different look needs to be taken toward international trade policy. The Burke-Hartke bill is one approach to the problem. Many people—from academic theoreticians to pragmatic businessmen—consider it to be dead wrong; but it represents an honest approach to the issue of what the United States needs today.

Key Questions to Consider

■ Why is the theory of comparative advantage inappropriate as a basis for free trade according to the author?

■ What has happened to weaken the argument that the kind of goods imported into the U.S. would be in the highly labor-intensive industries?

■ Has the author considered the effects of his proposals on all sectors of society, that is, labor, agriculture, business, consumers, etc.?

■ How, according to the author, has support of the most favored nation treatment affected the United States' trade position?

■ Why does labor support the Burke-Hartke bill?

_____

* Reprinted with permission from *American Federationist*, AFL-CIO, **80,** No. 2 (February 1973), pp. 1–7.

Updating the World of Trade

The trouble with trade today—or at least with any serious discussion of the problems the United States faces as a major participant in world trade—is that some people are "hung up" with outmoded, outdated concepts which may have been true 30, 20, or even 10 years ago, but which no longer fit the realities of today's world. Much of the current debate today is unfortunately no more than a knee-jerk reaction to worn out shibboleths, an unthinking rote recital of lessons learned long ago.

The world has changed since the current conventional wisdom became conventional. The concepts which were developed in the 1930s under the aegis of the "good grey" Cordell Hull, and which have guided U.S. foreign trade policy ever since, are no longer valid. If the United States is to have a foreign trade policy which is relevant to today and more especially which is consistent with U.S. goals, a whole new conceptual framework on which to hang that policy must be developed. This framework must recognize the newly emerging economic and political institutions, keep pace with swift changes in the developing world technocracy and enable the United States to continue to be on the leading edge of social advance.

The first step in the development of a new and more pertinent trade policy is a full and free discussion of all of the issues involved. The following are some of the familiar concepts which have formed the basis of our foreign trade policy for almost 40 years; events and changing conditions in the past 10 years have worked to undermine the validity of these concepts.

One: The fundamental theoretical basis for our trade policy has always been the theory of comparative advantage, as enunciated in the 18th and 19th centuries, first by Adam Smith, later by David Ricardo. The theory holds that in order to achieve optimum utilization of the world's resources, and thereby achieve maximum economic benefit for the world's peoples, each nation should—and in a perfect society, would—concentrate on the production of those goods and services which it could produce most efficiently in relation to the total demand for such goods and services. International trade being completely free would assure that the benefits of such concentration would be equitably distributed around the world to the greater comfort of all the world's peoples.

The theory of comparative advantage, of course, assumes that the factors of production—capital, technology and management, labor and land—are fixed and also that international trade could be conducted without national barriers or hindrances of any kind.

It is not certain that these assumptions were ever

correct. Certainly neither is in accord with the realities of today.

The great advances which have been made in communication and transportation have made possible a mobility of capital and technology never dreamed of in Ricardo's day. Only land and labor are fixed—and as a matter of fact, both are only relatively so. Through technology the productive capacity of both land and labor can be changed; formerly barren deserts have been made to bloom; and previously illiterate, unskilled labor has been trained to perform highly skilled tasks. However, labor is still considerably less mobile than the other factors of production and therefore remains particularly vulnerable. As the law of comparative advantage ceases to function— that is assuming it ever did or could—it not only cannot assure optimum utilization of the world's economic resources, but also it cannot provide a defensible rationale for policy formation.

Two: As the theory of comparative advantage begins to evaporate into a cloud of wishful thinking, so do the related arguments that formerly were used to supplement the Ricardian theories. As a corollary to the adherence to the theory of comparative advantage, liberals used to argue that the U.S. position as the most industrialized society in the world would inevitably assure that the goods imported into the United States would be in the highly labor intensive industries (the greatest U.S. advantage being in capital formation and advanced technology) and that as part of the pursuit of a higher standard of living for all workers, the workers in similar labor intensive U.S. industries could or should find jobs in the high technology and capital intensive industries in which the United States excelled. However, since the 1960s, two things have happened to make these earlier bland assumptions highly questionable.

First, it is clear that U.S. imports are no longer limited to high labor intensive products. On the basis of U.S. Department of Labor figures relating exports and competitive imports to employment, it took 71,000 jobs in 1966 to produce $1 billion worth of exports, while 90,000 jobs (in terms of U.S. standards) were needed to produce the same amount of imports. In other words, 19,000 more year-round jobs could be related to the manufacture and marketing of each $1 billion worth of goods imported in the United States than were required for each $1 billion worth of exports. (The comparison omits all of the non-competitive imports which, of course, would be even more labor intensive; it includes those imports that are directly comparable with U.S.-produced goods.)

By the end of 1972 it could be estimated that the ratio of jobs to exports decreased to 55,000 per $1 billion, while the import-related job ratio had declined to 60,000—a difference of only 5,000. The gap has narrowed by 75 percent. What this means is that in 1966 U.S. imports were 27 percent more labor intensive than exports, but by 1972, imports were only 9 percent more labor intensive.

Relation of Exports and Imports to Employment
Jobs Per $1 Billion Worth of Trade

	1966	1972
Import-related jobs (Competitive imports only)	90,000	60,000
Export-related jobs	71,000	55,000
Difference	19,000	5,000

If additional proof is needed, a special study by the Department of Commerce in 1971 showed that imports of products the government defines as technology intensive were growing at a much faster rate than imports of what the Commerce Department called non-technology intensive products. Between 1964 and 1970, the period which the study covered, imports of non-technology intensive manufactured products were doubled, but imports of technology intensive manufactured products shot up to four times the 1964 level. Moreover, during that same period, exports of technology intensive products grew by only 85 percent. Obviously U.S. imports are no longer confined to labor intensive categories; they now include sophisticated production.

Three: Another corollary concept of the comparative advantage theory, which was used to lull Americans into complacency about U.S. position in world trade, was based on the unshakable faith in a constantly rising rate of productivity; that U.S. industries (even including some of the labor intensive industries) could always count on higher productivity than other countries and therefore could always compete successfully in world markets. It was argued that the higher labor costs that prevailed in this country would not seriously impair U.S. ability to compete in world markets because our productivity was so much greater that unit labor costs would still be lower than in other countries. This may have been true once. It is far less true today, even though U.S. wages have been increasing at a slower rate than wages in other countries.

For the past 20 years, the other major developed countries of the world have increased productivity at a faster rate than has the United States. By the last half of the 1960s, the United States had dropped far behind in average annual productivity growth. The average annual growth for the United States between 1965 and 1969 was only 2.5 percent compared to a growth rate of 13.4 percent in Japan, 6.9 percent in France, 6.4 percent in Germany, 4.3 percent in the United Kingdom and 3.2 percent in Canada.

Some of this can be attributed to the inherent bias of statistical measurements—a growth rate measured from a very low starting point is bound to be greater than the same absolute growth starting from a higher base. And in this case the starting point for the European countries and Japan was very low. Some of the difference is also due to the U.S. economic slowdown in 1966–67 and the recession of 1969–70.

Nevertheless, the faster rate of productivity growth in other nations unquestionably has been aided and assisted by the export of investment funds and technology from the United States. Unless this trend can be tempered, the gap will narrow between the United States and its major competitors; indeed, in some industries this has already happened.

During the same period, 1965–69, unit labor costs in the United States were increasing at a faster rate than any of its major competitors except Canada. Indeed, in Germany, Italy and the United Kingdom, unit labor costs actually declined. In Japan, the average annual increase was only one-eighth that of the United States. Under present conditions, productivity increases can no longer be counted on to make up for our high standard of living and concomitant high labor costs.

Four: Underlying confidence in the invincibility of the United States in high productivity was the certainty that U.S. technology was—and could continue to be—more advanced than that of any other nation.

This theory said the U.S. competitive advantage could be maintained because it was the most highly developed nation in the world. U.S. technology was more advanced than any other country's and was therefore in a stronger competitive position. Aside from the purely chauvinistic fallacies of this argument (after all, who invented the Wankel, penicillin, the jet engine, the radial tire, cassette tapes?) it is clear now that the United States does not have a monopoly on technology. More important, even if it did, with the new mobility of resources, any monopoly would be short-lived. Frequently using the vehicle of multinational corporate organization, U.S. technology today moves quickly across national borders. One indication of the tremendous increase in the flow of U.S. technology abroad in the past decade is seen in the increase in revenues from license fees and royalties that shows up on our balance of payments. In 1960, this revenue amounted to only $840 million. By 1971, this amount had increased to almost $3 billion—3½ times as much as a decade before. It is ironic that frequently the technology that moves so easily outside the United States was initially financed through U.S. government support of industrial research and development programs. A case in point is the electronics industry, where two-thirds of the development activity between 1957 and 1965 was paid for with federal funds.

Another indication of the tenuous hold the United States has on the world technology lead is seen in recent trends in patent applications. While total applications to the U.S. Patent Office have increased only slightly over the decade of the 1960s, patent applications from foreigners nearly doubled. In 1961, about 25 percent of all applications for U.S. patents came from foreigners. By 1971, this ratio had increased to more than 40 percent.

Five: Backing up the argument that superior technology would always provide a competitive advantage was the fact that the United States spent more money, from both public and private sources, for research and development. But here again conditions have changed. No longer can we claim supremacy in this area. A 1967 study showed that the U.S. research and development activities financed by business were at about the same level as those of most of our major competitors. In addition, the bulk of government research and development money has gone into defense and aerospace programs and the development of products which are less likely to find their way into the regular flow of international trade, although there are some spin-offs from military and space technology.

Six: Even the most dedicated proponents of the theory of comparative advantage—with all of its ramifications—recognized that "freer" trade would cause temporary disruptions in normal marketing and production patterns which would hurt some individuals and some companies. Adjustment assistance was to be the answer to increased imports that resulted from a slavish adherence to the so-called "freer trade" policies. Indeed, confidence in the ability of adjustment assistance to correct whatever dislocations resulted from increased imports was what kept the labor movement on the side of the Trade Expansion Act of 1962. Little did labor suspect that imports would flood into the country in such volume that full utilization of adjustment assistance would push the cost of federal support through the roof. If adjustment assistance had ever been fully implemented—to provide meaningful

assistance in every case where workers were pushed out of their jobs by a flood of competitive imports, or in every case where companies were either forced to shut down or chose to move away—the cost to the federal government would have been prohibitive. All of this assumes, of course, that companies and industries will exist to provide all the displaced workers with jobs. But rather than face the issue squarely, the government chose to put off the day of reckoning by making it almost impossible for workers and companies to qualify for help under the act.

Seven: A good example of the government's faith in the ability of adjustment assistance to solve the problems of constantly shifting trade patterns is the Canadian auto agreement. Essentially this agreement proposed that each country concentrate on the production of certain models on one or the other side of the border, with the products of this specialization then being allowed to move duty-free across the border. On both sides, companion legislation further provided that any disruptions that occurred would be taken care of by enlarged and more leniently administered adjustment assistance programs.

At the time it was signed in 1965, the Automotive Products Agreement was considered by its supporters—which did not include the AFL-CIO—to be a reasonable, if not clever and innovative, arrangement to assure the most effective utilization and development of automotive productive capacity in both the United States and Canada. Despite a noted lack of enthusiasm for the concept within the labor movement, many people felt that the agreement would produce maximum benefits for both countries.

However, we now find that the labor movement's fears have been borne out. In the first five years of the program, the favorable balance the United States previously enjoyed in passenger car trade with Canada has moved from a surplus of 14,000 cars in 1965 to a deficit of 385,000 in 1969—when Canada shipped 676,000 cars to the United States, while the United States shipped only 291,000 to Canada.

In that period adjustment assistance which was supposed to alleviate the dislocation that took place as a result of the agreement was made available to only 2,500 workers in six states on the U.S. side of the border. At the same time, 8,600 Canadian workers were certified eligible for assistance under a similar Canadian provision. The point is not that we were all wrong about the automotive agreement, but rather that we did not think far enough ahead and think through the probable consequences of our actions. Lacking experience and guided by an inappropriate and irrelevant conceptual framework, we have watched what looked like a really good idea turn out to be something less than expected.

Eight: Paralleling the unquestioning belief in the eventual correctness of the theory of comparative advantage was an unshakable support of the theory of unconditional most favored nation (MFN) treatment. This theory—that the trade advantages given to one nation must be given to all if the free market is to play its role as the best and final arbiter of international trade—lies at the heart of the GATT, the General Agreement on Trade and Tariffs. GATT now has 77 members, one provisional member and 13 nations which follow its rules de facto, but despite the size and scope of the organization, its 25 years as an international institution have been marked by more exceptions than observances of the rule.

Successful application of the most favored nation principle implies a political and economic balance among nations—a balance that does not exist. As conceived, MFN would overlook both historical relationships and geographic realities. It is not necessary to derogate the ideals behind the theory of the MFN, but merely to ask whether the United States can continue to blindly pursue the ideal without at least recognizing the problems of fitting that ideal to the practical realities of the world as it is.

Nine: For more than 30 years, the United States has followed a reciprocal trade program first propounded by Cordell Hull. Reciprocal trade agreements were to be the vehicle for the achievement of freer trade and realization of the concepts of the most favored nation treatment. The reciprocal program, it was believed, would let the United States ignore existing realities because if we just led the way in developing free trade, other countries would surely follow our lead. Time and again, authority to negotiate tariff reductions was passed by Congress on the strength of this argument. As the largest and most advanced industrial country in the world, it was said, the United States must set the example; open its doors to freer trade first; apply the principle of most favored nation and then other countries would follow suit and world trade could be carried on in a way that would make the theory of comparative advantage fully functional. Since 1947, six different rounds of negotiations have been carried out under the GATT umbrella; the last one being the Kennedy Round completed in 1967. Each time, the U.S. negotiating team was authorized to lower tariffs and extend the most favored nation treatment concept in the name of leading the way to freer trade. But it hasn't happened that way. It is true that there have been tariff reductions. But instead of freer trade, what has developed has been an increase in the number and size of the preferential trading blocs—which of course exclude the United States—and in the spread of non-tariff barriers. Instead of following the U.S. lead, other countries appear to have been so intent on developing and protecting their own economies as not to notice where the United States was leading. Not only has the United States not led anybody anywhere, but while the United States was going one direction, everyone else has been going in quite the opposite direction.

Ten: Standing in the way of effective implementation of the most favored nation concept was the need for special treatment toward the war-torn countries in the immediate post-war period. From the outset, it was recognized by the GATT signatories that exceptions to unconditional most favored nation treatment would have to be made if the war-ravaged countries of Europe and Japan were to make a quick and full recovery. Various concessions were made at that time —to which the United States readily agreed—so that those countries could get back on their feet. Other concessions were—and are—made to the less developed countries to help them along in the process of industrialization. Only the United States has held relatively firmly to the original principles of GATT, the principles first enunciated by Hull.

Eleven: One of the major variations from GATT principles was the encouragement of regional trading groups, specifically the European Economic Community (EEC) or Common Market. In this case, the United States was more than willing to permit exceptions to its general principles of "freer" international trade because of the firm belief that by promoting the economic unity of Europe, international tensions would be lessened and the chances for peace strengthened. In the interest of creating a united Europe—somewhat in the mold of a United States of America—the United States agreed to exceptions from the most favored nation treatment, as well as to other concessions which would strengthen the European economies. However, with the addition of three more countries in January (the United Kingdom, Ireland and Denmark) to the original six (France, Germany, Italy, Belgium, The Netherlands and Luxembourg) the EEC is now one of the most powerful economic forces in the world, if not the most powerful. It has evolved into an institution quite different from its beginnings.

The impact of some of the changes can now be seen; others are still unknown. For example, the mechanism of a common external tariff and the elimination of internal tariffs which seemed innocent enough at the outset must now be looked at in a very different way. For one thing, this mechanism has itself led to the rise of the multinational corporations whose rapid growth must be attributed at least in part to the desire to get over the external tariff barrier and to take advantage of the zero internal tariff. Initially, this development was justified on the grounds that such investments were necessary to help the European countries in their recovery effort. But,

in addition to the concern that is being voiced in this country as we see our capital and most advanced technology being exported to other countries, there is also the concern of the other countries that they may be losing control of their own destinies. As former Secretary of Commerce Peter Peterson has said, "To nationalists in developed and developing countries alike—but particularly in the latter—they (the multinationals) represent a threat of foreign dominance of the national economy."

Another example of the long-range impact of U.S. concessions made in the name of promoting European recovery and world peace is seen in the Common Agricultural Policy of the EEC. In this case the CAP instrument, a variable levy on agricultural products, was accepted in order to help agricultural interests in the separate countries that made up the EEC adjust to the changing trade patterns that were expected to develop as the result of the EEC union. The motivation behind the CAP was both political and economic, part of the management by western European governments to prevent the sharp dislocations that took place in the United States.

The result of the variable levy, however, has been to produce a situation that completely contradicts the principles of freer trade, of most favored nation treatment and of comparative advantage. By maintaining an artificially high price for Common Market agricultural products, the CAP provides an incentive for uneconomic production which not only hurts the United States in terms of its agricultural exports to Europe but also creates a problem in third country markets. The European subsidy generates agricultural surpluses that compete unfairly with U.S. products.

The value-added tax adopted by some western European governments is another exception to the GATT principles, accepted because it was interpreted to be an internal tax to which the GATT rules did not apply. Indeed, it was on these terms that the United States did not object to the value-added tax at the time it was adopted. But instead of being used as a strictly internal tax to raise revenue, it is now being used as a subsidy for exports and a border tax on all imports.

In this reverse logic, the subsidy occurs not because of the application of the tax, but because goods produced for export are exempted, thereby receiving what amounts to a subsidy. This, of course, is not in accord with GATT rules and principles. It is another example of national economic management.

Another mutation of the Common Market—which has serious implications for the United States—is the development of the associated memberships, as for example the former French colonies of Africa, which are deemed to have a special relationship with the EEC because of their former relationship with France. This kind of arrangement was not dreamed of when the EEC was first conceived—and when the United States was working so hard to help the infant trade association off the ground. But these developments are realities which must be taken into consideration today.

Twelve: Last, but not least, among the outdated concepts on which our trade policy is based is the notion that the United States need not worry about its balance of payments because it would always have a trade surplus big enough to offset the deficits that grew out of U.S. economic, military and other foreign aid commitments. An adjunct of this was that if the trade surplus was not quite large enough to cover the whole deficit, the rest could be taken out of our large $24 billion gold reserve (which with the gold window now shut, is down to some $10.5 billion). Little did the United States realize that large trade surpluses would not be tolerated for long by the deficit countries. In 1971, for the first time since 1893, the U.S. trade balance slipped into the red by some $2.7 billion. Far from being able to make up the deficit incurred through other U.S. international transactions, the trade balance only added to the total deficit of $30 billion. In 1972, the trade deficit jumped to $6.4 billion.

These are some of the most obvious of the outdated concepts which have shaped public thinking in the past but which we can no longer use as guideposts for the future. All of this adds up to saying that a new, fresh and different look needs to be taken toward international trade policy. The Burke-Hartke bill is one approach to the problem. Many people—from academic theoreticians to pragmatic business interests—consider it to be dead wrong; but it represents an honest approach to the issue of what the United States needs today rather than more of the same reciprocal trade-GATT-Cordell Hull approach. I challenge these people to rethink these issues. If they don't like the Burke-Hartke approach, then let them come up with other alternatives. A State Department expert, Leonard Weiss, put the issue clearly in a paper he prepared last year for the Commission on International Trade and Investment Policy. He wrote, "No one questions the importance of full employment and freer trade, practically all if not all of us would undoubtedly come down for full employment."

Then he added his belief that, "This is not a necessary choice." If he is right and it is not a necessary choice, how then do we achieve both goals? Burke-Hartke certainly comes down on the side of full employment. If that is not acceptable—if that does not seem the right choice—find other alternatives. Continued mouthing of arguments of the past cannot provide the solutions that are needed today.

Business and the labor movement can join in three possible courses in developing the new policies and programs which will make the United States more competitive and which can then lead to full employment.

Business says that it would prefer to produce goods within U.S. borders but cannot profitably do so because of the need to get behind existing tariff walls, or to comply with content laws, or to overcome other restrictive trade barriers. We need to find a way to make those barriers come down. We cannot just sit back and say, "well, that's the way it is—we'll have to accept it." We must get rid of the barriers. Burke-

Hartke tries to do this. For years we have tried to wish the barriers away—hoping that our good example would be a magic wand. But we know now that there is no magic wand; that wishing does not work. Perhaps now is the time to put up some barriers of our own—hopefully temporary ones—but in sufficient strength to give us a bargaining position with other nations. Barrier reduction could then be done on a joint basis.

A second problem to which business should address itself is the issue of the ability of the United States to compete in world markets. Many businessmen will argue that it is not just the existence of trade barriers erected by other nations which has led to the declining U.S. position in the world trade, but the high costs of production in the United States and consequent declining productivity relative to other countries. Some may argue that even if barriers are removed, the United States still will be unable to compete successfully because our costs are too high. I challenge business to join with labor to help the United States regain and maintain its competitive edge. To do this, we must even the odds—odds which are now against us. We must take the steps necessary to change the conditions which now favor U.S. investment and manufacture abroad and consequently give other nations advantages which are not reciprocated.

We cannot—and do not—expect American business to operate their businesses solely for altruistic, societal or patriotic purposes. Under our system, business must, of course, maximize its profits. At the present time, it is obvious that the search for profits is enticing many American businesses overseas. The incentives for investment abroad—tax and otherwise—have introduced inequities that make it more attractive to produce overseas than to stay here at home. We must re-set the balance. We must eliminate those incentives and make it just as profitable for business to produce at home—and maybe more profitable—as it is to leave our shores. Burke-Hartke attempts to do

this by wiping out the special advantages that now accrue to U.S. companies with overseas investments. Burke-Hartke would treat income earned abroad in the same way it would be treated if it were earned in the United States, whether such income comes from direct investments or from the sale or license of U.S. technology and management.

My third proposal also has to do with the need to make our economy more competitive. The way things are now, U.S. business seems to have been lulled into a mistaken complacency about the need for increasing research and development. U.S. companies, like business everywhere, must continually expand their markets in order to maintain their own economic health. As long as they can move production freely to other parts of the world, markets will of course be expanded and the need to compete fiercely for an expanding share of the U.S. market will be alleviated.

Those world markets, generally less sophisticated than the U.S. market, may be willing to accept yesterday's product—never having had the product of the day before—and the pressure on the U.S. company to invest in research and development or to develop new products is also alleviated. The result is not only a gradual erosion of U.S. competitiveness and a relaxation of efforts to improve productivity, but also a slowing down of the technological advance that we must have in order to cope with the emerging crisis posed by the need to rationalize a rising standard of living with the protection and preservation of our environment.

For example, to the extent that the system encourages U.S. business to shift production abroad—there to produce the same product in the same way that it was formerly produced in the United States—attention will be diverted from the need to develop new products or new techniques of production.

We will be able to, and probably will, export some pollution. We will be able to, and probably will, waste foreign resources instead of ours. We will be able to, and probably will, exploit their labor, not ours. But in the long run, we will not have done anything for U.S. business, nor for jobs, nor for ourselves. Burke-Hartke tries to get at this problem by equalizing the opportunity for investment and production. By making it equally attractive to remain at home, it is expected that U.S. business will once again invest heavily in research and development and find the way to take a commanding lead in technology.

The U.S. business stake in this is just as high as that of U.S. labor. It should join with labor in making the U.S. economy strong, healthy and competitive; in taking the steps that are necessary to really reduce the barriers to free trade; and in shaping a foreign trade policy that makes sense by recognizing the realities of today.

Reading 38

The Growing Impact of International Forces upon the Economy of the United States*

By Philip E. Coldwell

Summary

Perhaps it was a result of our heritage, our abundance of natural resources, or our geographic isolation from other population centers of the world, but —whatever the reason—until recently, some Americans operated almost as if they were in an economic vacuum. People became accustomed to primarily domestic forces as the principal factors of change, and, to a great extent, international forces were treated with benign neglect. Other than the financial impact of our roles as policeman and benefactor, the nation's economic policies were set largely to meet the domestic situation. And yet, the international financial and economic changes in the postwar period have steadily exerted more and more influence on the underlying progress and long-run health of the American economy. Certain industries, unions, and limited segments of our population, mainly on the coastal areas, became acutely aware of the growing international competition in sales and jobs, but, by and large, the hinterland of the United States remained inwardly oriented in its attitudes and views on the U.S. economy.

In 1971, this isolationist attitude suffered a severe setback, and in 1973, the extent of United States dependence on world trade and international financial cooperation finally registered with most Americans. To many people, this was a sudden shift in economic forces, but to the knowledgeable observer, the buildup of competitive positions in Europe and Japan, the foreign accumulation of dollars from heavy U.S. balance-of-payments deficits, and the steady erosion of U.S. raw-material resources had forecast a United States shift in policies and practices to accommodate the international pressures.

The positions and policies of the United States on international finance, trade, foreign aid, and corporate reciprocity will all need to be reconsidered with great care to assure us that the internationalization of our economy is reflected in those policies. More specifically, our policies need to recognize the essential U.S. interests in continuing free trade, unhampered credit flows, and a strengthened export position to pay for imports critical to our continuing economic progress.

Key Questions to Consider

- What is the impact of international trade on the economic activity in the U.S.?
- What major classes of items does the U.S. export and import?
- What should the future thrust of our economy be?

- What are the alternatives facing the oil-consuming countries as they attempt to cope with the long-run problem of payment?

* Reprinted with permission from *Business Review*, Federal Reserve Bank of Dallas, August 1974, pp. 1–5.

The Growing Impact of International Forces upon the Economy of the United States

Perhaps it was a result of our heritage, our abundance of natural resources, or our geographic isolation from other population centers of the world, but—whatever the reason—until recently, some Americans operated almost as if they were in an economic vacuum. People became accustomed to primarily domestic forces as the principal factors of change, and, to a great extent, international forces were treated with benign neglect. Other than the financial impact of our roles as policeman and benefactor, the nation's economic policies were set largely to meet the domestic situation. And yet, the international financial and economic changes in the postwar period have steadily exerted more and more influence on the underlying progress and long-run health of the American economy. Certain industries, unions, and limited segments of our population, mainly on the coastal areas, became acutely aware of the growing international competition in sales and jobs, but, by and large, the hinterland of the United States remained inwardly oriented in its attitudes and views on the U.S. economy.

In 1971, this isolationist attitude suffered a severe setback, and in 1973, the extent of United States dependence on world trade and international financial cooperation finally registered with most Americans. To many people, this was a sudden shift in economic forces, but to the knowledgeable observer, the buildup of competitive positions in Europe and Japan, the foreign accumulation of dollars from heavy U.S. balance-of-payments deficits, and the steady erosion of U.S. raw-material resources had forecast a United States shift in policies and practices to accommodate the international pressures.

There is, of course, a danger of overreaction to the now highly visible international influences. One might be tempted to blame all our recent problems on these forces, or, alternatively, one might view the recent upsets as purely transitory, with only a temporary impact. Both extremes seem to me to be unwarranted. Instead, a middle ground of proper concern balanced with recognition of some of the unusual aspects of the present situation is probably an appropriate policy position.

Let us measure the impact of international trade on the production and consumption of the United States. In the broadest terms, both U.S. merchandise exports and imports are about 7 percent of the gross national product. In dollars, U.S. exports and imports in early 1974 were each at an annual rate of about $90 billion, or about $20 billion above the 1973 total and $30 billion above the first four months of the past year. Through April, the 1974 merchandise trade balance showed a minor surplus of $778 million, contrasted with a deficit in the first four months of 1973 and a surplus of $2.5 billion in the final four months of last year.

Among the principal items of export, the primary sales increases have been for agricultural products and machinery—especially computers, agricultural and construction machinery, and electric power and telecommunications equipment. Total nonagricultural exports rose 14 percent above the final third of 1973, and agricultural exports rose an identical percentage. On the import side, industrial supplies showed a 43-percent gain, led by petroleum, steel, copper, newsprint, and chemicals.

To a considerable extent, these export and import items reflect the changing U.S. position. With years of heavy production of some minerals and scarcity of domestic deposits of others, the United States is now at least 50 percent dependent on foreign sources for basic minerals such as bauxite, manganese, nickel, copper, and tin. In addition, there is a rising dependence for others, particularly petroleum, natural gas, chemicals, and sulfur.

It is just no longer possible for the United States to operate in an isolationist environment and maintain the current standards of living of its people. Our future thrust should be toward developing and refining our capacity as a processor, rather than a producer, of raw materials. To pay for these enlarged imports, the United States will need to expand exports in sectors where this nation has a natural or technological advantage. Again, the list of exports provides an excellent survey of the sophisticated machines and basic agricultural products that will need to be exported in ever greater volume to pay for our imports.

Thus, merchandise trade patterns that reflect the growing internationalization of our economy will have a profound impact on U.S. trade policies and practices. Only at our own peril could we neglect or ignore the world forces and their influence on the economic progress of our nation. But perhaps the strongest changes in policies and attitudes in the United States are likely to come from the realization that the international financial forces have, in some ways, become dominant to the domestic financial forces.

Part of the background for this important development is the postwar accumulation of dollars in foreign hands as dollars were being used as both the primary reserve and vehicle currency. The continued outflow of dollars from persistent balance-of-payments deficits caused a surplus of dollars in world financial markets and a concomitant reduction in value. By 1971, with U.S. trade surpluses declining sharply and the dollar under strong pressure in exchange markets, the United States suspended convertibility and then devalued the dollar. These actions by the United States brought a severe shock to the international financial community. But as pressures continued against the dollar, a further devaluation occurred in early 1973, and the dollar subsequently deteriorated in exchange markets to a low point in July 1973.

With the suspension of convertibility, the Bretton Woods mechanism of a gold-dollar exchange standard ceased functioning and, by 1973, fixed exchange rates for the currencies of many countries had been replaced by floating arrangements. For nearly three years, then, the international payments mechanism has relied on market-oriented pressures to determine relative values of currencies, though central bank intervention has played an increasing role to prevent disorderliness in the markets.

Throughout this period of turmoil, the changing international value of the dollar has had significant effects on the domestic position of the American economy. The declining value of the dollar in terms of foreign currencies has meant that prices of American products sold abroad were effectively reduced and demand was thereby stimulated. As competition increased between foreign and domestic buyers of U.S. goods, domestic prices advanced sharply. Aggravating this demand pressure was the fact that all major industrialized nations shifted to a coincident cyclical position of expansion—a situation not evident at any other time in the postwar period. The effect of the dollar depreciation was also felt in the higher prices paid for imported goods. Foreign producers were faced with a need to cover the past devaluations of the dollar and protect against further exchange rate erosion.

As if these changes were not enough, the world faced a new crisis in late 1973, when politically inspired oil embargoes and price increases were imposed by the principal oil-producing nations in the Middle East. While the embargoes and reduced output phases of the policy have been suspended, the world was left with a new and sharply higher price structure for petroleum and its derivative products. Although in a more favored position than many other nations by virtue of our domestic oil production, which supplies nearly two-thirds of our demand, the United States is a primary user of petroleum and its demand has been accelerating.

Not only have basic prices of oil and gasoline advanced sharply, but these products form a large part of the ongoing costs of business in transporting its products to consumer outlets. In addition, the by-products of petroleum refining are the source of feed-stock for the production of plastics, fertilizers, chemicals, and a host of other business and consumer products. Thus, the initial petroleum price increase had a pervasive effect on many other goods and services marketed throughout the world and was especially significant in the United States because of our heavy dependence on oil and gas for energy supplies.

Moreover, the petroleum price increases triggered price advances for other basic raw materials, especially bauxite, iron ore, and copper. In modern industrialized nations geared to heavy use of such raw materials, the price increases served as a catalyst for a new and particularly virulent inflationary spiral. Consequently, all major nations are presently contending with inflationary pressures, and only a few have been able to contain their rates of inflation below a double-digit position.

While the United States may be less directly affected by oil imports because of its productive capacity, there are special factors in the U.S. position that reinforce the indirect effects of the oil price problem. Despite the breakdown of the Bretton Woods system, the dollar is still used as the primary vehicle, or transactions, currency of the Free World. Payments for oil are made primarily in dollars, and—given the weakened state of our currency—the oil-producing nations converted some into sterling and have sought purchasing power guarantees. Moreover, since a very large stock of dollars is held in foreign official reserves, other major industrialized nations are using these funds for oil payments, thus redirecting the dollar overhang to the principal oil-producing nations. As such dollar payments are made, either in a transactions sense or from foreign official reserves, there appear to be further exchange rate pressures against the dollar. Even oil payment dollars placed in the Eurodollar market can contribute some pressure as such dollars may be converted into other currencies.

It is much too early to assess all the implications of this feature of the oil price problem, but suffice it to say that the real test will come in the disposition of such dollar revenues, whether the dollars are reinvested in U.S. securities or purchases, sold in the open market for other currencies, or neutralized in international accounts of the Bank for International Settlements or International Monetary Fund. There is hope that some of the surplus will be used to help the underdeveloped nations.

However the oil producers use the funds, the oil-consuming nations have a long-run problem of payment. The alternatives are difficult at best and could be of major concern. First, if exports to the oil-producing nations could be sharply increased, payment for the oil imports would be partially achievable. But the payments for oil are so massive—variously estimated for the OPEC nations at a gross of $60 billion to $80 billion for 1974—that imports could scarcely meet half of this cost. Moreover, the principal oil-producing nations are relatively underdeveloped and have only small populations. Therefore, the amount of imports they would absorb is likely to be small.

Secondly, the oil-consuming nations could raise the prices of their principal exports to help pay for their oil imports. This would be helpful for some nations but would aggravate the inflationary impact for other nations, especially those without exports that are in widespread demand. Nevertheless, such a broad rise in prices of basic raw materials and other exports could have a strong impact on the price levels of all nations. In relation to payments for oil imports, the advance in prices of other world trade commodities is not likely to generate sufficient income to meet a sizable share of the oil import bill. For the United States, these patterns of price retaliation may be less difficult but still of major significance in terms of the inflationary potential from both internal impetus as workers seek to maintain standards of living through higher wages and external impetus as we pay for the increasing dependence on foreign sources of vital raw materials.

Two other approaches to payment involve quite unacceptable risks. First, currency devaluation could be used to pay part of the bill, but this runs the risk of future rejections or even higher prices and might create an atmosphere conducive to competitive devaluations. Another approach might be a resort to barter, but, even here, there would need to be an agreement on the relative values of the bartered goods. The primary problem with this approach, though, is its limited use. After all, how many jet airplanes, computers, or even tons of wheat can be absorbed by relatively small countries?

Finally, of course, the preferred plan embraces a reduction in oil prices, both as a contribution to world economic stability and as a means of avoiding heavy deficits in balances of payments for most oil-consuming nations.

In this overall context of a world in transition to a new and differential pattern of prices, official reserves, and financial power, the international exchanges become even more significant. And yet, there is no real stability at this time, nor any new agreed-on mechanism of international settlement. Preliminary plans for use of Special Drawing Rights, valued according to a market basket of 16 currencies, have been developed by the Committee of Twenty of the IMF and finance ministers over the past few months. But this is an untried element of settlement, and many problems of use and relationships need definition before this mechanism is accepted. Full faith and confidence in the mechanism will, of course, require years of successful operation and will entail difficult decisions on the rate and purpose of issuance of SDR's, on the underdeveloped country link, and on the internal balance between the currencies in the market basket.

At the same time, there continues to be a sizable body of world opinion that gold should remain the centerpiece of the international payments mechanism. If the new market basket approach completely denies a role to gold in the international mechanism, there is likely to be less support than if gold were included. One new dimension to this problem has been the recent decision to allow official gold holdings to be used as collateral at a market-related price. It is, obviously, sheer speculation to forecast future gold moves, but a broader spirit of accommodation may be developing that would certainly augur well for greater cooperation in creating a viable international financial structure.

Meanwhile, the pressures from international financial disruptions, exchange rate volatility, and massive capital flows have brought price increases in the United States and, in fact, throughout the world. The universality of the world's credit markets, with their almost instantaneous shifting of funds and competitive rates of interest, has permitted, if not encouraged, movements of funds across borders. The unpredictable nature of such flows introduces an element of instability into the supply and demand for dollars. Of course, one of the primary movers of funds is the relative interest rate levels in the principal markets of the world, and, to some extent, this fact operates as a constraining force on domestic policies.

Of more continuing influence for the United States is the flow of funds to and from foreign central banks, especially the movement into and out of Treasury securities. Such investments have had a sharp influence on the Treasury financing program and quite often have an impact on the Government securities market, particularly when large amounts are sold or purchased in a short time frame. Foreign official holdings of dollars have had a smaller impact on our markets and credit positions, however, than the very large Eurodollar holdings and the capital flows for investments, loans, and payments abroad.

The massive amount of dollars in the Eurodollar market has exerted a formidable force on currency exchange rates as holders have shifted from one currency to another. Confidence in U.S. currency values has waned over the past ten years and was seriously eroded in the 1970–74 period. As such confidence declined, more dollars were offered for sale and exchange rates shifted against the dollar. One measure of the Eurodollar market is the dollar liabilities of banks reporting to the BIS. These liabilities amounted to only $18 billion in 1967 but more than doubled to $58 billion in 1970 and had doubled again to $130 billion by the end of 1973.

American banks and American branches of foreign banks have become heavily involved in the movement of funds into and out of the Eurodollar market. At times, United States banks have borrowed Eurodollars as a temporary escape mechanism from the monetary restraint exercised domestically and have used such funds both to meet foreign commitments and to alleviate the pressure for domestic credit demands. In recent months, with strong Eurodollar market demands, some funds have flowed from the United States to feed that market. Naturally, any large volume of funds moving into or out of the United States credit market can have a strong effect on interest rates and even availability of credit in the United States.

In a somewhat longer time frame, capital investments of U.S. companies abroad have also had a marked impact on our international position. With American companies investing in new plant and equipment abroad and steadily shifting labor-intensive production to foreign countries where labor is less expensive, there have been profound effects on the types of jobs available in this country and a reinforcement of the high-technology output at which this country excels. This move has meant more high-paying professional positions and fewer low-paying factory jobs open in the United States. The shift of production to foreign subsidiaries has also had a significant impact on U.S. imports and exports. However, in view of U.S. dependence on foreign sources of raw materials, we have little choice but to continue our efforts toward free trade among all nations.

One of the often unnoticed results of these capital investments abroad has been the volume of funds returned in the form of profits and dividends to U.S. corporations. Often, however, such investments also require payments out of the home office for salaries, fees, royalties, and purchases. In fact, recurring oil company payments are one of the routine factors influencing the demand for sterling.

Perhaps we have covered enough of the changing relationships to convince you that the U.S. economy is no longer—if, indeed, it ever was—an isolationist economy and, in fact, would suffer severely if a national policy of isolationism were to be established. Nevertheless, there is one other element of our world interdependence that should be mentioned. The credit markets of the Free World are still largely free, and, despite some exchange and finance controls, credit moves around the world with great facility. But if oil import payments become such a burden that the bulk of international liquidity is accumulated by only a handful of oil-producing nations, there could be moves to severely limit international financial flows. These actions would force nations into world trade by barter, would do untold harm to the ongoing development of the poorer nations, and would impact heavily on the U.S. position as a raw-material importer.

The positions and policies of the United States on international finance, trade, foreign aid, and corporate reciprocity will all need to be reconsidered with great care to assure us that the internationalization of our economy is reflected in those policies. More specifically, our policies need to recognize the essential U.S. interests in continuing free trade, unhampered credit flows, and a strengthened export position to pay for imports critical to our continuing economic progress.

Economic Consequences of the OPEC Cartel*

By Adrian W. Throop

Summary

The Organization of Petroleum Exporting Countries may be the most successful international cartel in history. Supplying more than 85 percent of the oil traded in world markets, it faces little immediate competition from other sources of crude oil.

When the 12 OPEC members cut production last year—reducing their output 21 percent from 1973 levels against a world demand that was rising more than 8 percent a year—prices skyrocketed. The posted price of Saudi Arabian light crude oil, for example, rose from $2.59 a barrel in early 1973 to $11.25 at the beginning of 1975.

The impact of higher oil prices on the importing countries depends greatly on what the recipients of dollars or pounds in the OPEC countries decide to do with them.

Key Questions to Consider

■ What will be the effect of higher oil prices on importing countries if the recipients buy domestic goods and services?

■ What would be the effect of higher oil prices on importing countries if the recipients make investments in the oil consuming countries?

■ How were OPEC revenues used in 1974?

_____

* Reprinted with permission from *Business Review*, Federal Reserve Bank of Dallas, May 1975, pp. 1–10.

Economic Consequences of the OPEC Cartel

The Organization of Petroleum Exporting Countries may be the most successful international cartel in history. Supplying more than 85 percent of the oil traded in world markets, it faces little immediate competition from other sources of crude oil.

When the 12 OPEC members cut production last year—reducing their output 21 percent from 1973 levels against a world demand that was rising more than 8 percent a year—prices skyrocketed. The posted price of Saudi Arabian light crude oil, for example, rose from $2.59 a barrel in early 1973 to $11.25 at the beginning of 1975.

Members of the cartel appropriated the lion's share of the increased revenue in the form of royalties, taxes, and participating crude and by the acquisition of more producing properties. The result was an increase in total export earnings of OPEC members of $75 billion—from about $30 billion in 1973 to about $105 billion in 1974.

The relative price of oil is, nevertheless, very apt to come down. While price hikes have been extremely profitable for OPEC, the quantity of oil demanded could fall over the next five to ten years by about the same proportion as the increase in price, leaving total revenue to producers largely unaffected over the long haul. Meanwhile, higher oil prices are

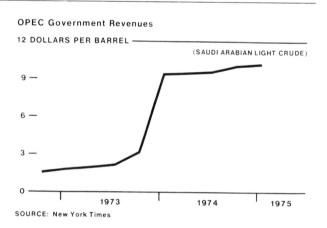

OPEC Government Revenues

SOURCE: New York Times

stimulating the search for more oil from outside the cartel.

The cartel may well decide on a strategy of gradually lowering prices as other fuels and other sources of oil are developed. This would help reconcile the interests of two groups within OPEC.

Countries with large populations and ambitious plans for development—such as Iran, Venezuela, Iraq, and Algeria—would apparently like to make as much as they can now. They are less concerned about long-run erosion of the market by high prices than countries like Saudi Arabia, Kuwait, and the Persian Gulf sheikdoms, which have more money coming in than they can currently use. If oil prices were allowed to fall slowly, current revenues could still be enhanced without sacrificing as much future income.

The world price of oil could also turn down for an entirely different reason. As efforts to maintain current prices call for more and more cutbacks in production, individual members of the cartel could try to hold on to their markets by making concessions in the sale of some oil.

There is considerable incentive for such a move. For most of the OPEC countries, the incremental costs of producing an extra barrel of oil is extremely low. It is only about 20 cents in the Persian Gulf—and that includes a reasonable return on investment.

OVERALL CONSEQUENCES . . .

Even if relative oil prices fall from current levels, importing countries will have to make continuing economic and financial adjustments to high oil prices for some time to come.

Although OPEC receives payment for its oil in U.S. dollars, and to some extent in the British pound sterling, the particular currency used as a means of payment does not change the adjustments oil-importing countries have to make. Nor does it materially affect the economic position of the United States.

Take, for example, a situation where an Italian company buys OPEC oil with dollars that OPEC then invests in the German capital market. In world currency markets, the Italian purchase of dollars is offset by the OPEC sale, so there is no tendency for the average value of the dollar to change. But these transactions put downward pressure on the lira relative to the mark.

Alternatively, if central banks do not allow the mark-lira exchange rate to vary, the German Federal Bank would gain reserves at the expense of the Bank of Italy. But neither the value of the dollar nor the U.S. balance of payments would be affected.

The impact of higher oil prices on the importing countries depends greatly on what the recipients of dollars or pounds in the OPEC countries decide to do with them. If the recipients are mostly corporations and individuals, much of the money might be exchanged for local currencies and used to buy domestic goods and services or investments.

In this case, if OPEC countries continued to peg the value of their currencies to those of the oil importers, their central banks would have to furnish the local currencies, causing their money supplies to expand and eventually creating inflationary pressures. But as the central banks would normally invest their new reserves in earning assets abroad, the dollars or pounds would be kept in circulation there even when the recipients in OPEC countries decide to spend their new revenues at home.

Practically all the oil payments, in fact, are going to OPEC governments. And as they recognize the inflationary implications of such large amounts of money being spent in their own economies, it is probably safe to assume that most petromoney will not be exchanged for local currencies but, instead, will be used by OPEC governments to buy goods and services or make investments abroad.

. . . OF OPEC IMPORTS . . .

Since the $75 billion in extra payments for foreign oil in 1974 would otherwise have been used to buy goods and services in oil-importing countries, the higher oil prices tended to create shortfalls in aggregate demand in their economies, in addition to the deficits in their trade balances. But if OPEC had used all the $75 billion to buy exports from the importing countries, there would have been no net deficiency of demand or balance-of-payments deficit for these countries, at least as a group.

Because the goods demanded by oil-exporting countries would not necessarily have been those in immediate excess supply in oil-importing countries, a major real-location of resources would have been needed. But once these adjustments were made, the importing countries would pay the higher price for oil on a current basis by devoting less of their production to their own use and more to exports.

The reduction in the standard of living of oil-importing countries would be less under this adjustment than might be thought—at least for industrial countries. An increase of $75 billion a year nearly doubles the income of the OPEC group. The loss in economic welfare from cutting back on the absorption of domestic goods and services by this amount comes out to about 2 percent of the national income of industrial countries.[1] And it comes to about 3 percent of the income of less developed countries.

As 2 percent of national income is no more than the normal annual increase in labor productivity in industrial countries, the cost to them amounts to no more than a year's growth in per capita income. However, not only is the increase in the cost of oil greater relative to the national incomes of underdeveloped countries, but their normal rate of growth in per capita income is less than in industrial countries—close to zero in some cases. So, the overall impact of higher oil prices on their standard of living is generally more severe.

----

[1] As the price of domestic oil rises to meet that of international oil, significant transfers of income take place between producers and consumers within oil-importing countries. But the transfers net to zero as far as the overall standard of living of these countries is concerned.

In the United States, this redistribution has been blunted by a two-price system for petroleum. Imported oil, oil from new wells, and oil from wells producing less than 10 barrels a day sell at the world price. But the price of other domestically produced petroleum is controlled at $5.25 a barrel. However its effects on the distribution of income are regarded, this system has the disadvantage of tending to suppress the domestic supply compared with what it would be under a single price. This is true because the system encourages investment in new wells even when an equal amount of investment in old wells would be more productive.

... AND OPEC INVESTMENTS

If, on the other hand, OPEC used all the $75 billion of new petromoney for investments in oil-consuming countries while waiting to spend the money on future imports, the effect on the standard of living of the importing countries would depend on the national economic policies of their governments. If petromoney were allowed to flow back into capital investment projects in these countries, the impact on their standard of living would be about the same as if the money were spent on their exports.

To facilitate the complete absorption of petromoney, central banks in oil-importing countries might have to let interest rates fall. But the increased demand for capital needed to expand domestic energy supplies might be enough to offset this normal tendency.

In any case, the increase in expenditures on capital goods would tend to offset the deficiency in aggregate demand created by the higher cost of foreign oil. Once again, a significant reallocation of resources from their present uses would be required. But the extra saving would increase the capital stock of oil-importing countries enough to produce exports in the future that would pay the interest and principal on petromoney debt.

However, the extra $75 billion in saving from petromoney investments would not be enough to generate a significant increase in the future standard of living of the importing countries. The greater output in the future would be absorbed almost entirely by demands of the OPEC countries when they spend the interest and principal of petromoney debt on imports.[2]

----

[2] If OPEC capital is paid a return equal to its marginal product and the inflows from OPEC are large relative to the capital stock of the importing countries, the increase in the productive capacity of the oil importers could substantially exceed the amount needed to service the petrodebt. And the standard of living of the countries could be signficantly enhanced as long as the petromoney remains invested in them. Actually, however, OPEC is expected to own no more than 2 to 4 percent of the world's capital stock by 1980, at which

And their current standard of living would suffer because $75 billion of current output would no longer be available for either current consumption or capital accumulation to produce goods and services for their own use in the future. Consequently, the effect on both the present and future standard of living of oil-importing countries would be about the same in this case as when OPEC countries use the petromoney to buy imports.

The immediate effect on the standard of living would be lifted if governments of oil-importing countries cut taxes and increased expenditures enough to increase current consumption by $75 billion. Either way—whether by cutting taxes or by increasing government spending—the governments could finance their budget deficits by borrowing petromoney from OPEC.

The disadvantage of such a policy is that OPEC would accumulate claims against the future output of oil-importing countries—with interest—without any addition being made to the productive capacities of these countries. Instead of suffering a decline of $75 billion in their standard of living initially, the countries would incur a loss of $75 billion plus accumulated interest on petromoney debts in the future.

The difference between the two policies amounts to a difference in the time path of the amount of economic goods available to oil-importing countries. When petromoney is borrowed and used for productive investment, there is a once-and-for-all decline in the standard of living equal to the added cost of oil imports. Advances in the standard of living, however, can resume at the same rate as before. But if the petromoney is borrowed by governments simply to prevent a decline in the current standard of living, its growth rate will be slower.

Which policy is better depends on how much a country values current consumption over future consumption. Oil-importing countries that are satisfied with their current rates of economic growth would do well not to reduce their growth by borrowing petrodollars to support current consumption at the expense of investment. Instead of cutting taxes or increasing government services to offset the deflationary effects of oil payments, they would do better to allow the return flow of petromoney to be channeled into capital projects.

Actually, OPEC countries were able to increase their imports of goods and services by only about $20 billion in 1974. That left roughly $55 billion of the return flow of petromoney to be invested in financial assets and the real assets of oil-importing countries.

How long such huge trade surpluses and accompanying capital flows will last depends on such things as the future price of oil, which of the OPEC countries absorb any production cutbacks, and the speed with which their development programs get started. A return to a near-zero trade balance for OPEC could come, however, as soon as 1980.

Whatever the exact path of OPEC's trade balance, the surplus will probably decline relatively slowly at first. As a result, world financial markets will still have to cope with large petromoney investments for at least several years more.

IMPORTER ADJUSTMENTS...

Since petromoney paid to OPEC returns to the oil-importing countries as a demand for goods, services, or financial assets, there can be no balance-of-payments problem from petromoney flows for these countries as a group. It would be purely coincidental, however, if OPEC purchases of economic goods and financial assets exactly matched the increased oil payments of each country. Further adjustments, therefore, will probably be needed for individual countries.

Individual adjustments cannot eliminate the overall trade deficit with OPEC countries. That can come only when the OPEC countries increase their

---

point its export surplus and petromoney investments are expected to diminish greatly, if not disappear. Consequently, substantial enhancement of the standard of living of the oil-importing countries from the use of OPEC capital does not appear to be very likely.

import demands. But individual importing countries will have to adjust to the net impact of the higher cost of oil and reflows of petromoney on their balances of payments. In these adjustments, some countries are apt to benefit at the expense of others.

...TO EXPORT DEMANDS...

If individual oil-importing countries increase sales to OPEC countries less rapidly than they increase their imports from OPEC—without the difference being made up by investments—their balances of payments will deteriorate. In running payments deficits, these countries will see their foreign exchange reserves run down—something that cannot go on forever.

Various kinds of adjustments are possible. Policies reducing demand would help these countries cut back their imports, but at the cost of unemployment and unused capacity. And tariffs on imports could be used to help eliminate their deficits, but at the expense of reduced benefits from international specialization.

A better form of adjustment would be for such countries to allow their currencies to depreciate in foreign exchange markets. With a depreciated currency, they could export to other oil-importing coun-

tries goods they were unable to sell to OPEC. Similarly, countries that increase exports to OPEC more rapidly than they increase imports would let their currencies appreciate.

Expenditure choices of OPEC, then, determine both the total trade deficit of oil-importing countries with OPEC and the distribution of that deficit among importing countries. But adjustments in exchange rates can induce deficits and surpluses between importing countries that tend to offset those with OPEC, leaving each importing country to achieve an overall balance in its own international payments.

Still, some oil-importing countries will benefit at the expense of others. Countries not favored by OPEC demand for their goods will find the prices of their exports falling relative to the prices of their imports. And the depreciation of their currencies required for balancing their payments will usually reduce the relative prices of their exports even more.

A currency devaluation reduces prices of exports in terms of foreign exchange, allowing more goods to be sold abroad. It also lowers demands for imports, reducing their prices in terms of foreign currencies. But since most countries are more dominant in the world supply of goods they export than in the world demand

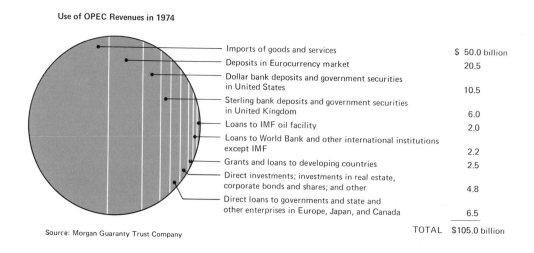

Use of OPEC Revenues in 1974

Imports of goods and services	$ 50.0 billion
Deposits in Eurocurrency market	20.5
Dollar bank deposits and government securities in United States	10.5
Sterling bank deposits and government securities in United Kingdom	6.0
Loans to IMF oil facility	2.0
Loans to World Bank and other international institutions except IMF	2.2
Grants and loans to developing countries	2.5
Direct investments; investments in real estate, corporate bonds and shares; and other	4.8
Direct loans to governments and state and other enterprises in Europe, Japan, and Canada	6.5
	TOTAL $105.0 billion

Source: Morgan Guaranty Trust Company

for goods they import, export prices usually fall more.[3]

A decline in the relative price of exports increases the amount of exports a country must produce to consume any particular quantity of imports. Such a deterioration in its terms of trade reduces the benefits that can be derived from international trade.

So, in addition to the burden of high oil costs, importing countries that do not share equally in sales to OPEC must also carry the burden of worsening terms of trade. Countries favored by sales to OPEC, on the other hand, will have gained in the adjustment process, seeing improvements in their terms of trade.

...AND CAPITAL INFLOWS

Investments of petromoney could also benefit some countries at the expense of others. Oil-importing countries that receive more petromoney through investments than their initial trade deficits with OPEC countries will develop balance-of-payments surpluses. Currencies of countries in this position will tend to appreciate, the effect usually being an improvement in their terms of trade.

Such improvements, however, will be at the ex-

pense of countries not favored by petromoney investments. Thus, uneven flows of petromoney investments could be an additional cause of income redistributions among oil-importing countries.

An important difference, however, exists between initial payments imbalances created by OPEC investments and those due to OPEC demands for goods. When petromoney flows into a country's money or capital markets, interest rates in that country tend to fall, causing investors to withdraw their money for investment in countries where rates are higher. If that happens, the effect of the inflow of petromoney on the payments balance is offset, to some extent, by a compensating outflow of funds. And there is less need for any further adjustment—including changes in the terms of trade—to restore a balance in international payments.

The extent to which capital moves internationally in response to differences in interest rates was lessened, however, by the abandonment in 1973 of fixed exchange rates among the major currencies. Under that system, there was less risk that the profit to be made from differences in interest rates would be wiped out by changes in exchange rates. The result was a stronger tendency for capital to flow between countries until interest rates were nearly equalized.

Under the current system of managed floating of exchange rates, there are no official parities that monetary authorities must defend. Investors that want to profit from differences in interest rates are more likely to hedge against exchange risk by covering their transactions in the forward market.

For example, if interest rates are higher abroad, investors sell foreign exchange for future delivery—the amount being equal to the principal and expected interest on the investment—at the same time as they buy foreign exchange in the spot market. This pushes the price of foreign exchange in the forward market to a discount. Capital then tends to flow out of the country until the discount on the forward exchange rate equals the difference in interest rates. But the movement of the discount on forward foreign ex-

---

[3] A country that plays a major role in the world supply of goods it exports will face an export demand that is relatively inelastic with respect to price. When its costs of production in terms of foreign currency are reduced by the depreciation, the country will experience a relatively large decline in export prices in terms of foreign currencies. If the country is less dominant in the world market for the goods it imports, the decline in import demand produced by the currency depreciation will gain little for the country in the way of reductions in foreign prices. As a result, its ratio of export prices to import prices—or terms of trade—will worsen.

The terms of trade may be measured in either the foreign currency or the home currency, the result being identical at any exchange rate. The important thing is that the same currency be used for both exports and imports. It is incorrect to argue that just because a depreciation increases import prices in the home currency and reduces export prices in the foreign currency, it necessarily worsens the terms of trade.

change limits the amount of capital that will move in response to the initial difference in interest rates.

Under floating exchange rates, if an inflow of petromoney depresses interest rates, there is still likely to be some incentive for opposite outflows of capital. But the incentive will be blunted by the movement of forward rates. So, an inflow of petromoney is more likely now to result in a net inflow of capital, an appreciation of the currency, and an improvement in the country's terms of trade than under the older system of fixed exchange rates.

U.S. PAYMENTS IN 1974

The main effects of the increased cost of oil on international payments began to be felt in early 1974. A reasonably good picture of the impact of petromoney flows on various countries may be obtained, therefore, by comparing their balances of payments in 1973 and 1974.

The official reserve transactions balance is a

U.S. Official Settlements Balance
(Billion dollars)

Credits (+), debits (−)	1973	1974
Merchandise trade balance	$0.5	−$5.9
Balance on services	3.9	9.1
Balance on transfer payments	−3.9	−7.2
Balance on long-term capital	−1.5	−6.6
Balance on short-term capital	−2.0	−2.7
Errors and omissions	−2.3	5.2
Official reserve transactions balance	−$5.3	−$8.1
Liabilities to foreign official agencies		
OPEC countries	$0.7	$10.2
Other countries	4.4	−0.7
U.S. official reserve assets	0.2	−1.4
Settlement items	$5.3	$8.1

Source: U.S. Department of Commerce

widely used measure of the international payments position of the United States and takes into account the role of the United States as a reserve currency country. This balance treats changes in liabilities to foreign official agencies—as well as changes in U.S. official reserve assets—as settlement items, which go below the line. All other transactions go above the line, their net total equaling the deficit or surplus on the official transactions balance.

Under fixed exchange rates—and before the increase in the cost of imported oil—the official reserve transactions balance was a useful measure of the country's payments position. If international payments exceeded receipts, foreign central banks usually bought the excess to keep the value of the dollar from falling below parity. These dollars were then either exchanged for gold or Special Drawing Rights or used to buy securities in the United States. The excess of payments over receipts showed up as a deficit in the official transactions balance and as an opposite movement in settlement items, below the line.

In 1973, the official reserve transactions balance of the United States registered a deficit of $5.3 billion. This deficit was due largely to a speculative outflow of funds in the first quarter, as roughly $7.4 billion left the country in anticipation of the February devaluation of the dollar. Had it not been for this outflow, the balance of payments for 1973 would have been in surplus by $2.1 billion. Sales of goods and services that year were more than enough to cover normal transfer payments and capital outflows.

In 1974, the official reserve transactions balance registered a deficit of $8.1 billion. However, the inflow of petromoney investments contributed heavily to this deficit. According to Commerce Department estimates, OPEC countries invested $10.2 billion in liquid and readily marketable form in the United States last year, compared with only $0.7 billion the year before. Had this inflow been handled above the line as an ordinary capital item instead of below the line as a settlement item, the official reserve transactions balance would have shown a surplus of $2.2 billion in 1974.

When OPEC investments are treated as ordinary movements of capital, then, the overall U.S. balance of payments was roughly the same in 1974 as in 1973, except for the speculative flows in 1973. Nor was there much change in the trade-weighted value of the dollar, which declined only 1.4 percent relative to the currencies of other major industrial countries between 1973 and 1974. Nevertheless, petromoney flows did not balance themselves out but, instead, were offset by changes in other items.

Contrary to some expectations, the $10.2 billion direct reflow of petromoney investments into the United States in 1974 fell considerably short of the $17.6 billion addition to the cost of imported oil. But because of lagged effects of the dollar devaluation and a weakening in the U.S. economy, the nonoil trade balance simultaneously increased $11.4 billion. Thus, if OPEC investments are treated as a normal capital flow, the total change in the trade balance combined with the direct reflow of petromoney was enough to improve the balance of payments by $4 billion in 1974.

This gain was almost entirely offset, however, by an increased net capital outflow from banks, which was associated mainly with the removal of controls over U.S. lending abroad. Foreign commercial banks expanded their lending in the United States by $9 billion in 1974. But U.S. banks simultaneously expanded their lending to foreigners by $12 billion, resulting in an increased net outflow of $3 billion.

Private financial markets have adjusted to petromoney flows remarkably well so far. Adjustments in patterns of resource use and trade, however, have only just begun to be made by oil-importing countries. Production and trade in these countries will have to be adjusted to the future pattern of petromoney invest-

ments and, eventually and more permanently, to increased OPEC demands for goods and services.

The longer-run adjustment mechanism will, in the main, be changes in exchange rates. But a full response of trade balances to exchange rate changes can take as much as two years. So, the change in the value of a currency needed to achieve payments balance in the short run may be considerably more than is necessary in the long run. Temporary official financing can be used to keep rates from changing more than is needed for the long run, helping to promote smoother shifts of resources to their new uses. Various new official financing arrangements are in use or have been agreed to in principle.

The International Monetary Fund has established a special oil facility that received about $3 billion in deposits from OPEC countries last year for loans to oil-importing countries that might otherwise have trouble obtaining reflows of petromoney. The facility was expanded to $6.2 billion this year. In addition, agreement has been reached to increase the regular IMF quotas by 32.5 percent next year. This increase in the pool of currencies paid into IMF will make still more money available to member countries with temporary payments problems.

New official financing from sources other than the IMF will also be available. Tentative agreement has been reached for the 24 countries belonging to the Organization for Economic Cooperation and Development to establish a $25 billion mutual insurance fund for the protection of members that have exhausted other avenues to financing. And the European Economic Community has agreed to back a $3 billion bond issue subscribed to by OPEC countries, the proceeds of which are to go to member countries with the greatest needs.

Policy Issues in the International Economy of the 1970s*

By H. S. Houthakker

Summary

There is room for argument whether the 1970s started on January 1, 1970, or January 1, 1971, but one thing is certain: neither date was significant for international economic policy. If we have to periodize by decades at all, then the 1970s probably began on August 15, 1971—and not only in international economics. On that date the United States in effect brought an end to the existing international monetary system by suspending the convertibility of the dollar into gold. The immediate purpose of this move was to bring about a worldwide realignment of par values and particularly a fall in the value of the dollar relative to other currencies.

The results of the August 15 decision have not had an equally satisfying impact on the international monetary system. We had to pull down the house because it was no longer adapted to the needs of the time, but putting something better in its place has not been easy. For nearly a year we have been living with floating rates, a device long favored by a majority of academic economists. So far floating rates have worked reasonably well; although there have been some excessive rate fluctuations of speculative origin, the growth of world trade and capital movements does not appear to have been impeded.

Key Questions to Consider

- Why are exchange rates still not allowed to fluctuate freely?

- What is the international liquidity problem?

- What has been the effect of the Arab oil embargo?

* Reprinted with permission from *The American Economic Review* (Papers and Proceedings) **LXIV**, No. 2 (May 1974), 138–140.

Policy Issues in the International Economy of the 1970s

There is room for argument whether the 1970's started on January 1, 1970, or January 1, 1971, but one thing is certain: neither date was significant for international economic policy. If we have to periodize by decades at all, then the 1970's probably began on August 15, 1971—and not only in international economics. On that date the United States in effect brought an end to the existing international monetary system by suspending the convertibility of the dollar into gold. The immediate purpose of this move was to bring about a worldwide realignment of par values and particularly a fall in the value of the dollar relative to other currencies. This purpose was accomplished in two or three stages, depending on how one interprets the appreciation of the European currencies during the summer of 1973. The results of that action are already exceeding the most optimistic predictions —our balance of payments, after causing us and other countries endless (though frequently exaggerated) concern during the 1960's, is now in solid surplus and likely to remain so for the remainder of the decade. The principal qualification that should be made relates to the energy problem, on which I shall say more later. Our surplus will not be burdensome as long as other countries can run down their previously accumulated dollar assets.

But the results of the August 15 decision have not had an equally satisfying impact on the international monetary system. We had to pull down the house because it was no longer adapted to the needs of the time, but putting something better in its place has not been easy. For nearly a year we have been living with floating rates, a device long favored by a majority of academic economists. So far floating rates have worked reasonably well; although there have been some excessive rate fluctuations of speculative origin, the growth of world trade and capital movements does not appear to have been impeded. However, we do not have *freely* floating rates, the system many economists advocate, but rather dirty or managed floating, with strong remnants of fixed rates, especially in Europe. Official intervention in the foreign exchange markets has not come to an end, nor is it likely to. The notion that the exchange rate can be left entirely to market forces is anathema to most governments who fear that this would result in a loss of control over their domestic policies. We still need a new monetary *system*, as distinct from the unco-ordinated operations now being practiced by all major countries. Our government has made detailed and thoughtful proposals for a new system that would combine reasonable predictability of exchange rates with a capacity to make needed adjustments promptly and with a minimum of turmoil. These proposals have not been accepted by other countries, and since the United States can live with the present interim situation, we have not pressed them very hard. Perhaps we should take comfort in the French saying that only provisional arrangements can last, but the risks of disintegration of the world economy cannot be overlooked. Despite all its defects the Bretton Woods system had the merit of being universal, whereas the prevailing conditions encourage regional groupings such as the European "snake in the tunnel" experiment. This is the main reason why international monetary reform should remain on the agenda.

A related issue is international liquidity, particularly as it affects the worldwide inflation we are now going through. In the 1960's there was considerable agitation over an alleged shortage of liquidity, in response to which the Special Drawing Rights were created. Actually the evidence for such a shortage was never impressive; while net official reserve assets may not have grown much, there was a huge creation of private international liquidity in the Eurodollar market. Moreover, official liquidity would have been more than adequate if greater reliance had been placed on exchange rates in the adjustment of imbalances. Now that exchange rates are being used more freely, the need for official liquidity is much reduced, and for the time being we should abstain from creating more. In the meantime, however, private international liquidity continues to expand. Since much of it is footloose, it does not show up in published money supply data, which in any case show excessive growth. Nevertheless it almost certainly contributes powerfully to the inflationary pressures that no nation has succeeded in keeping under control. If the world is ever going to take hold of the general price level, the question of international liquidity needs a more searching examination than it has had in the past.

Apart from the problem of inflation, which is only partly of an international nature, the most serious international problems are likely to be in particular markets. To no one's surprise I shall first say something about the petroleum market. The basic fact, as every economist should know, is not that the world

is running out of energy resources, as the Club of Rome would have us believe. We are not running out, and even if we were, higher prices could easily take care of that since both supply and demand are price-elastic. The problem, rather, is the attempt by the oil-producing countries to cartelize the supply side. This attempt is now coming to a climax, and it would be rash indeed to make predictions about its ultimate success. The embargo by certain Arab producers against the United States and the Netherlands was proclaimed on political grounds, but it is already clear that its main effects will be economic. The world petroleum market is fairly well integrated; if one or two countries are denied access to certain sources of supply, they will simply outbid the other importers for alternative supplies. Those importers who continue to receive Arab oil, therefore, will get less from other sources, and the net result is a more or less equal reduction of supply to all countries, whether friendly to the Arabs or not. This reallocation is currently being carried out by the international oil companies since there is no open market in crude oil, but these companies can hardly be blamed for doing what elementary economics dictates. Even though the favored importers are therefore receiving less oil (assuming the embargo is effective and the cutback is not fully made up by increased supplies from other producers), they may still have an advantage over the "hostile" importers if they get the Arab oil at a lower price. However, recent pricing actions by the Organization of Petroleum Exporting Countries (*OPEC*) would seem to have wiped out this advantage.

Indeed, it now appears that the selective embargo, far from being inspired by lofty motives of Arab solidarity, was essentially a move to create discord among the importing countries, thus torpedoing any contemplated consumer cartel and making it easier for *OPEC* to double and triple the price. In this respect it has so far been successful. Although members of the Organization for Economic Cooperation and Development (*OECD*) apparently had a prior agreement to share oil in case of a supply interruption, our allies across the Atlantic and the Pacific broke ranks at the first shot. The European Community also turned out to be a sham when one of its members was cut off from Arab oil. Now our allies are being presented by their new friends with the bill for their shortsightedness; the producers are gradually terminating the embargo which has served its real economic purpose without accomplishing any of its stated political goals. The producers' main concern is now what to do with their vastly increased revenues.

Of course this is not the end of the story. There may be markets where the price can be doubled or tripled without changing the balance of supply and demand, but the petroleum market is certainly not one of them. The incentives for increasing production are tremendous, and no matter what the Club of Rome may say, the potential for greater output exists, not only in the currently exporting countries, but also in the United States. In the very short run not much can be done, but at prevailing *OPEC* prices we are likely to see a surplus of oil within the next year or two. Normal responses to higher prices on the demand side will work in the same direction. The producer cartel will then have to adopt prorationing if it wants to keep the price up. The abstention of Iraq and Libya from the present embargo suggests that cohesion among the exporters may be as hard to achieve as cohesion among the importers.

This episode has wider ramifications. The United States has made self-sufficiency in energy an official policy goal, though one must hope that this means a *potential* for self-sufficiency to forestall extortion by *OPEC*, rather than actual autarchy which would cost too much and disrupt our international economic relations. The balance of payments of Europe, Japan and most of the developing countries will be strained by higher oil prices, and this may in turn affect our exports to these countries; at the same time, however, it will make their exports less competitive in the *U.S.* market, so that the net effect on our balance of payments is likely to be small.

I have not said anything about agriculture or the more traditional trade problems, particularly tariffs and nontariff barriers to trade. The message is the same as with respect to the problems I have already discussed: without more effective international cooperation the world economy may break into regional blocks. The atmosphere has deteriorated and meaningful new agreements among the Western countries appear to be harder and harder to negotiate. The Europeans are increasingly looking inward to the construction of their Community, but the results achieved have not been commensurate with the negotiating efforts. Japan has not yet found a posture befitting its importance in the world economy. Our own strong-arm tactics over the dollar—even though justified by their results and by the tendency of other countries to turn a blind eye to our problems—have hardly promoted international understanding; our autarchic pronouncements about energy, equally understandable in the circumstances, are also open to misinterpretation. To reverse these tendencies will be the major challenge to the international economy in the 1970's.